Vital Statistics
on the Presidency

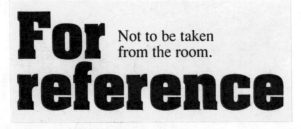

Vital Statistics on the Presidency

Washington to Clinton

Lyn Ragsdale
University of Arizona

Congressional Quarterly Inc.
Washington, D.C.

Library of Congress Cataloging-in-Publication Data

Ragsdale, Lyn, 1954–
    Vital statistics on the presidency : Washington to Clinton / Lyn Ragsdale.
        p. cm.
    Includes bibliographical references (p.   ) and index.
    ISBN 1-56802-050-3 (c : alk. paper). — ISBN 1-56802-049-X (p : alk. paper)
        1. Presidents—United States—History—Handbooks, manuals, etc.
    2. Presidents—United States—Statistics—Handbooks, manuals, etc.
    I. Title.
JK518.R34   1995
324.6'3'0973021—dc20   95-33031
                                                                          CIP

For my mother

Contents

Tables and Figures

Chapter 3   Presidential Elections

Chapter 4   Public Appearances

Chapter 5   Public Opinions

Chapter 6   Presidential Organization and the Executive Branch

Chapter 7   Presidential Policy Making

Chapter 8   Congressional Relations

Chapter 9   The Presidency and the Judiciary

Acknowledgments

Vital Statistics on the Presidency is a thoroughly revised and updated version of *The Elusive Executive,* which Gary King and I published with Congressional Quarterly in 1988. My sincere thanks go to Gary for all his efforts in the earlier collaboration, which made this current volume possible. His indefatigable work on *The Elusive Executive* is still evident in many of the pages of the new book.

This book could not have been completed without the fine data-gathering skills of David Colnic, Diana Rix, Gwen Torges, David White, and Richard Witmer. My special thanks go to Lara Brown and Cynthia Kleback, who updated several of the most complicated and lengthy data series. Both did so promptly, accurately, and with remarkably good humor. The book also reflects the labor and data collection efforts of John J. Theis III of Avila College, as part of our project on the institutionalization of the presidency. Barbara Hinckley, David Lublins, Richard Niemi, Barbara Norrander, and Harold Stanley graciously shared data they had collected, and Mark Petracca and Harold Stanley provided extensive and exceptionally helpful comments on the manuscript.

I am also grateful to the team at Congressional Quarterly, especially Shana Wagger for her enthusiasm about the book, her editorial acumen, and her willingness to work out the countless details that brought the book to fruition. Martha Hawley-Bertsch was instrumental in finding data that were difficult to obtain. Kerry Kern enhanced the book with her careful production skills, just as she did with *The Elusive Executive.* Tracy Villano's painstaking copy editing unquestionably improved the manuscript.

Finally, this book has been a family enterprise. I thank my husband, Jerry Rusk, who lovingly whisked our two-year-old son Matthew off to the park as various deadlines for the book approached. I would like to thank Matthew, too, for just being himself. This book is dedicated to my mother—a true friend who has provided me encouragement and inspiration for a lifetime.

Introduction

This book presents a comprehensive statistical description of the American presidency. It offers a perspective on the presidency that de-emphasizes the uniqueness of individual presidents and focuses instead on the presidency as an institution. This perspective suggests that institutions are "political actors in their own right" (March and Olsen, 1984, 738). Institutions are not simply the sum total of the behavior of individual participants. Rather, they have lives of their own that illuminate individual actions. Institutions are collections of regularly occurring patterns of behavior that help explain and predict the conduct of individual actors. Theoretically, the study of the presidency as an institution highlights continuities and patterns that can be observed from one president to the next. These patterns characterize the presidency as an elected office and offer an explanation of the organization of the Executive Office of the President, its relations with the public, its policy decisions, and its dealings with other institutions, such as Congress and the courts. The chapters of this book provide readers not only with comprehensive quantitative data on various aspects of the presidency, but also with information about change and continuity within the institutional presidency.

Changing Directions in Presidency Research

For the past two decades, presidency scholars have implored each other to engage in more rigorous, systematic forms of research. They have charged that the field is largely devoid of theory and have challenged each other to offer theoretical approaches to the topic that would direct such efforts. Researchers have denounced their own field as lagging behind other fields in political science (for example, the field of congressional studies) in adequately addressing questions through scientific explanation. Critics have charged that presidency research has been remiss in its development of theory, gathering of quantitative data, and presentation of statistical analyses across numerous presidents.

When these charges were first leveled in the 1970s and into the early 1980s, they were seemingly true. Many presidency scholars concentrated on questions about the personalities, power, and leadership of individual presidents. These concepts afforded incumbent-specific approaches to the study of the office that saw each president as different, bringing unique talents, foibles, and goals to the office and leaving with distinctive accomplishments and failures. From this perspective, the presidency was a composite of such heroic leaders as George Washington and Abraham Lincoln and their more feeble counterparts, such as James Buchanan and Franklin Pierce. No two presidents were alike. In effect, presidents were the presidency. To the extent that discussions of the office were offered, they were couched in the language of individual incumbents' power and leadership—the imperial presidency (too much power and malevolent leadership), the imperiled presidency (too little power and docile leadership), the impossible presidency (considerable power, but docile leadership), and the impressive presidency (considerable power and benevolent leadership).

This political-actor perspective preempted systematic data analysis across presidents and hindered relevant generalizations, because presidents were scrutinized one at a time. The central theoretical question asked in much of this literature was how presidents differed in their decisions. Studies addressed the personality characteristics that most influenced decision making, the management styles presidents adopted to make their decisions, and the strategies they employed to convince others of the decisions' merits. Yet, such a perspective "promotes enormous complications in theory and research, opening a Pandora's box of individual motivation and behavior and orienting the field around causal mysteries that we are unlikely to solve" (Edwards, Kessel, and Rockman, 1993, 8). The question about how presidents differ in their decisions, if not the wrong question to ask, is surely too narrow a question that looks at the presidency through a fun house mirror—accentuating the sizes and shapes of the presidents, but leaving the actual office they hold a blur.

It is not surprising, then, that the answers scholars gave stressed variations among presidents. The analyses were often simply descriptions of events; qualitative case studies; or comparisons of case studies of single presidents based on anecdotes, personality sketches, and insiders' reminiscences. Many books included sequential chapters on presidents since Franklin Roosevelt, laying out how each office holder shaped various aspects of the office.

Today, the charge of inadequate systematic research is no longer as easy to level. The study of the American presidency is now at a complicated crossroads. While some scholars continue to address president-specific questions, others have begun to ask different types of questions than those about personality, power, and leadership. And they seek answers using different research techniques.

Asking New Questions

Presidency scholars have begun to ask questions that deemphasize the uniqueness of individual presidents and focus instead on the presidency as an institution. Scholars are now asking how the institution of the presidency can affect political outcomes, including presidents' behavior. The answer researchers have given is that institutional regularities prompt all presidents, regardless of personality, leadership style, or ambition, to behave similarly in fundamental ways (Moe, 1985, 1994; Ragsdale, 1993). In addition, scholars are asking how the environment within which the presidency operates affects presidents' actions and public approval of their performances in office (Ostrom and Job, 1986; Brace and Hinckley, 1992). The conclusion they have reached is that political, social, and economic environmental constraints profoundly limit a president's latitude to make a difference as an individual. Both questions consider presidential actions—whether they are legislative initiatives, vetoes, public appearances, civil rights commitments, or the use of military force—as the unit of analysis, rather than the president who is effecting the action. These new questions are directing researchers' attention to the patterns that characterize the office rather than the idiosyncrasies of its occupants.

Consider as examples three regular patterns that scholars have found to characterize the institutional presidency. Perhaps the most widely known pattern is that the longer a president has been in office, the lower is his public approval. Although explanations of this pattern have differed sharply (cf. Mueller, 1970; Kernell, 1978), no one disputes the general trend in presidential popularity. This finding points to institutional continuities facing all presidents, regardless of their political party, election success, and policy accomplishments or lack thereof. Another pattern is that the giving of a major public address increases presidents' public approval (Ragsdale, 1984; Brace and Hinckley, 1992). This occurs no matter what the presidents' skills at delivering the message or the content of the message. A third pattern is that the smaller the number of initiatives a president undertakes in Congress, the higher is the president's legislative success (Ostrom and Simon, 1985). This occurs regardless of the size of the president's party in Congress or the specific legislative initiatives considered. There are certainly differences among presidents within each of these broad patterns. For instance, not all presidents begin their terms with approval ratings at or near the same level. Nonetheless, the universality of the downward trend is apparently of great significance in understanding the institution of the presidency.

Looking for Answers

Scholars have obtained answers to their questions about the institutional presidency and its environment in ways different from methods used in the past. The institutional perspective helps advance the gathering of data across time because such a viewpoint suggests there will be longitudinal continuities in the way presidents behave. Moreover, because the unit of analysis is often a particular presidential action there is an underlying assumption that any one of these actions taken by one president can be compared to the same action taken by another president.

Thus, worthwhile data on the institutional presidency are emerging across time, spanning numerous individual presidencies. The data make comparisons across presidents more precise and generalizations about the institution more clear-cut. Researchers have become familiar with the wealth of publicly available data in the *Public Papers of the Presidents*, the *Code of Federal Regulations*, the *Budget of the United States*, and the *Statistical Abstract of the United States*, among other comprehensive sources, that reveal the size and actions of the presidency. In addition, some scholars have gathered systematic data through extensive searches of material at presidential libraries. Although there is limited comparability in the data culled from one presidential library to the next, these data can nonetheless add to the picture of the presidency as an institution. The quantitative and qualitative sources are invaluable, even though they may not be as fun to read as staff members' firsthand accounts of administration intrigues. Research using these sources dispels the infamous "N = 1" problem—one president in office at a time—and the complementary complaint that White House decision making is done privately. In addition, the systematic data on the presidency culled from these sources are increasingly being analyzed with more sophisticated and vigorous methodologies.

The progress that has been made triggers an uneasy tension among presidency scholars. Some continue to concentrate on finding out how individual presidents contribute to the presidency—What is Bill Clinton really like? Others see Bill Clinton as someone who will come and go; they consider that many of the factors that influence his success in Congress, his approval amongst the American public, and his policy achievements are not unique to him, but general to the presidency. As George Edwards, John Kessel, and Bert Rockman have noted, "presidency research lacks a powerful consensus on appropriate methodology and theoretical approaches" (1991, 11). Yet, in many ways this lack of consensus has insured progress toward more systematic and rigorous research.

A Less Elusive Executive

The two central goals of this book are to clarify the concept of institution as it applies to the presidency and to identify key statistical patterns characterizing the presidency as an institution. Presidency scholars, like researchers in political science generally, run the risk of overusing the term *institution* without truly understanding what it means. The term has become a handy buzz word that may well be added to the pool of other such terms that the discipline has seen come, and sometimes go, such as *power, system, inputs, outputs, role, culture,* and *rationality*. Often these terms are invoked to lend a theoretical framework to research that otherwise might be charged with stark empiricism. Adopted as a matter of convenience rather than as an element of theoretical rigor, writers employ their own common-sense definitions of the word, making it cover more and more situations and in so doing causing it to be less and less helpful in distinguishing political phenomena.

The Study of Institutions

Across the large number of people writing about political institutions, there is little agreement on how the term should be conceptualized. Three different perspectives exist. One view sees institutions as "humanly devised constraints that shape human interaction" or "the rules of the game" (North, 1990, 3). According to this view, institutions include all rules, from informal norms and conventions, such as the seniority system in Congress, to formal constraints, such as constitutions. Such rules are in place as rational responses to collective action problems; the rules become agreements used to structure cooperation and reduce the costs of making decisions and carrying out other transactions. In contemporary social science, this perspective emerges from economics and has become the basis for what is typed the "new institutionalism" in political science, especially current in the study of Congress.

Yet, the new institutionalism is not all that new. Ironically, its precursors are evident in early political science writings on the American presidency. Edward Corwin (1957), Pendelton Herring (1940), Louis Koenig (1944), and Clinton Rossiter (1960) foreshadow the current work with a focus on the constitutional foundations, powers, and precedents of the presidency—the rules by which the office developed. Although these scholars do not adopt notions of rationality, they nonetheless offer a traditional approach to institutionalism in political science.

Furthermore, this view of institutions rests on a slim conceptual reed. Kenneth Shepsle and Barry Weingast (1987), in a widely cited work that has been taken as an archetypical example of the new institutionalism, never define the term institution, but merely assume that their audience knows what it means. In response, Keith Krehbiel provides some help in identifying "'institutional foundations' (i.e., formal rules and precedents)" (1987, 929). Yet this parenthetical phrase is all that is offered.

References in economics are more definitive, but no more satisfying. Douglass North categorically distinguishes institutions (the rules) from organizations, which are the game and players (1990, 4–5). Thus, an organization cannot be an institution. This divorce of organization from institution prohibits the quite common explanation of an institution as a well-established social organization. From the economics viewpoint, entities such as schools, churches, universities, hospitals, legislatures, and executive offices cannot be considered institutions, although the rules by which they operate can.

A second view of institutions maintains that an institution is a stable organization that has established patterns of behavior over time that fulfill certain functions in society. Sociologists in the 1950s and 1960s identified institutions according to their lack of expendability, the creation of norms and routines, and maintenance of boundaries (Selznick, 1957; Eisenstadt, 1964). Institutions do not exist to resolve collective action problems; rather, they adapt self-images that are extensions of cultural and social expectations. Political scientists applied this concept to political organizations such as legislatures, cabinets, and political parties (Huntington, 1965; Polsby, 1968). Research using this perspective considered aspects of institutions such as autonomy (the independence of an organization from other social groupings), complexity (differentiation and multiplication of organizational subunits), coherence (consensus about the internal procedures of an organization), and adaptability (age of the organization and changes it has withstood).

A third view of institutions, which also emerged in sociology, is at once more narrow than the economics view and more broad than the old sociological view (Powell and DiMaggio, 1991). Today, sociologists, too, write of a new institutionalism, but their version directly counters that of economics and political science. The new institutionalism in sociology expressly rejects notions of rational choice as the basis for the formation and maintenance of institutions. According to this view, institutions are not formal and informal rules designed for the expedient reduction of decision costs. Instead, they are social relationships and actions that come to be taken for granted to the extent that they achieve rulelike status in social thought and action. These include such conventions as the handshake, marriage, attending college, the "No Smoking" sign, and the Nobel Prize (Meyer and Rowan, 1991). Indeed, "taken for grantedness" is a common, if curious, noun used by many in the field. Thus, institutions have cultural and symbolic, not rational, foundations.

The new institutionalism in sociology also broadens the traditional sociological attention to organizations by examining "organizational fields." These are homogenous practices and arrangements found across a wide variety of similarly situated organizations. Such fields include the university, the corporation, the art museum, and the industry. They demonstrate similar characteristics and share a consensus about goals and boundaries of the field across a wide variety of specific organizations. For instance, the form and functions of universities are more alike than different in their approach to departmental units, tenure, the granting of degrees, and so on and thus are said to constitute a field (DiMaggio, 1991).

The Presidency as an Institution

The literature on the presidency shows no clear direction or choice among these three approaches to institutions. Presidency scholars mix and match views without necessarily recognizing their differences or even acknowledging their existence. Terry Moe adopts the traditional sociological view in a brief footnote and writes of institutions as regularized behavior patterns (1985, 236n). In later works (1989; 1993), he drops the sociological view in favor of rational choice institutionalism but does not explain why. Others retain the traditional sociological perspective (Burke, 1992; Pika, 1988; Hart; 1987; Wayne, 1978). Yet, elements of the new sociological perspective also creep into some of these writings. Although authors are seemingly unaware of the new institutionalism in sociology, they often consider the presidency as having characteristics of a bureaucracy, and thus of being part of a larger organizational field. Some of the confusion stems from the ambiguity of the three views. But the difficulty also rests with presidency scholars themselves who have not clearly articulated or agreed upon the dimensions of the presidency as an institution.

To help resolve these issues, this book considers the presidency as an institution from the traditional sociological view, but also enlarges that view. The traditional sociological view defies the tendency of the new sociological perspective to be overly broad and label almost anything as an institution. Designating the handshake, the "No Smoking" sign, and the Nobel Prize as institutions confuses what may be more aptly considered symbols for institutions. The traditional sociological approach does not mistake the characteristics of an institution for the institution itself, a problem with the economics view. For instance, the use of the informal rule of seniority in Congress is indicative of Congress as an institution rather than seniority as an institution. The traditional sociological view permits the identification of two dimensions of an institution: organizational and behavioral. It recognizes the intuitive understanding already in place in much of the presidency literature that an organization imbued "with value beyond the technical requirements of the task at hand" is an institution (Selznick, 1957, 17). It also suggests that regular behavior patterns accompany, but are distinct from, the organizational dynamics.

Yet, the traditional sociological view falters in not fully recognizing a third dimension of institutions—structure. The organizational and behavioral dimensions of an institution do not simply come about on their own. Structural elements are the intrinsic, defining characteristics of the institution that provide the parameters within which the organization and institutional behavior occur. These structures are not so broad as to identify an organizational field; instead, they describe the most typical features of a single institution. For instance, there are certain elements that distinguish the American presidency from the German or French presidencies. The structures guiding the American office include quadrennial indirect elections, separation of powers, and the combination of head of state with policy actor. These structures establish the parameters within which the institutional organization and behavior occur. Thus, this book identifies three dimensions of the presidency as an institution: organizational, behavioral, and structural.

The *organizational dimension* reveals how an institution is fused with value as an end in itself. Applied to the presidency, it involves the routines, procedures, and units that comprise the Executive Office of the President. Although presidents often make marginal changes within the organization, the office is not reinvented each time a president arrives at the White House (see Chapter 6). Because of the tangible qualities of the organization, this dimension is especially important in juxtaposing the presidency as an institution against presidents as individuals.

The *behavioral dimension* involves the extent to which presidents faced with similar environmental circumstances respond in similar ways. Perhaps one of the most well-defined behavioral aspects of the contemporary presidency is the use of public persuasion. Scholars often concentrate on the uniqueness of individual presidents' public leadership. Yet, institutional behavior—in the form of major national addresses, news conferences, and ceremonial appearances—guides much of these individual actions. In addition, imagery attached to the office—that is, the image of the president as the one person in charge of the government and as the representative of the people—creates consistency in the way presidents present themselves to the public (see Chapter 4).

The *structural dimension* defines how the U.S. Constitution, historical precedents, and temporal orderings shape the presidency. Most fundamentally, the presidency is structured as an electoral and representative office, independent from the legislature. As an electoral office, the presidency runs on a four-year clock set by the most recent and the next presidential election. Time systematically defines how the office operates. Political resources and opportunities decrease as time moves further away from the election victory and the "honeymoon" ends (Light, 1991). As a representative office, the presidency rests on a symbolic connection between the people and the president; the president is a symbol of the nation and is thereby identified with its achievements and misfortunes. As an independent office, the presidency reflects separation of powers. This independence has allowed the presidency to garner more power than the Framers originally envisioned, though the executive's gain has not necessarily been at the expense of Congress, which itself benefits from the separation of powers. These three dimensions—organizational, behavioral, and structural—define the manner in which the presidential institution has a life of its own.

Statistical Patterns of the Presidency

The statistical patterns revealed in this book show that the institution of the presidency shapes presidents as much as presidents, during their short tenures, shape the institution. Both the resources and constraints inherent in the institution make the actions of individual presidents far more similar than different to the actions of their immediate predecessors and successors. In addition, the institutional presidency may even act independently of presidents in making policy decisions or shaping presidents' public activities. While it is true that some presidents have fashioned significant innovations, such one-time reforms often become commonplace practices for future presidents and thus a part of the institution. This book attempts to place these president-specific changes within the context of an evolving presidency. It is also true that exogenous events in the national and international environment are important. These events may shape both presidents' actions and the institution itself. The data presented here provide the necessary foundation for fashioning explanations about the connections among the presidency, presidents, and the political environment. Readers will find three sets of statistical patterns in the book: institutional patterns, environmental patterns, and incumbent-specific patterns. Of course, data are not self-interpreting. Scholars may find other statistical patterns than those highlighted here. In either case, the data may allow them to pursue answers to questions they have not thought about in the past.

Institutional Continuity

The transition between administrations provides one of the strongest tests of the validity of institutional patterns. How can the presidency truly exist as an ongoing institution when, on January 20 following the election of a new president, virtually every important White House office changes occupants? The turnover is dramatic and takes place whether or not the successive executives belong to different political parties. Even when a president begins a second term, changes abound. A new chief establishes a new direction.

Still, the outlook of the new administration reflects past campaigns, administrations, and policies, all of which provide continuity. In addition, as broad new themes shape specific relationships among (new) individuals in (old) organizations, many arrangements and procedures persist from previous administrations. When one incumbent replaces another, the newcomer may well perpetuate established practices out of a need to respond quickly in a context of limited information and expertise.

The executive apparatus shows even more systematic continuity. Although members of the White House staff change with some frequency, the broader institution of the presidency is hardly recreated each time a new administration enters office. Many, if not all, top staffers change during a transition, but the career personnel stay. As an example, on January 6, 1977, the International Trade Commission recommended to President Gerald Ford that tariffs be placed on shoes imported from abroad. Ford decided not to act on the matter but instead left it to his successor. The day after Jimmy Carter took office, he received a memo from the National Security Council on shoe import quotas. On February 4, the office of the United States Trade Representative—a unit within the Executive Office of the President charged with advising presidents on trade—provided Carter with a background memo. In both instances, action was being taken on material inherited from the Ford administration (see DiClerico 1985, 248–249). This item on the national policy agenda continued to be addressed, regardless of who was president.

Yet, incumbent change surely remains prominent even amidst this continuity. Ultimately, the most appropriate way of viewing the change wrought by a new incumbent and administration is to see it as a structural cycle of the institution, *not* a feature of the presidential entourage. Quadrennial change is merely one of the regularly occurring patterns that constitute the presidency and help explain the behavior of old and new alike at the White House. While every president enters office determined to make a difference, students of the presidency are deceived if they think that this is a function of an individual president. Instead, it is much more reflective of the electoral and representative nature of the office. Election cycle change is actually a very regular and well-known aspect of the presidency—it inheres in the office, not in its incumbents.

Environmental Influences

The overall environment plays a role in establishing some of the most compelling patterns in the presidency. These patterns derive from the way national politics depends on exogenous events and conditions, such as wars, economic booms and busts, rising crime rates, hefty trade imbalances, and the collapse of longstanding governments abroad. Such circumstances are not wholly or even principally under presidents' control, although they are sometimes mistakenly assumed to be so. Herbert Hoover made this point when he said, "Once upon a time my political opponents honored me as possessing the fabulous intellectual and economic power by which I created a world-wide depression all by myself." Sharing Hoover's sentiments, William Howard Taft observed,

> There is a class of people that . . . visit the President with responsibility for everything that is done and that is not done. If poverty prevails where, in their judgment, it should not prevail, then the President is responsible. If other people are richer than they ought to be, the President is responsible. While the President's powers are broad, he cannot do everything. . . . This would be ludicrous if it did not sometimes take serious results. The President cannot make clouds to rain, he cannot make the corn to grow, he cannot make business to be good. (1916, 47–50)

In many ways, the success or failure attributed to individual presidents may well be the result of conditions in the broader social, political, and economic environment that make presidents look good and bad, or better and worse, than they would otherwise.

Incumbent Differences

President-specific dynamics comprise a third set of patterns derived from the data. General patterns take on recognizable forms across different administrations, though individual incumbents may give them distinct character. An example from Chapter 4 reveals that President Richard Nixon made significantly fewer news conferences than did other presidents. Another example from Chapter 5 indicates that President George Bush's public approval ratings started high, soared even higher, then dropped precipitously. A final example from Chapter 6 shows that President Ford sharply cut the size of the Executive Office of the President upon taking office.

Yet each of these incumbent-specific patterns must be placed in the larger context of the office. Nixon made fewer news conferences, but he did not abandon these sessions with the press because he could not. The practice of giving news conferences is an institutional feature of the presidency that a president—even Nixon, who bitterly distrusted the press—would stop only at his political peril. Bush obtained the highest approval rating of any president in the middle of his third year in office, yet the institutional pattern still caught up with him when public expectations went unmet on domestic and economic issues after the Persian Gulf War. President Ford drastically cut the size of the White House staff, but he did not cut its budget.

None of these examples are meant to suggest that the institution has some kind of magical power over individual incumbents. Rather, the institution represents an encompassing set of offices, procedures, and relationships within which presidents act and react and which help to guide their behavior.

Systematic Research on the Presidency

Although this book contains many statistics, data points, trend lines, and counts, this does not suggest that all research on the presidency should be quantitative or that all quantitative research is better than qualitative research. Indeed, not all questions worthy of being asked can be answered with quantitative data. Quantitative or qualitative work done shoddily reveals nothing. Quantitative and qualitative work done thoroughly can provide (and has provided) important insights into the office. It is surely possible for presidency scholars to develop theoretically driven, systematic analyses using either type of data. There is nothing intrinsically more rigorous, difficult, or informative about quantitative research relative to qualitative research (King, 1993; King, Keohane, Verba, 1994). But, ultimately, this book stands as a reminder that there is little room left in the study of the presidency for research based on unsystematic, albeit absorbing, anecdotes and passing observations. Researchers often masquerade such anecdotal evidence as systematically gathered and analyzed qualitative data, which it is not.

Anecdotal observation has at least two negative consequences. First, it leads observers to make misinformed judgments and statements. For example, the 1980 and 1984 elections were widely perceived as two of the largest presidential election victories ever. Accordingly, Democrats and Republicans alike believed that the American public supported Ronald Reagan's policies wholeheartedly. Although his 1984 victory was a substantial electoral college win, fully one-third of all election victories in this century were decided by *larger* popular vote margins (see Chapter 3). Moreover, two-thirds of all presidential elections in this century were decided by larger popular vote margins than Reagan's 1980 victory.

Second, anecdotal observation leaves scholars without a reliable basis for comparison and analysis. Presidential behavior, reporters' comments, newspaper editorials, presidents' biographies and autobiographies, and political arguments by members of Congress or the administration are impossible to evaluate adequately without knowledge of comparable situations and statistics. For example, commentators often overstated Carter's unpopularity, portraying him as unable to lead the country during trying times. In an equally overstated fashion, observers pointed to Reagan's exceptional popularity, dubbing him the "Teflon" president when his personal popularity remained seemingly untouched by the relative unpopularity of his political positions. Yet systematic analysis of the evidence reveals that these characterizations of the two presidents were erroneous. Data in Chapter 5 make clear that during the first two years of their terms, these two presidents had similar public approval ratings.

Thoroughgoing data analysis—whether quantitative or qualitative— of an individual president's term or across several presidents' terms alleviates these twin problems. Comparisons are routine and evaluations of the evidence are more reliable. Presidency watchers of all kinds have an interest in eliminating anecdotal observation to reduce the chasm between information about American presidents and information about the presidency. As more presidency scholars test theories and hypotheses with appropriate data, generalizations about the presidency become more numerous and more trustworthy. Many of these generalizations are already in place (Ragsdale, 1994). Such research provides the opportunity for cumulative scientific study that will move the field toward a consensus about which questions *not* to ask and about *how* to ask new questions and away from past squabbles about the second-class status of the field.

Outline of the Book

The book is organized into nine chapters. Data in the chapters are presented in as long a time frame as possible. Chapter 1 offers a brief look at presidents from George Washington to Clinton—their personal backgrounds and their political experience. The chapter reminds readers of who these men were and the significance of the eras in which they lived.

Chapters 2 and 3 consider how elections create structural aspects of the presidency as an institution. Chapter 2 offers a view of the presidential selection process, providing data on presidential nominating conventions beginning in 1832. It continues with an examination of the rise in importance of presidential primaries since 1912. Media coverage of the 1988 and 1992 nominations is also addressed, showing that what was once a heavily party-dominant task is now a much more candidate-driven process. Chapter 3 examines general election outcomes since 1789 and offers information on modern-day presidential campaigns.

Chapters 4 and 5 consider the nature of institutional behavior, first from the perspective of presidents' activities and then from the perspective of the public's reactions to these activities. Chapter 4 provides an analysis of presidents' public appearances since Calvin Coolidge as a form of institutional behavior. Chapter 5 offers public opinion data on presidents since Harry Truman that reveal a downward trend over time. This public institutional behavior may shape subsequent presidential behavior.

Chapters 6 and 7 look at the organization as a pivotal part of the presidency as an institution. Chapter 6 considers the size and shape of the office of the president, its budget, and the units within it since its inception in 1924. The chapter also examines the broad outlines of the executive branch and stresses that the organization of the presidency is not the same thing as the executive branch, nor is it in control of the executive branch. Chapter 7 continues this look at the organization of the presidency with an examination of the independent decisions that the presidential institution makes on behalf of the president. These decisions involve diplomacy, military affairs, the economy, and domestic matters. Treaties, executive agreements, and executive orders from Washington to Clinton are highlighted.

The final two chapters examine relations between the presidency and the other institutions of government. The structural, behavioral, and organizational dimensions of the presidency are evident in relations between the presidency and Congress (Chapter 8) and between the presidency and the courts (Chapter 9). Chapter 8 lists presidential requests to Congress and presidential positions on legislation before Congress since Dwight Eisenhower and notes vetoes taken since Washington. Chapter 9 depicts the judicial nominations of presidents and examines court rulings against presidents since Washington.

1

Presidents of the United States

Can anyone grow up to be president, as the old adage suggests? The tables of this chapter present data with which to examine this question. Table 1-1 lists the presidents and vice presidents of the United States; Table 1-2 examines the personal backgrounds of the presidents; and Tables 1-3, 1-4, and 1-5 offer accounts of the presidents' political lives. The data reveal that the forty-one presidents of the United States have come from every conceivable set of circumstances. Apparently, it does not matter whether one is 5 feet, 4 inches tall (Madison) or 6 feet, 4 inches tall (Bush, Clinton). It does not matter whether one goes to Ivy League schools such as Harvard (Adams) or Yale (Bush) or to no school at all (Washington). One can be young (Tyler, Kennedy, Clinton) or old (Harrison, Eisenhower, Reagan). There have been presidents with no political experience (Taylor, Grant) and presidents with lengthy political careers behind them (Lyndon Johnson, Ford). These differences would seem to lend credence to the political-actor perspective discussed in the introduction—namely, that no two presidents are alike and they all arrive and leave the presidency via distinctive paths. The political-actor perspective contends that this uniqueness is worthy of study.

Yet, most of these characteristics do not have much to offer in our search to understand how presidents will act in office. Table 1-6, which looks at the various ratings of presidents, indicates that neither personal nor political characteristics are good predictors of success (as defined in the several polls). The six polls share considerable similarity in naming the very best presidents. Yet nothing in the presidents' immediate personal or political backgrounds provides clues to their so-called greatness.

So are there any useful patterns to be observed? Three are most noteworthy: First, there is a clear bias in who has become (and can become) president. Anyone can become president who is *not* female, black, hispanic, Jewish, or openly homosexual. The presidency, more than any other elected and appointed office in America, enforces a strong, white-men-only restriction.

Second, Table 1-6 reveals that several presidents who were judged "great" were in fact caught up in circumstances beyond their control—Lincoln faced the Civil War, Wilson encountered World War I, and Franklin Roosevelt confronted the Great Depression and World War II. As noted in the introduction, it is important to consider the environment within which presidents act. Social, economic, and political events and conditions may force, as much as allow, presidents to behave boldly. A note of caution is also in order regarding interpretation. Greatness is surely in the eye of the beholder. Although the polls show agreement on the top four or five presidents, there is little consensus thereafter. A person's judgment of greatness varies depending on his or her own background, political interests, partisanship, and view of the office.

Finally, historical eras are important in studying individual presidents. As an example, drawn from Tables 1-3 and 1-4, the twentieth-century presidency attracts a particular type of office-seeker who is far different from that of the nineteenth century. Twentieth-century presidents are less likely to have served in Congress than those of the nineteenth century; indeed, they are less likely to have had any lengthy political experience at all prior to running for office. Researchers should bear in mind that eighteenth- and nineteenth-century presidents and their twentieth-century counterparts are unlike, largely because the office they have held has radically changed over time (Ragsdale, 1993).

The nineteenth-century presidency operated under a doctrine of presidential restraint in which presidents did not take the lead in government, but instead deferred to Congress. This view of presidential restraint closely followed the intent of the Framers—in the U.S. Constitution the chief executive is given a limited set of specified powers rather than any inherent executive authority. As such, it is no accident that twenty of the twenty-five presidents of the nineteenth century were not activists. Only Washington, Jefferson, Jackson, Polk, and Lincoln are exceptions to this nineteenth-century rule of restraint. This is not because those twenty presidents were especially prosaic or unhappy men, unable to champion the office they held. Nor is it because the five other presidents were keenly charismatic, energetic, or intelligent. Instead, conceptions of the Constitution strongly restricted the institution in which all twenty-five served. On occasion, circumstances, such as the founding of government, the outbreak of war, or internal crises, have allowed presidents to move beyond the restrictions. Yet decades separated these precedents, and they were not incorporated together.

At the opening of the twentieth century, ideas about the presidency and government changed. A theory of presidential activism replaced that of presidential restraint. Presidents should use their power to act, in Theodore Roosevelt's words, as "the steward of the people bound actively and affirmatively to do all he could for the people" (1913, 389). The twentieth-century office is one that has expanded presidents' activities far beyond what they were in the previous century. Thus, in thinking about presidents, it is important to consider the times in which they sought and held the office.

Table 1-1 U.S. Presidents and Vice Presidents

President (political party)	President's term of service	Vice president	Vice president's term of service
George Washington (F)	April 30, 1789–March 4, 1793	John Adams	April 30, 1789–March 4, 1793
George Washington (F)	March 4, 1793–March 4, 1797	John Adams	March 4, 1793–March 4, 1797
John Adams (F)	March 4, 1797–March 4, 1801	Thomas Jefferson	March 4, 1797–March 4, 1801
Thomas Jefferson (DR)	March 4, 1801–March 4, 1805	Aaron Burr	March 4, 1801–March 4, 1805
Thomas Jefferson (DR)	March 4, 1805–March 4, 1809	George Clinton	March 4, 1805–March 4, 1809
James Madison (DR)	March 4, 1809–March 4, 1813	George Clinton[a]	March 4, 1809–April 12, 1812
James Madison (DR)	March 4, 1813–March 4, 1817	Elbridge Gerry[a]	March 4, 1813–Nov. 23, 1814
James Monroe (DR)	March 4, 1817–March 4, 1821	Daniel D. Tompkins	March 4, 1817–March 4, 1821
James Monroe (DR)	March 4, 1821–March 4, 1825	Daniel D. Tompkins	March 4, 1821–March 4, 1825
John Quincy Adams (DR)	March 4, 1825–March 4, 1829	John C. Calhoun	March 4, 1825–March 4, 1829
Andrew Jackson (D)	March 4, 1829–March 4, 1833	John C. Calhoun[b]	March 4, 1829–Dec. 28, 1832
Andrew Jackson (D)	March 4, 1833–March 4, 1837	Martin Van Buren	March 4, 1833–March 4, 1837
Martin Van Buren (D)	March 4, 1837–March 4, 1841	Richard M. Johnson[c]	March 4, 1837–March 4, 1841
William H. Harrison[a] (W)	March 4, 1841–April 4, 1841	John Tyler[c]	March 4, 1841–April 6, 1841
John Tyler (W)	April 6, 1841–March 4, 1845		
James K. Polk (D)	March 4, 1845–March 4, 1849	George M. Dallas[c]	March 4, 1845–March 4, 1849
Zachary Taylor[a] (W)	March 4, 1849–July 9, 1850	Millard Fillmore[c]	March 4, 1849–July 10, 1850
Millard Fillmore (W)	July 10, 1850–March 4, 1853		
Franklin Pierce (D)	March 4, 1853–March 4, 1857	William R. King[a]	March 24, 1853–April 18, 1853
James Buchanan (D)	March 4, 1857–March 4, 1861	John C. Breckinridge	March 4, 1857–March 4, 1861
Abraham Lincoln (R)	March 4, 1861–March 4, 1865	Hannibal Hamlin	March 4, 1861–March 4, 1865
Abraham Lincoln[a] (R)	March 4, 1865–April 15, 1865	Andrew Johnson[c]	March 4, 1865–April 15, 1865
Andrew Johnson (R)	April 15, 1865–March 4, 1869		
Ulysses S. Grant (R)	March 4, 1869–March 4, 1873	Schuyler Colfax	March 4, 1869–March 4, 1873
Ulysses S. Grant (R)	March 4, 1873–March 4, 1877	Henry Wilson[a]	March 4, 1873–Nov. 22, 1875
Rutherford B. Hayes (R)	March 4, 1877–March 4, 1881	William A. Wheeler[c]	March 4, 1877–March 4, 1881
James A. Garfield[a] (R)	March 4, 1881–Sept. 19, 1881	Chester A. Arthur[c]	March 4, 1881–Sept. 20, 1881

President	Term	Vice President	Term
Chester A. Arthur (R)	Sept. 20, 1881–March 4, 1885		
Grover Cleveland (D)	March 4, 1885–March 4, 1889	Thomas A. Hendricks[a]	March 4, 1885–Nov. 25, 1885
Benjamin Harrison (R)	March 4, 1889–March 4, 1893	Levi P. Morton	March 4, 1889–March 4, 1893
Grover Cleveland (D)	March 4, 1893–March 4, 1897	Adlai E. Stevenson	March 4, 1893–March 4, 1897
William McKinley (R)	March 4, 1897–March 4, 1901	Garret A. Hobart[a]	March 4, 1897–Nov. 21, 1899
William McKinley[a] (R)	March 4, 1901–Sept. 14, 1901	Theodore Roosevelt[c]	March 4, 1901–Sept. 14, 1901
Theodore Roosevelt (R)	Sept. 14, 1901–March 4, 1905		
Theodore Roosevelt (R)	March 4, 1905–March 4, 1909	Charles W. Fairbanks	March 4, 1905–March 4, 1909
William H. Taft (R)	March 4, 1909–March 4, 1913	James S. Sherman[a]	March 4, 1909–Oct. 30, 1912
Woodrow Wilson (D)	March 4, 1913–March 4, 1917	Thomas R. Marshall	March 4, 1913–March 4, 1917
Woodrow Wilson (D)	March 4, 1917–March 4, 1921	Thomas R. Marshall	March 4, 1917–March 4, 1921
Warren G. Harding[a] (R)	March 4, 1921–Aug. 2, 1923	Calvin Coolidge[c]	March 4, 1921–Aug. 3, 1923
Calvin Coolidge (R)	Aug. 3, 1923–March 4, 1925		
Calvin Coolidge (R)	March 4, 1925–March 4, 1929	Charles G. Dawes	March 4, 1925–March 4, 1929
Herbert Hoover (R)	March 4, 1929–March 4, 1933	Charles Curtis	March 4, 1929–March 4, 1933
Franklin D. Roosevelt (D)	March 4, 1933–Jan. 20, 1937	John N. Garner	March 4, 1933–Jan. 20, 1937
Franklin D. Roosevelt (D)	Jan. 20, 1937–Jan. 20, 1941	John N. Garner	Jan. 20, 1937–Jan. 20, 1941
Franklin D. Roosevelt (D)	Jan. 20, 1941–Jan. 20, 1945	Henry A. Wallace	Jan. 20, 1941–Jan. 20, 1945
Franklin D. Roosevelt[a] (D)	Jan. 20, 1945–April 12, 1945	Harry S. Truman[c]	Jan. 20, 1945–April 12, 1945
Harry S. Truman (D)	April 12, 1945–Jan. 20, 1949		
Harry S. Truman (D)	Jan. 20, 1949–Jan. 20, 1953	Alben W. Barkley	Jan. 20, 1949–Jan. 20, 1953
Dwight D. Eisenhower (R)	Jan. 20, 1953–Jan. 20, 1957	Richard Nixon	Jan. 20, 1953–Jan. 20, 1957
Dwight D. Eisenhower (R)	Jan. 20, 1957–Jan. 20, 1961	Richard Nixon	Jan. 20, 1957–Jan. 20, 1961
John F. Kennedy[a] (D)	Jan. 20, 1961–Nov. 22, 1963	Lyndon B. Johnson[c]	Jan. 20, 1961–Nov. 22, 1963
Lyndon B. Johnson (D)	Nov. 22, 1963–Jan. 20, 1965		
Lyndon B. Johnson (D)	Jan. 20, 1965–Jan. 20, 1969	Hubert H. Humphrey	Jan. 20, 1965–Jan. 20, 1969
Richard Nixon (R)	Jan. 20, 1969–Jan. 20, 1973	Spiro T. Agnew	Jan. 20, 1969–Jan. 20, 1973
Richard Nixon[b] (R)	Jan. 20, 1973–Aug. 9, 1974	Spiro T. Agnew[b]	Jan. 20, 1973–Oct. 10, 1973
		Gerald R. Ford[c]	Dec. 6, 1973–Aug. 9, 1974
Gerald R. Ford[c] (R)	Aug. 9, 1974–Jan. 20, 1977	Nelson A. Rockefeller	Dec. 19, 1974–Jan. 20, 1977
Jimmy Carter (D)	Jan. 20, 1977–Jan. 20, 1981	Walter F. Mondale	Jan. 20, 1977–Jan. 20, 1981

(Table continues)

Table 1-1 *(Continued)*

President (political party)	President's term of service	Vice president	Vice president's term of service
Ronald Reagan (R)	Jan. 20, 1981–Jan. 20, 1985	George Bush	Jan. 20, 1981–Jan. 20, 1985
Ronald Reagan (R)	Jan. 20, 1985–Jan. 20, 1989	George Bush	Jan. 20, 1985–Jan. 20, 1989
George Bush (R)	Jan. 20, 1989–Jan. 20, 1993	Dan Quayle	Jan. 20, 1989–Jan. 20, 1993
Bill Clinton (D)	Jan. 20, 1993–	Albert Gore	Jan. 20, 1993–

Sources: Presidential Elections Since 1789, 4th ed. (Washington, D.C.: Congressional Quarterly, 1987), 4.; Daniel C. Diller, "Biographies of the Vice Presidents," in *Guide to the Presidency,* ed. Michael Nelson (Washington, D.C.: Congressional Quarterly, 1989), 1319–1346.

Note: D—Democrat; DR—Democratic-Republican; F—Federalist; R—Republican; W—Whig.

a Died in office.
b Resigned.
c Succeeded to the presidency.

Table 1-2 Personal Backgrounds of U.S. Presidents, Washington to Clinton

President	Date of birth	Place of birth	Date of death	Age at death	Higher education	Occupation	Number of children	Height in inches
1. George Washington	Feb. 22, 1732	Va.	Dec. 14, 1799	67	None	Farmer/surveyor	0	74
2. John Adams	Oct. 30, 1735	Mass.	July 4, 1826	90	Harvard	Farmer/lawyer	5	67
3. Thomas Jefferson	April 13, 1743	Va.	July 4, 1826	83	William & Mary	Farmer/lawyer	6	75
4. James Madison	March 16, 1751	Va.	June 28, 1836	85	Princeton	Farmer	0	64
5. James Monroe	April 28, 1758	Va.	July 4, 1831	73	William & Mary	Farmer/lawyer	2	72
6. John Quincy Adams	July 11, 1767	Mass.	Feb. 23, 1848	80	Harvard	Lawyer	4	67
7. Andrew Jackson	March 15, 1767	S.C.	June 8, 1845	78	None	Lawyer	0	73
8. Martin Van Buren	Dec. 5, 1782	N.Y.	Jan. 18, 1862	71	None	Lawyer	4	66
9. William H. Harrison	Feb. 9, 1773	Va.	April 4, 1841	68	Hampden	Military	10	N/A
10. John Tyler	March 29, 1790	Va.	Jan. 18, 1862	71	William & Mary	Lawyer	15	72
11. James K. Polk	Nov. 2, 1795	N.C.	June 15, 1849	53	North Carolina	Lawyer	0	68
12. Zachary Taylor	Nov. 24, 1784	Va.	July 9, 1850	65	None	Military	6	68
13. Millard Fillmore	Jan. 7, 1800	N.Y.	March 8, 1874	74	None	Lawyer	2	69
14. Franklin Pierce	Nov. 23, 1804	N.H.	Oct. 8, 1869	64	Bowdoin	Lawyer	3	70
15. James Buchanan	April 23, 1791	Pa.	June 1, 1868	77	Dickinson	Lawyer	0[a]	72
16. Abraham Lincoln	Feb. 12, 1809	Ky.	April 15, 1865	56	None	Lawyer	4	74
17. Andrew Johnson	Dec. 29, 1808	N.C.	July 31, 1875	66	None	Tailor	5	70
18. Ulysses S. Grant	April 27, 1822	Ohio	July 23, 1885	63	West Point	Military	4	68
19. Rutherford B. Hayes	Oct. 4, 1822	Ohio	Jan. 17, 1893	70	Kenyon	Lawyer	8	68
20. James A. Garfield	Nov. 19, 1831	Ohio	Sep. 19, 1881	49	Williams	Educator/lawyer	5	N/A
21. Chester A. Arthur	Oct. 5, 1829	Vt.	Nov. 18, 1886	57	Union	Lawyer	3	74
22. Grover Cleveland	March 18, 1837	N.J.	June 24, 1908	71	None	Lawyer	5	71
23. Benjamin Harrison	Aug. 20, 1833	Ohio	March 13, 1901	67	Miami (Ohio)	Lawyer	3	66
24. Grover Cleveland	March 18, 1837	N.J.	June 24, 1908	71	None	Lawyer	5	71
25. William McKinley	Jan. 29, 1843	Ohio	Sep. 14, 1901	58	Allegheny	Lawyer	2	67
26. Theodore Roosevelt	Oct. 27, 1858	N.Y.	Jan. 6, 1919	60	Harvard	Lawyer/author	6	70

(Table continues)

Table 1-2 *(Continued)*

President	Date of birth	Place of birth	Date of death	Age at death	Higher education	Occupation	Number of children	Height in inches
27. William H. Taft	Sep. 15, 1857	Ohio	March 8, 1930	72	Yale	Lawyer	3	72
28. Woodrow Wilson	Dec. 28, 1856	Va.	Feb. 3, 1924	67	Princeton	Educator	3	71
29. Warren G. Harding	Nov. 2, 1865	Ohio	Aug. 2, 1923	57	Ohio Central	Newspaper editor	0	72
30. Calvin Coolidge	July 4, 1872	Vt.	Jan. 5, 1933	60	Amherst	Lawyer	2	70
31. Herbert Hoover	Aug. 10, 1874	Iowa	Oct. 20, 1964	90	Stanford	Engineer	2	71
32. Franklin D. Roosevelt	Jan. 30, 1882	N.Y.	April 12, 1945	63	Harvard	Lawyer	5	74
33. Harry S. Truman	May 8, 1884	Mo.	Dec. 26, 1972	88	None	Clerk/Store owner	1	69
34. Dwight D. Eisenhower	Oct. 14, 1890	Texas	March 28, 1969	78	West Point	Military	1	70
35. John F. Kennedy	May 29, 1917	Mass.	Nov. 22, 1963	46	Harvard	Lawyer	2	72
36. Lyndon B. Johnson	Aug 27, 1908	Texas	Jan. 22, 1973	64	Southwest Texas State Teachers' College	Educator	2	75
37. Richard Nixon	Jan. 9, 1913	Calif.	Apr. 22, 1994	81	Whittier	Lawyer	2	72
38. Gerald R. Ford	July 14, 1913	Neb.			Michigan	Lawyer	4	72
39. Jimmy Carter	Oct. 1, 1924	Ga.			Annapolis	Farmer/businessman	4	69
40. Ronald Reagan	Feb. 6, 1911	Ill.			Eureka	Actor	4	74
41. George Bush	June 12, 1924	Mass.			Yale	Businessman	6	76
42. Bill Clinton	Aug. 19, 1946	Ark.			Georgetown	Lawyer	1	76

Sources: Adapted from *Congressional Quarterly's Guide to U.S. Elections*, 2d ed. (Washington, D.C.: Congressional Quarterly, 1985), 252; Jack E. Holmes and Robert Elder, "Our Best and Worst Presidents" (paper presented at the annual meeting of the American Political Science Association, September 1986).

Note: N/A—Not available.

Table 1-3 Political Careers of U.S. Presidents Prior to Their Presidencies, Washington to Clinton

President	Party	Age at first political office	First political office/last political office	Years in Congress	Years as governor	Years as vice president	Age at becoming president
1. George Washington	F	17	County surveyor/military general	2	0	0	57
2. John Adams	F	39	Highway surveyor/vice president	5	0	4	61
3. Thomas Jefferson	DR	26	State legislator/vice president	5	3	4	58
4. James Madison	DR	25	State legislator/secretary of state	15	0	0	58
5. James Monroe	DR	24	State legislator/secretary of state	7	4	0	59
6. John Quincy Adams	DR	27	Minister to Netherlands/secretary of state	0a	0	0	58
7. Andrew Jackson	D	21	Prosecuting attorney/U.S. Senate	4	0	0	62
8. Martin Van Buren	D	30	County surrogate/vice president	8	0	4	55
9. William H. Harrison	W	26	Territorial delegate/minister to Colombia	0	0	0	68
10. John Tyler	W	21	State legislator/vice president	12	2	0	51
11. James K. Polk	D	28	State legislator/governor	14	3	0	50
12. Zachary Taylor	W	—	None/military general	0	0	0	65
13. Millard Fillmore	W	28	State legislator/vice president	8	0	1	50
14. Franklin Pierce	D	25	State legislator/district attorney	9	0	0	48
15. James Buchanan	D	22	County prosecutor/minister to Great Britain	20	0	0	65
16. Abraham Lincoln	R	25	State legislator/U.S. House	2	0	0	52
17. Andrew Johnson	D	20	City alderman/vice president	14	4	0	57
18. Ulysses S. Grant	R	—	None/military general	0	0	0	47
19. Rutherford B. Hayes	R	36	City solicitor/governor	3	6	0	55
20. James A. Garfield	R	28	State legislator/U.S. Senate	18	0	0	50
21. Chester A. Arthur	R	31	State engineer/vice president	0	0	1	51
22. Grover Cleveland	D	26	District attorney/governor	0	2	0	48
23. Benjamin Harrison	R	24	City attorney/U.S. Senate	6	0	0	56

(Table continues)

Table 1-3 *(Continued)*

President	Party	Age at first political office	First political office/last political office	Years in Congress	Years as governor	Years as vice president	Age at becoming president
24. Grover Cleveland	D	26	District attorney/governor	0	2	0	53
25. William McKinley	R	26	Prosecuting attorney/governor	14	4	0	54
26. Theodore Roosevelt	R	24	State legislator/vice president	0	2	1	43
27. William H. Taft	R	24	Prosecuting attorney/secretary of war	0	0	0	52
28. Woodrow Wilson	D	54	Governor/governor	0	2	0	56
29. Warren G. Harding	R	35	State legislator/U.S. Senate	6	0	0	56
30. Calvin Coolidge	R	26	City council/vice president	0	2	3	51
31. Herbert Hoover	R	43	Relief administrator/secretary of commerce	0	0	0	55
32. Franklin D. Roosevelt	D	28	State legislator/governor	0	4	0	49
33. Harry S. Truman	D	38	County judge/vice president	10	0	0	61
34. Dwight D. Eisenhower	R	—	None/military general	0	0	0	63
35. John F. Kennedy	D	29	U.S. House/U.S. Senate	14	0	0	43
36. Lyndon B. Johnson	D	28	U.S. House/U.S. Senate	24	0	3	55
37. Richard Nixon	R	34	U.S. House/vice president	6	0	8	56
38. Gerald R. Ford	R	36	U.S. House/vice president	25	0	2	61
39. Jimmy Carter	D	38	Member, County Board of Education/governor	0	4	0	52
40. Ronald Reagan	R	55	Governor/governor	0	8	0	69
41. George Bush	R	42	U.S. House/vice president	4	0	8	64
42. Bill Clinton	D	30	State attorney general/governor	0	12	0	46

Sources: Adapted from *Presidential Elections Since 1789*, 4th ed. (Washington D.C.: Congressional Quarterly, 1987), 4; Norman Thomas, Joseph Pika, and Richard Watson, *The Politics of the Presidency*, 3d ed. (Washington, D.C.: CQ Press, 1993), 490.

Note: D—Democrat; DR—Democratic-Republican; F—Federalist; W—Whig.

[a] Adams served in the U.S. House for six years after leaving the presidency.

Table 1-4   Presidents' Previous Public Positions, Washington to Clinton

	Number of presidents holding position prior to presidency	
Position	Pre-1900 (24)	Post-1900 (17)
Vice president	7	7
Cabinet member	7	3
U.S. representative	13	5
U.S. senator	9	5
Federal judge	0	1
Governor	11	7
State legislator	16	5
State judge	1	2
Mayor	2	1
Diplomat, ambassador	7	2
Military general	11	1

	Last public position held before presidency	
Position	Pre-1900 (24)	Post-1900 (17)
Vice president		
Succeeded to presidency	4	5
Won presidency in own right	3	2
Congress		
House	1	0
Senate	3	2
Appointive federal office		
Military general	3	1
Cabinet secretary	3	2
Ambassador	2	0
Other civilian	1	0
Governor	4	5

Source: Harold Stanley and Richard Niemi, *Vital Statistics on American Politics*, 4th ed. (Washington, D.C.: CQ Press, 1994), 262.

Table 1-5   Presidents Who Died in Office

President	Year of death	Portion of term served (in months)	Age	Cause
William H. Harrison	1841	1	68	Illness
Zachary Taylor	1850	16	65	Illness
Abraham Lincoln	1865	1	56	Assassination
James A. Garfield	1881	6	49	Assassination
William McKinley	1901	6	58	Assassination
Warren G. Harding	1923	29	57	Illness
Franklin D. Roosevelt	1945	1	63	Illness
John F. Kennedy	1963	35	46	Assassination

Source: Adapted from *Congressional Quarterly's Guide to U.S. Elections*, 2d ed. (Washington, D.C.: Congressional Quarterly, 1985), 252.

Table 1-6 Ratings of U.S. Presidents, Washington to Reagan

Schlesinger poll (1948)	Schlesinger poll (1962)	Maranell-Dodder poll (1970)	DiClerico poll (1977)	Tribune poll (1982)	Murray-Blessing poll[a] (1982)
Great	*Great*	*Accomplishments of administration*	*Ten greatest presidents*	*Ten best presidents*	*Great*
1. Lincoln	1. Lincoln	1. Lincoln	1. Lincoln	1. Lincoln (best)	1. Lincoln
2. Washington	2. Washington	2. F. Roosevelt	2. Washington	2. Washington	2. F. Roosevelt
3. F. Roosevelt	3. F. Roosevelt	3. Washington	3. F. Roosevelt	3. F. Roosevelt	3. Washington
4. Wilson	4. Wilson	4. Jefferson	4. Jefferson	4. T. Roosevelt	4. Jefferson
5. Jefferson	5. Jefferson	5. T. Roosevelt	5. T. Roosevelt	5. Jefferson	*Near great* 5. T. Roosevelt
6. Jackson	*Near great* 6. Jackson	6. Truman	6. Wilson	6. Wilson	6. Wilson
Near great 7. T. Roosevelt	7. T. Roosevelt	7. Wilson	7. Jackson	7. Jackson	7. Jackson
8. Cleveland	8. Polk / Truman (tie)	8. Jackson	8. Truman	8. Truman	8. Truman
9. J. Adams	9. J. Adams	9. L. Johnson	9. Polk	9. Eisenhower	*Above average* 9. J. Adams
10. Polk	10. Cleveland	10. Polk	10. J. Adams	10. Polk (10th best)	10. L. Johnson
Average 11. J. Q. Adams	*Average* 11. Madison	11. J. Adams			11. Eisenhower
12. Monroe	12. J. Q. Adams	12. Kennedy			12. Polk
13. Hayes	13. Hayes	13. Monroe			13. Kennedy
14. Madison	14. McKinley	14. Cleveland			14. Madison
15. Van Buren	15. Taft	15. Madison			15. Monroe
16. Taft	16. Van Buren	16. Taft			16. J. Q. Adams
17. Arthur	17. Monroe	17. McKinley			17. Cleveland
18. McKinley	18. Hoover	18. J. Q. Adams			*Average* 18. McKinley
19. A. Johnson	19. B. Harrison	19. Hoover			19. Taft
20. Hoover	20. Arthur / Eisenhower (tie)	20. Eisenhower			
21. B. Harrison	21. A. Johnson	21. A. Johnson			
		22. Van Buren			
		23. Arthur			
		24. Hayes			
		25. Tyler			

Tribune poll (1982) — *Ten worst presidents*

1. Harding (worst)
2. Nixon
3. Buchanan
4. Pierce
5. Grant
6. Fillmore
7. A. Johnson
8. Coolidge
9. Tyler
10. Carter (10th worst)

(Table continues)

Table 1-6 *(Continued)*

Schlesinger poll (1948)	Schlesinger poll (1962)	Maranell-Dodder poll (1970)	Murray-Blessing poll[a] (1982)
Below average	**Below average**	26. B. Harrison	20. Van Buren
22. Tyler	22. Taylor	27. Taylor	21. Hoover
23. Coolidge	23. Tyler	28. Buchanan	22. Hayes
24. Fillmore	24. Fillmore	29. Fillmore	23. Arthur
25. Taylor	25. Coolidge	30. Coolidge	24. Ford
26. Buchanan	26. Pierce	31. Pierce	25. Carter
27. Pierce	27. Buchanan	32. Grant	26. B. Harrison
		33. Harding	
Failure	**Failure**		**Below average**
28. Grant	28. Grant		27. Taylor
29. Harding	29. Harding		28. Reagan
			29. Tyler
			30. Fillmore
			31. Coolidge
			32. Pierce
			Failure
			33. A. Johnson
			34. Buchanan
			35. Nixon
			36. Grant
			37. Harding

Source: Harold Stanley and Richard Niemi, *Vital Statistics on American Politics*, 4th ed. (Washington, D.C.: CQ Press, 1994), 260–261.

Note: These ratings result from surveys of scholars and range in number from 49 to 846. Data for Bush and Clinton not available.

[a] The rating of President Reagan was obtained in a separate poll conducted in 1989.

2

Presidential Selection

The introduction outlined three dimensions of an institution: organization (the institution's routines, procedures, and units), behavior (its regular patterns of activity), and structure (its intrinsic, identifying characteristics). Each dimension distinguishes one institution from another and ensures that the institution is both taken for granted and indispensable. One of the central structural features of the presidential institution is periodic, regularly scheduled elections. These elections are held at four-year intervals, in races separate from those for the legislature, largely between two parties, with results determined indirectly by the electoral college. It is commonplace to discuss how these electoral peculiarities set up the rules by which the game is played, and thereby determine who wins and goes on to hold office. While one cannot argue against this almost tautological observation, the focus tends to fall on the victorious presidential candidates as individuals, highlighting their personal and political backgrounds and the techniques they used to master the game. However, this perspective misses how the elections themselves direct the presidency, no matter who is elected to the office.

This chapter examines a central feature of the electoral structure, one that helps shape the presidential institution: ambivalence toward political parties. There is a tendency to characterize Americans as antipathetic, rather than ambivalent, toward parties, which has led inexorably to the parties' decline. Writers rush to quote George Washington, who once spoke of "the baneful effects of the spirit of party . . . a spirit not to be encouraged" (quoted in Chambers, 1963, 6–7). Yet, such a characterization understates the practical need for parties in organizing voters, espousing policy positions, and staffing government and the speed with which they developed, the longevity they have enjoyed, and the excitement they have generated in the voting public. This ambivalence is marked by both a spirited philosophical distrust of parties and a practical embrace of them. The electoral structure plainly sets up a governing institution that is wholly different from one in which other structural features are employed, such as a strong multi-party system. Furthermore, changes in these structural elements have guided how the institution has evolved.

Selecting the Nominees

Two basic features of the presidential nomination process—the method of selection and the role of the national nominating convention—permit an assessment of this characteristic ambivalence toward parties. Four distinct historical periods show evidence of ambivalence: (1) the congressional caucus period from 1800 to 1824, (2) the brokered convention period from 1828 to 1908, (3) the emergent primary period from 1912 to 1968, and (4) the media primary period from 1972 to the present.

The first nomination system was the simplest and most nationally party-dominant. Caucuses of members of Congress from the two principal parties—the Democratic-Republicans and the Federalists—met to select their presidential nominees, many of whom were former members of Congress. The selection process did not readily take into account the preferences of rank-and-file party members or the popular support of an outside candidate such as Andrew Jackson. The caucus system broke down in 1824 with the demise of the Federalist party and the rise of factions among the Democratic-Republicans. Although the 1824 caucus named a candidate, William Crawford of Georgia, state legislatures disregarded this choice and supported three regional candidates instead.

During the brokered convention system, state and national conventions replaced the congressional caucus. State party leaders, wielding large blocs of delegates, competed with each other at the national nominating conventions. Tables 2-1 and 2-2 list ballots taken at the national conventions for the Democrats since 1832 and the Republicans since 1856, respectively. The nature of the brokered convention period is readily evident. On average, the Democrats required ten ballots to select their nominees, and the Republicans five. Prior to the Civil War, the Democrats had a particularly difficult time getting the Southern and Northern wings of the party to cooperate in selecting a nominee. This is revealed by the 49 ballots required to nominate Franklin Pierce and the 17 needed to nominate James Buchanan.

The demands of the Progressive era, which heralded a more open and democratic electoral process, led to the party primary period. In the primary, voters affiliated with a party cast their ballots directly to nominate delegates to the national party convention. The data in Table 2-3 permit an examination of the growth of presidential primaries. During this emergent primary period, less than half of the states adopted primaries, which were often "beauty contests" or "advisory." In 1912, a dozen states adopted presidential primaries; in 1916, this number almost doubled and over 50 percent of convention delegates for the two parties were selected in primaries. The movement stalled during World War I, and some states moved to repeal their presidential primary laws. During this period, delegates selected in the primaries were not pledged to a specific candidate, nor were the ballots cast by party voters binding on the party. This allowed room for negotiation between candidates and state party leaders, and brokered party politics continued. As Tables 2-1 and 2-2 indicate, the number of ballots needed to secure a nomination dropped by half, but multiple ballots were still frequent. The Democrats required an average of five ballots and the Republicans an average of two to select their nominees.[1]

The 1968 presidential election was the last time a candidate, Democrat Hubert Humphrey, secured a party nomination without running in a single primary. Relying on commitments from state party leaders, the method of Humphrey's nomination stood in stark contrast to the primary victories of Sen. Eugene McCarthy of Minnesota and Sen. Robert Kennedy of New York, before his assassination (see Table 2-7). Many Democrats were disturbed by the hollowness of the primaries in the nomination process. This led to Democratic party reforms after the 1968 election that saw many states adopt primaries or open up their caucuses and conventions to grass-roots supporters.

In the current media primary period, existing since 1972, primaries have become *the* road to the White House. The nomination is typified by one long, continuous primary covered ardently by the media, especially television. As seen in Table 2-3, over 85 percent of the delegates for the two parties in 1992 were selected in primaries, including those held in the eleven largest states—California, New York, Texas, Pennsylvania, Illinois, Ohio, Florida, Michigan, New Jersey, North Carolina, and Georgia. The national conventions have merely ratified rather than determined the nominees of the parties, all of whom have been selected on the first ballot. Indeed, the Republicans have not taken a second ballot since 1948 and the Democrats have not taken a second ballot since 1952.

As one phase has blurred into another, the ambivalence toward parties has endured. During each of the four periods, parties have been seen as both barriers against democracy and vehicles for democracy. These two views are in constant tension. When the congressional caucus was denounced as a "cabal," its demise left a void that state parties quickly filled with the appearance of greater openness and representativeness. But the appearance was largely just that. Although the state conventions were more broad-based in membership than had been "King Caucus," state party bosses nonetheless controlled the newly opened nominating conventions. The caucus was condemned as a barrier against democracy, while state conventions were touted as vehicles for democracy. Yet, party-boss control itself created a new and formidable barrier against democracy.

Ambivalence toward parties continued. In the emergent primary period, party primaries were a novel democratic device, but state party leaders maintained control of the nomination process. The media primary period, which we will discuss in greater depth below, has heightened this ambivalence. The increasing preeminence of primaries, both in sheer numbers and in the intensity of media coverage, has diminished party control over the nomination and increased the importance of individual candidates. Yet, parties retain importance in sponsoring the nomination process.

These four phases suggest that there has been a historical reconfiguration of the significance of political parties. While party elites have lost more and more control of the nomination process, the nomination system nevertheless demonstrates the persistence of American political parties. For over 140 years, the Republican and Democratic party labels have existed at national and state levels. Would-be presidents still must channel their hopes through the nomination process of one of the two main parties. It has been difficult for even an exceedingly well-financed, self-anointed, third-party candidate campaign to make inroads into the durability of the two major parties. In Leon Epstein's words, the key to the parties' persistence is their "permeability"—they are "readily entered by individuals and groups who want [their] electoral labels" (1986, 5).

Elements of the Media Primary

Primaries and Candidate Success

The next set of tables provides a closer look at several aspects of the media primary period. Table 2-4 shows that although primaries have become the preferred method of nomination, states have entertained a great deal of flexibility in switching from a caucus/convention system to a primary system from one election year to the next. For example, Kansas used the caucus/convention approach in 1976, switched to an independent primary in 1980, switched back to the caucus in 1984 and 1988, and adopted an open primary in 1992. The states also choose among several different types of primaries. To make matters even more complex, some states give parties the option of selecting their own method of nomination rather than mandating a single method for all parties in the state.

Three facts emerge from Table 2-5, which aggregates the data from Table 2-4. First, while the number of states using the caucus/convention system declined from 1972 to 1992, the caucus system still accounts for one-quarter of the nominating processes used in the states. Second, relative to the open and independent primaries, closed primaries have increased in number and are the most common type of primary. There were 20 closed primaries in 1992; this compares to 13 independent primaries and 8 open primaries. Third, the number of independent primaries has also risen, doubling since 1980. These three facts again stress ambivalence toward parties at work in the media primary era. The presence of the caucuses and the closed primaries maintain the integrity of the parties more than do open and independent primaries. At the same time, the rise in independent primaries indicates that the parties are permitting voters who are not affiliated with any party to help make the nomination decisions.

Table 2-6 shows that selection method does make a difference in who ultimately succeeds in a candidacy. To be sure, the differences between primaries and caucuses/conventions should not be overstated. In Everett Ladd's words, current party caucuses may be little more than "restrictive primaries" (1981, 34). Many enjoy large numbers of participants who differ from their primary counterparts only in that they spend several hours rather than several minutes casting their ballots. Nonetheless, caucuses and primaries do create differences in candidates' strategies. Some candidates may spend considerable time devising plans to capture key primaries while avoiding caucuses; others may plan the reverse. Perhaps the clearest example of the caucus-primary difference occurred in the 1976 Republican nomination, in which Gerald Ford did much better in primary states than caucus states, while his chief rival, Ronald Reagan, found success pursuing the caucus states.

In theory, primaries should advance democracy; in practice, they simply sharpen candidate independence from the parties and its other members. As shown in Figure 2-1, the growth of primaries has put pressure on presidential aspirants to begin their campaigns early. A quick start is important because candidates are no longer building internal party coalitions. They have traded these party candidacies for their own media visibility, fundraising, campaign organization, and standing in public opinion polls, all of which take a great deal of time to develop. Note the contrast in Figure 2-1 between the 1968 and the 1972 and 1976 Democratic nomination time lines. Humphrey started his campaign after President Lyndon Johnson announced in late March 1968 that he would not seek a second term. As noted above, Humphrey secured a first-ballot victory by winning uncommitted delegates in party convention states. In 1972 and again in 1976, the eventual nominees—George McGovern and Jimmy Carter—ran outside the established party and started campaigning nearly two years before the election.

Upon entering the media primary, candidate success is subject to the vagaries of "momentum" (Aldrich, 1980). The sequential arrangement of primaries creates a self-propelling campaign dynamic. Doing well in an early primary generates resources for later primaries. These necessary resources include money, media coverage, endorsements, poll results, and campaign staffing. Doing poorly often shuts off the flow of these resources.

This creates the patterns evident in Tables 2-7 through 2-13: the importance of success in early primaries, the rapid winnowing out of contenders, and the bolstering of candidates who emerge from being unknowns to being recognized as major contenders.

For primary states, the complement of momentum is "frontloading." States jockey for the earliest and best time slots to maximize media coverage of their races and maximize their impact on the final outcome. Several southern states in 1980 began to hold primaries simultaneously on the second Tuesday in March. By 1988, what became known as Super Tuesday was a regional fixture of the nominating process (Norrander, 1992). By 1992, several states had moved their primaries and caucuses to the week before Super Tuesday (dubbed Junior Tuesday) to dull the impact of the South and at the same time take part in the effort to narrow the field. Frontloading on Junior Tuesday and Super Tuesday is evident in Tables 2-14 and 2-15, which show that nearly half of the Democratic convention delegates and slightly more than one-third of the Republican delegates were decided on or before Super Tuesday in 1992. Frontloading opens the nomination to a wider range of candidates, all of whom hope they can do well in at least one early contest. For instance, Table 2-13 shows that in 1992 Paul Tsongas won the New Hampshire primary on February 18; Bob Kerrey won the South Dakota primary on February 25; and Bill Clinton, Jerry Brown, and Tsongas split the results of the Colorado primary on March 3. Frontloading also closes the nomination by discouraging aspirants who do not do well early on and who therefore will not be considered a serious contender in later rounds. Kerrey withdrew from the race on March 5 and Tsongas withdrew on March 19. Clinton was all but assured the nomination after victories in the Illinois and Michigan primaries on March 17.

Media Coverage

The growth of media coverage has matched the growth of primaries. Television, in particular, has the same effects on presidential selection as the primaries. It opens the nomination to a broader pool of hopeful candidates by providing lesser-known or unknown candidates the chance to gain instantaneous recognition among the party's electorate. But it rapidly closes the nomination to candidates who cannot afford the high price of television campaigning or lack the organization or the primary showings to get their message across. Journalists following the campaign become substitutes for the old party power-brokers—what they cover, how they cover it, and what they do not cover become a major determinant of the outcome.

Table 2-16 shows that a considerable amount of coverage during the 1988 and 1992 primary season focused on the horse race element of these contests—who was ahead, who was behind, who was going to win. The horse race consumed one-half of the coverage in 1988 and nearly one-third of the coverage in 1992. Tables 2-17 and 2-18 report positive television coverage of primary candidates in 1988 and 1992. However, positive television coverage is not per se a good indicator of the all-important momentum that helps determine the eventual nominee. For example, Michael Dukakis received uniformly positive coverage throughout the entire nomination period, while coverage of George Bush was more erratic. In 1992, Bush received universally negative coverage while Clinton's was decidedly lukewarm.

Independent Partisanship

Primaries combine with media coverage to create an "independent partisanship" that typifies presidential candidacies.[2] Although many observers of presidential elections comment on the independence of presidential candidates, they neglect to recognize the continued importance of parties. Both words of the phrase, *independent* and *partisanship*, are equally significant. Independence dictates that candidates raise their own money, develop their own campaign strategies, take their own polls, hire their own media consultants and staff, and reach out to a network of volunteers on their own. These candidates do not depend even marginally on building a coalition of state and local party leaders and public officials. As Richard Neustadt puts it, "We have left the age of barons and entered the age of candidates. Its hallmarks are management by private firms, exposure through the tube, funding by direct-mail drives as well as fat-cats, and canvassing by zealous volunteers" (1975, 434).

Despite the independent nature of candidates' campaigns, candidates are still partisans, Republican or Democrat. The average Republican candidate continues to disagree with the average Democratic candidate on contentious issues in the campaign. The two appeal to different voters, and voters perceive the two parties differently. So while the old-style party organization, brokers, and deals no longer hold sway, the permeability of the parties nonetheless continues to attract candidates. Independent partisanship is a modern sign of the longstanding ambivalence.

The End of Conventions?

Although parties themselves have not declined as much as some may think, party conventions have. The media primary has eliminated much of the importance of party conventions as venues for candidates' coalition-building. Conventions retain only nominal, and highly ceremonial, authority over the party's choice for president. As Tables 2-1 and 2-2 make clear, party nomination fights today do not occur on the floor of the convention. The extent to which party conventions are becoming less crucial in the nomination of presidents is also witnessed by the declining amount of television coverage they receive. Table 2-19 shows that in 1952 the networks dedicated 119 hours of coverage to the two parties' conventions; forty years later in 1992 they gave a scant 15 hours of coverage to the Democratic and Republican conventions.

Although the importance of the convention as a decision-making body has declined, it continues to reflect the party to the nation. Table 2-20 offers a profile of convention delegates since 1968. The parties, in varying degrees, have made an effort to open their conventions to a wider group of people. The number of women attending the Democratic and Republican conventions has increased. Blacks have become more prominent at the Democratic party convention. Neither party, however, has done especially well in adding young people to its ranks of delegates.

The final tables in the chapter (Tables 2-21 through 2-27) document the balloting of the conventions from 1968 to 1992. Although all of the nominations listed were won on the first ballot, the results reveal conflicts within the parties that the nominees have had to resolve to successfully begin the general election phase of the campaign and ultimately win the election. They also reveal the regional bases of some of the nominees' internal party support. Conventions, then, alert nominees to the intraparty challenges they face. This reinforces the independent partisanship of the presidential nominees. They do come to the convention as their own candidates, but they leave it carrying many party bags.

Conclusion

This ongoing ambivalence toward parties, and its accompanying manifestations in primaries, media coverage, weakened national conventions, and independent partisanship, has a paradoxical effect on the presidency as an institution. The view of parties as barriers against democracy allows presidents to develop direct appeals to the American people. Presidents portray themselves as above party politics and freely criticize parties as key obstacles to national progress. This places great emphasis on presidents as individuals who are no longer attached to conventional party moorings. It casts the presidency as a plebiscitary office rather than a partisan one.

Still, partisanship remains central to the way the White House is run. Data in Chapter 4 indicate the number of partisan appearances presidents have made and data in Chapter 5 show the advantage presidents have received from people who identified with the president's party in public approval ratings. Data in Chapters 6 and 9 show that almost all people who have immediately surrounded the president have been of the president's party; over 90 percent of presidential appointments to executive branch and judicial branch positions have also been partisan. Data in Chapter 7 reveal that policy solutions, especially on domestic and economic affairs, have a partisan cast. And, data in Chapter 8 demonstrate that presidents have been routinely more successful with their party in Congress than with the opposing party.

Thus, ambivalence toward parties in the nomination process is molded as a structural feature of the presidency. Contemporary presidents come to Washington as intensely independent politicians. They have their own campaign organizations, and many do not have strong ties to others in their party. Yet, while often having campaigned against government, outside Washington, and above party politics, presidential candidates turned presidents face the nagging realization that they are now squarely in the midst of all three. In fact, their very independence prompts work in the White House and in Washington to go on in an intensely partisan fashion, acting as the glue that holds people together and defines the sides of an issue.

Notes

1. The Democratic number excludes the extraordinary 103 ballots taken to nominate John Davis in 1924.
2. The term was first used to apply to voters in Jack Dennis, "Political Independence in America, Part I: On Being an Independent Partisan Supporter," *British Journal of Political Science* 18 (March 1988): 77–109.

Table 2-1   Democratic National Conventions, 1832–1992

Year	City	Date	Presidential nominee	Ballots[a]
1832	Baltimore	May 21	Andrew Jackson	1
1835	Baltimore	May 20	Martin Van Buren	1
1840	Baltimore	May 5	Martin Van Buren	1
1844	Baltimore	May 27–29	James K. Polk	9
1848	Baltimore	May 22–26	Lewis Cass	4
1852	Baltimore	June 1–6	Franklin Pierce	49
1856	Cincinnati	June 2–6	James Buchanan	17
1860	Baltimore	June 18–23	Stephen A. Douglas	2
1864	Chicago	August 29	George B. McClellan	1
1868	New York	July 4–11	Horatio Seymour	22
1872	Baltimore	July 9	Horace Greeley	1
1876	St. Louis	June 27–29	Samuel J. Tilden	2
1880	Cincinnati	June 22–24	Winfield S. Hancock	2
1884	Chicago	July 8–11	Grover Cleveland	2
1888	St. Louis	June 5	Grover Cleveland	1
1892	Chicago	June 21	Grover Cleveland	1
1896	Chicago	July 7	William J. Bryan	5
1900	Kansas City	July 4–6	William J. Bryan	1
1904	St. Louis	July 6–9	Alton S. Parker	1
1908	Denver	July 7–10	William J. Bryan	1
1912	Baltimore	June 25–July 2	Woodrow Wilson	46
1916	St. Louis	June 14–16	Woodrow Wilson	1
1920	San Francisco	June 28–July 6	James M. Cox	43
1924	New York	June 24–July 9	John W. Davis	103
1928	Houston	June 26–29	Alfred E. Smith	1
1932	Chicago	June 27–July 2	Franklin D. Roosevelt	4
1936	Philadelphia	June 23–27	Franklin D. Roosevelt	b
1940	Chicago	July 15–18	Franklin D. Roosevelt	1
1944	Chicago	July 19–21	Franklin D. Roosevelt	1
1948	Philadelphia	July 12–14	Harry S. Truman	1
1952	Chicago	July 21–26	Adlai E. Stevenson	3
1956	Chicago	August 13–17	Adlai E. Stevenson	1
1960	Los Angeles	July 11–15	John F. Kennedy	1
1964	Atlantic City	August 24–27	Lyndon B. Johnson	b
1968	Chicago	August 26–29	Hubert H. Humphrey	1
1972	Miami Beach	July 10–13	George McGovern	1
1976	New York	July 12–15	Jimmy Carter	1
1980	New York	August 11–14	Jimmy Carter	1
1984	San Francisco	July 16–19	Walter Mondale	1
1988	Atlanta	July 18–21	Michael Dukakis	1
1992	New York	July 13–16	Bill Clinton	1

Source: Adapted from *Congressional Quarterly's Guide to U.S. Elections,* 2d ed. (Washington, D.C.: Congressional Quarterly, 1985), updated by the author.

[a] Number of ballots required to select nominee.
[b] Acclamation.

Table 2-2   Republican National Conventions, 1856–1992

Year	City	Date	Presidential nominee	Ballots[a]
1856	Philadelphia	June 17–19	John C. Fremont	2
1860	Chicago	May 16–19	Abraham Lincoln	3
1864	Baltimore	June 7–8	Abraham Lincoln	1
1868	Chicago	May 20–21	Ulysses S. Grant	1
1872	Philadelphia	June 5–6	Ulysses S. Grant	1
1876	Cincinnati	June 14–16	Rutherford B. Hayes	7
1880	Chicago	June 2–8	James A. Garfield	36
1884	Chicago	June 3–6	James G. Blaine	4
1888	Chicago	June 19–25	Benjamin Harrison	8
1892	Minneapolis	June 7–10	Benjamin Harrison	1
1896	St. Louis	June 16–18	William McKinley	1
1900	Philadelphia	June 19–21	William McKinley	1
1904	Chicago	June 21–23	Theodore Rooosevelt	1
1908	Chicago	June 16–19	William H. Taft	1
1912	Chicago	June 18–22	William H. Taft	1
1916	Chicago	June 7–10	Charles E. Hughes	3
1920	Chicago	June 8–12	Warren G. Harding	10
1924	Cleveland	June 10–12	Calvin Coolidge	1
1928	Kansas City	June 12–15	Herbert Hoover	1
1932	Chicago	June 14–16	Herbert Hoover	1
1936	Cleveland	June 9–12	Alfred M. Landon	1
1940	Philadelphia	June 24–28	Wendell L. Willkie	6
1944	Chicago	June 24–28	Thomas E. Dewey	1
1948	Philadelphia	June 21–25	Thomas E. Dewey	3
1952	Chicago	July 7–11	Dwight D. Eisenhower	1
1956	San Francisco	August 20–23	Dwight D. Eisenhower	1
1960	Chicago	July 25–28	Richard Nixon	1
1964	San Francisco	July 13–16	Barry Goldwater	1
1968	Miami Beach	August 5–8	Richard Nixon	1
1972	Miami Beach	August 21–22	Richard Nixon	1
1976	Kansas City	August 16–19	Gerald R. Ford	1
1980	Detroit	July 14–17	Ronald Reagan	1
1984	Dallas	August 20–23	Ronald Reagan	1
1988	New Orleans	August 15–18	George Bush	1
1992	Houston	August 17–20	George Bush	1

Source: Adapted from *Congressional Quarterly's Guide to U.S. Elections,* 2d ed. (Washington, D.C.: Congressional Quarterly, 1985), updated by the author.

[a] Number of ballots required to select nominee.

Table 2-3   The Growth of Presidential Primaries, 1912–1992

Year	Democratic Party		Republican Party	
	Number of primaries	Percentage of delegates selected in primaries	Number of primaries	Percentage of delegates selected in primaries
1912	12	32.9	13	41.7
1916	20	53.5	20	58.9
1920	16	44.6	20	57.8
1924	14	35.5	17	45.3
1928	17	42.2	16	44.9
1932	16	40.0	14	37.7
1936	14	36.5	12	37.5
1940	13	35.8	13	38.8
1944	14	36.7	13	38.7
1948	14	36.3	12	36.0
1952	16	39.2	13	39.0
1956	19	41.3	19	43.5
1960	16	38.4	15	38.6
1964	16	41.4	17	45.6
1968	17	48.7	17	47.0
1972	23	66.5	22	58.2
1976	30	76.1	29	70.4
1980	35	81.1	36	78.0
1984	30	67.1	29	66.6
1988	37	81.4	38	80.7
1992	40	88.0	39	85.4

Source: Adapted from Harold Stanley and Richard Niemi, *Vital Statistics on American Politics,* 4th ed. (Washington, D.C.: CQ Press, 1994), 148.

Note: Primaries include binding and nonbinding presidential preference primaries as well as primaries selecting national convention delegates only without indication of presidential preference.

Table 2-4 Presidential Nomination Methods by State, 1968–1992

State	1968	1972	1976	1980	1984	1988	1992
Alabama	CP	CP	OP	OP	IP	IP	IP
Alaska	CC	CC	CC	CC	CC	CC	CC
Arizona	CO-D CC-R	CC	CC	CC	CC	CC	CC
Arkansas	CC	CC	OP	OP-D CC-R	CC	OP	OP
California	CP	CP	CP	CP	CP	CP	CP
Colorado	CC	CC	CC	CC	CC	CC	OP
Connecticut	CC	CC	CC	CP	CP-D CC-R	CP	CP
Delaware	CC	CC	CC	CC	CC	CC	CC
Florida	CP	CP	CP	CP	CP	CP	CP
Georgia	CO-D CC-R	CC	OP	OP	IP	IP	IP
Hawaii	CC	CC	CC	CC	CC	CC	CC
Idaho	CC	CC	OP	CC-D OP-R	IP-D OP-R	NB-D OP-R	NB-D OP-R
Illinois	CP	CP	OP	OP	CP	CP	CP
Indiana	OP	OP	OP	OP	IP	IP	IP
Iowa	CC	CC	CC	CC	CC	CC	CC
Kansas	CC	CC	CC	IP	CC	CC	OP
Kentucky	CC	CC	CC	IP	CC	CP	CP
Louisiana	CO	CC	CC	CP	CP	CP	CP
Maine	CC	CC	CC	CC	CC	CC	CC
Maryland	CO-D CC-R	CP	CP	CP	CP	CP	CP
Massachusetts	IP	IP	IP	IP	IP	IP	IP
Michigan	CC	OP	OP	CC-D OP-R	CC	CC-D NB-R	CP
Minnesota	CC	CC	CC	CC	CC	CC	CC
Mississippi	CC	CC	CC	CC-D CP-R	CC	IP	IP
Missouri	CC/CO-D CC-R	CC	CC	CC	CC	IP	CC
Montana	CC	CC	OP	OP	OP	IP-D NB-R	OP-D NB-R
Nebraska	OP	OP	OP	OP	CP	CP	CP
Nevada	CC	CC	CP	CP	CC	CC	CC
New Hampshire	IP	IP	IP	IP	IP	IP	IP
New Jersey	IP	IP	IP	IP	CP	CP	CP
New Mexico	CC	CP	CC	CP	CP	CP	CP
New York	CO/CP	CO/CP	CP	CP	CP	CP	CP
North Carolina	CC	CP	CP	CP	CP	CP	CP
North Dakota	CC	CC	CC	CC	CP	NB-D OP-R	NB-D OP-R
Ohio	OP	OP	OP	OP	IP	IP	IP
Oklahoma	CC	CC	CC	CC	CC	CP	CP
Oregon	CP	CP	CP	CP	CP	CP	CP
Pennsylvania	CO/CP	CP	CP	CP	CP	CP	CP

(Table continues)

Table 2-4   *(Continued)*

State	1968	1972	1976	1980	1984	1988	1992
Rhode Island	CO-D CC-R	IP	IP	IP	IP	IP	IP
South Carolina	CC	CC	CC	CC	CC-D OP-R	CC	OP-D CC-R
South Dakota	CP	CP	CP	CP	CP	CP	CP
Tennessee	CC	OP	OP	OP	IP	IP	IP
Texas	CC	CC	OP	CP	CC-D OP-R	IP	IP
Utah	CC	CC	CC	CC	CC	CC	CC
Vermont	CC	CC	NB	NB	NB	NB	NB
Virginia	CC	CC	CC	CC	CC	IP-D NB-R	CC
Washington	CO/CC-D CC-R	CC	CC	CC	CC	CC	CP
West Virginia	CP	CP	CP	CP	CP	CP	CP-D IP-R
Wisconsin	OP	OP	OP	OP	NB-D OP-R	IP-D OP-R	IP-D OP-R
Wyoming	CC	CC	CC	CC	CC	CC	CC
District of Columbia	CP	CP	CP	CP	CP	CP	CP
Puerto Rico	CC	CC	CC	OP	IP-D CC-R	IP	IP

Source: Adapted from Harold Stanley and Richard Niemi, *Vital Statistics on American Politics,* 4th ed. (Washington, D.C.: CQ Press, 1994), 98–99.

Note: CC—delegates chosen by local caucuses and state conventions; CO—delegates chosen by state party committee; CP—closed primary in which only voters registered to a party may vote in that party's primary; IP—independent primary in which voters registered to a party and independents may vote in that party's primary, but voters registered to other parties may not; OP—open primary in which any registered voter may vote, regardless of party affiliation; NB—nonbinding presidential primary (delegates are actually chosen by caucuses and conventions). D—Democrat; R—Republican.

Table 2-5 Types of Presidential Nomination Methods, 1968–1992

Method of selection[a]	1968	1972	1976	1980	1984	1988	1992
Caucus/convention	30 4 (R)	29	23	15 1 (R) 3 (D)	20 2 (R) 2 (D)	14 1 (D)	12 1 (R)
Party committee	1 4 (D)	0	0	0	0	0	0
Closed primary	10	13	11	16 1 (R)	16 1 (D)	18	19 1 (D)
Independent primary	3	4	4	6	8 2 (D)	12 3 (D)	11 1 (R) 1 (D)
Open primary	4	6	13	10 2 (R) 1 (D)	1 4 (R)	1 3 (R)	3 3 (R) 2 (D)
Nonbinding primary	0	0	1	1	1 1 (D)	1 3 (R) 1 (D)	1 1 (R) 2 (D)

Source: Adapted from Harold Stanley and Richard Niemi, *Vital Statistics on American Politics,* 4th ed. (Washington, D.C.: CQ Press, 1994), 98–99.

Note: Numbers denoted with (R) or (D) (Republican and Democrat, respectively) indicate states in which the two parties used different methods of selection. These are in addition to the number of states in which both parties adopted the same method. For example, in 1968 30 states adopted the convention method and in 4 additional states only the Republicans used this method. Hence, in that year, there was a total of 34 states in which at least one party used the convention method.

[a] *Caucus/convention* denotes delegates chosen by local caucuses and state conventions; *party committee* denotes delegates chosen by state party committee; *closed primary* denotes contest in which only voters registered to a party may vote in that party's primary; *independent primary* denotes contest in which voters registered to a party and independents may vote in that party's primary, but voters registered to other parties may not; *open primary* denotes contest in which any registered voter may vote, regardless of party affiliation; *nonbinding primary* denotes nonbinding presidential primary—delegates are actually chosen by caucuses and conventions.

Table 2-6   Presidential Candidates' Delegate Strength from Caucus
States and Primary States, 1968–1992

Year/candidate	Caucus states	Primary states	Number of convention votes	Percentage of convention
1968 Democratic convention				
Humphrey	80.2%	53.4%	1,760.25	67.1
McCarthy	12.1	34.4	601	22.9
McGovern	3.8	7.5	146.5	5.6
Others	4.0	4.7	114.25	4.4
Total	N = 1,346	N = 1,276	2,622	100.0
1968 Republican convention				
Nixon	59.6	43.2	692	51.9
Rockefeller	14.4	27.9	277	20.8
Reagan	11.2	16.4	182	13.7
Others	14.7	12.4	182	13.7
Total	N = 706	N = 627	1,333	100.0
1972 Democratic convention				
McGovern	41.0	64.9	1,715.4	56.9
Jackson	30.0	11.5	534	17.7
Wallace	7.3	15.5	385.7	12.8
Others	21.7	8.1	380.9	12.6
Total	N = 1,009	N = 2,007	3,016	100.0
1976 Republican convention				
Ford	44.9	55.9	1,187	52.5
Reagan	55.1	43.9	1,070	47.4
Others	0.0	0.1	2	0.1
Total	N = 693	N = 1,566	2,259	100.0
1980 Democratic convention				
Carter	71.0	60.8	2,123	63.7
Kennedy	24.3	38.6	1,150.5	34.5
Others	4.7	0.5	57.5	1.7
Total	N = 953	N = 2,378	3,331	100.0
1984 Democratic convention				
Mondale	56.3	55.6	2,191	55.9
Hart	29.6	31.2	1,200.5	30.6
Jackson	11.9	11.9	465.5	11.9
Others	2.3	1.3	66	1.7
Total	N = 1,460	N = 2,463	3,923	100.0
1988 Democratic convention				
Dukakis	62.6	71.5	2,876.25	69.9
Jackson	36.2	28.1	1,218.50	29.6
Others	1.2	0.4	23	0.6
Total	N = 766.75	N = 3,351.00	4,117.75	100.0

Table 2-6   (*Continued*)

Year/candidate	Caucus states	Primary states	Number of convention votes	Percentage of convention
1992 Democratic convention				
Brown	10.9%	14.2%	596	13.9
Clinton	84.4	77.8	3,372	78.6
Tsongas	3.7	5.5	209	4.9
Others	1.0	2.5	111	2.6
Total	N = 514	N = 3,774	4,288	100.0

Source: Harold Stanley and Richard Niemi, *Vital Statistics on American Politics*, 4th ed. (Washington, D.C.: CQ Press, 1994) 102–103.

Note: Shown are major presidential candidates with substantial opposition. The table is based on first-ballot votes before switches. For 1984–1992, votes of Democratic superdelegates not chosen through caucuses or primaries are counted as if they were chosen by the delegate selection method in their state. States holding both primaries and caucuses are counted among primary states in these calculations. ("States" include all jurisdictions having delegates.)

Figure 2-1   Length of Campaign for Presidential Candidates, 1968-1992

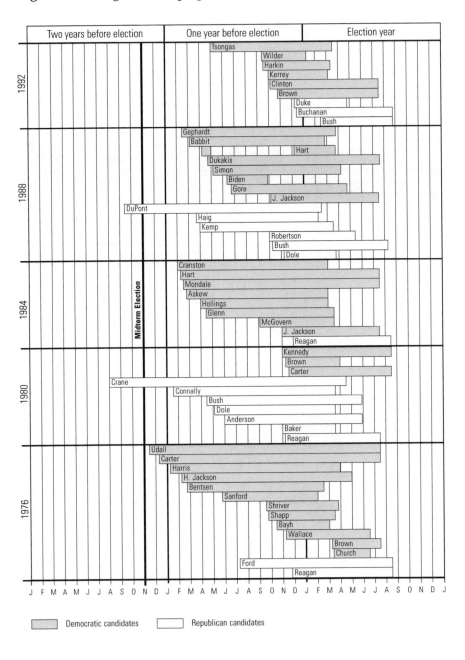

Figure 2-1   (Continued)

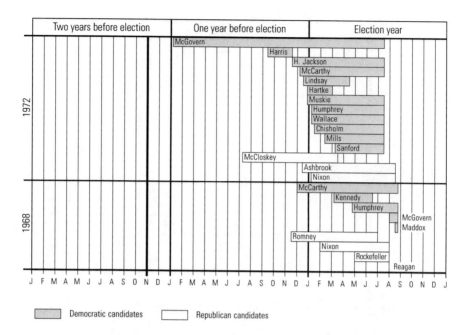

	Two years before election	One year before election	Election year

Democratic candidates   Republican candidates

Sources: Congressional Quarterly's Guide to U.S. Elections (Washington, D.C.: Congressional Quarterly, 1994), 562; Harold Stanley and Richard Niemi, *Vital Statistics on American Politics,* 4th ed. (Washington, D.C.: CQ Press, 1994), 96–97.

Note: Start of the candidates' campaigns is denoted by their formal announcement. End of their candidacies is denoted by their withdrawal from the race or the party nomination.

Table 2-7 Leading Candidates in Presidential Primaries, 1968 (percent)

		Democrats					Republicans			
Date	*State*	Eugene McCarthy	Robert Kennedy	Hubert Humphrey	Lyndon Johnson	Others	Ronald Reagan	Richard Nixon	Nelson Rockefeller	Others
March 12	N.H.	41.9	—	—	49.6	8.5	—	77.6	10.8	11.6
April 2	Wis.	56.2	6.3	0.5	34.6	2.8	10.4	79.7	1.6	8.3
April 23	Pa.	71.7	11.0[a]	8.7[a]	3.6[a]	5.0	2.8[a]	59.7[a]	18.4[a]	19.1[a]
April 30	Mass.	49.3	27.6[a]	17.7[a]	2.8	2.7	1.7[a]	25.8[a]	30.0[a]	42.5[b]
May 7	D.C.	—	62.5[c]	37.5[c]	—	—	—	90.1[d]	[d]	9.9[d]
	Ind.	27.0	42.3	—	—	30.7[e]	—	100.0	—	100.0[f]
	Ohio	—	—	—	—	100.0[f]	—	—	—	—
May 14	Neb.	31.2	51.7	7.4	5.6	4.1	21.3	70.0	5.1[a]	3.6
	W. Va.	—	—	—	—	100.0[e]	—	—	—	100.0[g]
May 28	Fla.	28.7	—	—	—	71.3[h]	—	—	—	100.0[g]
	Ore.	44.0	38.0	3.3[a]	12.1	2.7	20.4	65.0	11.6[a]	3.0
June 4	Calif.	41.8	46.3	—	—	12.0[g]	100.0	—	—	—
	N.J.	36.1[a]	31.3[a]	20.3[a]	—	12.3	3.1[a]	81.1[a]	13.0[a]	2.8
	S.D.	20.4	49.5	—	30.0	—	—	100.0	—	—
June 11	Ill.	38.6	—	17.1	—	44.3[i]	7.1[a]	78.1[a]	9.7[a]	5.1[a]

Source: Adapted from *Congressional Quarterly's Guide to U.S. Elections*, 2d ed. (Washington, D.C.: Congressional Quarterly, 1985).

Note: "—" indicates candidate did not enter primary.

[a] Write-in.
[b] John A. Volpe (Massachusetts) received 29.5 percent of the vote.
[c] Source: District of Columbia Board of Elections. No figures are available for vote for delegates to Republican convention.

d Prior to the primary, the District Republican organization agreed to divide the nine delegate votes, with six going to Rockefeller, according to the 1968 *Congressional Quarterly Almanac*, vol. 24.

f Roger D. Branigin (Indiana) received 30.7 percent of the vote.

f One candidate in each party's primary received 100 percent of the vote: in the Democratic primary, Stephen M. Young (Ohio), and in the Republican primary, James A. Rhodes (Ohio).

g Unpledged delegates at large.

h George A. Smathers (Florida) received 46.1 percent of the vote, and 25.2 percent were unpledged delegates at large.

i Edward M. Kennedy (Massachusetts) received 33.7 percent of the vote.

Table 2-8 Leading Candidates in Presidential Primaries, 1972 (percent)

		Democrats					Republicans			
Date	State	Hubert Humphrey	George McGovern	George Wallace	Edmund Muskie	Others[a]	Richard Nixon	John Ashbrook	Paul McCloskey	Others[b]
March 7	N.H.	0.4[c]	37.1	0.2[c]	46.4	15.9	67.6	9.7	19.8	2.9
March 14	Fla.	18.6	6.2	41.6	8.9	24.8	87.0	8.8	4.2	—
March 21	Ill.	0.1[c]	0.3[c]	0.6[c]	62.6	36.4[d]	97.0[c]	0.5[c]	0.1[c]	2.4[c]
April 4	Wis.	20.7	29.6	22.0	10.3	17.4	96.9	0.9	1.3	0.8
April 25	Mass.	7.9	52.7	7.4	21.3	10.6	81.2	4.0	13.5	1.4
	Pa.	35.1	20.4	21.3	20.4	2.8	83.3[c]	—	—	16.8
May 2	D.C.[e]	—	—	—	—	100.0[f]	—	—	—	—
	Ind.	47.1	—	41.2	11.7	—	100.0	—	—	—
	Ohio	41.2	39.6	—	8.9	10.2	100.0	—	—	—
May 4	Tenn.	15.9	7.2	68.2	2.0	6.7	95.8	2.1	2.1	—
May 6	N.C.	—	—	50.3	3.7	45.9[g]	94.8	—	5.2	0.4
May 9	Neb.	34.3	41.3	12.4	3.6	8.3	92.4	2.6	4.6	—
	W. Va.	66.9	—	33.1	—	—	—	—	—	100.0[h]
May 16	Md.	26.8	22.4	38.7	2.4	9.8	86.2	5.8	8.0	—
	Mich.	15.7	26.8	51.0	2.4	4.1	95.5	—	2.9	1.6
May 23	Ore.	12.5	50.2	20.0	2.5	14.7	82.0	5.9	10.4	1.7
	R.I.	20.3	41.2	15.3	20.7	2.4	88.3	3.1	6.0	2.6
June 6	Calif.	38.6	43.5	7.5[c]	2.0	8.3	90.1	9.8	—	—
	N.J.	—	—	—	—	100.0[i]	—	—	—	100.0[h]
	N.M.	25.9	33.3	29.3	4.2	7.4	88.5	—	6.1	5.5
	S.D.	—	100.0	—	—	—	100.0	—	—	—

Source: Adapted from *Congressional Quarterly's Guide to U.S. Elections*, 2d ed. (Washington, D.C.: Congressional Quarterly, 1985).

Note: "—" indicates candidate did not enter primary.

[a] In addition to scattered votes, "others" includes Patrick Paulsen, who received 1,211 votes in the New Hampshire primary.

[b] In addition to scattered votes, "others" includes Edward T. Coll, who received 280 votes in the New Hampshire primary and 589 votes in the Massachusetts primary.

[c] Write-in.

[d] Eugene McCarthy received 36.3 percent of the vote.

[e] No Republican primary was held in 1972.

[f] Walter E. Fauntroy (District of Columbia) received 71.8 percent of the vote.

[g] Terry Sanford (North Carolina) received 37.3 percent of the vote.

[h] Unpledged delegates at large.

[i] Shirley Chisholm (New York) received 66.9 percent of the vote; and Sanford (North Carolina) received 33.1 percent of the vote.

Table 2-9 Leading Candidates in Presidential Primaries, 1976 (percent)

Date	State	Democrats					Republicans		
		Jimmy Carter	Frank Church	Morris Udall	George Wallace	Others	Gerald Ford	Ronald Reagan	Others
February 24	N.H.	28.4	—	22.7	1.3[a]	37.7[b]	49.4	48.0	2.6
March 2	Mass.	13.9	—	17.7	16.7	49.6[c]	61.2	33.7	5.0
	Vt.	42.2	—	2.1	—	48.8[d]	84.0	15.2	—
March 9	Fla.	34.5	0.4	—	30.5	30.8[e]	52.8	47.2	—
March 16	Ill.	48.1	—	2.3	27.6	23.8	58.9	40.1	1.0
March 23	N.C.	53.6	—	—	34.7	9.1	52.4	45.9	1.7
April 6	Wis.	36.6	—	35.6	12.5	13.1	55.2	44.3	0.3
April 27	Pa.	37.0	—	18.7	11.3	31.8[f]	92.1	5.1	2.8
May 4	D.C.	39.7	—	26.0	—	1.6[g]	100.0[o]	—	—
	Ga.	83.4	0.5	1.9	11.5	1.4	31.7	68.3	—
	Ind.	68.0	—	—	15.2	16.9	48.7	51.3	—
May 11	Neb.	37.6	38.5	2.7	3.2	5.8	45.4	54.5	0.1
	W. Va.	—	—	—	11.0	[h]	56.8	43.2	—
May 18	Md.	37.1	—	5.5	4.1	53.3[i]	58.0	42.0	—
	Mich.	43.4	—	43.1	6.9	6.2	64.9	34.3	0.8
May 25	Ark.	62.6	—	7.5	16.5	13.3	35.1	63.4	1.5
	Idaho	11.9	78.7	1.3	1.5	4.4	24.9	74.3	0.8
	Ky.	59.4	9.0	10.9	16.8	12.2	50.9	46.9	2.1
	Nev.	23.3	—	3.0	3.3	61.3[j]	28.8	66.3	5.0
	Ore.	26.7	33.6	2.7	1.3	27.3[k]	50.3	45.8	3.9
	Tenn.	77.6	2.4	3.7	10.9	5.3	49.8	49.1	1.1
June 1	Mont.	24.6	59.4	6.3	3.4	6.3	34.6	63.1	2.2
	R.I.	30.2	27.2	4.2	0.8	37.5	65.3	31.2	3.5
	S.D.	41.2	—	33.3	2.4	23.2	44.0	51.2	4.8
June 8	Calif.	20.5	7.4	5.0	3.0	64.1[l]	34.5	65.5	—
	N.J.	58.4	13.6	—	8.6	14.8	100.0	—	—
	Ohio[m]	39.0	5.3	10.1	12.5	30.0[n]	55.2	44.8	—

Source: Adapted from *Congressional Quarterly's Guide to U.S. Elections,* 2d ed. (Washington, D.C.: Congressional Quarterly, 1985).

Note: "—" indicates candidate did not enter primary.

a Write-in votes.

b Birch Bayh received 15.2 percent of the vote and Sargent Shriver received 8.2 percent of the vote.

c Henry M. Jackson received 22.3 percent of the vote.

d Shriver received 27.6 percent of the vote.

e Jackson received 23.9 percent of the vote.

f Jackson received 24.6 percent of the vote. Jackson suspended his campaign May 1.

g Uncommitted slate headed by delegate Walter E. Fauntroy received 21.6 percent of the vote; another uncommitted slate headed by Mayor Walter E. Washington received 11.1 percent.

h Senator Robert C. Byrd received 89.0 percent of the vote. Byrd was also on the ballot in Florida, where he received 0.4 percent, and in Georgia, where he received 0.7 percent.

i Edmund G. Brown received 48.4 percent of the vote.

j Brown received 52.7 percent of the vote.

k Brown received 24.7 percent of the vote; these were write-in votes.

l Brown received 59.0 percent of the vote.

m State Treasurer Gertrude W. Donahey headed an at-large slate that received 4.0 percent.

n Brown received 15.2 percent of the vote.

o Ford unopposed; no primary held.

Table 2-10 Leading Candidates in Presidential Primaries, 1980 (percent)

Date	State	Democrats				Republicans				
		Jimmy Carter	Edward Kennedy	Jerry Brown	Others	Ronald Reagan	George Bush	John Anderson	Howard Baker	Others
February 17	P.R.	51.7	48.0	0.2	0.1	—	60.1	—	37.0	22.1
February 26	N.H.	47.1	37.3	9.6	6.0	49.6	22.7	9.8	12.1	5.8
March 4	Mass.	28.7	65.1	3.5	2.7	28.8	31.0	30.7	4.8	4.7
	Vt.	73.1	25.5	0.09	1.31	30.1	21.7	29.0	12.3	6.9
March 8	S.C.	—	—	—	—	54.7	14.8	—	0.5	30.0
March 11	Fla.	60.7	23.2	4.9	11.2	56.2	30.2	9.2	1.0	3.4
	Ga.	88.0	8.4	1.9	1.7	73.2	12.6	8.4	0.4	5.4
	Ala.	81.6	13.2	4.0	1.2	69.7	25.9	0.9	0.9	2.6
March 18	Ill.	65.0	30.0	3.0	2.0	48.4	11.0	36.7	1.0	2.9
March 25	N.Y.[a]	41.1	58.9	—	—	—	—	—	—	—
	Conn.	41.5	46.9	2.6	9.0	33.9	38.6	22.1	1.3	4.1
April 1	Wis.	56.2	30.1	11.8	1.9	40.2	30.4	27.4	0.4	1.6
	Kans.	56.6	31.6	4.9	6.9	63.0	12.6	18.2	1.3	4.9
April 5	La.	55.7	22.5	4.7	17.1	74.9	18.8	—	—	6.3
April 22	Pa.	45.4	45.7	2.3	6.6	42.5	50.5	2.1	2.5	2.4
May 3	Texas	55.9	22.8	2.6	18.7	51.0	47.4	—	—	1.6
May 6	Ind.	67.7	32.3	—	—	73.7	16.4	9.9	1.5	—
	N.C.	70.1	17.7	2.9	9.3	67.6	21.8	5.1	—	4.0
	D.C.	36.9	61.7	—	1.4	—	66.1	26.9	—	7.0
	Tenn.	75.2	18.1	1.9	4.8	74.1	18.1	4.5	—	3.3
May 13	Md.	47.5	38.0	3.0	11.5	48.2	40.9	9.7	—	1.2
	Neb.	46.9	37.6	3.6	11.9	76.0	15.3	5.8	—	2.9
May 20	Mich.	—	—	29.4	70.6	31.8	57.5	8.2	—	2.5
	Ore.[b]	56.7	31.1	9.3	2.9	54.0	34.6	10.2	—	1.2
May 27	Ark.[b]	60.1	17.5	—	22.4	—	—	—	—	—

Idaho	62.0	22.0	4.0	12.0	82.3	4.0	9.7	—	4.0
Ky.	66.9	23.0	—	10.1	82.4	7.2	5.1	—	5.3
Nev.	37.6	28.8	—	33.6	83.0	6.5	—	—	10.5
June 3 Calif.	37.6	44.8	4.0	13.5	80.3	4.9	13.6	—	1.2
Miss.	—	—	—	—	89.4	8.2	—	—	2.4
Mont.	51.0	37.0	—	12.0	87.0	10.0	—	—	4.0
N.J.	38.0	56.0	—	6.0	81.0	17.0	—	—	2.0
N.M.	41.8	46.3	—	11.9	63.8	9.9	12.0	—	14.3
Ohio	51.1	44.4	—	4.5	80.8	9.9	—	—	—
R.I.	25.8	68.3	0.8	5.1	72.8	19.2	—	—	8.6
S.D.	45.4	48.6	—	6.0	82.2	18.6	—	—	13.6
W.V.	62.2	37.8	—	—	83.6	4.2	—	—	2.3
						14.1			

Source: Adapted from *Congressional Quarterly's Guide to U.S. Elections,* 2d ed. (Washington, D.C.: Congressional Quarterly, 1985).

Note: "—" indicates candidate did not enter primary.

[a] No Republican primary was held in New York.
[b] No Republican primary was held in Arkansas.

Table 2-11 Leading Candidates in Presidential Primaries, 1984 (percent)

Date	State	Democrats				Republicans	
		Walter Mondale	Gary Hart	Jesse Jackson	Others[a]	Ronald Reagan[b]	Others[a]
February 28	N.H.	27.9	37.3	5.3	29.5[c]	86.1	13.9
March 6	Vt.	20.0	70.0	7.8	2.2	98.7	1.3
March 13	Ala.[d]	34.6	20.7	19.6	24.1	—	—
	Fla.	33.4	39.2	12.2	15.2	100.0	0.0
	Ga.	30.5	27.3	21.0	20.8	100.0	0.0
	Mass.	25.5	39.0	5.0	30.5[e]	89.5	10.5
	R.I.	34.5	45.0	8.7	11.8	90.7	9.3
March 18	P.R.[f]	99.1	0.6	—	0.3	—	—
March 20	Ill.	40.4	35.2	21.0	3.4	99.9	0.1
March 27	Conn.[d]	29.1	52.7	12.0	6.2	—	—
April 3	N.Y.[d]	44.8	27.4	25.6	2.2	—	—
	Wis.	41.1	44.4	9.8	4.7	95.2	4.8
April 10	Pa.	45.1	33.3	16.0	5.6	99.3	0.7
May 1	D.C.	25.6	7.1	67.3	—	100.0	—
	Tenn.	41.0	29.1	25.3	4.6	90.9	9.1
May 5	La.	22.3	25.0	42.9	9.8	89.7	10.3
	Texas[g]	—	—	—	—	96.5	3.5
May 8	Ind.	40.9	41.8	13.7	3.6	100.0	0.0
	Md.	42.5	24.3	25.5	7.7	100.0	0.0
	N.C.[d]	35.6	30.2	25.4	8.8	—	—
	Ohio	40.3	42.0	16.4	1.3	100.0	0.0
May 15	Neb.	26.6	58.2	9.1	6.1	99.0	1.0
	Ore.	27.3	58.5	9.3	4.9	98.0	2.0
May 22	Idaho	30.1	58.0	5.7	6.2	92.2	7.8

June 5						
Calif.	35.3	38.9	18.4	7.4	100.0	0.0
Mont.	5.9	9.0	1.1	84.0	92.4	7.6
N.J.	45.1	29.7	23.6	1.6	100.0	0.0
N.M.	36.1	46.7	11.8	5.4	94.9	5.1
S.D.[d]	39.0	50.7	5.2	5.1	—	—
W.Va.	53.8	37.3	6.7	2.2	91.8	8.2
N.D.	2.8	85.1	0.2	11.9	100.0	0.0

Source: Adapted from *Congressional Quarterly's Guide to U.S. Elections,* 2d ed. (Washington, D.C.: Congressional Quarterly, 1985).

Note: "—" indicates candidate did not enter primary.

[a] "Others" includes uncommitted voters.

[b] Reagan won all twenty-four primaries with at least 86 percent of the vote in each.

[c] John Glenn received 12 percent of the vote, and George McGovern received 5 percent of the vote.

[d] No Republican primary was held.

[e] McGovern received 21 percent of the vote.

[f] No Republican primary was held in Puerto Rico.

[g] No Democratic primary was held.

Table 2-12 Leading Candidates in Presidential Primaries, 1988 (percent)

Date	State	Democrats				Republicans			
		Michael Dukakis	Jesse Jackson	Albert Gore	Others[a]	George Bush	Bob Dole	Pat Robertson	Others[a]
February 16	N.H.	35.8	7.8	6.8	49.7[b]	37.6	28.4	9.4	24.6
February 23	S.D.	31.2	5.4	8.4	55.0[c]	18.6	55.2	19.6	6.5
March 1	Vt.	55.8	25.7	—	18.5	49.3	39.0	5.1	6.6
March 5	S.C.	d	d	d	d	48.5	20.6	19.1	11.8
March 8	Ala.	7.7	43.6	37.4	11.3	64.5	16.3	13.9	5.2
	Ark.	18.9	17.1	37.3	26.6	47.0	25.9	18.9	8.2
	Fla.	40.9	20.0	12.7	26.5	62.1	21.2	10.6	6.0
	Ga.	15.6	39.8	32.4	12.2	53.8	23.6	16.3	6.3
	Ky.	18.6	15.6	45.8	19.9	59.3	23.0	11.1	6.5
	La.	15.3	35.5	28.0	21.1	57.8	17.7	18.2	6.3
	Md.	45.6	28.7	8.7	16.9	53.3	32.4	6.4	7.9
	Mass.	58.6	18.7	4.4	18.3	58.5	26.3	4.5	10.7
	Miss.	8.3	44.4	33.3	14.1	66.0	16.9	13.5	3.6
	Mo.	11.6	20.2	2.8	65.5[e]	42.2	41.1	11.2	5.6
	N.C.	20.3	33.0	34.7	12.1	45.4	39.1	9.8	5.6
	Okla.	16.9	13.3	41.4	28.4	37.4	34.9	21.1	6.5
	R.I.	69.8	15.2	4.0	11.1	64.9	22.6	5.7	6.8
	Tenn.	3.4	20.7	72.3	3.6	60.0	21.6	12.6	5.8
	Texas	32.8	24.5	20.2	22.6	63.9	13.9	15.3	6.9
	Va.	22.0	45.1	22.3	9.6	53.3	26.0	13.7	7.0
March 15	Ill.	16.3	32.3	5.1	46.2[f]	54.7	36.0	6.8	2.5
March 20	P.R.	22.9	29.0	14.4	33.7	97.1	2.7	0.1	0.1
March 29	Conn.	58.1	28.3	7.7	5.9	70.6	20.2	3.1	6.2[g]
April 5	Wis.	47.6	28.2	17.4	6.9	82.2	7.9	6.9	3.1
April 19	N.Y.	50.9	37.1	10.0	2.1	h	h	h	h

Date	State								
April 26	Penn.	66.5	27.3	3.0	3.3	79.0	11.9	9.1	0.0
May 3	D.C.	17.9	80.0	0.8	1.3	87.6	7.0	4.0	1.4
	Ind.	69.6	22.5	3.4	4.5	80.4	9.8	6.6	3.3
	Ohio	62.7	27.5	2.2	7.7	81.0	11.9	7.1	0.0
May 10	Neb.	62.9	25.7	1.5	9.8	68.0	22.3	5.1	4.9
	W. Va.	78.9	14.0	3.6	3.5	77.3	10.9	7.3	3.5
May 17	Ore.	56.8	38.1	1.4	3.6	72.9	17.9	7.7	1.5
May 24	Idaho	73.4	15.7	3.7	7.2	81.2	—	8.6	10.2
June 7	Calif.	60.8	35.2	1.8	2.2	82.9	12.9	4.2	0.0
	Mont.	68.7	22.1	1.8	7.3	73.0	19.4	0.0	7.5
	N.J.	63.2	32.9	2.8	1.1	100.0	—	—	—
	N.M.	61.0	28.1	2.5	8.4	78.2	10.5	6.0	5.3
June 14	N.D.	84.9	15.1	—	—	94.0	—	—	6.0

Source: (Democratic data) Adapted from *Congressional Quarterly Weekly Report*, July 9, 1988, 1894; (Republican data) adapted from *CQWR*, August 13, 1988, 2254.

Note: Entries may not total 100 percent due to rounding. "—" indicates candidate did not enter primary.

a "Others" include uncommitted delegates.
b Richard Gephardt received 19.8 percent of the vote, and Paul Simon received 17.1 percent of the vote.
c Gephardt received 43.5 percent of the vote.
d No Democratic primary was held.
e Gephardt received 57.8 percent of the vote.
f Simon received 42.3 percent of the vote.
g Gephardt withdrew from the Democratic race on March 28, Simon withdrew on April 17, and Gore on April 21. Dole withdrew from the Republican race on March 29 and Robertson on May 16.
h No Republican primary was held.

Table 2-13 Leading Candidates in Presidential Primaries, 1992 (percent)

| | | Democrats | | | | Republicans | | |
| | | Bill Clinton | Paul Tsongas | Jerry Brown | Others[a] | George Bush | Patrick Buchanan | Others[a] |
Date	State							
February 18	N.H.	24.7	33.2	8.1	34.0	53.0	37.4	9.7
February 25	S.D.	19.1	9.6	3.9	67.4[b]	69.3	—	30.7[c]
March 3	Colo.	26.9	25.6	28.8	18.8	67.5	30.0	2.5
	Ga.	57.2	24.0	8.1	10.7	64.3	35.7	0.0
	Md.	33.5	40.6	8.2	17.8	70.1	29.9	0.0
March 7	S.C.	62.9	18.3	6.0	12.8	66.9	25.7	7.4
March 10	Fla.	50.8	34.5	12.4	2.3	68.1	31.9	0.0
	La.	69.5	11.1	6.6	12.8	62.0	27.0	10.9
	Mass.	10.9	66.3	14.6	8.2	65.6	27.7	6.8
	Miss.	73.1	8.1	9.6	9.2	72.3	16.7	11.0
	Okla.	70.5	—	16.7	18.5	69.6	26.6	3.8
	R.I.	21.2	52.9	18.8	7.0	63.0	31.8	5.2
	Tenn.	67.3	19.4	8.0	5.2	72.5	22.2	5.1
	Texas	65.6	19.2	8.0	7.2	69.8	23.9	6.3
March 17	Ill.	51.6	25.8	14.6	7.9	76.4	22.5	1.2
	Mich.	50.7	16.6[d]	25.8	6.9	67.2	25.0	7.8
March 24	Conn.	35.6	19.5	37.2	7.6	66.7	21.9	11.4
April 5	P.R.	95.6	0.1	1.6	2.6	99.2	0.4	0.4
April 7	Kan.	51.3	15.2	13.0	20.5	62.0	14.8	23.2
	Minn.	31.1	21.3	30.6	17.0	63.9	24.2	11.9
	N.Y.	40.9	28.6	26.2	4.2	e	e	e
	Wis.	37.2	21.8	34.5	6.5	75.6	16.3	8.2
April 28	Penn.	56.5	12.8	25.7	5.0	76.8	23.2	0.0
May 5	D.C.	73.8	10.4	7.2	8.5	81.5	18.5	0.0
	Ind.	63.3	12.2	21.5	3.0	80.1	19.9	0.0
	N.C.	64.1	8.3	10.4	17.2	70.7	19.5	9.8

May 12	Neb.	45.5	7.1	21.0	19.2	81.4	13.5	5.2
	W. Va.	74.2	6.9	11.9	6.9	80.5	14.6	4.9
May 19	Ore.	45.3	10.5	31.4	12.7	67.1	19.0	14.0
	Wash.	42.0	12.8	23.1	22.1	67.0	10.2	22.8
May 26	Ark.	68.0	—	11.0	20.9	83.1	11.9	5.0
	Idaho	49.0	—	16.7	34.3	63.5	13.1	23.4
	Ky.	56.0	4.9	8.3	30.8	74.5	—	25.5
June 2	Ala.	68.2	—	6.8	25.0	74.3	7.6	18.1
	Calif.	47.5	7.4	40.2	5.0	73.6	26.4	0.0
	Mont.	46.9	10.8	18.5	23.9	71.6	11.8	16.6
	N.J.	59.2	11.1	19.5	10.2	77.5	15.0	7.5
	N.M.	52.8	6.3	16.9	24.1	63.8	9.1	27.1
	Ohio	61.2	10.6	19.0	9.2	83.2	16.8	27.1
June 9	N.D.	12.6[f]	—	—	87.4	83.4	—	16.6

Source: (Democratic data) Adapted from *Congressional Quarterly Weekly Report*, July 4, 1992, 69; (Republican data) adapted from *CQWR*, August 8, 1992, 63.

Note: Entries may not total 100 percent due to rounding. "—" indicates candidate did not enter primary.

[a] "Others" include uncommitted delegates.
[b] Bob Kerrey received 40.2 percent of the vote, and Tom Harkin received 25.2 percent of the vote.
[c] All uncommitted delegates.
[d] Tsongas withdrew from the race on March 19; Kerrey withdrew on March 5, and Harkin on March 9.
[e] No Republican primary was held.
[f] Clinton's votes were write-ins.

Table 2-14   Democrats' Delegate Selection Calendar, 1992

Date	State	Method	Delegates	Percentage of total
February 10	Iowa	C	59	1.4
February 18	New Hampshire	P	24	0.6
February 23	Maine	C	31	0.7
February 25	South Dakota	P	21	0.5
March 3	Colorado	P	58	1.4
	Georgia	P	96	2.2
	Maryland	P	85	2.0
	Idaho	C	26	0.6
	Minnesota	C	92	2.1
	Utah	C	29	6.8
	Washington	C	84	2.0
	American Samoa	C	5	0.1
Total for Junior Tuesday				17.2
Total as of Junior Tuesday				20.4
March 5	North Dakota	C	22	0.5
March 7	South Carolina	P	54	1.3
	Arizona	C	49	1.1
	Wyoming	C	19	0.4
	Democrats abroad	C	9	0.2
March 8	Nevada	C	27	0.6
March 10	Florida	P	167	3.9
	Louisiana	P	75	1.7
	Massachusetts	P	119	2.8
	Mississippi	P	46	1.1
	Oklahoma	P	58	1.4
	Rhode Island	P	29	0.7
	Tennessee	P	85	2.0
	Texas	P	232	5.4
	Delaware	C	21	0.5
	Hawaii	C	28	0.7
	Missouri	C	92	2.1
Total for Super Tuesday				22.3
Total as of Super Tuesday				46.8
March 17	Illinois	P	195	4.5
	Michigan	P	159	3.7
March 24	Connecticut	P	66	1.5
March 28	Virgin Islands	C	5	0.1
March 31	Vermont	C	21	0.5
April 2	Arkansas	C	18	0.4
April 5	Puerto Rico	P	58	1.4
April 7	Kansas	P	44	1.0
	Minnesota	P	92	2.1
	New York	P	290	6.8
	Wisconsin	P	94	2.2

Table 2-14   (*Continued*)

Date	State	Method	Delegates	Percentage of total
April 11	Virginia	C	97	2.3
April 28	Pennsylvania	P	194	4.5
May 3	Guam	C	4	0.1
May 5	District of Columbia	P	31	0.7
	Indiana	P	93	2.2
	North Carolina	P	99	2.3
May 12	Nebraska	P	33	0.8
	West Virginia	P	41	1.0
May 19	Oregon	P	57	1.3
	Washington	P	84	2.0
May 26	Arkansas	P	48	1.1
	Idaho	P	26	0.6
	Kentucky	P	64	1.5
June 2	Alabama	P	67	1.6
	California	P	406	9.5
	Montana	P	24	0.6
	New Jersey	P	126	2.9
	New Mexico	P	34	0.8
	Ohio	P	178	4.2
June 9	North Dakota	P	22	0.5
Total delegates			4,288	

Source: Adapted from Congressional Quarterly, *Guide to the 1992 Democratic National Convention* (Washington, D.C.: Congressional Quarterly, 1992), 70.

Note: C—caucus; P—primary.

Table 2-15 Republicans' Delegate Selection Calendar, 1992

Date	State	Method	Delegates	Percentage of total
November 1–30, 1990	Arizona	C	37	1.7
March 1–31, 1991	South Carolina	C	36	1.6
January 1–31, 1992	Hawaii	C	14	0.6
January 1–May 31	Delaware	C	19	0.8
January 1–March 30	Maine	C	22	1.0
January 26–February 15	Nevada	C	21	1.0
February 10	Iowa	C	23	1.0
February 16–29	Wyoming	C	11	0.5
February 18	New Hampshire	P	23	1.0
February 25	South Dakota	P	21	1.0
March 3	Colorado	P	37	1.7
	Maryland	P	42	1.9
	Minnesota	C	32	1.4
Total for Junior Tuesday				5.0
Total as of Junior Tuesday				15.2
March 10	Florida	P	97	4.4
	Georgia	P	52	2.4
	Louisiana	P	38	1.7
	Massachusetts	P	38	1.7
	Mississippi	P	32	1.4
	Oklahoma	P	34	1.5
	Rhode Island	P	15	0.7
	Tennessee	P	45	2.0
	Texas	P	121	5.5
Total for Super Tuesday				21.3
Total as of Super Tuesday				36.5
March 17	Illinois	P	85	3.8
	Michigan	P	72	3.3
March 24	Connecticut	P	35	1.6
April 1–30	Missouri	C	47	2.1
April 1–30	Vermont	C	19	0.9
April 1–May 31	Virginia	C	33	1.5
April 7	Kansas	P	30	1.3
	New York	P	100	4.5
	Wisconsin	P	35	1.6
April 20	Utah	C	27	1.2
April 28	Pennsylvania	P	35	1.6
May 1–31	Pennsylvania	SC	27	1.2
May 2	Wyoming	CO	9	0.4
May 5	District of Columbia	P	14	0.6
	Indiana	P	51	2.3
	North Carolina	P	57	2.6
	Ohio	P	83	3.8

Table 2-15 *(Continued)*

Date	State	Method	Delegates	Percentage of total
May 12	Nebraska	P	24	1.1
	West Virginia	P	18	.8
May 19	Oregon	P	23	1.0
	Washington	P	35	1.6
May 26	Arkansas	P	27	1.2
	Idaho	P	18	0.8
	Kentucky	P	35	1.6
	Virginia	CO	21	1.0
June 2	Alabama	P	38	1.7
	California	P	201	9.1
	Montana	P	20	0.9
	New Jersey	P	60	2.7
	New Mexico	P	25	1.1
June 9	North Dakota	P	17	0.8
June 18–20	Idaho	CO	4	0.2
Total delegates			2,210	

Source: Adapted from Michael Goldstein, *Guide to the 1992 Presidential Election* (Washington, D.C.: Congressional Quarterly, 1991), 28–29.

Note: C—caucus; P—primary; SC—state committee; CO—convention.

Table 2-16   Content of Television News Coverage of Primary
Campaigns, 1988 and 1992

| Time period | News content | | | Total number of news stories |
	Candidate character	Policy issues	Horse race[a]	
Preelection year				
1987	48%	19%	33%	258
1991	33	47	20	211
Pre–New Hampshire				
Jan. 1–Feb. 16, 1988	38	22	39	238
Jan. 1–Feb. 17, 1992	35	43	22	190
New Hampshire				
Feb. 16, 1988	22	7	70	108
Feb. 18, 1992	31	18	51	104
Super Tuesday				
March 8, 1988	23	18	58	130
March 10, 1992	17	22	62	76
Midwest				
March–May 1988	8	10	82	148
March–May 1992	40	21	40	54
New York				
April 19, 1988	22	22	56	59
April 7, 1992	45	28	28	131
California				
June 7, 1988	15	43	41	123
June 2, 1992	31	39	30	273
Primary total				
1988	29	20	50	1,064
1992	33	36	31	1,039

Source: (1988 data) Adapted from Harold Stanley and Richard Niemi, *Vital Statistics on American Politics*, 3d ed. (Washington, D.C.: CQ Press, 1992), 63; (1992 data) adapted from Stanley and Niemi, *Vital Statistics on American Politics*, 4th ed. (Washington, D.C.: CQ Press, 1994), 63.

Note: Data are derived from content analysis of the ABC, CBS, and NBC evening news broadcasts conducted by the Center for Media and Public Affairs.

[a] News stories in which focus was on who was leading—or trailing—in the polls.

Table 2-17 Positive Television News Coverage of Presidential Candidates, 1988 Primaries

Party/candidate	1987 (2/8–12/31)		Iowa (1/1–2/8)		New Hampshire (2/9–2/16)		Super Tuesday (2/17–3/8)		Midwest (3/9–4/5)		New York (4/6–4/18)		New York to California (4/19–6/7)	
Democrats														
Babbitt	84%	(19)	91%	(11)	100%	(1)	100%	(2)	N/A		N/A		N/A	
Biden	54	(61)	N/A		N/A		N/A		N/A		N/A		N/A	
Dukakis	64	(22)	53	(15)	45	(20)	42	(52)	63%	(40)	53%	(36)	61%	(64)
Gephardt	78	(23)	48	(48)	40	(25)	41	(49)	38	(16)	N/A		N/A	
Gore	75	(4)	33	(3)	100	(3)	50	(14)	42	(12)	55	(20)	100	(1)
Hart	38	(151)	34	(32)	0	(1)	0	(1)	0	(1)	N/A		N/A	
Jackson	84	(31)	86	(7)	100	(3)	73	(41)	79	(85)	60	(47)	69	(35)
Simon	92	(13)	31	(16)	39	(23)	0	(1)	100	(4)	N/A		N/A	
Republicans														
Bush	48	(89)	41	(98)	67	(64)	44	(55)	67	(15)	14	(7)	61	(51)
Dole	80	(35)	54	(61)	66	(38)	56	(27)	75	(20)	N/A		N/A	
du Pont	40	(10)	75	(4)	N/A		N/A		N/A		N/A		N/A	
Haig	85	(7)	60	(5)	33	(3)	N/A		N/A		N/A		N/A	
Kemp	79	(19)	46	(24)	50	(2)	40	(5)	N/A		N/A		N/A	
Robertson	59	(29)	82	(11)	65	(26)	33	(52)	0	(4)	N/A		N/A	

Source: Harold Stanley and Richard Niemi, *Vital Statistics on American Politics*, 3d ed. (Washington, D.C.: CQ Press, 1992), 70.

Note: Entries are the percentage of positive television news stories calculated from the total of all clearly positive and negative stories aired on the ABC, CBS, and NBC evening news broadcasts. Based on a content analysis conducted by the Center for Media and Public Affairs. The number in parentheses is the total number of stories. "Horse race" assessments are excluded. N/A—not available.

Table 2-18 Positive Television News Coverage of Presidential Candidates, 1992 Primaries

Party/candidate	1991 (1/1–12/31)		New Hampshire (1/1–2/17)		Junior Tuesday (2/18–3/2)		Super Tuesday (3/3–3/9)		Midwest (3/10–3/16)		New York (3/17–4/16)		California (4/7–6/2)	
Republicans														
Bush	28	(224)	25	(210)	25	(87)	18	(66)	19	(36)	24	(63)	16	(160)
Quayle	49	(35)	38	(8)	N/A		N/A		N/A		N/A		44	(18)
Buchanan	64	(11)	50	(40)	23	(64)	44	(25)	18	(11)	40	(5)	100	(1)
Duke	24	(17)	N/A		100	(1)	0	(1)	0	(1)	N/A		N/A	
Democrats														
Clinton	56	(9)	40	(81)	36	(39)	37	(49)	28	(39)	35	(141)	58	(116)
Gore	N/A		N/A		N/A		N/A		N/A		N/A		N/A	
Brown	40	(5)	79	(14)	100	(5)	100	(1)	50	(26)	35	(119)	31	(36)
Tsongas	71	(7)	60	(40)	63	(40)	55	(49)	41	(22)	81	(21)	100	(5)
Kerrey	67	(9)	56	(32)	75	(8)	50	(10)	N/A		N/A		N/A	
Harkin	53	(15)	56	(27)	N/A		N/A		N/A		N/A		N/A	
Wilder	50	(10)	N/A		N/A		N/A		N/A		N/A		N/A	
Independent														
Perot	N/A		N/A		N/A		N/A		N/A		100	(4)	63	(124)
Stockdale	N/A		N/A		N/A		N/A		N/A		N/A		N/A	

Source: Harold Stanley and Richard Niemi, *Vital Statistics on American Politics*, 4th ed. (Washington, D.C.: CQ Press, 1994), 70.

Note: Entries are the percentage of positive television news stories calculated from the total of all clearly positive and negative stories aired on the ABC, CBS, and NBC evening news broadcasts. Based on a content analysis conducted by the Center for Media and Public Affairs. The number in parentheses is the total number of stories. "Horse race" assessments are excluded. N/A—not available.

Table 2-19   Television Coverage and Viewership of National Party
Conventions, 1952–1992

Year/party	Audience rating[a]	Average hours viewed by household	Network hours telecast[b]
1952			
Republicans	N/A	10.5	57.5
Democrats	N/A	13.1	61.1
1956			
Republicans	N/A	6.4	22.8
Democrats	N/A	8.4	37.6
1960			
Republicans	N/A	6.2	25.5
Democrats	N/A	8.3	29.3
1964			
Republicans	N/A	7.0	36.5
Democrats	N/A	6.4	23.5
1968			
Republicans	28.5%	6.5	34.0
Democrats	26.4	8.5	39.1
1972			
Republicans	18.3	3.5	19.8
Democrats	23.4	5.8	36.7
1976			
Republicans	25.2	6.3	29.5
Democrats	31.5	5.2	30.4
1980			
Republicans	27.0	3.8	22.7
Democrats	21.6	4.4	24.1
1984			
Republicans	23.4	1.9	11.9
Democrats	19.2	2.5	12.9
1988			
Republicans	19.8	2.2	12.6
Democrats	18.3	2.3	12.8
1992			
Republicans	22.0	N/A	7.3
Democrats	20.5	N/A	8.0

Source: Harold Stanley and Richard Niemi, *Vital Statistics on American Politics,* 4th ed. (Washington, D.C.: CQ Press, 1994), 75.

Note: N/A—not available.

[a] Percentage of television households viewing the convention during an average minute. Through 1988, based on viewing of ABC, CBS, and NBC; for 1992, based on viewing the three networks plus PBS and CNN.
[b] Number of hours during which one or more of ABC, CBS, or NBC was broadcasting the convention. In 1988, CNN broadcast 30.0 hours of the Democratic convention and 14.5 hours of the Republican convention. In 1992, CNN broadcast 8.0 hours of each convention.

Table 2-20 Profile of National Party Convention Delegates, 1968–1992 (percent)

	1968		1972		1976		1980		1984		1988		1992	
	D	R	D	R	D	R	D	R	D	R	D	R	D	R
Women	13	16	40	29	33	31	49	29	49	44	48	33	50	43
Black	5	2	15	4	11	3	15	3	18	4	23	4	18	5
Under thirty	3	4	22	8	15	7	11	5	8	4	4	3	5	N/A
Lawyer	28	22	12	N/A	16	15	13	15	17	14	16	17	12	N/A
Teacher	8	2	11	N/A	12	4	15	4	16	6	14	5	9	N/A
Union member	N/A	N/A	16	N/A	21	3	27	4	25	4	25	3	28	N/A
Attending first convention	67	66	83	78	80	78	87	84	78	69	65	68	62	N/A
Protestant	N/A	N/A	42	N/A	47	73	47	72	49	71	50	69	49	N/A
Catholic	N/A	N/A	26	N/A	34	18	37	22	29	22	30	22	31	N/A
Jewish	N/A	N/A	9	N/A	9	3	8	3	8	2	7	2	9	N/A
Liberal	N/A	N/A	N/A	N/A	40	3	46	2	48	1	43	0	47	1
Moderate	N/A	N/A	N/A	N/A	47	45	42	36	42	35	43	35	44	32
Conservative	N/A	N/A	N/A	N/A	8	48	6	58	4	60	5	58	5	63
Median age	49	49	42	N/A	43	48	44	49	43	51	46	51	46	N/A

Source: Harold Stanley and Richard Niemi, *Vital Statistics on American Politics,* 4th ed. (Washington, D.C.: CQ Press, 1994), 149.

Note: D—Democrat; R—Republican; N/A—not available.

Table 2-21 The 1968 National Political Party Conventions

| | Democratic first ballot[a] | | | | | Republican first ballot[b] | | | |
State	Total	Hubert Humphrey	Eugene McCarthy	George McGovern	Channing Phillips	Total	Richard Nixon	Nelson Rockefeller	Ronald Reagan
Alabama	32	23	0	0	0	26	14	0	12
Alaska	22	17	2	3	0	12	11	1	0
Arizona	19	14.5	2.5	2	0	16	16	0	0
Arkansas	33	30	2	0	0	18	0	0	0
California	174	14	91	51	17	86	0	0	86
Colorado	35	16.5	10	5.5	3	18	14	3	1
Connecticut	44	35	8	0	1	16	4	12	0
Delaware	22	21	0	0	0	12	9	3	0
Florida	63	58	5	0	0	34	32	1	1
Georgia	43	19.5	13.5	1	3	30	21	2	7
Hawaii	26	26	0	0	0	14	0	0	0
Idaho	25	21	3.5	0.5	0	14	9	0	5
Illinois	118	112	3	3	0	58	50	5	3
Indiana	63	49	11	2	1	26	26	0	0
Iowa	46	18.5	19.5	5	0	24	13	8	3
Kansas	38	34	1	3	0	20	0	0	0
Kentucky	46	41	5	0	0	24	22	2	0
Louisiana	36	35	0	0	0	26	19	0	7
Maine	27	23	4	0	0	14	7	7	0
Maryland	49	45	2	2	0	26	18	8	0
Massachusetts	72	2	70	0	0	34	0	34	0
Michigan	96	72.5	9.5	7.5	6.5	48	4	0	0
Minnesota	52	38	11.5	0	2.5	26	9	15	0
Mississippi	24	9.5	6.5	4	2	20	20	0	0
Missouri	60	56	3.5	0	0.5	24	16	5	3
Montana	26	23.5	2.5	0	0	14	11	0	3
Nebraska	30	15	6	9	0	16	16	0	0

(Table continues)

Table 2-21 (*Continued*)

State	Democratic first ballot[a]					Republican first ballot[b]			
	Total	Hubert Humphrey	Eugene McCarthy	George McGovern	Channing Phillips	Total	Richard Nixon	Nelson Rockefeller	Ronald Reagan
Nevada	22	18.5	2.5	1	0	12	9	3	0
New Hampshire	26	6	20	0	0	8	8	0	0
New Jersey	82	62	19	0	1	40	18	0	0
New Mexico	26	15	11	0	0	14	8	1	5
New York	190	96.5	87	1.5	2	92	4	88	0
North Carolina	59	44.5	2	0.5	0	26	9	1	16
North Dakota	25	18	7	0	0	8	5	2	1
Ohio	115	94	18	2	0	58	2	0	0
Oklahoma	41	37.5	2.5	0.5	0.5	22	14	1	7
Oregon	35	0	35	0	0	18	18	0	0
Pennsylvania	130	103.75	21.5	2.5	1.5	64	22	41	1
Rhode Island	27	23.5	2.5	0	0	14	0	14	0
South Carolina	28	28	0	0	0	22	22	0	0
South Dakota	26	2	0.5	24	0	14	14	0	0
Tennessee	51	49.5	2.5	1	0	28	28	0	0
Texas	104	100.5	2	0	1	56	41	0	15
Utah	26	23	2	0	1	8	2	0	0
Vermont	22	8	6	7	0	12	9	3	0
Virginia	54	42.5	5.5	0	2	24	22	2	0
Washington	47	32.5	8.5	6	0	24	15	3	6
West Virginia	38	34	3	0	0	14	11	3	0
Wisconsin	59	8	49	1	1	30	30	0	0
Wyoming	22	18.5	3.5	0	0	12	12	0	0
Canal Zone[c]	5	4	0	1	0	0	0	0	0
District of Columbia	23	2	0	0	21	9	6	3	0
Guam	5	5	0	0	0	0	0	0	0

	2,622	1,759.25	601	146.5	67.5	1,333	692	277	182
Puerto Rico	8	8	0	0	0	5	0	5	0
Virgin Islands	5	5	0	0	0	3	2	1	0
Total	2,622	1,759.25	601	146.5	67.5	1,333	692	277	182

Source: Adapted from *Congressional Quarterly's Guide to U.S. Elections*, 2d ed. (Washington, D.C.: Congressional Quarterly, 1985).

[a] Other candidates: Dan K. Moore, 17.5 (12 in North Carolina, 3 in Virginia, 2 in Georgia, 0.5 in Alabama); Edward M. Kennedy, 12.75 (proceedings record, 12.5) (3.5 in Alabama, 3 in Iowa, 3 in New York, 1 in Ohio, 1 in West Virginia, 0.75 in Pennsylvania, 0.5 in Georgia); Paul Bryant, 1.5 (Alabama); George Wallace, 0.5 (Alabama); James H. Gray, 0.5 (Georgia). Not voting, 15 (3 in Alabama, 3 in Georgia, 2 in Mississippi, 1 in Arkansas, 1 in California, 1 in Delaware, 1 in Louisiana, 1 in Rhode Island, 1 in Vermont, 1 in Virginia).

[b] Other candidates: James A. Rhodes, 55 (Ohio); George Romney, 50 (44 in Michigan, 6 in Utah); Clifford P. Case, 22 (New Jersey); Frank Carlson, 20 (Kansas); Winthrop Rockefeller, 18 (Arkansas); Hiram L. Fong, 14 (Hawaii); Harold Stassen, 2 (1 in Minnesota, 1 in Ohio); John V. Lindsay, 11 (Minnesota).

[c] There were no Republican delegates from the Canal Zone.

Table 2-22 The 1972 National Political Party Conventions

| | Democratic first ballot[a] | | | | | | Republican first ballot | | |
State	Total	George McGovern	Jesse Jackson	George Wallace	Shirley Chisholm	Terry Sanford	Total	Richard Nixon	Paul McCloskey
Alabama	37	9	1	24	0	1	18	18	0
Alaska	10	6.50	3.25	0	0	0	12	12	0
Arizona	25	21	3	0	0	1	18	18	0
Arkansas	27	1	1	0	0	0	18	18	0
California	271	0	0	0	0	0	96	96	0
Colorado	36	27	0	0	7	0	20	20	0
Connecticut	51	30	20	0	0	1	22	22	0
Delaware	13	5.85	6.50	0	0.65	0	12	12	0
Florida	81	2	0	75	2	1	40	40	0
Georgia	53	14.50	14.50	11	12	1	24	24	0
Hawaii	17	6.50	8.50	0	1	0	14	14	0
Idaho	17	12.50	2.50	0	2	0	14	14	0
Illinois	170	119	30.50	0.50	4.50	2	58	58	0
Indiana	76	26	20	26	1	0	32	32	0
Iowa	46	35	0	0	3	4	22	22	0
Kansas	35	20	10	0	2	1	20	20	0
Kentucky	47	10	35	0	0	2	24	24	0
Louisiana	44	10.25	10.25	3	18.50	2	20	20	0
Maine	20	5	0	0	0	0	8	8	0
Maryland	53	13	0	38	2	0	26	26	0
Massachusetts	102	102	0	0	0	0	34	34	0
Michigan	132	50.50	7	67.50	3	1	48	48	0
Minnesota	64	11	0	0	6	0	26	26	0
Mississippi	25	10	0	0	12	3	14	14	0
Missouri	73	24.50	48.50	0	0	0	30	30	0
Montana	17	16	0	0	1	0	14	14	0
Nebraska	24	21	3	0	0	0	16	16	0
Nevada	11	5.75	5.25	0	0	0	12	12	0

State									
New Hampshire	18	10.80	5.40	0	0	0	14	14	0
New Jersey	109	89	11.50	0	4	1.50	40	40	0
New Mexico	18	10	0	8	0	0	14	13	1
New York	278	263	9	0	6	0	88	88	0
North Carolina	64	0	0	37	0	27	32	32	0
North Dakota	14	8.40	2.80	0.70	0.70	0	12	12	0
Ohio	153	77	39	0	23	3	56	56	0
Oklahoma	39	10.50	23.50	0	1	4	22	22	0
Oregon	34	34	0	0	0	0	18	18	0
Pennsylvania	182	81	86.50	2	9.50	1	60	60	0
Rhode Island	22	22	0	0	0	0	8	8	0
South Carolina	32	6	10	6	4	6	22	22	0
South Dakota	17	17	0	0	0	0	14	14	0
Tennessee	49	0	0	33	10	0	26	26	0
Texas	130	54	23	48	4	0	52	52	0
Utah	19	14	1	0	0	0	14	14	0
Vermont	12	12	0	0	0	0	12	12	0
Virginia	53	33.50	4	1	5.50	3	30	30	0
Washington	52	0	52	0	0	9	24	24	0
West Virginia	35	16	14	1	0	0	18	18	0
Wisconsin	67	55	3	0	5	4	28	28	0
Wyoming	11	3.30	6.05	0	1.10	0	12	12	0
Canal Zone	3	3	0	0	0	0	0	0	0
District of Columbia	15	13.50	1.50	0	0	0	9	9	0
Guam	3	1.50	1.50	0	0	0	3	3	0
Puerto Rico	7	7	0	0	0	0	5	5	0
Virgin Islands	3	1	1.50	0	0.50	0	3	3	0
Total	3,016	1,728.35	525.00	381.70	151.95	77.50	1,348	1,347	1

Source: Adapted from *Congressional Quarterly's Guide to U.S. Elections*, 2d ed. (Washington, D.C.: Congressional Quarterly, 1985).

a Other candidates: Humphrey, 66.70 (46 in Minnesota, 4 in Ohio, 4 in Wisconsin, 3 in Michigan, 2 in Indiana, 2 in Florida, 1 in Colorado, 1 in Hawaii, 0.70 in North Dakota); Mills, 33.80 (25 in Arkansas, 3 in Illinois, 3 in New Jersey, 2 in Alabama, 0.55 in Wyoming, 0.25 in Alaska); Muskie, 24.30 (15 in Maine, 5.50 in Illinois, 1.80 in New Hampshire, 1 in Texas, 1 in Colorado); Kennedy, 12.70 (4 in Iowa, 3 in Illinois, 2 in Ohio, 1 in Kansas, 1 in Indiana, 1 in Tennessee, 0.70 in North Dakota); Hays, 5 (Ohio); McCarthy, 2 (Illinois); Mondale, 1 (Minnesota); Clark, 1 (Minnesota); not voting, 5 (Tennessee).

Table 2-23 The 1976 National Political Party Conventions

State	Democratic first ballot						Republican first ballot		
	Total	Jimmy Carter	Morris Udall	Jerry Brown	Ellen McCormack	Others[a]	Total	Gerald Ford	Ronald Reagan
Alabama	35	30	0	0	0	5	37	0	37
Alaska	10	10	0	0	0	0	19	17	2
Arizona	25	6	19	0	0	0	29	2	27
Arkansas	26	25	1	0	0	0	27	10	17
California	280	73	2	205	0	0	167	0	167
Colorado	35	15	6	11	0	3	31	5	26
Connecticut	51	35	16	0	0	0	35	35	0
Delaware	12	10.5	0	1.5	0	0	17	15	2
Florida	81	70	0	1	0	10	66	43	23
Georgia	50	50	0	0	0	0	48	0	48
Hawaii	17	17	0	0	0	0	19	18	1
Idaho	16	16	0	0	0	0	21	4	17
Illinois	169	164	1	2	1	1	101	86	14
Indiana	75	72	0	0	0	3	54	9	45
Iowa	47	25	20	1	0	1	36	19	17
Kansas	34	32	2	0	0	0	34	30	4
Kentucky	46	39	2	0	0	5	37	19	18
Louisiana	41	18	0	18	0	5	41	5	36
Maine	20	15	5	0	0	0	20	15	5
Maryland	53	44	6	3	0	0	43	43	0
Massachusetts[b]	104	65	21	0	2	16	43	28	15
Michigan	133	75	58	0	0	0	84	55	29
Minnesota	65	37	2	1	11	14	42	32	10
Mississippi[c]	24	23	0	0	0	0	30	16	14
Missouri	71	58	4	2	7	0	49	18	31
Montana	17	11	2	0	0	4	20	0	20
Nebraska	23	20	0	3	0	0	25	7	18
Nevada	11	3	0	6.5	0	1.5	18	5	13
New Hampshire	17	15	2	0	0	0	21	18	3
New Jersey	108	41	0	0	0	67	63	4	0
New Mexico	18	14	4	0	0	0	21	0	21
New York	274	209.5	56.5	4	0	4	154	133	20

North Carolina[d]	61	56	0	0	0	3	54	25	29
North Dakota	13	13	0	0	0	0	18	11	7
Ohio	152	132	20	0	0	0	97	91	6
Oklahoma	37	32	1	0	0	4	36	0	36
Oregon	34	16	0	10	0	8	30	16	14
Pennsylvania	178	151	21	6	0	0	103	93	10
Rhode Island	22	14	0	8	0	0	19	19	0
South Carolina	31	28	0	1	0	2	36	9	27
South Dakota	17	11	5	0	0	1	20	9	11
Tennessee	46	45	0	0	0	1	43	21	22
Texas	130	124	0	4	0	2	100	0	100
Utah	18	10	0	5	0	3	20	0	20
Vermont	12	5	4	3	0	0	18	18	0
Virginia	54	48	6	0	0	3	51	16	35
Washington	53	36	11	3	0	2	38	7	31
West Virginia	33	30	1	0	0	13	28	20	8
Wisconsin	68	29	25	0	1	0	45	45	0
Wyoming	10	8	1	1	0	0	17	7	10
Canal Zone[e]	3	3	0	0	0	0	0	0	0
Democrats abroad	3	2.5	0	0.5	0	0	0	0	0
District of Columbia	17	12	5	0	0	0	14	14	0
Guam	3	3	0	0	0	0	4	4	0
Puerto Rico	22	22	0	0	0	0	8	8	0
Virgin Islands	3	3	0	0	0	0	4	4	0
Total	3,008	2,238.5	329.5	300.5	22.0	114.5	2,259	1,187	1,070

Source: Adapted from *Congressional Quarterly's Guide to U.S. Elections*, 2d ed. (Washington, D.C.: Congressional Quarterly, 1985).

[a] Other votes: George Wallace, 57 (Alabama 5, Florida 10, Illinois 1, Indiana 3, Kentucky 5, Louisiana 5, Massachusetts 11, North Carolina 3, South Carolina 2, Tennessee 1, Texas 1, Wisconsin 10); Frank Church, 19 (Colorado 3, Montana 4, Nevada 1, Oregon 8, Utah 1, Washington 2); Hubert Humphrey, 10 (Minnesota 9, South Dakota 1); Henry M. Jackson, 10 (Massachusetts 2, New York 4, Washington 1, Wisconsin 3); Fred Harris, 9 (Massachusetts 2, Minnesota 4, Oklahoma 3); Milton J. Shapp, 2 (Massachusetts 1, Utah 1). Receiving one vote each: Robert C. Byrd (West Virginia); Cesar Chavez (Utah); Leon Jaworski (Texas); Barbara C. Jordan (Oklahoma); Edward M. Kennedy (Iowa); Jennings Randolph (West Virginia); Fred Stover (Minnesota). In addition, a Nevada delegate cast one-half vote for nobody.

[b] Massachusetts passed when it was first called and cast its vote at the end of the ballot.

[c] One abstention.

[d] Two abstentions.

[e] There were no Republican delegates from the Canal Zone.

Table 2-24 The 1980 National Political Party Conventions

	Democratic first ballot[a]				Republican first ballot				
State	Total	Jimmy Carter	Edward Kennedy	Other[b]	Total	Ronald Reagan	John Anderson	George Bush	Other[c]
Alabama	45	43	2	0	27	27	0	0	0
Alaska	11	8.4	2.6	0	19	19	0	0	0
Arizona	29	13	16	0	28	28	0	0	0
Arkansas	33	25	6	2	19	19	0	0	0
California	306	140	166	0	168	168	0	0	0
Colorado	40	27	10	3	31	31	0	0	0
Connecticut	54	26	28	0	35	35	0	0	0
Delaware	14	10	4	0	12	12	0	0	0
Florida	100	75	25	0	51	51	0	0	0
Georgia	63	62	0	1	36	36	0	0	0
Hawaii	19	16	2	1	14	14	0	0	0
Idaho	17	9	7	1	21	21	0	0	0
Illinois	179	163	16	0	102	81	21	0	0
Indiana	80	53	27	0	54	54	0	0	0
Iowa	50	31	17	2	37	37	0	0	0
Kansas	37	23	14	0	32	32	0	0	0
Kentucky	50	45	5	0	27	27	0	0	0
Louisiana	51	50	1	0	31	31	0	0	0
Maine	22	11	11	0	21	21	0	0	0
Maryland	59	34	24	1	30	30	0	0	0
Massachusetts	111	34	77	0	42	33	9	0	0
Michigan	141	102	38	1	82[d]	67	9	13	1[d]
Minnesota	75	41	14	20	34	33	0	0	1
Mississippi	32	32	0	0	22	22	0	0	0
Missouri	77	58	19	0	37	37	0	0	0
Montana	19	13	6	0	20	20	0	0	0
Nebraska	24	14	10	0	25	25	0	0	0
Nevada	12	8.12	3.88	0	17	17	0	0	0

State									
New Hampshire	19	10	9	0	22	22	0	0	0
New Jersey	113	45	68	0	66	66	0	0	0
New Mexico	20	10	10	0	22	22	0	0	0
New York	282	129	151	2	123	121	0	0	0
North Carolina	69	66	3	0	40	40	0	0	0
North Dakota	14	5	7	2	17	17	0	0	0
Ohio	161	89	72	0	77	77	0	0	0
Oklahoma	42	36	3	2	34	34	0	0	0
Oregon	39	26	13	0	29	29	0	0	0
Pennsylvania	185	95	90	0	83	83	0	0	0
Rhode Island	23	6	17	0	13	13	0	0	0
South Carolina	37	37	0	0	25	25	0	0	0
South Dakota	19	9	10	0	22	22	0	0	0
Tennessee	55	51	4	0	32	32	0	0	0
Texas	152	108	38	6	80	80	0	0	0
Utah	20	11	4	5	21	21	0	0	0
Vermont	12	5	7	0	19	19	0	0	0
Virginia	64	59	5	0	51	51	0	0	0
Washington	58	36	22	0	51	51	1	0	0
West Virginia	35	21	10	4	37	36	0	0	0
Wisconsin	75	48	26	1	18	18	6	0	0
Wyoming	11	8	3	0.5	34	34	0	0	0
Democrats abroad	4	1.5	2	0.5	19	19	0	0	0
District of Columbia	19	12	5	2	—	—	—	—	—
Guam	4	4	0	0	14	14	0	0	0
Puerto Rico	41	21	20	0	4	4	0	0	0
Virgin Islands	4	4	0	0	14	14	0	0	0
					4	4	0	0	0
Total	3,331	2,123.02	1,150.48	54.5[e]	1,994	1,939	37	13	1

Source: Adapted from Congressional Quarterly's Guide to U.S. Elections, 2d ed. (Washington, D.C.: Congressional Quarterly, 1985).

[a] Other votes: uncommitted, 10 (3 in Texas, 2 in Colorado, 2 in North Dakota, 1 in Arkansas, 1 in Maryland, and 1 in Idaho); William Proxmire, 10 (Minnesota); Scott M. Matheson 5 (Utah); Koryne Horbal, 5 (Minnesota); abstentions, 4 (2 in the District of Columbia, 1 in Hawaii, 1 in Michigan); Ronald V. Dellums, 2.5 (2 in New York, 0.5 from Democrats abroad). Receiving 2 votes each were: John C. Culver (Iowa); Warren Spannaus (Minnesota); Alice Tripp (Minnesota); Kent

(Table continues)

Table 2-24 (*Continued*)

Hance (Texas); Robert C. Byrd (West Virginia); Jennings Randolph (West Virginia). Receiving 1 vote each were: Dale Bumpers (Arkansas); Edmund S. Muskie (Colorado); Walter F. Mondale (Minnesota); Hugh L. Carey (Oklahoma); Tom Steed (Oklahoma); Edmund G. Brown, Jr. (Wisconsin).

[b] At the conclusion of the roll call, Delaware switched to 14 for Carter and none for Kennedy. Iowa switched to 33 for Carter and 17 for Kennedy. Totals after switches: Carter, 2,129; Kennedy, 1,146.5. The votes received by other candidates did not change. After the switches, Carter was nominated by acclamation following a motion to that effect by the Massachusetts delegation.

[c] Other votes: Alabama, 1 for Philip Crane; Alaska, 1 for Henry Hyde, 4 abstentions; Colorado, 2 abstentions, 1 for Eugene Schroeder; Florida, 2 abstentions, 1 for Jack Kemp; Georgia, 11 for Jack Kemp, 1 for Donald Rumsfeld, 2 abstentions; Idaho, 2 for Crane, 1 for Kemp; Illinois, 8 for Crane, 6 for Kemp, 5 for Jim Thompson, 4 abstentions; Kansas, 4 abstentions; Kentucky, 2 for Crane; Massachusetts, 1 for Kemp; New Mexico, 1 for Kemp, 1 abstention; New York, 1 for Crane; Pennsylvania, 1 for Howard Baker; Rhode Island, 5 for Crane; South Carolina, 2 abstentions; Virginia, 6 for Kemp; Washington, 2 for Crane, 3 for Kemp, 1 for William Simon, 1 abstention; Wisconsin, 4 abstentions; Wyoming, 1 abstention. Totals: 42 for Kemp, 30 abstentions, 23 for Crane, 5 for Thompson; 1 for Hyde, 1 for Schroeder, 1 for Rumsfeld, 1 for Simon, 1 for Ashbrook, 1 for Vander Jagt, 1 for Baker, and 1 opposed.

[d] One vote for Anne Armstrong. Four not voting.

[e] This figure does not include: 2 absent (1 in Georgia, 1 in Oklahoma) and 1 not voting (Texas).

Table 2-25 The 1984 National Political Party Conventions

| | Democratic first ballot | | | | | Republican first ballot: |
State	Total	Walter Mondale	Gary Hart	Jesse Jackson	Other[a]	Abstained[b]	Ronald Reagan (total)
Alabama	62	39	13	9	1	0	38
Alaska	14	9	4	1	0	0	18
Arizona	40	20	16	2	0	2	32
Arkansas	42	26	9	7	0	0	29
California	345	95	190	33	0	27	176
Colorado	51	1	42	1	0	7	35
Connecticut	60	23	36	1	0	0	35
Delaware	18	13	5	0	0	0	19
Florida	143	82	55	3	0	2	82
Georgia	84	40	24	20	0	0	37
Hawaii	27	27	0	0	0	0	14
Idaho	22	10	12	0	0	0	21
Illinois	194	114	41	39	0	0	93[c]
Indiana	88	42	38	8	0	0	52
Iowa	58	37	18	2	1	0	37
Kansas	44	25	16	3	0	0	32
Kentucky	63	51	5	7	0	0	37
Louisiana	69	26	19	24	0	0	41
Maine	27	13	13	0	1	0	20
Maryland	74	54	3	17	1	0	31
Massachusetts	116	59	49	5	3	0	52
Michigan	155	96	49	10	0	0	77
Minnesota	86	63	3	4	16	0	32
Mississippi	43	26	4	13	0	0	30
Missouri	86	55	14	16	0	0	47
Montana	25	11	13	1	0	0	20

(Table continues)

Table 2-25 (Continued)

| State | Total | Democratic first ballot | | | | | Republican first ballot: Ronald Reagan (total) |
		Walter Mondale	Gary Hart	Jesse Jackson	Other[a]	Abstained[b]	
Nebraska	30	12	17	1	0	0	24
Nevada	20	9	10	1	0	0	22
New Hampshire	22	12	0	0	0	0	22
New Jersey	122	115	0	7	0	0	64
New Mexico	28	13	13	2	0	0	24
New York	285	156	75	52	0	0	136
North Carolina	88	53	19	16	0	0	53
North Dakota	18	10	5	1	0	0	18
Ohio	175	84	80	11	0	0	89
Oklahoma	53	24	26	3	0	0	35
Oregon	50	16	31	2	0	0	32[c]
Pennsylvania	195	177	0	18	0	0	98[c]
Rhode Island	27	14	12	0	0	0	14
South Carolina	48	16	13	19	0	0	35
South Dakota	19	9	10	0	0	0	19
Tennessee	76	39	20	17	0	0	46
Texas	200	119	40	36	2	0	109
Utah	27	8	19	0	0	1	26
Vermont	17	5	8	0	0	0	19
Virginia	78	34	18	25	0	0	50
Washington	70	31	36	3	0	0	44
West Virginia	44	30	14	0	0	0	19
Wisconsin	89	58	25	6	0	0	46
Wyoming	15	7	7	0	0	1	18
American Samoa[d]	6	6	0	0	0	0	—
Democrats abroad	5	3	1.5	0.5	0	0	—
District of Columbia	19	5	0	14	0	0	14
Guam	7	7	0	0	0	0	4

Latin America[d]	5	5	0	0	0	—	
Puerto Rico	53	53	—	—	—	14	
Virgin Islands	6	4	0	2	0	4	
Total	3,923	2,191	1,200.5	465.5	26	40	2,235[e]

Source: Adapted from *Congressional Quarterly's Guide to U.S. Elections,* 2d ed. (Washington, D.C.: Congressional Quarterly, 1985).

[a] Other votes: Alabama, 1 for Martha Kirkland; Iowa, 1 for George McGovern; Maine, 1 for Joseph R. Biden, Jr.; Massachusetts, 3 for McGovern; Minnesota, 16 for Thomas F. Eagleton; North Dakota, 2 for Eagleton; Texas, 2 for John Glenn.

[b] This figure does not include the following absences: Florida, 1; Missouri, 1; New York, 2; Oregon, 1; Rhode Island, 1; Texas, 3; and Virginia, 1. One delegate in Illinois and one in Pennsylvania abstained; there were 92 votes for Reagan in Illinois and 97 for Reagan in Pennsylvania.

[c] American Samoa and Latin America did not have any Republican delegates.

[d]

[e] This is the total number of ballots. Reagan received 2,233 because of two abstentions—one in Pennsylvania and one in Illinois.

Table 2-26 The 1988 National Political Party Conventions

| | Democratic first ballot | | | | | Republican first ballot: |
State	Total[a]	Michael Dukakis	Jesse Jackson	Other	Abstained	George Bush (total)
Alabama	65	37	28	0	0	38
Alaska	17	9	7	1	0	19
Arizona	43	28	14	0	0	33
Arkansas	48	31	11	0	1	27
California	363	235	122	0	0	175
Colorado	55	37	18	0	0	36
Connecticut	63	47	16	0	0	35
Delaware	19	9	7	2	1	17
Florida	154	116	35	0	0	82
Georgia	94	50	42	0	0	48
Hawaii	28	19	8	0	0	20
Idaho	24	20	3	0	0	22
Illinois	200	138	57	0	0	92
Indiana	89	70	18	0	0	51
Iowa	61	49	12	0	0	37
Kansas	45	30	15	0	0	34
Kentucky	65	59	6	0	0	38
Louisiana	76	41	33	1	0	41
Maine	29	17	12	0	0	22
Maryland	84	59	25	0	0	41
Massachusetts	119	99	19	0	0	52
Michigan	162	80	80	0	2	77
Minnesota	91	57	29	3	0	31
Mississippi	47	19	26	0	0	31
Missouri	88	50	37	0	0	47
Montana	28	22	5	0	0	20
Nebraska	30	22	8	0	0	25
Nevada	23	16	5	0	0	20

New Hampshire	22	22	0	0	0	23
New Jersey	126	107	19	0	0	64
New Mexico	30	22	8	0	0	26
New York	292	194	97	0	0	136
North Carolina	95	58	35	0	0	54
North Dakota	22	17	3	0	2	16
Ohio	183	136	46	0	1	88
Oklahoma	56	52	4	0	0	36
Oregon	54	35	18	0	0	32
Pennsylvania	202	179	23	0	0	96
Rhode Island	28	24	3	0	1	21
South Carolina	53	22	31	0	0	37
South Dakota	20	19	1	0	0	18
Tennessee	84	63	20	0	0	45
Texas	211	135	71	1	4	111
Utah	28	25	3	1	0	26
Vermont	20	9	9	0	0	17
Virginia	86	42	42	1	2	50
Washington	77	50	27	0	0	41
West Virginia	47	47	0	0	0	28
Wisconsin	91	65	25	0	0	47
Wyoming	18	14	4	0	0	18
American Samoa	6	6	0	0	0	—
Democrats abroad	9	8	1	0	0	—
District of Columbia	25	7	18	0	0	14
Guam	4	4	0	0	0	4
Puerto Rico	57	49	8	0	0	14
Virgin Islands	5	0	5	0	0	4
Total	4,162	2,876	1,219	9	14	2,277

Source: (Democratic data) *Congressional Quarterly Weekly Report,* July 23, 1988, 2033; (Republican data) *Congressional Quarterly's Guide to U.S. Elections,* 3d ed. (Washington, D.C.: Congressional Quarterly, 1994) 254.

[a] Figures may not add to totals due to absences.

Table 2-27 The 1992 National Political Party Conventions

	Democratic first ballot					Republican first ballot			
State	Total[a]	Bill Clinton	Jerry Brown	Paul Tsongas	Others/ Abstentions	Total	George Bush	Patrick Buchanan	Others/ Abstentions
Alabama	67	67	0	0	0	38	38	0	0
Alaska	18	18	0	0	0	19	19	0	0
Arizona	49	23	12	14	0	37	37	0	0
Arkansas	48	48	0	0	0	27	27	0	0
California	406	211	160	0	35	201	201	0	0
Colorado	58	26	19	13	0	37	31	5	1
Connecticut	66	45	21	0	0	35	35	0	0
Delaware	21	17	3	1	0	19	19	0	0
Florida	167	141	3	15	8	97	97	0	0
Georgia	96	96	0	0	0	52	52	0	0
Hawaii	28	24	2	0	2	14	14	0	0
Idaho	26	22	0	1	3	22	22	0	0
Illinois	195	155	9	29	2	85	85	0	0
Indiana	93	73	20	0	0	51	51	0	0
Iowa	59	55	2	0	2	23	23	0	0
Kansas	44	43	0	0	1	30	30	0	0
Kentucky	64	63	0	0	1	35	35	0	0
Louisiana	75	75	0	0	0	38	38	0	0
Maine	31	14	13	4	0	22	22	0	0
Maryland	85	83	0	2	0	42	42	0	0
Massachusetts	119	109	6	1	3	38	35	1	2
Michigan	159	120	35	0	4	72	72	0	0
Minnesota	92	61	8	2	21	32	32	0	0
Mississippi	46	46	0	0	0	34	34	0	0
Missouri	92	91	1	0	0	47	47	0	0
Montana	24	21	2	0	1	20	20	0	0
Nebraska	33	24	9	0	0	24	24	0	0
Nevada	27	23	4	0	0	21	21	0	0

New Hampshire	24	17	0	7	0	23	0	0	23
New Jersey	126	102	24	0	0	60	60	0	0
New Mexico	34	30	3	0	1	25	25	0	0
New York	290	155	67	64	4	100	100	0	0
North Carolina	99	95	1	0	3	57	57	0	0
North Dakota	22	18	0	19	4	17	17	0	0
Ohio	178	144	34	0	0	83	83	0	0
Oklahoma	58	56	2	0	0	34	34	0	0
Oregon	57	38	19	0	0	23	23	1	0
Pennsylvania	194	139	43	4	8	91	90	0	0
Rhode Island	58	57	0	0	1	15	15	0	0
South Carolina	54	54	0	0	0	36	36	0	0
South Dakota	21	21	0	0	0	19	19	11	0
Tennessee	85	85	0	0	4	45	34	0	0
Texas	232	204	4	20	0	121	121	0	0
Utah	29	20	9	0	0	27	27	0	0
Vermont	21	14	7	0	0	19	19	0	0
Virginia	97	94	3	0	3	55	55	0	0
Washington	84	49	18	14	0	35	35	0	0
West Virginia	41	41	0	0	0	18	18	0	0
Wisconsin	94	46	30	18	0	35	35	0	0
Wyoming	19	18	1	0	0	20	20	0	0
American Samoa	5	5	0	0	0	4	4	0	0
Democrats abroad	9	9	0	0	0	—	—	—	—
District of Columbia	31	31	0	0	0	14	14	0	0
Guam	4	4	0	0	0	4	4	0	0
Puerto Rico	58	57	0	0	1	14	14	0	0
Virgin Islands	5	5	0	0	0	4	4	0	0
Total	4,288	3,372	596	209	111	2,210	2,166	18	26

Source: (Democratic data) *Congressional Quarterly Weekly Report,* July 25, 1992, 2,220; (Republican data) *CQWR,* August 22, 1992, 2582.

[a] Figures may not add to totals due to absences.

3

Presidential Elections

The previous chapter discussed how periodic elections are a structural element of the presidency. It examined how ambivalence toward parties (a philosophical distrust of political parties in tandem with a practical embrace of them) has helped create an independent-partisan institution. This institution is at once plebiscitary, emphasizing the success and failure of individual incumbents, and tied to party, shaping political strategies and policy solutions along party lines. This chapter continues the discussion by focusing on the general election. It considers how seemingly mundane details of elections, and the loftier claims of democracy upon which they rest, structure the way the presidency operates.

Textbooks matter-of-factly describe the defining characteristics of American presidential elections—four-year intervals, a two-party system, separate executive and legislative elections, and results determined by the electoral college. These features are so obvious that they are often not recognized as relevant to the design of the presidential institution. Yet, each contributes to the way the presidential campaign is fought, how the general election is won, and the kind of electoral office that results.

A more keenly philosophical issue asserts that elections grant citizens the ability to control government. Equally important, they permit office-seekers and officeholders to claim themselves representatives of the people by characterizing their election victories as mandates from the citizenry. Candidates since Thomas Jefferson have claimed that election success allows the president to wield power, having "unite[d] in himself the confidence of the whole people" (Ford, 1892–1899, 8:26). This democratic promise intertwines with the ambivalence toward parties to highlight individual candidates and campaign imagery.

The chapter is divided into two parts. First, it examines how election details, the promise of democracy, and ambivalence toward parties have affected presidential election results since the early republic. The historical perspective permits an assessment of how these three factors have changed and how they have altered the presidency as an institution. Second, it outlines how these same three factors shape specific elements of contemporary campaigns—namely, imagery, issues, the media, polling, and money.

Elections and Reelections

Although only one person is elected president, presidential elections contain three distinct sets of results: the national popular vote, the national electoral college vote, and the state-by-state outcomes. While each can reveal a different pattern of results, the differences are not as remarkable as sometimes assumed. In addition, while ballots for president are being counted, results are also being tallied in congressional elections, which may strengthen or weaken the president's political position. Finally, turnout results can affect who wins and how effectively that person will be able to govern.

The Popular Vote

Table 3-1 presents the popular and electoral college results of presidential elections from 1789 to 1992. A glance down the popular vote column reveals the extent to which the presidency has been a strongly competitive two-party office. Over the course of time since 1824 during which popular votes have been cast, presidents have won with an average of 51.4 percent of the vote. The table also reveals the remarkable longevity of the two major parties. The Democrats fielded candidates as early as 1828; the Republicans emerged in 1856, and although they did not capture the White House, they fostered the collapse of the Whig party. From 1856 to 1992, Republicans have won 21 presidential elections; Democrats have won 14. The White House has swung from one party to the other a total of 17 times. In races in the twentieth century, from 1904 to 1992, Republicans garnered 12 victories, the Democrats 11, and the White House changed hands 9 times.[1]

There has been, however, a noticeable decline in competitiveness between the nineteenth century (the 20 elections from 1824 to 1900) and the twentieth century (the 23 elections from 1904 to 1992). Nineteenth-century presidents won by an average of 49 percent of the popular vote. While no nineteenth-century candidate won by more than 55 percent of the popular vote, the *average* victory margin in the twentieth century has been 54 percent. Indeed, as amplified in Table 3-2, in 10 of the 20 elections from 1824 to 1900, presidents were elected by less than 50 percent of the vote. The oft-cited period of Republican-party dominance after the Civil War looks much less robust when considered in relation to the popular election results during that period: Rutherford B. Hayes, James A. Garfield, and Benjamin Harrison were all minority presidents, and Grover Cleveland stole the office from the Republicans on two separate occasions, in both cases with a minority of the popular vote. In contrast, only 6 of the 23 elections of the twentieth century have seen victorious presidential candidates win with a minority of the popular vote.

As detailed in Table 3-3, winning candidates of the nineteenth century held a 6 percentage point advantage over their nearest rival. Victorious twentieth-century candidates have held nearly a 13 percentage point advantage over their chief foe. Competition has been particularly diminished during the twentieth century when seated incumbents have sought reelection. In the 11 instances in which victorious presidential candidates received at least 55 percent of the vote, 7 involved seated incumbents. Data in Table 3-4 show that in neither century have third-party candidates been a significant factor. Only 11 third-party candidates, who ran in just 9 presidential elections from 1824 to 1992, have received at least 10 percent of the popular vote.

Electoral Votes

Electoral college results amplify this decline in competitiveness. Since all states but Maine have adopted a winner-take-all provision in calculating the relationship between popular and electoral votes, victorious presidential candidates have always received a larger percentage of electoral votes than popular votes (see Table 3-1). In fact, over the entire time period from 1824 to 1992, winning presidential candidates have always received a 15 percentage point advantage in their electoral vote result compared with their popular vote result (see Table 3-3). The most dramatic example of this was in 1912 when Woodrow Wilson won only 41.8 percent of the national popular vote, but received 81.9 percent of the national electoral vote.

Much is made of the electoral college's ability to break the promise of democracy by skewing, if not subverting, popular vote results. The winner-take-all approach requires that a candidate merely receive one more popular vote than any other candidate to gain all of the electoral votes in a state. It is mathematically possible that a candidate be elected with a majority of the electoral votes, though not with a majority of the popular vote. Table 3-5 shows that this has occurred just once, in 1888, when Benjamin Harrison held an electoral vote majority and Grover Cleveland a popular vote majority. Another anomaly is when no candidate receives a majority of the electoral votes, which then places the election in the hands of the House of Representatives, as provided in the U. S. Constitution. This circumstance has occurred only twice in the 43 presidential elections from 1824 to 1992, once in 1824 as a result of a four-way race and again in 1876 when election returns were disputed in four states. Table 3-6 shows a final oddity of the electoral college process: electors who have failed to cast their votes for the candidate they were legally bound to vote for. This occurred as recently as 1988, when elector Margaret Leach cast a ballot for Lloyd Bentsen rather than Michael Dukakis. However, none of these instances altered the outcomes of the elections. Despite the peculiarities of the electoral college system, there have been only three significant distortions between the popular vote and the electoral vote since 1789. The curiosity of the electoral college, then, is not in that it skews results away from the popular vote winner, but in that it actually accentuates the winner's victory margin.

Results in the States

Changes in competitiveness are also evident in the states. Table 3-7 details the parties' strength in capturing states in presidential elections from 1789 to 1992. Tables 3-8 through 3-11 provide a more detailed breakdown of the popular vote from 1968 to 1992, while Tables 3-12 through 3-15 present data on state electoral votes from 1968 to 1992. The data in these tables are significant in two regards. First, they reveal how few states have been truly competitive during the several political eras (see Table 3-7, in particular). Instead, they have swung over time. For example, Massachusetts shifted from being a Republican stronghold in the 1896–1928 period to being a Democratic stronghold thereafter. Southern states have also shifted. They were consistently Democratic during the 1932–1964 period, but have shifted in favor of the Republican party in the most recent elections. The percentages at the bottom of Table 3-7 show that the parties' dominance of states has increased in the latter part of the twentieth century. During the period from 1968 to 1992 the Republicans captured all of the states 72 percent of the time, compared to capturing 59 percent of the states during the two periods from 1860 to 1892 and 1896 to 1928.

Second, the constitutional provision that the president must receive a majority of the electoral college vote provides candidates with a convenient road map that they must follow to win. Candidates must target large-population states, with high numbers of electoral votes, in which their party is competitive. As is readily apparent in Tables 3-12 through 3-15, from 1968 to 1992 the victorious presidential candidate captured these states 86 percent of the time. The candidate who will ultimately succeed and the campaign themes on which that candidate runs must be effective in these highly populated states. The electoral college, then, indirectly makes the presidency an institution that follows the population and demographic shifts of the country.

Congressional Outcomes

Constitutionally separate executive and legislative elections create an electoral prize that makes presidential candidates, and ultimately presidents, a unique focus of national politics. Yet these separate elections can also create a problem for presidents, whose party fortunes in one or both chambers of Congress may not match their own electoral strength. Matters invariably worsen at the midterm, when the president's party has lost congressional seats in every election (except 1934) since the Civil War. Table 3-16 shows how well the president's party fared in House elections from 1796 to 1992, and when it faced divided government (a time in which a majority of one or both houses was not of the president's party). Congressional competition has not diminished with the decline in presidential competitiveness. The president's party captured 52 percent of the vote in the nineteenth century and has captured 53 percent of the vote in the twentieth century. The strength of incumbency, which has been documented as a significant component of congressional voting, may insulate the parties from decline (Garand and Gross, 1984).[2] Presidents have faced divided government 34 times in one or both houses—an equal 17 times in each century. Divided government typically has occurred first in congressional midterm elections and then continued into subsequent presidential election years. Only since 1968 has divided government emerged in presidential election years and continued through midterm election years (Theis, 1994). A comparison of Tables 3-1 and 3-16 reveals that the most competitive period in American party history was between 1876 and 1896, when minority-elected presidents and divided government were exceedingly common (see also Table 8-1, which examines the actual seats won by the parties in the House and Senate).

Turnout

Turnout determines the results of both presidential and congressional races. As displayed in Figure 3-1, turnout steadily declined in the twentieth century in presidential elections, and, more notably, in midterm congressional elections. Presidential election turnout has dropped dramatically by as much as 25 percentage points since its peak in the nineteenth century. Tables 3-17 through 3-20 reveal the variation in turnout by state in presidential election years. Southern states have traditionally had lower turnout rates than non-Southern states, but that gap has closed in recent years as turnout in Southern states has gone up, while turnout in the rest of the country has declined.

Elections and Institutions Over Time

Historical statistics on presidential elections indicate both underlying continuity and fundamental change in outcomes between the nineteenth and twentieth centuries. The two major parties continue to battle for the White House with relative equality. Even when one party has not held the

White House for several terms, it ultimately has managed to take it back. Divided government has bedeviled presidents with regularity during the two centuries. Yet, the election winner, regardless of party, has gained a much larger popular vote margin in the twentieth century than that achieved in the nineteenth century. And that has been with fewer people going to the polls in both presidential and congressional races.

What accounts for these changes in institutional structure? Although data are not fully available to understand why they have occurred, it does appear, as many observers have noted, that the two major parties shaped the promise of democracy more clearly in the nineteenth century than they have in the twentieth century. During the nineteenth century the parties shaped notions of democracy, representativeness, and power. Political bosses controlled the presidential nomination process, wielding considerable clout in getting out the vote for both presidential and congressional candidates (Epstein, 1986). As the ambivalence toward parties has intensified, the focus of the democratic promise has shifted from party elites to the candidates themselves. Parties are no longer as successful in coordinating turnout efforts (Sorauf and Beck, 1993). Presidential and congressional outcomes diverge, not only because presidential candidates are running as independent partisans, but because congressional candidates are as well. Final election results are more likely to reflect momentum shifts that favor one candidate at the expense of another as the end of a campaign approaches. All of these factors lead to a more personal victory and, consequently, a more personal office.

Elements of the Campaign

Most statistical data about campaigns are available only for the contemporary period, thus the historical changes in presidential campaigns are more difficult to gauge than are changes in the actual election outcomes. Contemporary campaigns involve five key components: imagery, issues, media, polling, and money.

Candidate Imagery

Arguably, the central feature of modern presidential campaigns is candidate imagery. Candidates spend much of their campaign efforts developing an image to which voters will be attracted—impressionistic accounts of who the candidate is and the kinds of personal credentials he or she has. Presidential candidates attempt to display the qualities of a good president in their personal characteristics and in their ability to empathize with the voters. Citizens' perceptions of candidate characteristics and citizens' emotional responses to candidates are depicted in Tables 3-21 and 3-22, respectively. The data make clear that citizens indeed evaluate candidates very differently. For instance, Table 3-21 shows that individuals in 1984 considered Ronald Reagan far more inspiring, and a stronger leader, than Walter Mondale. In general, the winning candidate is perceived to have more favorable personal characteristics than the losing candidate. Not surprisingly, nonincumbents have stirred much less intense emotion than incumbents in the four races examined. Table 3-22 reveals that in 1980 Jimmy Carter angered many people (63.4 percent), while Reagan angered relatively few (23.7 percent). Figure 3-2 examines the overall positive and negative evaluations of presidential candidates from 1952 to 1992. These judgments correspond well to the eventual winners and losers in each campaign.

Issue Positions

Issues are important in presidential campaigns as well, although one must be careful in ascertaining whether what a candidate calls an issue is really that. Many "issues" are little more than emotional, symbolic themes, often intentionally vague, designed as extensions of the candidate's image and intended to resonate among as many voters as possible: "It's Morning in America" (Reagan in 1984), "Change" (Bill Clinton in 1992), "Patriotism" (George Bush in 1988), and "Family Values" (Bush in 1992) are examples of such pseudo issues. More traditional policy-oriented issues are discussed as well and may influence the vote. Figure 3-3 shows that voters in 1992 differed in who they believed would best handle the issues. Voters believed Bush would be most successful in handling foreign affairs; H. Ross Perot at handling the economy; and Clinton on health care, education, and the environment. Table 3-23 shows that issues also affected people's vote choices in the 1992 presidential election. Respondents who preferred a decrease in government services, little government help for blacks, and imposition of government restrictions on abortion were much more likely to vote for Bush than for Clinton or Perot. Ironically, those who wished to increase defense spending and those who wished to decrease it were both much more likely to support Clinton than either Bush or Perot. Clinton's campaign theme of change may have captured people's desire to modify the defense budget status quo.

Media Coverage

Media coverage of campaigns affects how candidates are able to emphasize certain personal characteristics, emotional themes, and substantive issues. Table 3-24 depicts television news coverage of the general election campaigns of 1988 and 1992. Candidate character and policy issues received significant treatment. The horse race aspect of the election—who is ahead and who will win—was more substantially covered during the primary period than during the general election period. Table 3-25 examines the extent of positive coverage of candidates in the 1988 and 1992 general election periods. It would be difficult to predict who would win the races based on this rather erratic positive news coverage. In 1992 Bush received only mildly positive coverage throughout the general election period. Clinton received glowing coverage prior to the Republican convention, but thereafter positive coverage declined, except during the debates. Judging from the data, even odds could have been laid on Bush and Clinton during the final weeks of the campaign. From the period of the Republican convention onwards, Perot received far more positive coverage than either of the two major-party candidates.

Public Opinion Polls

Public opinion polls are another central ingredient to presidential election campaigns. Table 3-26 examines the fluctuation in public opinion throughout the general election period for elections from 1948 to 1992. In 9 of the 12 races, the frontrunner in the earliest poll ultimately won the race. Only the 1960, 1980, and 1992 elections proved exceptions. Almost all frontrunners found their initial poll advantages narrowed by election day, with the exception of Richard Nixon in 1972 and Reagan in 1984, whose election support actually grew from the first poll trial heats. Figure 3-4 provides a closer look at the nature of momentum and its swings during the 1992 campaign. Clinton received a tremendous boost in July at the time of the Democratic convention and Perot's departure from the race. Although his percentage of support dropped thereafter, it did so slowly. At only one point was Bush able to catch up with Clinton, and that was shortly after the Republican convention. Figure 3-4 also reveals that support for Perot peaked sometime in mid-June; he never came close to regaining that strength after his return to the race in late September. Although Perot did well for a third-party candidate, clearly he never threatened either major-party candidate by the campaign's end.

Campaign Money

Fundraising is an important aspect of any election in America. The overall expenditures of Republican and Democratic presidential candidates in general elections, from 1860 to the present, appear in Table 3-27. In most of these years, Republican expenditures were higher than Democratic expenditures, though both parties exhibited increases up until 1964. At that point, the Republican party began spending more than twice the amount spent by the Democrats. In 1972, during the Nixon-McGovern campaign, the Republicans spent nearly triple the amount spent by the

Democrats. In response to this gap, and also in reaction to Watergate, Congress approved public funding of presidential campaigns in the Federal Election Campaign Act of 1974. Implementation of this law in 1976 brought about equality between the parties in expenditures for presidential campaigns.

Under this law, presidential candidates' expenditures are limited both nationally and within the states. Table 3-28 outlines the limits for candidates in presidential primary and general elections, for the parties' conventions, and for parties' efforts outside the conventions, including voter registration drives, polling, and advertising. While campaign money was largely channeled through the parties during the nineteenth century and well into the twentieth century, in the 1960s candidates began to set up in addition their own campaign fund-raising mechanisms that were wholly independent of the parties. This trend was typified by the 1972 Nixon campaign organization, known as the Committee to Reelect the President, which had no connection with the Republican party.

Campaigns over Time

Modern presidential campaigns are theatrical, candidate-centric affairs. Although systematic data do not exist about the campaigns of the nineteenth century (and the early twentieth century), there is evidence that these earlier campaigns were theater of a different sort (Schlesinger, 1973a). They, too, were fought on the basis of imagery, but it was party, not candidate, imagery. For instance, in one of the earliest party imagery elections, the election of 1840, the Whigs presented themselves as the party of the log cabin and hard cider. They then made their presidential candidate, the well-to-do, successful general William Henry Harrison, fit the party image. Harrison's simple life and love of cider became legendary (Lorant, 1951). Nineteenth-century campaigns were fought on the basis of issues as well, but presidential and congressional candidates did not advance their own themes and position papers. Instead, they held to their parties' positions on such matters as the national bank, tariffs, the national debt, and western land. No doubt the news coverage of campaigns in the nineteenth century was extensive, but it was reported in party-line papers. The news did not travel fast, nor was it nationally focused, making it difficult for momentum shifts to sweep the country (Rubin, 1981). The absence of public opinion polls made any momentum shifts that did occur difficult to detect. Campaign money was significant in the nineteenth century, but it was money that the parties, not the candidates, spent on developing party slogans, celebrations, rallies, newspaper circulation, and turnout.

Today, by contrast, imagery, issues, media coverage, polls, and money are unabashedly used to direct the voters' attention to individual candidates. A candidate's image may in fact magnify any mistakes made during the campaign. Dukakis' tank ride in an out-sized helmet and Bush's comment that he was not aware of how the deficit affected individual lives attest to this. However, the successful candidate can claim a public mandate grounded in that carefully crafted image. Invoking the promise of democracy, they can assert a strong mandate to govern in the name of the people, allowing them greater leeway to advance policy aims, but saddling them with a greater burden to succeed.

Conclusion

From the statistical descriptions of presidential nominations and elections two central features of the contemporary presidential institution have emerged. First, imagery is an important component of the institution. Candidate images blur into the image of a single executive who is the most powerful, unique, visible, and important political figure in the country, if not the world. This single executive image proceeds from the notion of the president as the only official elected by the entire country, and thus the truest representative of the people (Ragsdale, 1993). The president is a symbol of the nation, embodying America, its unity, values, and mission in the world. The chief executive is the one person in charge of the government. He (or one day she) is the nation's principal problem-solver who personally attempts to resolve intractable problems that mere mortals have failed to alleviate.

This personalization of the institution encourages an immediate and ongoing evaluation of its primary occupant. In an almost daily plebiscite, presidents are subject to the latest poll results, media assessments of their policy success and administrative competence, and constant speculations about their personal habits and tastes. In addition, the imagery becomes a part of the way in which the national policy debate is shaped. It is not simply a discussion of the issues, but of the way presidents present themselves as well. Do they convey sufficient competence, concern, trust, patriotism, or even anger? Can they convince the public that they are on the right side of a policy question and that it is the opposition that is misguided? The horse race continues even after the president has won the election.

A second feature of the contemporary presidential institution is an ongoing ambivalence toward parties. Party appears to matter both more and less to the presidency than it once did. More because it has become the lone reliable arbiter of policy disputes. Party provides some order to the muddle of views held by independent partisans in the White House and on Capitol Hill. Republicans still line up against Democrats. The intensity of the partisan debate is witnessed in perennial strife over presidential appointments. During the Reagan and Bush years, congressional Democrats conducted a proxy war against the White House over the Supreme Court nominations of Robert Bork and Clarence Thomas and the Secretary of Defense nomination of John Tower. During the Clinton administration, Republicans returned fire by attacking nominees Zoë Baird and Lani Guinier. In 1993 President Clinton further demonstrated the power of partisanship by constructing a Democrats-only coalition to pass the budget. Party matters less because journalists, public opinion polls, and campaign fund-raising strategies have replaced party brokers in deciding who has momentum in the nomination process and who is likely to be the front-runner going into the general election.

The tension between public imagery and partisanship presents twentieth-century presidents with a sharp irony. They win the office with larger victory margins and are more salient national figures than their nineteenth-century counterparts. Yet, the mandate that has placed them above party leaves them isolated from other politicians, both of their own party and of the opposition's. Current party politics deepens the irony. It is not uncommon for members of the president's party to attack the president in public debate and private negotiation. At the same time, presidents are still able to cut deals and settle policy issues through party. Contemporary presidential elections offer this baffling maze to presidents, many of whom have had little experience in Washington, or even of government of any kind. These elections, with their peculiarities of state-by-state calculations and popular and electoral vote differences, seem at times like an eccentric, somewhat confused old uncle, but they are very deeply entrenched structures of the presidential institution and direct how presidents act within it.

Notes

1. The election of 1900 is considered a nineteenth-century election for two reasons. First, it marked the reelection of William McKinley, who was first elected in 1896 and was a president steeped in the earlier century. Second, electoral votes were calculated from state population figures from the 1890 census, not the 1900 census.
2. Table 3-16 examines only party competitiveness; it does not consider incumbent-challenger competitiveness in congressional races. Although there is considerable debate on how to measure incumbent electoral strength, research indicates that this strength has increased and thus dampened candidate competition (Garand and Gross, 1984; Alford and Brady, 1993).

Table 3-1 Major Party Popular and Electoral Votes for President, 1789–1992

Year	Number of states	Total popular vote[a]	Total electoral votes	Winning candidate	Percentage of popular vote received by winning candidate[a]	Electoral votes received by winning candidate (N)	(%)	Losing candidate	Percentage of popular vote received by losing candidate[a]	Electoral votes received by losing candidate (N)	(%)
1789	10	—	69	Washington (F)	—	69	100.0	b	—	b	b
1792	15	—	135	Washington (F)	—	132	97.7	b	—	b	b
1796	16	—	139	J. Adams (F)	—	71	51.1	Jefferson (DR)	—	68	48.9
1800	16	—	137	Jefferson (DR)	—	73	53.3	J. Adams (F)	—	65	47.4
1804	17	—	176	Jefferson (DR)	—	162	92.0	Pinckney (F)	—	14	8.0
1808	17	—	176	Madison (DR)	—	122	69.3	Pinckney (F)	—	47	26.7
1812	18	—	218	Madison (DR)	—	128	58.7	Clinton (F)	—	89	40.8
1816	19	—	221	Monroe (DR)	—	183	82.8	King (F)	—	34	15.4
1820	24	—	235	Monroe (DR)	—	231	98.3	J. Q. Adams (I)	—	1	0.4
1824	24	365,833	261	J. Q. Adams (I)	30.9	84	32.2	Jackson (D)	41.3	99	37.9
1828	24	1,148,018	261	Jackson (D)	56.0	178	68.2	J. Q. Adams (NR)	43.6	83	31.8
1832	24	1,293,973	288	Jackson (D)	54.2	219	76.0	Clay (NR)	37.4	49	17.0
1836	26	1,503,534	294	Van Buren (D)	50.8	170	57.8	W. Harrison (W)	36.6	73	24.8
1840	26	2,411,808	294	W. Harrison (W)	52.8	234	79.6	Van Buren (D)	46.8	60	20.4
1844	26	2,703,659	275	Polk (D)	49.5	170	61.8	Clay (W)	48.1	105	38.2
1848	30	2,879,184	290	Taylor (W)	47.3	163	56.2	Cass (D)	42.5	127	43.8
1852	31	3,161,830	296	Pierce (D)	50.8	254	85.8	Scott (W)	43.9	42	14.2
1856	31	4,054,647	296	Buchanan (D)	45.3	174	58.8	Fremont (R)	33.1	114	38.5
1860	33	4,685,561	303	Lincoln (R)	39.8	180	59.4	Douglas (D)	29.5	12	4.0
1864	36	4,031,887	234	Lincoln (R)	55.0	212	90.6	McClellan (D)	45.0	21	9.0
1868	37	5,722,440	294	Grant (R)	52.7	214	72.8	Seymour (D)	47.3	80	27.2
1872	37	6,467,679	366	Grant (R)	55.6	286	78.1	Greeley (D)	43.8	c	c
1876	38	8,413,101	369	Hayes (R)	48.0	185	50.1	Tilden (D)	51.0	184	49.9

(Table continues)

Table 3-1 (Continued)

Year	Number of states	Total popular vote[a]	Total electoral votes	Winning candidate	Percentage of popular vote received by winning candidate[a]	Electoral votes received by winning candidate (N)	(%)	Losing candidate	Percentage of popular vote received by losing candidate[a]	Electoral votes received by losing candidate (N)	(%)
1880	38	9,210,420	369	Garfield (R)	48.3	214	58.0	Hancock (D)	48.2	155	42.0
1884	38	10,049,754	401	Cleveland (D)	48.5	219	54.6	Blaine (R)	48.2	182	45.3
1888	38	11,383,320	401	B. Harrison (R)	47.8	233	58.1	Cleveland (D)	48.6	168	42.0
1892	44	12,056,097	444	Cleveland (D)	46.1	277	62.4	B. Harrison (R)	43.0	145	32.7
1896	45	13,935,738	447	McKinley (R)	51.0	271	60.6	Bryan (D)	46.7	176	39.4
1900	45	13,970,470	447	McKinley (R)	51.7	292	65.3	Bryan (D)	45.5	155	34.7
1904	45	13,518,964	476	T. Roosevelt (R)	56.4	336	70.6	Parker (D)	37.6	140	29.4
1908	46	14,882,734	483	Taft (R)	51.6	321	66.5	Bryan (D)	43.0	162	33.5
1912	48	15,040,963	531	Wilson (D)	41.8	435	81.9	Taft (R)	23.2	8	1.5
1916	48	18,535,022	531	Wilson (D)	49.2	277	52.2	Hughes (R)	46.1	254	47.8
1920	48	26,753,786	531	Harding (R)	60.3	404	76.1	Cox (D)	34.2	127	23.9
1924	48	29,075,959	531	Coolidge (R)	54.1	382	71.9	David (D)	28.8	136	25.6
1928	48	36,790,364	531	Hoover (R)	58.2	444	83.6	Smith (D)	40.8	87	16.4
1932	48	39,749,382	531	F. Roosevelt (D)	57.4	472	88.9	Hoover (R)	39.6	59	11.1
1936	48	45,642,303	531	F. Roosevelt (D)	60.8	523	98.4	Landon (R)	36.5	8	1.5
1940	48	49,840,443	531	F. Roosevelt (D)	54.7	449	84.6	Willkie (R)	44.8	82	15.4
1944	48	47,974,819	531	F. Roosevelt (D)	53.3	432	81.4	Dewey (R)	45.9	99	18.6
1948	48	48,692,442	531	Truman (D)	49.5	303	57.1	Dewey (R)	45.1	189	35.6
1952	48	61,551,118	531	Eisenhower (R)	55.1	442	83.2	Stevenson (D)	44.4	89	16.8
1956	48	62,025,372	531	Eisenhower (R)	57.4	457	86.1	Stevenson (D)	42.0	73	13.7
1960	50	68,828,960	537	Kennedy (D)	49.7	303	56.4	Nixon (R)	49.5	219	40.8
1964[d]	50	70,641,104	538	L. Johnson (D)	61.1	486	90.3	Goldwater (R)	38.5	52	9.9
1968	50	73,203,370	538	Nixon (R)	43.4	301	55.9	Humphrey (D)	42.7	191	35.5
1972	50	77,727,590	538	Nixon (R)	60.7	520	96.7	McGovern (D)	37.5	17	3.2

1976	50	81,555,889	538	Carter (D)	50.1	297	55.2	Ford (R)	48.0	240	44.6
1980	50	86,515,221	538	Reagan (R)	50.7	489	90.9	Carter (D)	41.0	49	9.1
1984	50	92,652,793	538	Reagan (R)	58.8	525	97.6	Mondale (D)	40.6	13	2.4
1988	50	91,584,820	538	Bush (R)	53.4	426	79.2	Dukakis (D)	45.6	111	20.6
1992	50	104,425,014	538	Clinton (D)	43.0	370	68.8	Bush (R)	37.4	168	31.2

Source: Congressional Quarterly's Guide to U.S. Elections, 2d ed. (Washington, D.C.: Congressional Quarterly, 1985); updated by the author.

Note: Only the top two vote-getters are listed. For significant third-party contenders, see Table 3-3. F—Federalist; DR—Democratic-Republican; I—Independent Democrat-Republican; NR—National Republican; W—Whig; D—Democrat; R—Republican.

[a] Reliable data on the popular vote are not available before 1824.

[b] Washington ran unopposed in 1789 and 1792.

[c] Horace Greeley, the Democratic candidate, died between the popular vote and the meeting of the electoral college. The 66 Democratic electors split their votes among several candidates, including 3 votes cast for Greeley that Congress refused to count.

[d] The Twenty-third Amendment provided for three electoral college votes for the District of Columbia, beginning with the 1964 election.

Table 3-2   Candidates Who Won Presidency Without Popular Vote Majorities, 1824–1992

Year	Candidate	Percentage of popular vote received	Percentage of electoral vote received
1824	J. Q. Adams (I)	30.9	32.2
1844	Polk (D)	49.5	61.8
1848	Taylor (W)	47.3	56.2
1856	Buchanan (D)	45.3	58.8
1860	Lincoln (R)	39.8	59.4
1876	Hayes (R)	48.0	50.1
1880	Garfield (R)	48.3	58.0
1884	Cleveland (D)	48.5	54.6
1888	B. Harrison (R)	47.8	58.1
1892	Cleveland (D)	46.1	62.4
1912	Wilson (D)	41.8	81.9
1916	Wilson (D)	49.2	52.2
1948	Truman (D)	49.5	57.1
1960	Kennedy (D)	49.7	56.4
1968	Nixon (R)	43.4	55.9
1992	Clinton (D)	43.0	68.8

Source: Congressional Quarterly's Guide to U.S. Elections, 2d ed. (Washington, D.C.: Congressional Quarterly, 1985); updated by the author.

Note: Reliable data on the popular vote not available before 1824. I—Independent Democratic-Republican; W—Whig; D—Democrat; R—Republican.

Table 3-3 Comparison of Popular and Electoral Vote Mandates, 1824–1992

Year	Winning candidate	Percentage of popular vote received	Popular vote advantage[a]	Percentage of electoral vote received	Electoral vote advantage[a]	Percentage difference between electoral votes and popular votes
1824	J. Q. Adams (I)	30.9	-10.4	32.2	-5.7	1.3
1828	Jackson (D)	56.0	12.4	68.2	36.4	12.2
1832	Jackson (D)	54.2	16.8	76.0	59.0	21.8
1836	Van Buran (D)	50.8	14.2	57.8	33.0	7.0
1840	W. Harrison (W)	52.8	6.0	79.6	59.2	26.8
1844	Polk (D)	49.5	1.4	61.8	23.6	12.3
1848	Taylor (W)	47.3	4.8	56.2	12.4	8.9
1852	Pierce (D)	50.8	6.9	85.8	71.6	35.0
1856	Buchanan (D)	45.3	12.2	58.8	20.3	13.5
1860	Lincoln (R)	39.8	10.3	59.4	55.4	19.6
1864	Lincoln (R)	55.0	10.0	90.6	81.6	35.6
1868	Grant (R)	52.7	5.4	72.8	45.6	20.1
1872	Grant (R)	55.6	11.8	78.1	66.0	22.5
1876	Hayes (R)	48.0	-3.0	50.1	0.2	2.1
1880	Garfield (R)	48.3	0.1	58.0	16.0	9.7
1884	Cleveland (D)	48.5	0.3	54.6	9.3	6.1
1888	B. Harrison (R)	47.8	-0.8	58.1	16.1	10.3
1892	Cleveland (D)	46.1	3.1	62.4	29.7	16.3
1896	McKinley (R)	51.0	4.3	60.6	21.2	9.6
1900	McKinley (R)	51.7	6.2	65.3	30.6	13.6
1904	T. Roosevelt (R)	56.4	18.8	70.6	41.2	14.2
1908	Taft (R)	51.6	8.6	66.5	33.0	14.9
1912	Wilson (D)	41.8	18.6	81.9	80.4	40.1
1916	Wilson (D)	49.2	3.1	52.2	4.4	3.0
1920	Harding (R)	60.3	26.1	76.1	52.2	15.8

(Table continues)

Table 3-3 (Continued)

Year	Winning candidate	Percentage of popular vote received	Popular vote advantage[a]	Percentage of electoral vote received	Electoral vote advantage[a]	Percentage difference between electoral votes and popular votes
1924	Coolidge (R)	54.1	25.3	71.9	46.3	17.8
1928	Hoover (R)	58.2	17.4	83.6	67.2	25.4
1932	F. Roosevelt (D)	57.4	17.8	88.9	77.8	31.5
1936	F. Roosevelt (D)	60.8	24.3	98.4	96.9	37.6
1940	F. Roosevelt (D)	54.7	9.9	84.6	69.2	29.9
1944	F. Roosevelt (D)	53.3	7.4	81.4	62.8	28.1
1948	Truman (D)	49.5	4.4	57.1	21.5	7.6
1952	Eisenhower (R)	55.1	10.7	83.2	66.4	28.1
1956	Eisenhower (R)	57.4	15.4	86.1	72.4	28.7
1960	Kennedy (D)	49.7	0.2	56.4	15.6	6.7
1964	L. Johnson (D)	61.1	22.6	90.3	80.4	29.2
1968	Nixon (R)	43.4	0.7	55.9	20.4	12.5
1972	Nixon (R)	60.7	23.2	96.7	93.5	36.0
1976	Carter (D)	50.1	2.1	55.2	10.6	5.1
1980	Reagan (R)	50.7	9.7	90.9	81.8	40.2
1984	Reagan (R)	58.8	18.2	97.6	57.0	38.8
1988	Bush (R)	53.4	7.8	79.2	58.6	25.8
1992	Clinton (D)	43.0	5.6	68.8	37.6	25.8

Source: Congressional Quarterly's Guide to U.S. Elections, 2d ed. (Washington, D.C.: Congressional Quarterly, 1985); updated by the author.

Note: I—Independent Democratic-Republican; W—Whig; D—Democrat; R—Republican.

[a] Percentage point difference between winner and nearest rival.

Table 3-4   Significant Third-Party Presidential Candidates, 1824–1992

Year	Candidate	Party	Percentage of popular vote received	Electoral votes received
1824	Henry Clay	Democratic-Republican	13	37
	William Crawford	Democratic-Republican	11	41
1836	Hugh White	Whig	10	26
1848	Martin Van Buren	Free Soil	10	0
1856	Millard Fillmore	Whig-American	22	8
1860	John Breckinridge	Southern Democrat	18	72
	John Bell	Constitutional Union	13	39
1912	Theodore Roosevelt	Progressive	27	88
1924	Robert LaFollette	Progressive	17	13
1968	George Wallace	American Independent	14	46
1992	H. Ross Perot	Independent	19	0

Source: Congressional Quarterly's Guide to U.S. Elections, 2d ed. (Washington, D.C.: Congressional Quarterly, 1985); updated by the author.

Note: Only candidates who received at least 10 percent of the popular vote are listed. No significant third-party candidate prior to 1824.

Table 3-5   Electoral College Anomalies, 1789–1992

Year	Candidate	Percentage of popular vote received[a]	Percentage of electoral vote received	Winner
1800[b]	J. Adams	—	65	Jefferson
	Jefferson	—	73	
	Burr	—	73	
1824[c]	J. Q. Adams	31	32	J.Q. Adams
	Jackson	41	38	
1876[d]	Hayes	48	50	Hayes
	Tilden	51	50	
1888	Cleveland	49	42	B. Harrison
	B. Harrison	48	48	

Source: Adapted from *Congressional Quarterly's Guide to U.S. Elections,* 2d ed. (Washington, D.C.: Congressional Quarterly, 1985); updated by the author.

[a] Reliable data on the popular vote not available before 1824.
[b] Jefferson was elected by the House of Representatives.
[c] Adams was elected by the House of Representatives after a four-way race.
[d] The returns from Florida, Louisiana, Oregon, and South Carolina were disputed. Congress, in joint session, declared Hayes the winner.

Table 3-6 Faithless Electors, 1789–1992

Year	Elector	State	Elected to vote for	Voted for
1796	Unknown	Pennsylvania	John Adams	Thomas Jefferson
1820	Unknown	New Hampshire	James Monroe	John Quincy Adams
1948	Preston Parks	Tennessee	Harry Truman	Strom Thurmond
1956	W. F. Turner	Alabama	Adlai Stevenson	Walter E. Jones
1960	Henry D. Irwin	Oklahoma	Richard Nixon	Harry F. Byrd
1968	Dr. Lloyd W. Bailey	North Carolina	Richard Nixon	George C. Wallace
1972	Roger L. McBride	Virginia	Richard Nixon	John Hospers
1976	Mike Padden	Washington	Gerald Ford	Ronald Reagan
1988	Margaret Leach	West Virginia	Michael Dukakis	Lloyd Bentsen

Source: Adapted from *Congressional Quarterly's Guide to U.S. Elections,* 2d ed. (Washington, D.C.: Congressional Quarterly, 1985); updated by the author.

Table 3-7 Party Winning Presidential Election by State, 1789–1992

State	1789–1824 D	1789–1824 F	1789–1824 O	1828–1856 D	1828–1856 R	1828–1856 O	1860–1892 D	1860–1892 R	1860–1892 O	1896–1928 D	1896–1928 R	1896–1928 O	1932–1964 D	1932–1964 R	1932–1964 O	1968–1992 D	1968–1992 R	1968–1992 O
Alabama	2	0	0	8	0	0	6	2	0	9	0	0	7	1	1	1	5	1
Alaska	—	—	—	—	—	—	—	—	—	—	—	—	1	1	0	0	7	0
Arizona	—	—	—	—	—	—	—	—	—	2	3	0	5	4	0	2	7	0
Arkansas	—	—	—	6	0	0	6	1	0	9	0	0	9	0	0	2	4	1
California	—	—	—	2	0	0	2	7	0	1	7	1	6	3	0	1	6	0
Colorado	—	—	—	—	—	—	0	4	1	5	4	0	4	5	0	1	6	0
Connecticut	2	8	0	2	6	0	4	5	0	1	8	0	5	4	0	2	5	0
Delaware	2	8	0	2	6	0	7	1	1	1	8	0	5	4	0	2	5	0
District of Columbia[a]	—	—	—	—	—	—	—	—	—	—	—	—	1	0	0	7	0	0
Florida	—	—	—	2	1	0	4	3	1	8	1	0	6	3	0	1	6	0
Georgia	8	2	0	5	3	0	7	0	1	9	0	0	8	1	0	3	3	1
Hawaii	—	—	—	—	—	—	—	—	—	—	—	—	2	0	0	5	2	0
Idaho	—	—	—	—	—	—	1	0	1	4	5	0	6	3	0	0	7	0
Illinois	2	0	0	8	0	0	1	8	0	1	8	0	7	2	0	1	6	0
Indiana	3	0	0	6	2	0	3	6	0	1	8	0	3	6	0	0	7	0
Iowa	—	—	—	2	1	0	0	9	0	1	8	0	4	5	0	2	5	0
Kansas	—	—	—	—	—	—	0	7	1	3	6	0	3	6	0	0	7	0
Kentucky	8	1	0	2	6	0	8	0	1	6	3	0	7	2	0	2	5	0
Louisiana	4	0	0	6	2	0	5	1	1	9	0	0	6	2	1	2	4	1
Maine	2	0	0	5	3	0	0	9	0	1	8	0	1	8	0	2	5	0
Maryland	4	6	0	1	6	1	7	1	1	4	5	0	6	3	0	4	3	0
Massachusetts	3	7	0	0	8	0	0	9	0	2	7	0	7	2	0	5	2	0
Michigan	—	—	—	4	2	0	0	9	0	0	8	1	5	4	0	5	2	0
Minnesota	—	—	—	—	—	—	0	9	0	0	8	1	7	2	0	6	1	0

(*Table continues*)

Table 3-7 *(Continued)*

State	1789–1824 D	F	O	1828–1856 D	R	O	1860–1892 D	R	O	1896–1928 D	R	O	1932–1964 D	R	O	1968–1992 D	R	O
Mississippi	2	0	0	7	1	0	5	1	1	9	0	0	6	1	2	1	5	1
Missouri	—	—	—	8	0	0	7	2	0	4	5	0	8	1	0	2	5	0
Montana	—	—	—	—	—	—	0	1	0	4	5	0	6	3	0	1	6	0
Nebraska	—	—	—	—	—	—	0	7	0	4	5	0	3	6	0	0	7	0
Nevada	—	—	—	—	—	—	1	6	1	5	4	0	7	2	0	1	6	0
New Hampshire	4	6	0	6	2	0	0	9	0	2	7	0	4	5	0	1	6	0
New Jersey	5	5	0	3	5	0	7	2	0	1	8	0	6	3	0	1	6	0
New Mexico	—	—	—	—	—	—	—	—	—	2	3	0	7	2	0	1	6	0
New York	6	3	0	5	3	0	4	5	0	1	8	0	6	3	0	4	3	0
North Carolina	8	1	0	5	3	0	5	2	1	8	1	0	9	0	0	1	6	0
North Dakota	—	—	—	—	—	—	—	—	—	2	7	0	3	6	0	0	7	0
Ohio	6	0	0	4	4	0	0	9	0	2	7	0	5	4	0	2	5	0
Oklahoma	—	—	—	—	—	—	—	—	—	4	2	0	6	3	0	0	7	0
Oregon	—	—	—	—	—	—	1	8	0	1	8	1	5	4	0	2	5	0
Pennsylvania	8	2	0	6	2	0	0	9	0	0	8	0	5	4	0	3	4	0
Rhode Island	4	5	0	2	6	0	0	9	0	2	7	0	7	2	0	5	2	0
South Carolina	8	2	0	6	0	2	4	3	1	9	0	0	7	1	1	1	6	0
South Dakota	—	—	—	—	—	—	0	1	0	1	7	1	3	6	0	0	7	0
Tennessee	8	0	0	3	5	0	6	1	1	7	2	0	6	3	0	2	5	0
Texas	—	—	—	3	0	0	7	0	0	8	1	0	7	2	0	2	5	0
Utah	—	—	—	—	—	—	—	—	—	2	7	0	6	3	0	0	7	0
Vermont	6	3	0	7	1	0	0	9	0	0	9	0	1	8	0	1	6	0
Virginia	8	2	0	8	0	0	5	1	1	8	1	0	6	3	0	0	7	0
Washington	—	—	—	—	—	—	0	1	0	2	6	1	6	3	0	3	4	0
West Virginia	—	—	—	—	—	—	5	3	0	1	8	0	8	1	0	5	2	0

Wisconsin	—	—	2	1	0	1	8	0	1	7	1	5	4	0	3	4	0
Wyoming	—	—	1	—	—	0	1	0	3	6	0	5	4	0	0	7	0
Total[b]	113 (65%)	61 (35%)	136 (62%)	79 (36%)	3 (1%)	118 (37%)	189 (59%)	15 (5%)	170 (40%)	244 (58%)	7 (2%)	274 (63%)	158 (36%)	5 (1%)	96 (27%)	256 (72%)	5 (1%)

Source: Adapted from Harold Stanley and Richard Niemi, *Vital Statistics on American Politics*, 4th ed. (Washington, D.C.: CQ Press, 1994), 116–118.

Note: D—The Democratic-Republican party from 1796 to 1820 and in 1828, the Jackson faction in 1824, and the Democratic party in 1832 and later; F—the Federalists from 1792 to 1816, Independent Democratic-Republicans in 1820, and the J.Q. Adams faction in 1824; R—the National Republicans in 1828 and 1832, Whigs from 1836 to 1852, and the Republican party in 1856 and later; O—other (third-party) parties. Southern Democrats in 1860 are counted as Democratic. "—" indicates that the state was not yet admitted to the Union.

[a] Residents of the District of Columbia received the presidential vote in 1961.

[b] Fewer total votes for a given state within a party system indicate admission of the state during the party system or nonvoting in certain southern states in 1864, 1868, and 1872.

Table 3-8 Percentage of Popular Votes for President by State, 1968 and 1972

State	1968				1972		
	Richard M. Nixon (R)	Hubert H. Humphrey (D)	George C. Wallace (AI)	Other	Richard M. Nixon (R)	George S. McGovern (D)	Other
Alabama	14.0	18.8	65.8	1.4	48.8	47.5	3.7
Alaska	45.3	42.7	12.1	0.0	58.1	34.6	7.3
Arizona	54.8	35.0	9.6	0.6	61.6	30.4	8.0
Arkansas	30.8	30.4	38.9	0.0	68.9	30.7	0.4
California	47.8	44.7	6.7	0.7	55.0	41.5	3.5
Colorado	50.5	41.3	7.5	0.7	62.6	34.6	2.9
Connecticut	44.3	49.5	6.1	0.1	58.6	40.1	1.4
Delaware	45.1	41.6	13.3	0.0	59.6	39.2	1.2
Florida	40.5	30.9	28.5	0.0	71.9	27.8	0.3
Georgia	30.4	26.8	42.8	0.0	75.3	24.7	0.0
Hawaii	38.7	59.8	1.5	0.0	62.5	37.5	0.0
Idaho	56.8	30.7	12.6	0.0	64.2	26.0	9.7
Illinois	47.1	44.2	8.5	0.3	59.0	40.3	0.5
Indiana	50.3	38.0	11.5	0.3	66.1	33.3	0.5
Iowa	53.0	40.8	5.7	0.5	57.6	40.5	1.9
Kansas	54.8	34.7	10.2	0.3	67.7	29.5	2.9
Kentucky	43.8	37.7	18.3	0.3	63.4	34.8	1.9
Louisiana	23.5	28.2	48.3	0.0	66.0	28.6	5.4
Maine	43.1	55.3	1.6	0.0	61.5	38.5	0.0
Maryland	41.9	43.6	14.5	0.0	61.3	37.4	1.4
Massachusetts	32.9	63.0	3.7	0.4	45.2	54.2	0.6
Michigan	41.5	48.2	10.0	0.4	56.2	41.8	2.0
Minnesota	41.5	54.0	4.3	0.2	51.6	46.1	2.4
Mississippi	13.5	23.0	63.5	0.0	78.2	19.6	2.2
Missouri	44.9	43.7	11.4	0.0	62.3	37.7	0.0
Montana	50.6	41.6	7.3	0.5	57.9	37.9	4.2
Nebraska	59.8	31.8	8.4	0.0	70.5	29.5	0.0
Nevada	47.5	39.3	13.3	0.0	63.7	36.3	0.0

New Hampshire	52.1	43.9	3.8	0.2	64.0	34.9	1.2
New Jersey	46.1	44.0	9.1	0.8	61.6	36.8	1.7
New Mexico	51.9	39.8	7.9	0.5	61.1	36.6	2.4
New York	44.3	49.8	5.3	0.6	57.3	40.3	0.3
North Carolina	39.5	29.2	31.3	0.0	69.5	28.9	1.7
North Dakota	55.8	38.2	5.8	0.1	62.1	35.8	2.1
Ohio	45.2	43.0	11.8	0.0	59.6	38.1	2.3
Oklahoma	47.7	32.0	20.3	0.0	73.7	24.0	2.3
Oregon	49.8	43.8	6.1	0.3	52.5	42.3	5.3
Pennsylvania	44.0	47.6	8.0	0.4	59.1	39.1	1.7
Rhode Island	31.8	64.0	4.1	0.0	53.0	46.8	0.2
South Carolina	38.1	29.6	32.3	0.0	70.8	27.7	1.5
South Dakota	53.3	42.0	4.8	0.0	54.2	45.5	0.3
Tennessee	37.9	28.1	34.0	0.0	67.7	29.8	2.5
Texas	39.9	41.1	19.0	0.0	66.2	33.3	0.6
Utah	56.5	37.1	6.4	0.1	67.6	26.4	6.0
Vermont	52.8	43.5	3.2	0.6	62.9	36.6	0.5
Virginia	43.4	32.5	23.6	0.5	67.8	30.1	2.1
Washington	45.2	47.3	7.4	0.2	56.9	38.6	4.5
West Virginia	40.8	49.6	9.6	0.0	63.6	36.4	0.0
Wisconsin	47.9	44.3	7.6	0.3	53.4	43.7	2.9
Wyoming	55.8	35.5	8.7	0.0	69.0	30.5	0.5
District of Columbia	18.2	81.8	0.0	0.0	21.6	78.1	0.3
Total	43.4	42.7	13.5	0.3	60.7	37.5	1.8

Source: Adapted from *Congressional Quarterly's Guide to U.S. Elections,* 2d ed. (Washington, D.C.: Congressional Quarterly, 1985).

Note: AI—American Independent; D—Democrat; R—Republican.

Table 3-9 Percentage of Popular Votes for President by State, 1976 and 1980

State	1976				1980			
	Jimmy Carter (D)	Gerald R. Ford (R)	Eugene J. McCarthy (I)	Other	Ronald Reagan (R)	Jimmy Carter (D)	John Anderson (I)	Other
Alabama	55.7	42.6	0.0	1.6	48.8	47.5	1.2	2.5
Alaska	35.7	57.9	0.0	6.5	54.3	26.4	7.0	12.3
Arizona	39.8	56.4	2.6	1.2	60.6	28.2	8.8	2.4
Arkansas	65.0	34.9	0.1	0.1	48.1	47.5	2.7	1.7
California	47.6	49.3	0.7	2.3	52.7	35.9	8.6	2.8
Colorado	42.6	54.0	2.4	1.0	55.1	31.1	11.0	2.8
Connecticut	46.9	52.1	0.3	0.8	48.2	38.5	12.2	1.1
Delaware	52.0	46.6	1.0	0.4	47.2	44.8	6.9	1.1
Florida	51.9	46.6	0.8	0.7	55.5	38.5	5.2	0.8
Georgia	66.7	33.0	0.1	0.2	41.0	55.8	2.2	1.0
Hawaii	50.6	48.1	0.0	1.3	42.9	44.8	10.6	1.7
Idaho	36.8	59.3	0.3	3.5	66.4	25.2	6.2	2.2
Illinois	48.1	50.1	1.2	0.6	49.7	41.7	7.3	1.3
Indiana	45.7	53.3	0.0	1.0	56.0	37.7	5.0	1.3
Iowa	48.5	49.5	1.6	0.5	51.3	38.6	8.8	1.3
Kansas	44.9	52.5	1.4	1.2	57.8	33.3	7.0	1.9
Kentucky	52.8	45.6	0.6	1.1	49.1	47.6	2.4	0.9
Louisiana	51.7	46.0	0.5	1.8	51.2	45.8	1.7	1.3
Maine	48.1	48.9	2.3	0.8	45.6	42.3	10.2	1.9
Maryland	52.8	46.7	0.3	0.2	44.2	47.1	7.8	0.9
Massachusetts	56.1	40.4	2.6	0.9	41.9	41.7	15.2	1.2
Michigan	46.4	51.8	1.3	0.4	49.0	42.5	7.0	1.5
Minnesota	54.9	42.0	1.8	1.3	42.6	46.5	8.5	2.4
Mississippi	49.6	47.7	0.5	2.3	49.4	48.1	1.3	1.2
Missouri	51.1	47.5	1.2	0.2	51.2	44.3	3.7	0.8
Montana	45.4	52.8	0.0	1.8	56.8	32.4	8.1	2.7

State								
Nebraska	38.5	59.2	1.5	0.8	65.9	26.0	7.0	1.1
Nevada	45.8	50.2	0.0	4.1	62.5	26.9	7.1	3.5
New Hampshire	43.5	54.7	1.2	0.6	57.7	28.4	12.9	1.0
New Jersey	47.9	50.1	1.1	0.9	52.0	38.6	7.9	1.5
New Mexico	48.1	50.5	0.3	1.2	54.9	36.7	6.5	1.9
New York	51.9	47.5	0.1	0.6	46.7	44.0	7.5	1.8
North Carolina	55.2	44.2	0.0	0.5	49.3	47.2	2.9	0.6
North Dakota	45.8	51.6	1.0	1.6	64.2	26.3	7.8	1.7
Ohio	48.9	48.7	1.4	1.0	51.5	40.9	5.9	1.7
Oklahoma	48.7	50.0	1.3	0.0	60.5	35.0	3.3	1.2
Oregon	47.6	47.8	3.9	0.7	48.3	38.7	9.5	3.5
Pennsylvania	50.4	47.7	1.1	0.8	49.6	42.5	6.4	1.5
Rhode Island	55.4	44.1	0.1	0.5	37.2	47.7	14.4	0.7
South Carolina	56.2	43.1	0.0	0.7	49.4	48.2	1.6	0.8
South Dakota	48.9	50.4	0.0	0.7	60.5	31.7	6.5	1.3
Tennessee	55.9	42.9	0.3	0.8	48.7	48.4	2.2	0.7
Texas	51.1	48.0	0.5	0.4	55.3	41.4	2.5	0.8
Utah	33.6	62.4	0.7	3.2	72.8	20.6	5.0	1.6
Vermont	43.1	54.4	2.1	0.4	44.4	38.4	14.9	2.3
Virginia	48.0	49.3	0.0	2.8	53.0	40.3	5.1	1.6
Washington	46.1	50.0	2.4	1.5	49.7	37.3	10.6	2.4
West Virginia	58.0	41.9	0.0	0.0	45.3	49.8	4.3	0.6
Wisconsin	49.4	47.8	1.7	1.2	47.9	43.2	7.1	1.8
Wyoming	39.8	59.3	0.4	0.5	62.6	28.0	6.8	2.6
District of Columbia	81.6	16.5	0.0	1.9	13.4	74.8	9.3	0.6
Total	50.1	48.0	0.9	1.0	50.7	41.0	6.6	7.1

Source: Adapted from *Congressional Quarterly's Guide to U.S. Elections*, 2d ed. (Washington, D.C.: Congressional Quarterly, 1985).

Table 3-10 Percentage of Popular Votes for President by State, 1984 and 1988

State	1984			1988		
	Ronald Reagan (R)	Walter Mondale (D)	Other	George Bush (R)	Michael Dukakis (D)	Other
Alabama	60.5	38.3	1.2	59.2	39.9	0.9
Alaska	66.6	29.9	3.5	59.7	36.2	4.1
Arizona	66.4	32.5	1.1	60.0	38.8	1.2
Arkansas	60.5	38.3	1.2	56.4	42.2	1.4
California	57.5	41.3	1.2	51.1	47.6	1.3
Colorado	63.4	35.1	1.5	53.1	45.3	1.6
Connecticut	60.7	38.8	0.5	52.0	46.9	1.1
Delaware	59.8	39.9	0.3	55.9	43.5	0.6
Florida	65.3	34.7	0.0	60.9	38.5	0.6
Georgia	60.2	39.8	0.0	59.7	39.5	0.8
Hawaii	55.1	43.8	1.1	44.7	54.3	1.0
Idaho	72.4	26.4	1.2	62.1	36.0	1.9
Illinois	56.2	43.3	0.5	50.7	48.6	0.7
Indiana	61.7	37.7	0.6	59.8	39.7	0.5
Iowa	53.3	45.9	0.8	44.5	54.7	0.8
Kansas	66.3	32.6	1.1	55.8	42.5	1.7
Kentucky	60.0	39.4	0.6	55.5	43.9	0.6
Louisiana	60.8	38.2	1.0	54.3	44.1	1.6
Maine	60.8	38.8	0.4	55.3	43.9	0.8
Maryland	52.5	47.0	0.5	51.1	48.2	0.7
Massachusetts	51.2	48.4	0.4	45.4	53.2	1.4
Michigan	59.2	40.2	0.6	53.5	45.7	0.8
Minnesota	49.5	49.7	0.8	45.9	52.9	1.2
Mississippi	61.9	37.4	0.7	59.9	39.1	1.0
Missouri	60.0	40.0	0.0	51.8	47.9	0.3
Montana	60.5	38.2	1.3	52.1	46.2	1.7
Nebraska	70.6	28.8	0.6	60.1	39.2	0.7
Nevada	65.8	32.0	2.2	58.9	37.9	3.2

New Hampshire	68.6	30.9	0.5	62.5	36.3	1.2
New Jersey	60.1	39.2	0.7	56.2	42.6	1.2
New Mexico	59.7	39.2	1.1	51.9	46.9	1.2
New York	53.8	45.8	0.4	47.5	51.6	0.9
North Carolina	61.9	37.9	0.2	58.0	41.7	0.3
North Dakota	64.8	33.8	1.4	56.0	43.0	1.0
Ohio	58.9	40.1	1.0	55.0	44.1	0.9
Oklahoma	68.6	30.7	0.7	57.9	41.3	0.8
Oregon	55.9	43.7	0.4	46.6	51.3	2.1
Pennsylvania	53.3	46.0	0.7	50.7	48.4	0.9
Rhode Island	51.8	47.9	0.3	43.9	55.7	0.4
South Carolina	63.6	35.6	0.8	61.5	37.6	0.9
South Dakota	63.0	36.5	0.5	52.9	46.5	0.6
Tennessee	57.8	41.6	0.6	57.9	41.5	0.6
Texas	63.6	36.1	0.3	56.0	43.3	0.7
Utah	74.5	24.7	0.8	66.2	32.0	1.8
Vermont	57.9	40.8	1.3	51.1	47.6	1.3
Virginia	62.3	37.1	0.6	59.7	39.2	1.1
Washington	56.2	42.9	0.9	48.5	50.0	1.5
West Virginia	54.7	44.3	1.0	47.5	52.2	0.3
Wisconsin	54.3	45.1	0.6	47.8	51.4	0.8
Wyoming	69.1	27.7	3.2	60.5	38.0	1.5
District of Columbia	13.7	85.4	0.9	14.3	82.6	3.1
Total	58.8	40.6	0.6	53.4	45.6	1.0

Source: (1984 data) Adapted from *Congressional Quarterly's Guide to U.S. Elections*, 2d ed. (Washington, D.C.: Congressional Quarterly, 1985); (1988 data) *Congressional Quarterly Weekly Report*, January 23, 1993, 190.

Table 3-11 Percentage of Popular Votes for President by State, 1992

State	George Bush (R)	Bill Clinton (D)	H. Ross Perot (United We Stand)	Other
Alabama	47.6	40.9	10.8	0.6
Alaska	39.5	30.3	28.4	1.8
Arizona	38.5	36.5	23.8	1.2
Arkansas	35.5	53.2	10.4	0.9
California	32.0	46.0	20.6	0.8
Colorado	35.9	40.1	23.3	0.7
Connecticut	35.8	42.2	21.6	0.4
Delaware	35.3	43.5	20.4	0.7
Florida	40.9	39.0	19.8	0.3
Georgia	42.9	43.5	13.3	0.3
Hawaii	36.7	48.1	14.2	1.0
Idaho	42.0	28.4	27.0	2.5
Illinois	34.3	48.6	16.6	0.4
Indiana	42.9	36.8	19.8	0.5
Iowa	37.3	43.3	18.7	0.7
Kansas	38.9	33.7	27.0	0.4
Kentucky	41.3	44.6	13.7	0.4
Louisiana	41.0	45.6	11.8	1.6
Maine	30.4	38.8	30.4	0.4
Maryland	35.6	49.8	14.2	0.4
Massachusetts	29.0	47.5	22.7	0.7
Michigan	36.4	43.8	19.3	0.6
Minnesota	31.9	43.5	24.0	0.7
Mississippi	49.7	40.8	8.7	0.8
Missouri	33.9	44.1	21.7	0.3
Montana	35.1	37.6	26.1	1.1
Nebraska	46.6	29.4	23.6	0.4
Nevada	34.7	37.4	26.2	1.7
New Hampshire	37.6	38.9	22.6	0.9
New Jersey	40.6	43.0	15.6	0.9
New Mexico	37.3	45.9	10.1	0.6
New York	33.9	49.7	15.7	0.6
North Carolina	43.4	42.7	13.7	0.2
North Dakota	44.2	32.2	23.1	0.5
Ohio	38.3	40.2	21.0	0.5
Oklahoma	42.6	34.0	23.0	0.3
Oregon	32.5	42.5	24.2	0.8
Pennsylvania	36.1	45.1	18.2	0.5
Rhode Island	29.0	47.0	23.2	0.8
South Carolina	48.0	39.9	11.5	0.6
South Dakota	40.2	37.1	21.8	0.4
Tennessee	42.4	47.1	10.1	0.4
Texas	40.6	37.1	22.0	0.3
Utah	43.4	24.7	27.3	4.6
Vermont	30.4	46.1	22.8	0.7
Virginia	45.0	40.6	13.6	0.8
Washington	32.0	43.4	23.7	1.0
West Virginia	35.4	46.7	15.9	0.3
Wisconsin	36.8	41.1	21.5	0.6
Wyoming	39.6	34.0	25.6	0.9
District of Columbia	9.1	84.6	4.3	2.0
Total	37.4	43.0	18.9	0.6

Source: Congressional Quarterly Weekly Report, January 23, 1993, 190.

Table 3-12   Electoral Votes by State, 1968

State	Electoral votes	1968 winner
Alabama	10	W
Alaska	3	N
Arizona	5	N
Arkansas	6	W
California[a]	40	N
Colorado	6	N
Connecticut	8	H
Delaware	3	N
District of Columbia	3	H
Florida[a]	14	N
Georgia	12	W
Hawaii	4	H
Idaho	4	N
Illinois[a]	26	N
Indiana[a]	13	N
Iowa	9	N
Kansas	7	N
Kentucky	9	N
Louisiana	10	W
Maine	4	H
Maryland	10	H
Massachusetts[a]	14	H
Michigan[a]	21	H
Minnesota	10	H
Mississippi	7	W
Missouri	12	N
Montana	4	N
Nebraska	5	N
Nevada	3	N
New Hampshire	4	N
New Jersey[a]	17	N
New Mexico	4	N
New York[a]	43	H
North Carolina[a]	13	N[b]
North Dakota	4	N
Ohio[a]	26	N
Oklahoma	8	N
Oregon	6	N
Pennsylvania[a]	29	H
Rhode Island	4	H
South Carolina	8	N
South Dakota	4	N
Tennessee	11	N
Texas[a]	25	H
Utah	4	N
Vermont	3	N
Virginia	12	N

(Table continues)

Table 3-12   *(Continued)*

State	Electoral votes	1968 winner
Washington	9	H
West Virginia	7	H
Wisconsin	12	N
Wyoming	3	N
Total votes	538	
Number of votes needed to win	270	
Winner (votes)	N (301)	
Number of large states won	7	

Source: Adapted from *Congressional Quarterly's Guide to U.S. Elections,* 2d ed. (Washington, D.C.: Congressional Quarterly, 1985).

Note: H—Humphrey; N—Nixon; W—Wallace.

[a] One of twelve states with highest number of electoral votes. Total votes from these states add to 281.
[b] One electoral vote went to Wallace.

Table 3-13   Electoral Votes by State, 1972, 1976, and 1980

State	Electoral votes	1972 winner	1976 winner	1980 winner
Alabama	9	N	C	R
Alaska	3	N	F	R
Arizona	6	N	F	R
Arkansas	6	N	C	R
California[a]	45	N	F	R
Colorado	7	N	F	R
Connecticut	8	N	F	R
Delaware	3	N	C	R
District of Columbia	3	M	C	C
Florida[a]	17	N	C	R
Georgia	12	N	C	C
Hawaii	4	N	C	C
Idaho	4	N	F	R
Illinois[a]	26	N	F	R
Indiana[a]	13	N	F	R
Iowa	8	N	F	R
Kansas	7	N	F	R
Kentucky	9	N	C	R
Louisiana	10	N	C	R
Maine	4	N	F	R
Maryland	10	N	C	C
Massachusetts[a]	14	M	C	R
Michigan[a]	21	N	F	R
Minnesota	10	N	C	C
Mississippi	7	N	C	R
Missouri	12	N	C	R
Montana	4	N	F	R
Nebraska	5	N	F	R
Nevada	3	N	F	R
New Hampshire	4	N	F	R
New Jersey[a]	17	N	F	R
New Mexico	4	N	F	R
New York[a]	41	N	C	R
North Carolina[a]	13	N	C	R
North Dakota	3	N	F	R
Ohio[a]	25	N	C	R
Oklahoma	8	N	F	R
Oregon	6	N	F	R
Pennsylvania[a]	27	N	C	R
Rhode Island	4	N	C	C
South Carolina	8	N	C	R
South Dakota	4	N	F	R
Tennessee	10	N	C	R
Texas[a]	26	N	C	R
Utah	4	N	F	R
Vermont	3	N	F	R

(Table continues)

Table 3-13   *(Continued)*

State	Electoral votes	1972 winner	1976 winner	1980 winner
Virginia	12	N[b]	F	R
Washington	9	N	F[c]	R
West Virginia	6	N	C	C
Wisconsin	11	N	C	R
Wyoming	3	N	F	R
Total votes	538			
Number of votes needed to win	270			
Winner (votes)		N (520)	C (297)	R (489)
Number of large states won		11	7	12

Source: Adapted from *Congressional Quarterly's Guide to U.S. Elections*, 2d ed. (Washington, D.C.: Congressional Quarterly, 1985).

Note: C—Carter; F—Ford; M—McGovern; N—Nixon; R—Reagan.

[a] One of twelve states with highest number of electoral votes. Total votes from these states add to 285.
[b] One electoral vote went to Hospers.
[c] One electoral vote went to Reagan.

Table 3-14   Electoral Votes by State, 1984 and 1988

State	Electoral votes	1984 winner	1988 winner
Alabama	9	R	B
Alaska	3	R	B
Arizona	7	R	B
Arkansas	6	R	B
California[a]	47	R	B
Colorado	8	R	B
Connecticut	8	R	B
Delaware	3	R	B
District of Columbia	3	M	D
Florida[a]	21	R	B
Georgia[a]	12	R	B
Hawaii	4	R	D
Idaho	4	R	B
Illinois[a]	24	R	B
Indiana[a]	12	R	B
Iowa	8	R	D
Kansas	7	R	B
Kentucky	9	R	B
Louisiana	10	R	B
Maine	4	R	B
Maryland	10	R	B
Massachusetts[a]	13	R	D
Michigan[a]	20	R	B
Minnesota	10	M	D
Mississippi	7	R	B
Missouri	11	R	B
Montana	4	R	B
Nebraska	5	R	B
Nevada	4	R	B
New Hampshire	4	R	B
New Jersey[a]	16	R	B
New Mexico	5	R	B
New York[a]	36	R	D
North Carolina[a]	13	R	B
North Dakota	3	R	B
Ohio[a]	23	R	B
Oklahoma	8	R	B
Oregon	7	R	D
Pennsylvania[a]	25	R	B
Rhode Island	4	R	D
South Carolina	8	R	B
South Dakota	3	R	B
Tennessee	11	R	B
Texas[a]	29	R	B
Utah	5	R	B
Vermont	3	R	B

(Table continues)

Table 3-14   *(Continued)*

State	Electoral votes	1984 winner	1988 winner
Virginia[a]	12	R	B
Washington	10	R	D
West Virginia	6	R	D[b]
Wisconsin	11	R	D
Wyoming	3	R	B
Total votes	538		
Number of votes needed to win	270		
Winner (votes)		R (525)	B (426)
Number of large states won		14	12

Source: (1984 data) Adapted from *Congressional Quarterly's Guide to U.S. Elections*, 2d ed. (Washington, D.C.: Congressional Quarterly, 1985); (1988 data) Bureau of the Census, *Statistical Abstract of the United States 1993* (Washington, D.C.: Government Printing Office, 1993), 264.

Note: B—Bush; D—Dukakis; M—Mondale; R—Reagan.

[a] One of fourteen states with highest number of electoral votes. Total votes from these states add to 274.
[b] One electoral vote went to Bentsen.

Table 3-15   Electoral Votes by State, 1992

State	Electoral votes	Winner
Alabama	9	B
Alaska	3	B
Arizona	8	B
Arkansas	6	C
California[a]	54	C
Colorado	8	C
Connecticut	8	C
Delaware	3	C
District of Columbia	3	C
Florida[a]	25	B
Georgia[a]	13	C
Hawaii	4	C
Idaho	4	B
Illinois[a]	22	C
Indiana	12	B
Iowa	7	C
Kansas	6	B
Kentucky	8	C
Louisiana	9	C
Maine	4	C
Maryland	10	C
Massachusetts	12	C
Michigan[a]	18	C
Minnesota	10	C
Mississippi	7	B
Missouri	11	C
Montana	3	C
Nebraska	5	B
Nevada	4	C
New Hampshire	4	C
New Jersey[a]	15	C
New Mexico	5	C
New York[a]	33	C
North Carolina[a]	14	B
North Dakota	3	B
Ohio[a]	21	C
Oklahoma	8	B
Oregon	7	C
Pennsylvania[a]	23	C
Rhode Island	4	C
South Carolina	8	B
South Dakota	3	B
Tennessee	11	C
Texas[a]	32	B
Utah	5	B
Vermont	3	C
Virginia[a]	13	B

(Table continues)

Table 3-15   *(Continued)*

State	Electoral votes	Winner
Washington	11	C
West Virginia	5	C
Wisconsin	11	C
Wyoming	3	B
Total votes	538	
Number of votes needed to win	270	
Winner (votes)		C (370)
Number of large states won		8

Source: Bureau of the Census, *Statistical Abstract of the United States 1993* (Washington, D.C.: Government Printing Office, 1993), 264.

Note: B—Bush; C—Clinton.

[a] One of twelve states with highest number of electoral votes. Total votes from these states add to 283.

Table 3-16   Representation of the President's Party in the Two-Party House Vote, 1824–1994

Year	President's party	Percentage of House vote[a]	Unified or Divided Government
1824	DR	58	UG
1826	DR	61	DG
1828	D	44	UG
1830	D	53	UG
1832	D	55	UG
1834	D	54	UG
1836	D	52	UG
1838	D	54	UG
1840	W	54	UG
1842	W	45	DG-H
1844	D	51	UG
1846	D	53	DG-H
1848	W	48	DG
1850	W	45	DG
1852	D	54	UG
1854	D	80	DG-H
1856	D	70	UG
1858	D	69	DG-H
1860	R	57	UG
1862	R	63	UG
1864	R	64	UG
1866	D	59	UG
1868	R	56	UG
1870	R	53	UG
1872	R	55	UG
1874	R	53	DG-H
1876	R	49	DG-H
1878	R	45	DG
1880	R	49	U
1882	R	43	DG-H
1884	D	47	DG-S
1886	D	44	DG-S
1888	R	49	DG-H
1890	R	45	DG-H
1892	D	53	UG
1894	D	45	DG
1896	R	48	UG
1898	R	46	UG
1900	R	50	UG
1902	R	48	UG
1904	R	53	UG
1906	R	49	UG
1908	R	48	UG
1910	R	46	DG-H
1912	D	61	UG
1914	D	57	UG
1916	D	55	UG

(Table continues)

Table 3-16   *(Continued)*

Year	President's party	Percentage of House vote[a]	Unified or Divided Government
1918	D	54	DG
1920	R	56	UG
1922	R	47	UG
1924	R	51	UG
1926	R	51	UG
1928	R	51	UG
1930	R	46	DG-H
1932	D	62	UG
1934	D	64	UG
1936	D	63	UG
1938	D	60	UG
1940	D	59	UG
1942	D	57	UG
1944	D	58	UG
1946	D	54	DG
1948	D	58	UG
1950	D	57	UG
1952	R	47	UG
1954	R	42	DG
1956	R	44	DG
1958	R	38	DG
1960	D	59	UG
1962	D	55	UG
1964	D	59	UG
1966	D	52	UG
1968	R	48	DG
1970	R	44	DG
1972	R	48	DG
1974	R	42	DG
1976	D	57	UG
1978	D	54	UG
1980	R	48	DG-H
1982	R	47	DG-H
1984	R	48	DG-H
1986	R	45	DG
1988	R	46	DG
1990	R	44	DG
1992	D	51	UG
1994	D	49	DG

Source: Compiled by the author.

Note: DR—Democratic-Republican; W—Whig; D—Democrat; R—Republican; DG—divided government; DG-H—divided government in the House; DG-S—divided government in the Senate; UG—unified government: a majority of congressional seats held by the president's party.

[a] The tally is the percentage of the two-party House vote representing the president's party.

Figure 3-1 Voter Turnout in Presidential and Congressional Elections, 1796–1994 (percent of eligible voting age population)

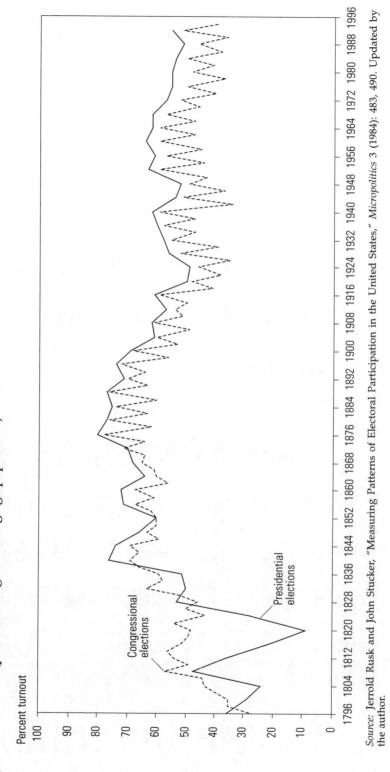

Source: Jerrold Rusk and John Stucker, "Measuring Patterns of Electoral Participation in the United States," *Micropolitics* 3 (1984): 483, 490. Updated by the author.

Table 3-17 State Voter Turnout in Presidential Elections, 1824–1876 (percent)

State	1824	1828	1832	1836	1840	1844	1848	1852	1856	1860	1864	1868	1872	1876
Alabama	49.1	54.6	31.5	64.9	89.7	80.3	69.7	45.3	71.0	78.7	a	77.9	79.6	72.8
Arkansas	—	—	—	28.9	67.6	63.5	55.9	48.6	60.2	79.5	a	49.0	67.6	64.7
California	—	—	—	—	—	—	—	75.7	81.6	71.2	64.6	72.3	57.9	75.9
Colorado	—	—	—	—	—	—	—	—	—	—	—	—	—	b
Connecticut	14.9	27.2	46.0	52.3	75.7	80.0	72.3	72.3	81.8	73.3	76.3	80.1	71.3	82.0
Delaware	—	—	67.1	69.5	82.8	85.8	80.4	75.0	78.5	79.5	79.8	84.3	73.3	73.4
Florida	—	—	—	—	—	—	64.0	56.9	77.6	79.5	a	b	77.0	93.5
Georgia	—	31.8	29.0	61.8	88.8	92.6	86.0	54.8	82.8	85.1	a	73.2	55.2	63.5
Illinois	24.3	52.4	46.0	43.5	86.0	76.0	70.5	64.7	72.4	80.5	69.2	76.7	75.0	87.5
Indiana	37.1	68.7	71.9	69.2	84.4	84.7	78.5	80.3	88.3	89.4	82.9	92.5	85.3	94.6
Iowa	—	—	—	—	—	—	90.7	80.2	87.0	94.2	95.4	97.7	79.0	99.1
Kansas	—	—	—	—	—	—	—	—	—	—	31.8	51.3	77.8	65.7
Kentucky	25.4	70.7	74.0	61.1	74.3	80.7	73.9	64.2	76.7	74.1	44.0	69.9	66.2	80.9
Louisiana	19.1	36.2	22.3	19.2	39.4	47.1	51.1	48.7	53.6	58.6	a	75.9	76.4	77.9
Maine	53.7	42.7	66.2	37.7	83.7	71.3	68.4	61.2	78.1	68.9	73.2	74.4	57.9	71.5
Maryland	29.0	70.3	55.7	67.6	84.5	81.4	76.0	72.8	80.0	81.1	57.7	72.6	75.0	82.7
Massachusetts	29.0	25.7	39.4	43.4	66.7	65.8	64.6	57.8	69.8	65.8	63.8	66.9	62.0	72.3
Michigan	—	—	—	35.0	84.9	79.8	74.5	71.3	81.1	80.0	66.2	77.4	64.0	78.0
Minnesota	—	—	—	—	—	—	—	—	—	74.9	57.5	71.1	67.5	71.3
Mississippi	41.3	56.6	28.0	64.4	88.2	86.1	80.7	61.7	78.3	89.5	a	c	71.1	79.7
Missouri	19.8	54.0	41.0	36.1	75.1	77.8	62.5	46.3	54.7	69.1	36.3	43.0	66.6	76.6
Nebraska	—	—	—	—	—	—	—	—	—	—	—	46.1	43.7	53.0
Nevada	—	—	—	—	—	—	—	—	—	—	57.5	73.7	74.4	90.0
New Hampshire	18.0	74.3	70.1	38.2	86.3	68.9	67.4	65.7	87.9	80.7	84.3	82.3	80.9	92.0
New Jersey	35.6	71.0	68.8	69.2	80.4	87.2	82.7	79.8	83.1	89.4	81.0	89.5	81.4	94.8
New York	—	80.2	84.2	70.5	91.9	92.1	79.6	84.7	89.9	95.5	89.3	91.7	80.5	89.6
North Carolina	41.8	56.9	31.3	53.0	82.4	78.8	71.4	65.8	66.7	70.9	a	91.2	71.9	90.1
Ohio	34.8	75.9	73.9	75.5	84.5	83.6	77.5	80.6	82.3	88.3	87.6	90.4	84.4	94.4

State														
Oregon	—	—	—	—	—	—	—	—	—	97.8	91.8	85.8	60.5	70.4
Pennsylvania	18.8	56.5	52.3	53.1	77.5	77.3	76.3	72.6	80.8	78.4	85.0	88.3	68.6	83.5
Rhode Island	12.0	17.1	26.3	23.8	33.2	45.1	41.1	57.8	62.9	59.4	58.8	46.6	40.2	49.4
South Carolina	—	—	—	—	d	d	d	d	d	d	a	79.6	60.4	e
Tennessee	28.3	55.0	31.3	57.3	89.7	89.8	83.4	72.9	82.9	80.9	a	39.7	66.2	74.6
Texas	—	—	—	—	—	—	69.6	42.6	58.1	67.4	a	c	56.3	54.6
Vermont	—	54.5	50.0	52.5	73.8	70.8	70.5	63.5	72.5	63.0	77.0	75.9	69.1	83.3
Virginia	11.6	27.7	31.1	35.2	54.7	54.2	47.3	63.3	67.8	71.5	a	c	66.2	77.6
West Virginia	—	—	—	—	—	—	—	—	—	—	51.6	58.0	61.2	83.6
Wisconsin	—	—	—	—	—	—	58.3	59.6	80.8	79.0	66.8	79.8	70.6	83.9
United States	26.9	57.6	55.4	57.8	80.2	78.9	72.7	69.6	78.9	81.2	73.8	78.1	71.3	81.8

Source: Adapted from U.S. Department of Commerce, *U.S. Historical Statistics: Colonial Times to 1970*, 2 vols. (Washington, D.C.: Government Printing Office, 1971), Y 27–78.

Note: "—" indicates state was not yet admitted to the Union.

a Confederate states did not participate in the 1864 election.
b Florida (in 1868) and Colorado (in 1876) cast three Republican electoral votes through its legislature rather than by popular vote.
c Mississippi, Texas, and Virginia did not participate in the 1868 election.
d South Carolina chose its electors through its legislature until 1868.
e Information not available.

Table 3-18 State Voter Turnout in Presidential Elections, 1880–1932 (percent)

State	1880	1884	1888	1892	1896	1900	1904	1908	1912	1916	1920	1924	1928	1932
Alabama	58.8	54.2	56.6	68.5	51.9	38.9	24.2	21.5	22.6	24.3	20.6	13.5	19.1	17.5
Arizona	—	—	—	—	—	—	—	—	38.6	48.7	46.8	44.4	47.9	55.1
Arkansas	59.5	59.1	68.9	55.0	48.2	40.8	33.8	40.2	30.7	40.0	20.9	15.3	21.4	22.1
California	67.1	68.8	76.5	73.8	75.0	69.9	61.7	60.2	46.9	58.0	47.2	50.8	59.0	64.0
Colorado	57.4	52.4	57.4	54.6	65.2	71.2	71.0	65.4	59.1	60.5	56.0	62.5	68.4	75.3
Connecticut	81.4	79.9	85.5	85.4	83.3	79.7	80.5	76.3	71.5	73.8	58.7	57.9	72.6	70.8
Delaware	81.9	76.0	68.8	80.4	64.6	81.9	82.0	86.2	84.1	86.1	75.1	68.1	75.3	76.3
Florida	85.9	83.1	85.0	35.3	40.0	29.9	24.4	26.2	24.2	33.8	30.3	17.0	33.0	30.5
Georgia	49.4	41.0	37.6	53.1	34.3	24.4	23.8	22.0	18.9	23.7	10.5	11.5	15.7	16.5
Idaho	—	—	—	63.1	76.1	77.8	65.3	65.8	59.8	67.4	61.1	65.2	66.0	74.4
Illinois	89.9	84.4	82.9	86.0	95.7	89.9	80.5	81.6	74.7	66.8	60.5	64.1	73.4	74.6
Indiana	94.4	92.2	93.3	89.0	95.1	92.1	89.7	89.9	77.8	81.9	71.0	70.7	74.9	78.9
Iowa	93.7	90.0	87.9	88.5	96.1	91.0	79.7	77.6	74.2	75.0	64.5	68.4	68.9	69.1
Kansas	80.8	85.1	88.2	80.7	85.5	91.2	78.1	82.5	76.3	65.8	58.0	64.1	65.9	71.1
Kentucky	75.5	70.8	81.1	73.8	89.2	87.0	77.7	84.0	74.6	82.8	71.8	61.0	67.7	67.4
Louisiana	50.3	49.8	50.0	45.1	35.8	21.7	15.6	19.8	19.3	21.6	14.1	12.4	20.1	23.4
Maine	85.0	75.0	71.7	63.5	63.0	56.0	49.5	53.2	63.4	65.1	46.9	44.9	60.2	66.3
Maryland	79.8	79.9	84.8	79.9	87.3	85.9	69.6	70.9	64.8	68.1	52.3	41.0	56.8	51.2
Massachusetts	71.2	69.3	71.7	74.6	70.6	67.4	67.6	65.1	63.4	62.8	53.3	56.6	74.0	69.5
Michigan	75.5	76.0	80.9	73.2	95.3	89.0	78.9	75.9	69.8	72.9	55.1	53.7	56.3	62.0
Minnesota	68.9	68.2	76.3	66.6	75.2	76.7	64.3	66.1	61.2	65.0	59.5	62.0	68.5	66.2
Mississippi	50.1	49.2	43.8	18.8	22.1	16.9	15.6	16.5	15.1	20.0	9.4	12.0	15.2	13.8
Missouri	78.0	77.0	81.8	77.4	88.5	83.1	74.9	79.7	74.9	81.5	67.6	63.3	69.1	70.9
Montana	—	—	—	74.2	73.8	75.3	65.8	61.9	63.3	68.0	61.4	59.2	65.3	70.3
Nebraska	67.7	67.8	75.9	66.2	74.1	80.2	70.1	77.8	77.1	84.5	55.7	63.8	71.5	72.1
Nevada	76.5	61.6	71.4	70.1	69.2	71.4	59.2	92.1	68.1	73.6	61.0	56.1	63.0	73.2
New Hampshire	93.3	87.4	90.2	85.8	78.1	83.9	81.6	80.8	78.2	77.3	67.5	67.4	77.8	77.5
New Jersey	95.4	88.6	91.9	90.3	88.4	85.9	83.6	82.4	69.1	70.7	59.1	60.7	75.6	72.0

New Mexico	—	—	—	—	—	—	—	—	59.6	77.8	62.3	61.8	60.3	69.7
New York	89.3	87.5	92.3	86.3	84.3	84.6	83.3	79.7	72.1	71.6	56.4	56.3	68.3	66.1
North Carolina	83.0	86.3	85.2	78.0	85.3	70.2	46.1	52.0	46.1	49.8	44.6	35.9	43.1	44.0
North Dakota	—	—	—	56.6	63.1	65.2	61.4	73.2	60.8	77.7	67.4	63.8	72.4	74.5
Ohio	94.4	93.4	91.9	86.2	95.5	91.5	83.1	87.5	74.8	76.5	62.6	57.8	66.9	65.5
Oklahoma	—	—	—	—	—	—	—	71.5	57.4	60.4	48.6	47.4	50.5	54.4
Oregon	79.1	63.0	53.5	58.4	69.9	58.3	47.6	47.3	51.8	54.2	52.3	55.3	57.7	60.7
Pennsylvania	88.8	82.3	83.0	75.7	81.8	75.0	74.3	71.8	64.4	63.4	42.8	45.8	62.7	53.1
Rhode Island	48.7	48.1	53.4	63.0	59.2	56.2	63.4	62.4	62.7	65.8	57.9	66.3	68.9	71.7
South Carolina	83.9	43.0	35.0	29.1	25.2	18.0	18.4	20.6	14.6	17.5	8.6	6.4	8.5	12.3
South Dakota	—	—	—	70.7	78.0	85.4	73.0	69.5	61.9	60.9	56.6	59.4	72.0	76.5
Tennessee	75.1	73.1	77.6	64.0	70.8	56.6	47.7	48.1	45.1	46.6	35.4	23.3	25.7	26.5
Texas	68.8	80.2	78.3	79.4	88.3	61.4	29.6	33.6	30.8	35.0	21.7	25.8	24.8	27.2
Utah	—	—	—	—	79.4	84.5	78.4	73.0	66.4	79.5	69.6	69.7	73.4	80.0
Vermont	81.6	70.5	71.4	60.4	67.5	57.9	50.7	48.9	56.8	58.2	45.3	51.3	66.8	66.6
Virginia	64.1	81.7	83.2	75.3	71.0	59.6	27.7	27.4	25.7	27.1	19.4	18.1	24.0	22.1
Washington	—	—	—	67.3	63.1	64.9	60.9	59.0	50.8	54.7	52.4	51.2	56.6	64.2
West Virginia	82.6	86.7	94.5	90.3	93.6	91.3	89.2	86.9	81.9	83.6	71.7	75.2	76.4	81.9
Wisconsin	82.4	82.2	81.1	76.8	84.9	77.5	72.0	68.7	68.7	70.2	52.3	57.3	65.9	65.1
Wyoming	—	—	—	47.7	50.7	51.1	50.8	49.2	50.3	54.9	52.3	71.0	68.7	74.9
United States	79.4	77.5	79.3	74.7	79.3	73.2	65.2	65.4	58.8	61.6	49.2	48.9	56.9	56.9

Source: Adapted from U.S. Department of Commerce, *U.S. Historical Statistics: Colonial Times to 1970*, 2 vols. (Washington, D.C.: Government Printing Office, 1971) Y 27–78.

Note: "—" indicates state was not yet admitted to the Union.

Table 3-19 State Voter Turnout in Presidential Elections, 1936–1984 (percent)

State	1936	1940	1944	1948	1952	1956	1960	1964	1968	1972	1976	1980	1984
Alabama	18.8	18.9	15.0	12.6	24.2	27.6	31.2	36.1	52.8	43.3	46.3	48.7	50.2
Alaska	—	—	—	—	—	—	59.2	48.0	53.0	46.9	48.1	57.2	60.3
Arizona	52.0	57.0	42.2	45.4	53.9	47.8	53.8	56.8	50.6	47.4	46.1	44.5	46.6
Arkansas	17.3	18.2	19.3	21.9	36.9	38.0	41.1	51.2	54.1	48.1	51.1	51.5	52.2
California	66.0	73.4	65.1	63.2	69.4	64.0	67.9	66.1	62.0	59.5	50.4	49.0	49.9
Colorado	75.5	79.7	67.9	64.5	76.2	69.2	71.7	67.6	64.0	59.5	58.8	55.8	54.8
Connecticut	74.6	77.2	73.9	71.2	80.9	75.8	77.1	71.3	68.8	66.2	62.8	61.0	61.0
Delaware	79.8	79.4	66.9	68.5	78.4	72.7	74.5	69.5	68.7	62.1	57.2	54.8	55.8
District of Columbia	—	—	—	—	—	—	—	39.4	34.7	30.4	32.2	35.4	43.8
Florida	31.3	40.9	33.5	34.1	47.6	43.6	50.0	51.9	53.8	48.6	49.2	48.7	49.0
Georgia	17.7	17.7	17.6	21.4	31.9	31.3	32.9	45.3	44.7	37.3	42.0	41.2	42.2
Hawaii	—	—	—	—	—	—	58.9	52.4	53.3	49.4	46.7	43.5	44.5
Idaho	71.8	77.0	64.5	63.1	78.2	75.2	80.6	75.2	71.9	63.3	60.7	67.8	60.4
Illinois	81.6	82.2	74.8	70.3	76.0	72.4	76.5	72.6	69.3	62.3	59.4	57.7	57.3
Indiana	78.7	81.1	71.7	67.2	75.7	73.7	76.9	71.7	69.5	60.8	60.1	57.6	56.3
Iowa	73.5	75.5	64.3	62.4	75.8	74.0	76.8	70.0	67.9	64.0	63.1	62.9	62.3
Kansas	76.6	75.1	62.2	65.0	71.7	67.4	71.8	63.6	63.4	59.5	58.8	56.7	57.0
Kentucky	56.9	59.5	51.9	47.9	57.0	60.5	60.5	54.8	51.3	48.0	48.0	49.9	50.7
Louisiana	27.3	29.4	25.1	27.5	40.2	36.0	45.1	47.1	54.9	44.0	48.7	53.1	54.2
Maine	64.4	65.0	57.3	49.0	63.1	61.8	74.0	65.0	66.4	60.3	63.7	64.6	65.2
Maryland	58.1	57.2	46.7	41.7	57.5	54.6	58.3	54.7	55.2	49.8	49.3	50.0	51.4
Massachusetts	75.9	78.7	71.0	71.5	75.0	72.0	76.9	68.4	66.4	62.0	61.7	59.0	57.9
Michigan	62.1	66.6	63.7	55.6	68.5	71.1	72.7	66.2	64.9	59.4	48.8	59.9	58.2
Minnesota	69.7	72.3	63.0	65.7	72.6	68.7	77.1	73.7	71.7	68.6	71.5	70.0	68.5
Mississippi	14.4	14.7	15.0	16.0	23.8	21.0	25.7	34.1	53.3	44.2	48.0	51.9	52.0
Missouri	77.3	74.4	62.2	61.0	71.8	68.8	72.6	65.2	64.9	57.3	57.3	58.7	57.7
Montana	70.8	72.2	59.0	62.3	71.8	71.6	71.7	70.6	68.4	67.6	63.3	65.0	65.0
Nebraska	75.6	75.4	67.9	58.2	71.9	67.6	72.1	66.6	60.0	56.4	56.2	56.7	56.1

Nevada	69.1	75.7	64.8	64.0	69.7	65.9	61.0	60.0	55.9	49.5	44.2	41.2	41.7
New Hampshire	77.8	79.6	73.5	70.3	79.2	74.4	80.2	71.4	68.5	63.6	57.3	57.2	53.9
New Jersey	75.0	76.1	69.1	63.0	72.3	68.9	71.8	69.2	65.8	59.8	57.7	54.9	56.9
New Mexico	68.7	66.6	48.8	53.4	60.5	56.8	64.5	62.8	60.0	57.7	53.4	50.8	51.6
New York	72.6	75.7	70.9	65.0	71.2	67.9	66.9	64.4	59.7	56.3	50.7	48.0	51.1
North Carolina	47.4	42.7	38.0	35.4	51.3	47.4	54.1	51.9	54.1	42.8	43.0	43.4	47.7
North Dakota	78.0	78.4	61.5	61.6	75.5	71.3	79.1	72.9	70.0	68.3	67.2	64.8	62.9
Ohio	71.8	75.4	66.9	58.4	69.7	66.4	71.3	65.3	62.7	57.3	55.1	55.4	58.0
Oklahoma	56.4	60.5	52.8	52.5	68.6	61.4	64.3	62.4	60.0	56.7	54.9	52.2	51.2
Oregon	62.5	67.1	58.4	56.5	69.6	71.1	72.4	67.2	64.6	62.1	61.3	61.3	62.6
Pennsylvania	72.5	67.6	59.8	56.0	66.5	65.5	70.7	66.6	64.3	56.0	54.2	51.9	53.9
Rhode Island	78.0	75.6	65.0	66.0	79.8	73.2	77.3	69.3	65.6	61.0	59.7	58.7	55.9
South Carolina	12.5	10.1	9.8	12.8	29.1	24.7	31.4	38.7	46.0	38.2	40.3	40.4	40.6
South Dakota	77.5	79.5	59.3	63.3	74.4	74.7	78.8	75.4	72.8	69.4	64.1	67.4	63.9
Tennessee	30.0	30.6	28.2	28.7	44.7	45.9	50.4	51.5	53.2	43.5	48.7	48.7	49.3
Texas	24.8	30.1	28.2	26.0	43.5	37.9	42.4	44.1	48.2	45.0	46.3	44.9	47.0
Utah	77.9	83.1	75.0	76.0	82.9	77.2	78.9	78.0	75.2	69.4	68.4	64.4	60.6
Vermont	68.5	66.8	56.9	54.5	66.8	66.5	72.9	67.0	62.9	60.7	55.7	57.6	60.1
Virginia	23.0	22.1	22.3	21.6	29.9	31.8	34.4	41.6	50.5	44.7	47.0	47.6	51.1
Washington	66.5	70.6	67.0	63.2	71.2	70.4	74.1	67.2	64.3	63.1	59.8	57.4	58.8
West Virginia	84.9	83.0	65.5	65.8	76.3	74.6	77.9	73.0	69.3	62.5	57.2	52.8	51.4
Wisconsin	68.9	72.4	65.7	59.8	72.5	67.8	73.5	68.6	65.6	62.5	66.5	67.3	63.4
Wyoming	74.0	74.8	63.3	59.6	72.5	67.4	73.9	74.1	65.3	64.4	58.6	53.3	51.8
United States	61.0	62.5	55.9	53.0	63.3	60.6	64.0	61.7	60.6	55.2	53.5	52.6	53.3

Source: Adapted from U.S. Department of Commerce, U.S. *Historical Statistics: Colonial Times to 1970,* 2 vols. (Washington, D.C.: Government Printing Office, 1971) Y 27–78; and U.S. Department of Commerce, *Statistical Abstract of the United States 1993* (Washington, D.C.: Government Printing Office, 1993), 285.

Note: "—" indicates state not yet admitted to the Union, or, for the District of Columbia, not yet able to vote for president.

Table 3-20   State Voter Turnout in Presidential Elections, 1988 and 1992 (percent)

State	1988	1992
Alabama	46.0	55.2
Alaska	55.7	65.4
Arizona	46.1	54.1
Arkansas	47.3	53.8
California	47.1	49.1
Colorado	56.2	62.7
Connecticut	58.3	63.8
Delaware	50.2	55.2
District of Columbia	40.9	49.6
Florida	44.7	50.2
Georgia	39.4	46.9
Hawaii	43.5	41.9
Idaho	58.2	65.2
Illinois	52.8	58.9
Indiana	52.8	55.2
Iowa	57.7	65.3
Kansas	53.7	63.0
Kentucky	48.1	53.7
Louisiana	52.3	59.8
Maine	61.1	72.0
Maryland	49.0	53.4
Massachusetts	57.7	60.2
Michigan	53.9	61.7
Minnesota	65.5	71.6
Mississippi	50.5	52.8
Missouri	54.5	62.0
Montana	62.4	70.1
Nebraska	55.9	63.2
Nevada	43.5	50.0
New Hampshire	55.2	63.1
New Jersey	52.6	56.3
New Mexico	48.9	51.6
New York	47.8	50.9
North Carolina	43.7	50.1
North Dakota	61.4	67.3
Ohio	54.5	60.6
Oklahoma	49.5	59.7
Oregon	57.3	65.7
Pennsylvania	49.5	54.3
Rhode Island	52.9	58.4
South Carolina	39.0	45.0
South Dakota	60.4	67.0
Tennessee	44.7	52.4
Texas	45.5	49.1
Utah	60.6	65.1
Vermont	57.9	67.5
Virginia	48.0	52.8
Washington	53.4	59.9
West Virginia	46.7	50.6
Wisconsin	61.0	69.0
Wyoming	52.1	62.3
United States	50.1	55.2

Source: Adapted from U.S. Department of Commerce, *Statistical Abstract of the United States 1993* (Washington, D.C.: Government Printing Office, 1993), 285.

Table 3-21   Personal Characteristics of Major-Party Candidates, 1980–1992

| | 1980 | | 1984 | | 1988 | | 1992 | |
Characteristic	Jimmy Carter (D)	Ronald Reagan (R)	Walter Mondale (D)	Ronald Reagan (R)	Michael Dukakis (D)	George Bush (R)	Bill Clinton (D)	George Bush (R)
Intelligent	—	—	79.5	80.9	82.1	75.3	82.2	80.7
Compassionate	—	—	68.9	57.2	65.0	55.5	71.5	58.0
Decent	—	—	83.1	81.1	79.2	82.1	46.0	57.9
Inspiring	35.1	45.8	29.3	56.9	44.7	36.6	55.4	39.1
Knowledgeable	73.2	67.1	74.8	74.4	75.9	79.2	78.1	81.2
Moral	78.2	65.9	74.2	77.3	69.1	69.9	43.9	77.4
Strong leadership	35.1	55.0	43.0	69.1	51.0	50.0	54.9	55.3
Cares about people	—	—	56.0	45.1	56.9	45.1	60.3	34.8

Source: Calculated by the author from the 1952–1990 Cumulative File for the American National Election Studies and the 1992 Pre-Post National Election Study.

Note: Entries are the percentage of respondents indicating that the characteristic fits the candidate "well" or "extremely well." — indicates question not asked.

Table 3-22 Emotional Responses to Major-Party Presidential Candidates, 1980–1992

	1980		1984		1988		1992	
Emotion	Jimmy Carter (D)	Ronald Reagan (R)	Walter Mondale (D)	Ronald Reagan (R)	Michael Dukakis (D)	George Bush (R)	Bill Clinton (D)	George Bush (R)
Anger	63.4	23.7	29.8	47.7	28.6	24.7	25.3	51.2
Fear	23.4	28.0	17.3	24.1	20.7	14.7	23.5	40.0
Hope	60.1	48.0	41.0	60.3	41.3	39.0	50.8	48.0
Pride	49.3	31.3	30.3	55.4	28.3	33.0	23.7	56.3

Source: Calculated by the author from the 1952–1990 Cumulative File for the American National Election Studies and the 1992 Pre-Post National Election Study.

Note: Entries are the percentage of respondents indicating that they have felt that emotion toward a candidate.

Figure 3-2   Images of the Democratic and Republican Presidential
Candidates, 1952–1992

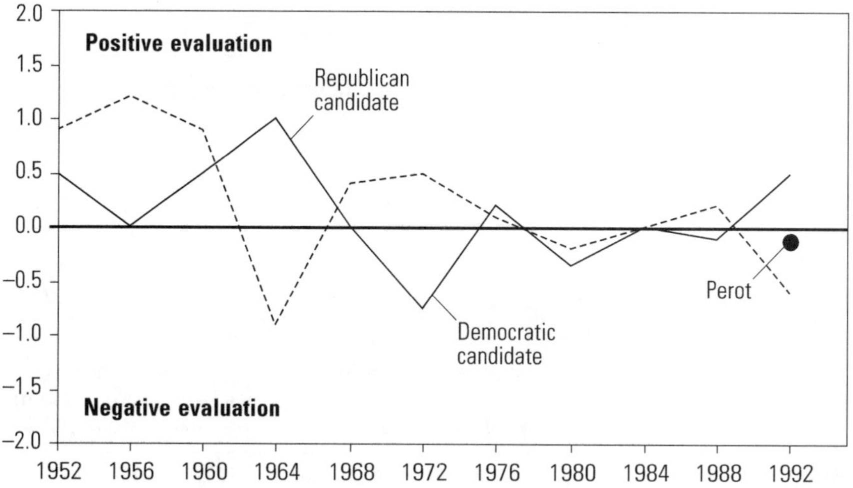

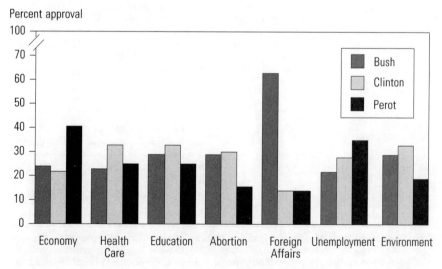

Source: William Flanigan and Nancy Zingale, *Political Behavior of the American Electorate,*
8th ed. (Washington, D.C.: CQ Press, 1993), 172.

Figure 3-3   Voter Perception of Candidates' Handling of Issues, 1992

Percent approval

Source: Adapted from *The Gallup Poll, Public Opinion 1992* (Wilmington, Del.: Scholarly
Resources, 1993), 120–121.

Note: Bars show percentage of respondents believing that that candidate would best
handle the issue. Results are from a survey conducted July 6–July 8, 1992.

Table 3-23 Issues and Voters' Presidential Preferences, 1992

Preferred candidate	*Issue*						
	Decrease government services	(7–point scale on government services)				Increase government services
Bush	59%	61%	49%	28%	22%	15%	19%
Clinton	23	17	27	53	65	63	68
Perot	18	22	24	20	13	22	13
Respondents (*N*)	86	155	240	468	263	125	110
	Decrease government aid to blacks	(7–point scale on government aid to blacks)				Increase government aid to blacks
Bush	42%	46%	46%	30%	22%	11%	10%
Clinton	38	30	38	51	61	72	83
Perot	20	24	16	19	17	17	7
Respondents (*N*)	299	224	229	426	180	82	83
	Decrease defense spending	(7–point scale on defense spending)				Increase defense spending
Bush	10%	13%	33%	45%	44%	41%	36%
Clinton	75	62	49	36	39	36	51
Perot	16	25	18	19	17	23	13
Respondents (*N*)	126	236	364	507	172	55	39

	Pro-life	(4–point scale on abortion)		Pro-choice
Bush	47%	46%	42%	22%
Clinton	40	38	39	58
Perot	12	16	19	20
Respondents (*N*)	139	435	236	801

Source: Adapted from William Flanigan and Nancy Zingale, *Political Behavior of the American Electorate*, 8th ed. (Washington, D.C.: CQ Press, 1993), 182–184. Results presented are from the 1992 American National Election Study conducted by the Center for Political Studies at the University of Michigan.

Table 3-24 Content of Television News Coverage of General Election, 1988 and 1992

Time period	News Content			Total number of news stories
	Candidate character	Policy issues	Horse race[a]	
Pre-Democratic Convention				
June 8–July 21, 1988	55%	33%	11%	248
June 3–July 10, 1992	34	49	17	247
Convention (Overall)				
July 22–August 18, 1988	43	38	18	200
July 11–August 23, 1992	36	45	19	505
Convention (Democrats),				
July 11–July 19, 1992	48	30	22	185
Pre-Republican Convention,				
July 20–August 14, 1992	32	57	11	182
Convention (Republican),				
August 15–August 23, 1992	25	50	25	138
Labor Day, August 24–				
Sept. 6, 1992	31	53	16	77
Pre-Debates, October 1–				
October 10, 1992[b]	35	35	30	365
Debates				
August 19–October 13, 1988	49	38	14	480
October 11–October 19, 1992	25	23	52	124
Post-Debates				
October 14–November 7, 1988	35	33	33	309
October 20–November 2, 1992	28	28	44	239
General Election Total				
1988	46	36	19	1,237
1992	33	28	27	1,558
Primary total				
1988	29	20	50	1,064
1992	33	36	31	1,039
Primary/General total				
1988	38	29	33	2,301
1992	33	38	29	2,597

Sources: (1988 data) Adapted from Harold Stanley and Richard Niemi, *Vital Statistics on American Politics*, 3d ed. (Washington, D.C.: CQ Press, 1988), 63; (1992 data) adapted from Stanley and Niemi, *Vital Statistics on American Politics*, 4th ed. (Washington, D.C.: CQ Press, 1994), 63.

Note: Data are derived from content analysis of the ABC, CBS, and NBC evening news broadcasts conducted by the Center for Media and Public Affairs.

[a] News stories in which focus was on who was leading—or trailing—in the polls.

Table 3-25 Positive Television News Coverage of Presidential and Vice-Presidential Candidates During the General Election 1988 and 1992

	Election year				
	1988		1992		
Time period	Bush/Quayle (R)	Dukakis/Bentsen (D)	Bush/Quayle (R)	Clinton/Gore (D)	Perot/Stockdale (I)
Pre-Democratic convention (June 8–July 21, 1988; June 3–July 10, 1992)	63%/NA	43%/82%	32%/22%	50%/100%	42%/NA
Democratic convention (July 16–July 31, 1988; July 11–July 19, 1992)	39/NA	64/73	46/29	67/79	33/NA
Pre-Republican convention (August 1–August 12, 1988; July 20–August 14, 1992)	37/NA	24/100	34/35	32/50	60/NA
Republican convention (August 13–August 28, 1988; August 15–August 23, 1992)	79/70	29/88	47/75	31/50	75/NA
Labor Day (August 24–September 6, 1992)	NA/NA	NA/NA	33/25	36/55	NA/NA
Pre-Debates (October 1–October 10, 1992)	NA/NA	NA/NA	32/42	35/70	41/NA
Debates (August 19–October 13, 1988; October 11–October 19, 1992)	26/42	30/53	34/50	47/45	62/53
Post-Debates (October 14–November 7, 1988; October 20–November 2, 1992)	36/25	38/96	34/NA	36/NA	49/NA

Source: (1988 data) Adapted from Harold Stanley and Richard Niemi, *Vital Statistics on American Politics,* 3d ed. (Washington, D.C.: CQ Press, 1988), 71; (1992 data) adapted from Stanley and Niemi, *Vital Statistics on American Politics,* 4th ed. (Washington, D.C.: CQ Press, 1992), 71.

Note: Entries are the percentage of positive television news stories calculated from the total of all clearly positive and negative stories aired on ABC, CBS, and NBC evening news broadcasts. Data are derived from content analysis of the network news broadcasts conducted by the Center for Media and Public Affairs. NA—not available; R—Republican; D—Democrat; I—Independent.

Table 3-26   Election Year Presidential Preferences, 1948–1992 (percent)

Year/candidate	First poll of year	First poll after conventions	Early October	Final survey	Election results
1948					
Truman (D)[a]	46 (+5)	37	40	45	50 (+5)
Dewey (R)	41	48 (+11)	46 (+6)	50 (+5)	45
1952					
Eisenhower (R)	59 (+28)	50 (+7)	53 (+12)	51 (+2)	55 (+11)
Stevenson (D)	31	43	41	49	44
1956					
Eisenhower (R)[a]	61 (+26)	52 (+11)	51 (+10)	60 (+19)	57 (+15)
Stevenson (D)	35	41	41	41	42
1960					
Kennedy (D)	43	44	49 (+3)	51 (+2)	50 (+0.2)
Nixon (R)	48 (+5)	50 (+6)	46	49	50
1964					
Johnson (D)[a]	75 (+57)	65 (+36)	64 (+35)	64 (+28)	61 (+23)
Goldwater (R)	18	29	29	36	38
1968					
Nixon (R)	43 (+9)	43 (+12)	43 (+12)	43 (+1)	43 (+.7)
Humphrey (D)	34	31	31	42	43
Wallace (AIP)	9	19	20	15	14
1972					
Nixon (R)[a]	53 (+19)	64 (+34)	60 (+26)	62 (+24)	61 (+23)
McGovern (D)	34	30	34	38	38
1976					
Carter (D)	47 (+5)	51 (+15)	47 (+2)	48	50 (+2)
Ford (R)[a]	42	36	45	49 (+1)	48
1980					
Reagan (R)	33	38	40	47 (+3)	51 (+10)
Carter (D)[a]	62 (+29)	39 (+1)	44 (+4)	44	41
Anderson (I)		13	9	8	7
1984					
Reagan (R)[a]	48 (+1)	55 (+15)	56 (+17)	59 (+18)	59 (+18)
Mondale (D)	47	40	39	41	41
1988					
Bush (R)	52 (+12)	48 (+4)	49 (+6)	53 (+11)	54 (+8)
Dukakis (D)	40	44	43	42	46
1992					
Bush (R)[a]	53 (+15)	42	35	37	37
Clinton (D)	38	52 (+10)	52 (+17)	49 (+12)	43 (+6)
Perot	—	—	7	14	19

Source: Harold Stanley and Richard Niemi, *Vital Statistics on American Politics*, 4th ed. (Washington, D.C.: CQ Press, 1994), 104.

Note: "—" indicates not included in survey question. D—Democrat; R—Republican; AIP—American Independent Party; I—Independent.

[a] Incumbent.

Figure 3-4 Results of Presidential Candidate Support Polls, March–October 1992

Percent support

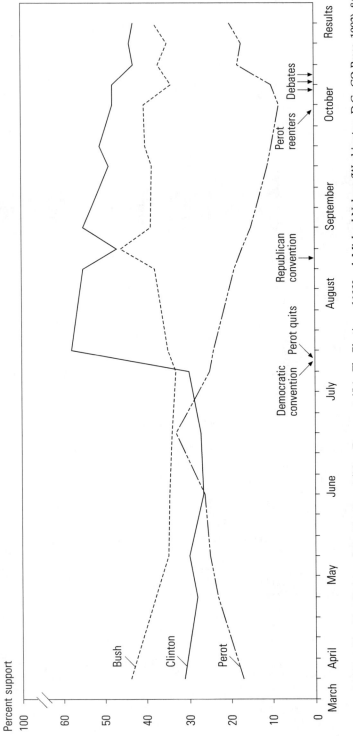

Source: Paul Quirk and Jon Dalager, "The Election: A 'New Democrat,'" in *The Elections of 1992,* ed. Michael Nelson (Washington, D.C.: CQ Press, 1993), 84.

Note: Data cited are from CBS News/*New York Times* polls.

Table 3-27   Financing Presidential General Elections, 1860–1992
(current dollars)

Year	Republicans	Democrats
1860	100,000	50,000
1864	125,000	50,000
1868	150,000	75,000
1872	250,000	50,000
1876	950,000	900,000
1880	1,100,000	355,000
1884	1,300,000	1,400,000
1888	1,350,000	855,000
1892	1,700,000	2,350,000
1896	3,350,000	675,000
1900	3,000,000	425,000
1904	2,096,000	700,000
1908	1,665,518	629,341
1912[a]	1,071,549	1,134,848
1916	2,441,565	2,284,590
1920	5,417,501	1,470,371
1924[b]	4,020,478	1,108,836
1928	6,256,111	5,342,350
1932	2,900,052	2,245,975
1936	8,892,972	5,194,741
1940	3,451,310	2,783,654
1944	2,828,652	2,169,077
1948[c]	2,127,296	2,736,334
1952	6,608,623	5,032,926
1956	7,778,702	5,106,651
1960	10,128,000	9,797,000
1964	16,026,000	8,757,000
1968[d]	25,402,000	11,594,000
1972	37,624,278	13,041,661
1976	21,820,000	21,820,000
1980	29,400,000	29,400,000
1984	40,400,000	40,400,000
1988	46,100,000	46,100,000
1992	55,200,000	55,200,000

Source: Adapted and updated from U.S. Department of Commerce, *U.S. Historical Statistics: Colonial Times to 1970,* 2 vols. (Washington, D.C.: Government Printing Office, 1971), Y 187–188; *Congressional Quarterly Weekly Report,* July 31, 1976, 2036; August 4, 1984, 1924; and U.S. Federal Election Commission press release, February 5, 1988 and February 12, 1992.

Note: Beginning in 1976, the major parties' presidential election campaigns were financed by the federal government. The parties' expenditures were also limited.

[a] Progressive party, with T. Roosevelt as candidate, spent $665,420.
[b] Progressive party, with R. M. LaFollette as candidate, spent $236,963.
[c] Progressive party, with Henry Wallace as candidate, spent $1,133,863; States' Rights, with Strom Thurmond as candidate, spent $163,442.
[d] American Independent party, with George Wallace as candidate, spent $7,223,000.

Table 3-28   Spending Limits in Presidential Elections, 1976–1992 (in millions of dollars)

Year	Candidate primary election[a]	Candidate general election[b]	Party convention[c]	Party general election[d]
1976	10.9	21.8	2.2	3.2
1980	14.7	29.4	4.4	4.6
1984	20.2	40.4	8.1	6.9
1988	27.7	46.1	9.2	8.3
1992	33.1	55.2	10.6	10.3

Sources: (1976–1984 data) U.S. Federal Election Commission, *Annual Report,* 1984 and 1985; (1988 data) Federal Election Commission press release, February 5, 1988, and Federal Election Commission, *Annual Report,* 1988; (1992 data) Federal Election Commission press release, January 30, 1992, and February 12, 1992.

[a] Refers to the amount of money candidates may spend during the primary season if they accept matching federal campaign funds.
[b] Refers to the amount of money candidates may spend during the general election season if they accept matching federal campaign funds.
[c] Refers to the amount of money the parties may spend on their conventions when receiving matching federal campaign funds.
[d] Refers to the amount of money the parties may spend during the general election when receiving matching federal campaign funds.

4

Public Appearances

Chapters 2 and 3 identified periodic elections as a key structural component of the institution of the presidency. As a structural component, elections contribute to two interrelated behavioral features of the presidency: the presentation of public imagery and the perpetual campaign. Ambivalence toward parties, which is an established feature of both the nomination process and the general election, poses a contradiction between a belief in the usefulness of parties and a disdain for their factional features. This disdain draws attention to individual candidates and the images they convey and away from their party affiliations, a process that is reinforced by the promise of democracy as candidates proclaim themselves representatives of the people. Presidential elections thus personalize the presidency and make imagery one of its cornerstones. Presidents advance an image of the single executive who is the most powerful, unique, important, and visible person in politics. This image portrays the president as the one who is in charge of government, who can identify the central problems of the nation and offer solutions to these problems. Partisanship remains a strong component of presidential elections and continues to direct presidential behavior, but it is far less vivid than the single executive image.

Public imagery is one of the most deceptive behavioral components of the presidency because it places inordinate attention on presidents as individuals. Personal trivia become public imperatives. News stories and street corner conversations cover presidents' favorite foods, their families and their pets, their temperaments and their habits. Thus, the very hallmark of the imagery is the uniqueness of each president, which is captured anew each time another president is elected. Consequently, people do not recognize that the imagery itself is a feature of the institution, and not a profile of individual presidents.

To convey the imagery, presidents conduct a perpetual campaign of public appearances. By one estimate, contemporary chief executives have spent one third of their time in office making public appearances (Kernell, 1984, 243). Roderick Hart calculates that from 1945 to 1985, presidents appeared in public nearly 10,000 times. Here, too, there is a tendency to focus on the differences between the presidents making the appearances. Scholars, journalists, and members of the public are apt to point to presidents' speaking styles and accents, how comfortable they look before the cameras, and the way they deliver their messages. The data analyzed in this chapter, however, suggest that attention to such differences is at best misleading and at worst irrelevant. The perpetual campaign is institutional behavior that shows different individuals facing similar circumstances and engaging in similar behavior. The presidents, despite their differences, become interchangeable actors all playing the same part. This chapter considers presidents' public appearances as a part of the perpetual campaign. Chapter 5 follows with an examination of public approval of presidents as an evaluative measure of their performances in the campaign and elsewhere.

National Appearances

With the advent of radio and television, presidents have become more public figures than they were in the nineteenth century. In the earlier period, one of the chief events of a president's term in office was to make a grand tour throughout the country to, in the words of James Monroe, "quicken and symbolize national identity" (Ketcham, 1984, 125–126). They would travel through major cities where thousands of cheering people would greet them. In contrast, modern presidents appear before millions of people via radio or television in what are truly national appearances. These appearances are of three principal types: major addresses and news conferences, both of which are broadcast live, and travel abroad, during which presidents portray themselves as envoys of the United States. These appearances bring attention to the presidency and make its occupant appear closely tied to the people.

Major National Addresses

Tables 4-1 through 4-3 provide a compilation of major national presidential addresses since Calvin Coolidge.[1] Indeed, the use of major addresses began with Coolidge, who, although nicknamed "Silent Cal," cultivated a large radio audience. As the *New York Times* noted in 1927, Coolidge had "spoken directly to more people than any other chief executive addressed in a lifetime." A major radio broadcaster of the day observed, "The people always want to listen to the President [Coolidge], because they know he always has something to say and there always is real food for thought in his remarks" (*New York Times*, September 4, 1927, 11).

These major addresses—delivered to a national audience during evening listening hours—are the most fully developed form of institutional public behavior and arguably the most important. In them, presidents announce decisions to go to war, inform the nation of international crises, discuss urgent economic travails, and outline their visions for the nation's future. The news media perceive these addresses as having such import that they receive coverage both before and after the president speaks. Because regular programming is preempted, large audiences hear them. Consequently, the speeches create a symbolic connection between presidents and the public more dramatically than any other type of public appearance. In so doing, they augment the single executive image as public and media attention turn toward the president.

As Table 4-2 shows, the number of major national speeches made by Presidents Coolidge to Clinton has been strikingly consistent and relatively infrequent at five per year (or roughly one national address every three months). Herbert Hoover made the fewest speeches (11), and Ronald Reagan, in his second term, made the most (27). This pattern is all the more significant considering that it transcends the development of different forms of mass media—from early radio for Coolidge to satellite television for Clinton. The limited use of major addresses by each of the presidents maximizes the impact of the speeches and minimizes problems of overexposure (Ragsdale, 1984).

Presidential News Conferences

Table 4-4 examines news conferences held by presidents from Coolidge to Clinton. These news conferences involve all formal exchanges with reporters during which a written transcript of questions asked is kept. News conferences are a longstanding, frequently used institutional activity. Begun by Theodore Roosevelt on an informal, irregular basis and transformed by Woodrow Wilson into a formal, twice-weekly event, Presidents Warren G. Harding, Coolidge, and Hoover continued to use the press conference, although all required reporters' questions to be submitted in writing in advance. Franklin Roosevelt eliminated this requirement, and it has never resurfaced since. President Harry S. Truman moved the news conference from the Oval Office, where it had traditionally been held, to an auditorium to better accommodate the expanding size of the White House press corps. During the Eisenhower administration the television networks began to film the press conferences, and many of them have been carried live since the Kennedy years (Cornwell, 1966; Grossman and Kumar, 1981).

This brief history reveals three phases in the development of the news conference as institutional behavior. First, the actions of Theodore Roosevelt and Woodrow Wilson created a presidential-press relationship that quickly became institutional behavior for presidents and members of the press corps alike. Subsequent presidents with far more limited views of the presidency than either Theodore Roosevelt or Wilson maintained these conferences as an official forum from which presidents could disseminate their version of the news. The spontaneous give-and-take of the press conference, which Theodore Roosevelt and Wilson initiated, and which Franklin Roosevelt resurrected, has contributed a second key element to the institutional behavior for both presidents and the press. To be sure, presidents have often complained of "flabby and dumb" questions, while the press has often protested evasive and overly rehearsed answers. Yet, the extemporaneous exchange offers both sides the opportunity to capture the public's attention in ways the more staged news conferences did not. Finally, live coverage has brought the exchange directly to the public, creating a more vivid forum for the presentation of the single executive image. Presidents can demonstrate how much they are in control of facts, figures, and certain contentious members of the press. The importance of presidents' relations with the press has also prompted all presidents since Hoover to designate a press secretary to help maintain communication (see Table 4-5).

Table 4-4 identifies three distinct periods in the use of news conferences. Presidents from Coolidge through Truman averaged five news conferences per month. In contrast, presidents from Dwight Eisenhower to Reagan gave slightly more than one press conference per month. This shift to fewer conferences may be the result of the introduction of television into the news conference format. With increased visibility attached to these press exchanges, presidents may have become reluctant to hold the sessions too often. The tables also reveal that individual variations during this period are not as unique as popular commentary would suggest. Many have said that Richard Nixon hid from the press because he sorely disliked them and that President Reagan stayed away from news conferences because he might bumble into an off-the-cuff mistake. The data do show that both presidents averaged fewer than one press conference per month during their terms. Yet neither abandoned the practice of holding news conferences altogether. If they had, they would have been criticized for violating expected institutional behavior. Furthermore, the data also indicate that other presidents, notably Gerald Ford and Jimmy Carter, averaged only slightly more than one news conference per month. The limited use of news conferences since Eisenhower is a pattern that transcends merely the individual profiles of Nixon and Reagan.

A third era appears to be unfolding with Presidents George Bush and Bill Clinton, who each averaged nearly three news conferences per month. This may reflect the use by both presidents of a significant number of regional and foreign news conferences, designed to promote the president's cause among reporters who are not a part of the White House, or even the Washington, press corps. If this trend of using more non-Washington news conferences continues, it may mark the development of another institutionalized behavior pattern that subsequent presidents will follow.

Foreign Travel

Presidents also travel and make appearances outside the United States. Table 4-6 shows the number of days of travel and the number of appearances made at foreign locales by Presidents Truman through Clinton. Presidents' foreign appearances have been at moderate levels since 1945. Foreign travel reflects an interplay between environmental changes, specifically technological advances in air transportation, and institutional behavior. To occur with any regularity at all, these trips depend on the ease and speed of air travel. But fast planes are not the only ingredient in understanding this behavior. Table 4-6 reveals that presidents have not gone abroad more frequently with improved air transportation. In fact, the yearly averages make clear that presidents have traveled abroad fairly infrequently, while scheduling numerous appearances for each day of travel. One of the reasons for the moderate use of foreign appearances is that presidents, acting as chief of state, are interested in capitalizing on foreign appearances at home. The image of the single executive representing the entire nation before the world is an especially powerful one when used with restraint.

Foreign travel can also prompt criticism. When presidents spend too much time outside the country, they may be accused of paying inadequate attention to domestic problems. Bush, who traveled abroad more than any other president since Truman, faced this charge during his term, in particular after the Persian Gulf War when many people felt the president should turn his attention to domestic affairs. Instead, Bush made several trips to Europe, Japan, and the Persian Gulf, and in so doing may have violated one of the parameters of the institutional behavior regarding the frequency of foreign travel.

Group Appearances

Presidents' perpetual campaigns continue in their appearances before groups in Washington and at locales throughout the country.[2] Presidents strive to construct nationwide support by obtaining constituent group approval in addition to appealing to the public as a whole. Collectively, these groups often take on the characteristics of the broader American middle class. Presidents appeal to group identities, but attempt to create a larger picture of groups working together for the common good. As an illustration, consider this passage from Reagan's inaugural address: "Our concern must be for a special interest group that has been too long neglected. It knows no sectional boundaries or ethnic and racial divisions, and it crosses party lines. It is made of men and women who raise our food, patrol our streets, man our mines and factories, teach our children, keep our homes and heal us when we're sick—professionals, industrialists, shopkeepers, clerks, cabbies, and truckdrivers. They are in short, 'We the people,' this breed called Americans." Presidents engage in two types of group activities: minor policy speeches and symbolic appearances in Washington, D.C., and across the country.

Minor Policy Speeches

Table 4-7 shows minor presidential speeches made from Truman to Clinton. These speeches involve substantive policy remarks made to a specific group or in a certain forum. Often given at university commencements or various labor, business, or professional association conventions, presidents use their remarks to outline concrete policy proposals. These speeches are usually as specific in discussing a national problem as are major addresses, but they are shorter and are not nationally broadcast. They can be used by a president to promote positions before groups who may be most supportive of the ideas conveyed. Less often, presidents go before hostile groups to promote cooperation. In some instances, presidents may actually seek to antagonize hostile groups and thereby cause other groups to coalesce behind the presidential position. Since the success of presidents' policy efforts in part rests on their ability to draw together a coalition of diverse groups, these minor addresses are important in allowing presidents to tailor remarks to specific audiences. Compared with major national addresses, these targeted appeals can be given with greater frequency and may succeed or fail in ways that major addresses to the entire public would not.

Table 4-7 reveals that presidents since Truman have made on average some twelve minor speeches annually. The data reveal two distinct periods in the delivery of minor speeches. Presidents from Truman to Nixon delivered on average seven minor speeches in a year, while presidents since Ford have made eighteen minor speeches annually. This increase may reflect a change in the presidency's approach to groups. The White House became more organized and strategic with respect to specific group interests during the Ford and Carter presidencies (Ragsdale, 1993). The Carter administration created the Office of Public Liaison to expand White House relations with key interest groups. This office and other efforts to court interest groups expanded in subsequent administrations.

Symbolic Appearances In and Out of Washington

Presidents engage in ceremonial appearances as a key form of institutional behavior that allows them to show their symbolic connection to the American people. Examples include bill signings, the greeting of foreign guests, the honoring of a group or individual, and the commemoration of a historical or seasonal event. Some of these appearances border on the trivial, for example, when a president congratulates the baseball team winning the World Series. But they demonstrate the importance of the president's role as chief of state domestically, just as foreign travel demonstrates it abroad. These appearances offer presidents the opportunity to project an image of caring and concern to the nation as a whole through television and newspaper coverage. Indeed, many of the ceremonial appearances are designed specifically for the broader national audience, rather than the immediate one. These ceremonial appearances occur in Washington, D.C., and at locales across the United States.

As shown in Table 4-8, presidents make numerous appearances before various groups in and around Washington. Two periods mark presidents' Washington appearances. Presidents Truman and Eisenhower made relatively few Washington appearances, an average of 36 annually. This is contrasted to the period since Kennedy, in which presidents have appeared before groups at the White House and elsewhere in Washington an average of 168 times annually, nearly a five-fold increase over the previous period. Nixon stands out as having made relatively few Washington appearances during the latter period. He particularly minimized public exposure during the Vietnam War and Watergate. Instead, Nixon relied on major addresses to the nation in which he presented his case without confronting specific groups.

Presidents also make appearances at locales outside of Washington, D.C. (see Table 4-9). These U.S. appearances, too, are largely ceremonial. Presidents travel to a particular community to commemorate a local event, meet civic groups and local leaders, or survey damage caused by natural disasters. The trend observed for Washington appearances repeats itself for U.S. public appearances. Truman and Eisenhower made far fewer U.S. appearances (an average of 13 per year) than did presidents since John F. Kennedy (an average of 53 per year).

Partisan Appearances

The national and group approaches are supplemented by a third type of appeal in which presidents act as party leaders. They do so in ways that nonetheless maintain the popular conception of the office. The party becomes the vehicle through which presidents satisfy the public. By this logic, democracy is best served by the competitive exchange of ideas between the parties. Presidents pursue a course of public appearances that include meetings with party leaders, fund raisers and rallies for party candidates, and gatherings of party workers. But presidents also continue to suggest on other occasions that they are above party and thereby maintain the uneasy balance in the ambivalence toward parties.

As Tables 4-10 and 4-11 show, presidents not surprisingly make roughly three times more partisan appearances during election years than during nonelection years. The number of partisan appearances increased dramatically beginning with Ford, who made some 400 political appearances in little more than two years. Presidents from Truman to Nixon made on average 19 political appearances a year, while presidents since Ford have made 69 partisan appearances a year. Presidents' use of these partisan appearances is not affected by their own election campaigns as party outsiders. Presidents Carter, Reagan, and Clinton, each of whom built their candidacies at least partly outside the traditional structure of the parties and against Washington party elites, nevertheless made significant numbers of party appearances.

The Mix of Public Activity

One final way of considering public appearances involves presidents' total domestic public activity. Table 4-12 is a compilation of presidents' major speeches, news conferences, minor addresses, Washington appearances, and U.S. appearances. The table is amplified by Figure 4-1, which depicts the annual rate of domestic appearances, taken separately and together. Partisan political appearances have been excluded because they involve presidents in activities of a nonofficial nature. Foreign appearances also do not figure in this tally because presidents often travel abroad for reasons other than public exposure back home (that is, matters of summitry, diplomacy, or war). The remaining items thus provide an overall measure of the level of presidents' official activity within the United States. Consistent with several earlier tables, the figure reveals two time periods: Truman and Eisenhower were far less active than presidents since Kennedy, who have made an average of almost one public appearance per day.

Conclusion

The data in this chapter reveal two important features of institutional behavior. First, presidents' public appearances are more alike than different. One may be tempted to analyze a chief executive's overtures to the public on a personal level and thereby concentrate on the uniqueness of a president—his specific contributions, style of communication, speaking skills, mannerisms, likability, and personality. The single executive image allows presidents to advance their own unique identities. Coolidge is not Johnson, and Johnson is not Clinton. Yet the public behavior sponsored by the single executive image says that indeed Coolidge is Johnson, and Johnson is Clinton. Contemporary presidents actively engage in all forms of public appearances. Even Eisenhower, who was the least active of the presidents studied, made seven domestic appearances per month. Presidents Coolidge, Johnson, and Clinton, with seemingly little in common, each gave five major addresses per year.

This similitude defies conventional wisdom about individual presidents and their unique public styles. Presidents such as Kennedy and Reagan, who were viewed as eloquent speakers, made no more major speeches than presidents such as Nixon and Carter, who were viewed as awkward speakers. Of course, this does not directly address the level of success achieved by presidents in making their public appearances. But evidence shows that presidents gain similar advantages no matter what their styles or personal skills (Ragsdale, 1984; Brace and Hinckley, 1992; Ragsdale, 1995). Institutional behavior overshadows individual differences.

Second, institutional behavior ineluctably changes over time. The similarities witnessed in a group of presidents do not imply that their behavior is fixed. Over the time period studied, the perpetual campaign became a much more intensive part of presidents' activities in office. Although Nixon creates something of an exception to prove the rule, presidents since Kennedy have been increasingly active. There is no evidence of a saturation point, a point at which presidents cannot physically add just one more public appearance into a day, week, or year. If anything, Presidents Bush and Clinton appear more active publicly than the earlier presidents. Yet, it is too soon to tell whether their behavior marks the beginning of a third distinct period, one in which the president's schedule of public appearances is all but frenetic.

The change in the perpetual campaign from the 1940s and 1950s to the 1960s and thereafter has apparently resulted from the interconnection of four factors, three within the political environment—television, public opinion polling, and group interests—and the fourth, a structural element of the presidency—election campaigns.

The advent of television has created a medium through which presidents can receive extensive coverage of each public appearance, from the most significant national addresses down to the merely celebratory meeting with a national spelling bee champion. Captured live and on evening news broadcasts, presidents enter Americans' living rooms daily in a form of mediated intimacy. The White House can strategically plan this intimacy based on the results of public opinion polls, which are conducted much more frequently now than in the past. The White House can gather information on how the public evaluates presidential performance. The perpetual campaign may counter slipping poll results. Interest groups, always at the core of American government, are more numerous and may well be more entrenched today than during any earlier period (Schlozman and Tierney, 1986). The perpetual campaign allows presidents to court as many groups as possible.

Joined to these three environmental factors is what presidents have learned about the intensity of campaigning from their election contests. They become familiar, if not comfortable, with particular types of appearances delivered at a feverish pace. They know the importance of television, polls, and meetings with organized groups. In addition, they apply one of the campaign's most critical lessons: election campaigners never really know whether bumper stickers, billboards, television advertisements, debates, or direct mail work. Instead they assume that trying every technique for which they have money and energy will pay off and at least not backfire.

This combination of factors makes increases in the perpetual campaign all but self-fulfilling. Like the earnest campaigners, presidents assume that the more appearances they make, the better off they will be in their ability to influence, increase, or maintain public support overall, among key groups within the public, and with key segments of their political party. As all presidents follow a similar logic, the number of public appearances will steadily increase over time. How successful the campaign is remains an open question. Evidence indicates that presidents from Truman to Reagan did not gain public approval from public appearances made, other than major national addresses (Ragsdale, 1993). Presidents may be applauded by the groups or regions targeted in their appeals, but their overall national approval level is not affected. Other patterns of public approval, more fully discussed in Chapter 5, indirectly confirm this finding. Recent presidents (Ford to Clinton) who are publicly quite active actually have lower average approval than their less active predecessors (Truman to Kennedy) (see Table 5-1).

When people are asked the question, "What do American presidents do on the job?" they think of critical decisions on such matters as military strategy, domestic legislation, budget allocations, and international diplomacy. Yet, the tables in this chapter reveal how presidents engage in a perpetual campaign of public appearances that consumes ever more of their time.

Notes

1. Throughout this chapter major addresses and news conferences are calculated beginning with Coolidge while other forms of appearances, such as foreign

travel, minor speeches, Washington appearances, and U.S. appearances, are calculated beginning with Truman. The earlier period, from Coolidge to Roosevelt, is not comparable to the more contemporary period with respect to these latter types of appearances, many of which were designed expressly for television coverage. The series starts, then, just as radio coverage of events is merging into television coverage.

2. In this chapter groups are defined broadly to include local communities, organized interests, and other less entrenched associations of individuals representing such associations.

Table 4-1   Description of Major Presidential Speeches by President,
Coolidge to Clinton

President	Speech
Coolidge	
February 23, 1924	George Washington address
April 15, 1924	Daughters of the American Revolution
April 23, 1924	Associated Press luncheon
May 11, 1924	Better homes movement
May 31, 1924	Memorial Day at Arlington Cemetery
September 2, 1924	Labor leaders at White House
October 24, 1924	Foreign and domestic policy
January 27, 1925	Budget Bureau
March 5, 1925	Inaugural address
April 19, 1925	Chicago World's Fair
April 21, 1925	Daughters of the American Revolution
May 31, 1925	Memorial Day at Arlington Cemetery
June 23, 1925	Business organization of government
February 23, 1926	National Education Association
April 20, 1926	Daughters of the American Revolution
June 1, 1926	Memorial Day at Arlington Cemetery
November 12, 1926	World Court
February 23, 1927	Washington's Birthday
June 11, 1927	Memorial Day at Arlington Cemetery
August 11, 1927	Mount Rushmore dedication
April 17, 1928	Daughters of the American Revolution
May 31, 1928	Gettysburg, Pennsylvania
November 12, 1928	Armistice Day
December 5, 1928	Budget message to congress
Hoover	
March 4, 1929	Inaugural address
September 18, 1929	Peace efforts and arms reduction
December 3, 1929	State of the Union
December 1, 1930	Economy
December 2, 1930	State of the Union
January 22, 1931	Drought relief
October 18, 1931	Employment
December 2, 1931	State of the Union
March 6, 1932	Hoarding money
October 16, 1932	Community funds relief
December 6, 1932	State of the Union
Roosevelt, I	
March 4, 1933	Inaugural address
March 12, 1933	Fireside chat—banking
May 7, 1933	Fireside chat—recovery
July 24, 1933	Fireside chat—recovery
October 22, 1933	Fireside chat—recovery
January 3, 1934	State of the Union
June 28, 1934	Fireside chat—economy
September 30, 1934	Fireside chat—recovery
January 4, 1935	State of the Union
April 28, 1935	Fireside chat—faith in government

Table 4-1   *(Continued)*

President	Speech
Roosevelt, I (continued)	
January 3, 1936	State of the Union
September 6, 1936	Fireside chat—drought, conserving soil and water
Roosevelt, II	
January 20, 1937	Inaugural address
March 9, 1937	Fireside chat—reorganizing the judiciary
October 12, 1937	Fireside chat—legislation in Congress
January 3, 1938	State of the Union
April 14, 1938	Fireside chat—economic conditions
June 24, 1938	Fireside chat—democratic candidates
August 15, 1938	Social security program
January 4, 1939	State of the Union
September 3, 1939	Fireside chat—war in Europe
January 3, 1940	State of the Union
April 15, 1940	World order—against terror and hatred
May 26, 1940	Fireside chat—time to build defenses
December 29, 1940	Fireside chat—national security
Roosevelt, III	
January 20, 1941	Inaugural address
May 27, 1941	Fireside chat—extended national emergency
September 1, 1941	Fireside chat—assist in every way
September 11, 1941	Fireside chat—nation cannot be passive
December 9, 1941	Fireside chat—declaration of war with Japan
January 6, 1942	State of the Union
February 23, 1942	Fireside chat—progress of war
April 28, 1942	Fireside chat—progress of war
September 7, 1942	Fireside chat—cost of living and progress of war
October 12, 1942	Fireside chat—reports on the home front
January 7, 1943	State of the Union
May 2, 1943	Fireside chat—seizure of coal mines
July 28, 1943	Fireside chat—progress of war
September 8, 1943	Fireside chat—war loan drive
December 24, 1943	Fireside chat—Teheran & Cairo conferences
January 11, 1944	State of the Union
June 5, 1944	Fireside chat—fall of Rome
June 12, 1944	Fireside chat—progress of war
October 5, 1944	Right to vote for everyone
Roosevelt, IV	
January 6, 1945	State of the Union
Truman, I	
April 16, 1945	State of the Union
April 25, 1945	United Nations Conference
May 8, 1945	Surrender of Germany
August 9, 1945	Potsdam conference
September 1, 1945	Surrender of Japan
October 30, 1945	Wages and prices during reconversion

(Table continues)

Table 4-1   *(Continued)*

President	Speech
Truman, I (continued)	
January 3, 1946	Status of reconversion
January 21, 1946	State of the Union
April 19, 1946	World hunger
May 24, 1946	Railroad strike emergency
June 29, 1946	Price controls
October 14, 1946	Lifting price controls
January 6, 1947	State of the Union
June 20, 1947	Veto of Taft-Hartley
October 29, 1947	Special session of Congress
January 7, 1948	State of the Union
April 14, 1948	Savings bonds
Truman, II	
January 20, 1949	Inaugural address
July 13, 1949	National economy
January 4, 1950	State of the Union
July 19, 1950	Korean War
September 1, 1950	Korean War
September 9, 1950	Signing of the Defense Production Act
December 15, 1950	Declares national emergency (Korea)
January 8, 1951	State of the Union
April 11, 1951	Korean War: Relieves MacArthur of command
June 14, 1951	Need to extend inflation controls
November 7, 1951	International arms reduction
January 9, 1952	State of the Union
March 6, 1952	Mutual security program
April 8, 1952	Steel mills (nation)
June 19, 1952	Steel mills (Congress)
Eisenhower, I	
January 20, 1953	Inaugural address
February 2, 1953	State of the Union
April 16, 1953	World peace
May 19, 1953	National security costs
June 3, 1953	Report with the cabinet
July 26, 1953	Korean armistice signed
August 6, 1953	Achievements of the administration and the Eighty-third Congress
January 4, 1954	Administration purposes and accomplishments
January 7, 1954	State of the Union
March 15, 1954	Tax program
April 15, 1954	National goals and problems
August 23, 1954	Achievements of the Eighty-third Congress
January 6, 1955	State of the Union
July 15, 1955	Departure for the Geneva conference
July 25, 1955	Return from Geneva
February 29, 1956	Decision on second term
April 16, 1956	Farm bill veto
August 3, 1956	DDE and Dulles on Suez
October 31, 1956	Middle East, Eastern Europe
January 5, 1957	Middle East (Congress)
January 10, 1957	State of the Union

Table 4-1   *(Continued)*

President	Speech
Eisenhower, II	
January 21, 1957	Inaugural address
February 20, 1957	Middle East and United Nations
May 14, 1957	Government costs
May 21, 1957	Mutual security programs
September 24, 1957	Desegregation in Little Rock
November 7, 1957	National security (advances in technology)
November 13, 1957	National security
December 23, 1957	Report on NATO conference in Paris
January 9, 1958	State of the Union
March 16, 1959	West Berlin and Soviet challenges to peace
August 6, 1959	Labor bill needed
September 10, 1959	Report on European trip
December 3, 1959	Departure on goodwill trip to Europe, Asia, Africa
January 7, 1960	State of the Union
February 21, 1960	South America departure
March 8, 1960	South America return
May 25, 1960	Events in Paris
January 17, 1961	Farewell address
Kennedy	
January 20, 1961	Inaugural address
January 30, 1961	State of the Union
May 25, 1961	National problems and needs
June 6, 1961	Return from Europe
July 25, 1961	Crisis in Berlin
January 11, 1962	State of the Union
March 2, 1962	Nuclear testing and disarmament
August 13, 1962	National economy
September 30, 1962	Situation at the University of Mississippi
October 22, 1962	Cuban missile crisis
January 14, 1963	State of the Union
May 12, 1963	Racial strife in Birmingham
June 11, 1963	Civil rights
July 26, 1963	Nuclear Test Ban Treaty
September 18, 1963	Nuclear Test Ban Treaty
Johnson[a]	
November 27, 1963	Joint session
January 8, 1964	State of the Union
February 26, 1964	Tax bill signing
April 9, 1964	Moratorium on railroad labor dispute
July 2, 1964	Civil rights signing
October 18, 1964	Events in Russia, China, Great Britain
January 4, 1965	State of the Union
January 20, 1965	Inaugural address
March 15, 1965	American hopes and goals
May 2, 1965	Dominican Republic situation
August 30, 1965	Postponement of steel industry shutdown
September 3, 1965	Announcement of steel settlement

(Table continues)

Table 4-1   *(Continued)*

President	Speech
Johnson[a] (continued)	
January 12, 1966	State of the Union
January 10, 1967	State of the Union
July 24, 1967	Detroit riot (authorization of federal troops)
July 27, 1967	Civil disorder
January 17, 1968	State of the Union
January 26, 1968	North Korea
March 31, 1968	Vietnam; will not run
April 5, 1968	Martin Luther King assassination
June 5, 1968	Robert Kennedy assassination
October 31, 1968	Bombing halt
January 14, 1969	State of the Union
Nixon, I	
January 20, 1969	Inaugural address
May 14, 1969	Vietnam War
August 8, 1969	Domestic programs (family assistance plan, revenue sharing)
November 3, 1969	Vietnam War
December 15, 1969	Vietnam War (troop reductions)
January 22, 1970	State of the Union
April 20, 1970	Vietnam War (troop reductions)
April 30, 1970	Cambodian invasion
June 3, 1970	Report on Cambodian invasion
June 17, 1970	Economic Policy
October 10, 1970	Vietnam War (peace initiatives)
January 22, 1971	State of the Union
April 7, 1971	Vietnam War (general)
August 15, 1971	Economic policy (wage-price freeze)
September 9, 1971	Economic stabilization
October 7, 1971	Economic stabilization (postfreeze)
January 20, 1972	State of the Union
January 25, 1972	Peace plan
February 28, 1972	China
March 16, 1972	Busing
April 16, 1972	Vietnam
May 8, 1972	Vietnam
June 1, 1972	Return from Soviet Union
Nixon, II	
January 20, 1973	Inaugural address
January 23, 1973	Paris peace accord
March 29, 1973	Vietnam and domestic problems
April 30, 1973	Watergate
June 13, 1973	Price controls
August 15, 1973	Watergate
October 12, 1973	Ford as vice president
November 7, 1973	Energy shortage
November 25, 1973	Energy policy
January 30, 1974	State of the Union
April 29, 1974	Taxes

Table 4-1   *(Continued)*

President	Speech
Nixon, II (continued)	
July 3, 1974	Return from Soviet Union
July 25, 1974	Inflation, economy
Ford	
August 9, 1974	Remarks on taking oath of office
August 12, 1974	Address to joint session of Congress
September 8, 1974	Nixon pardon
October 8, 1974	Economic policy (Whip Inflation Now program)
January 13, 1975	Energy and the economy
January 15, 1975	State of the Union
March 29, 1975	Signing of tax reduction bill
April 10, 1975	U.S. foreign policy
May 27, 1975	Energy programs
October 6, 1975	Federal tax and spending reductions
January 19, 1976	State of the Union
January 12, 1977	State of the Union
Carter	
January 20, 1977	Inaugural address
February 2, 1977	Report to the American people
April 18, 1977	Energy plan
April 20, 1977	Address to Congress on energy plan
November 8, 1977	Update on energy plan
January 19, 1978	State of the Union
February 1, 1978	Panama Canal treaties (benefits of)
September 18, 1978	Camp David Summit on Middle East
October 24, 1978	Anti-inflation program
January 23, 1979	State of the Union
April 5, 1979	Energy (decontrol of oil prices)
June 18, 1979	Report on Vienna Summit and SALT II
July 15, 1979	National goals
October 1, 1979	Soviet troops in Cuba and SALT II
January 4, 1980	Soviet invasion of Afghanistan
January 23, 1980	State of the Union
April 25, 1980	Hostage rescue attempt
Reagan, I	
January 20, 1981	Inaugural address
February 5, 1981	Economy
February 18, 1981	Program for economic recovery (Congress)
April 28, 1981	Economic recovery (Congress)
July 27, 1981	Tax reduction
September 24, 1981	Economic recovery
January 26, 1982	State of the Union
April 29, 1982	Federal budget
August 16, 1982	Tax and budget legislation
September 1, 1982	Middle East
September 20, 1982	Lebanon
October 13, 1982	Economy
November 22, 1982	Arms reduction and deterrence

(Table continues)

Table 4-1   *(Continued)*

President	Speech
Reagan, I (continued)	
January 25, 1983	State of the Union
March 23, 1983	National security
April 27, 1983	Central America
September 5, 1983	Soviet attack on Korean airline
October 27, 1983	Lebanon, Grenada
January 25, 1984	State of the Union
May 9, 1984	Central America
Reagan, II	
January 21, 1985	Inaugural address
February 6, 1985	State of the Union
April 24, 1985	Federal budget and deficit reduction
May 28, 1985	Tax reform
November 14, 1985	U.S.-Soviet summit in Geneva
November 21, 1985	U.S.-Soviet summit in Geneva
January 28, 1986	Explosion of space shuttle *Challenger*
February 4, 1986	State of the Union
February 26, 1986	National security
March 16, 1986	Nicaragua
April 14, 1986	Air strike against Libya
June 14, 1986	Nicaragua
July 4, 1986	Independence Day
September 14, 1986	Drug abuse
October 13, 1986	Iceland meetings with Gorbachev
November 13, 1986	Iran-contra controversy
December 2, 1986	Iran-contra controversy
January 27, 1987	State of the Union
March 4, 1987	Iran-contra controversy
June 15, 1987	Venice economic summit, arms control, and deficit
August 12, 1987	Iran-contra controversy
October 14, 1987	Supreme Court nominee Robert Bork
December 10, 1987	U.S.-Soviet summit
January 25, 1988	State of the Union
February 2, 1988	Nicaragua
January 11, 1989	Farewell address
Bush	
January 20, 1989	Inaugural address
February 9, 1989	State of the Union
September 5, 1989	Drug abuse
November 22, 1989	Thanksgiving address
December 20, 1989	Panama
January 31, 1990	State of the Union
September 11, 1990	Federal budget and Persian Gulf crisis
October 2, 1990	Federal budget
January 16, 1991	Allied air attacks in Persian Gulf
January 29, 1991	State of the Union
February 23, 1991	Allied ground offensive in Persian Gulf
February 26, 1991	Suspension of allied combat in Persian Gulf
March 6, 1991	Cessation of conflict in Persian Gulf
September 27, 1991	Nuclear weapons reduction

Table 4-1   *(Continued)*

President	Speech
Bush (continued)	
January 28, 1992	State of the Union
May 1, 1992	Los Angeles riots
Clinton[b]	
January 20, 1993	Inaugural address
February 15, 1993	Economic program
February 17, 1993	Administration goals
August 3, 1993	Economic program
September 22, 1993	Health care reform
January 25, 1994	State of the Union
September 15, 1994	Haiti
September 18, 1994	Haiti
October 18, 1994	Iraq
December 15, 1994	Middle Class Bill of Rights

Sources: Coded and calculated by the author from (Coolidge) H. Quint and R. Farrell, *The Talkative President* (Amherst: University of Massachusetts Press, 1964), and various issues of the *New York Times*; (Roosevelt) successive volumes of *The Public Papers of Franklin Roosevelt* (Washington, D.C.: Government Printing Office); (Hoover and Truman through Clinton) successive volumes of *The Public Papers of the Presidents* (Washington, D.C.: Government Printing Office).

[a] Includes full term from November 1963 to January 1969.
[b] 1993–1994 only.

Table 4-2 Major Presidential Speeches by Term, Coolidge to Clinton

President	All speeches			Discretionary speeches[a]		
	Total	Yearly average	Average interval between speeches (months)	Total	Yearly average	Average interval between speeches (months)
Coolidge	24	4.8	4.8	23	5.8	4.6
Hoover	11	2.2	4.4	6	1.5	8.0
Roosevelt, I	12	3.0	4.0	8	2.0	6.0
Roosevelt, II	13	3.3	3.7	9	2.3	5.3
Roosevelt, III	19	4.8	2.5	15	3.8	3.2
Roosevelt, IV	1	—	—	0	—	—
Truman, I	17	3.4	2.8	13	3.3	3.7
Truman, II	15	3.8	3.2	11	2.8	4.4
Eisenhower, I	21	5.3	2.3	16	4.0	3.0
Eisenhower, II	20	5.0	2.5	16	4.0	3.0
Kennedy	15	5.0	2.3	11	3.7	3.2
Johnson[b]	23	4.6	2.7	15	3.0	4.2
Nixon, I	23	5.8	2.1	19	4.8	2.5
Nixon, II	13	8.1	1.5	11	5.5	1.8
Ford	12	5.2	2.4	8	4.0	3.5
Carter	17	4.3	2.8	13	3.3	3.7
Reagan, I	20	5.0	2.4	16	4.0	3.0
Reagan, II	27	6.8	1.8	22	5.5	2.2
Bush	17	4.3	2.8	12	3.0	4.0
Clinton[c]	10	5.0	2.4	8	4.0	3.0
Total Average	330	4.7	2.6	252	3.7	3.3

Sources: Coded and calculated by the author from (Coolidge) H. Quint and R. Farrell, *The Talkative President* (Amherst: University of Massachusetts Press, 1964), and various issues of the *New York Times*; (Roosevelt) successive volumes of *The Public Papers of Franklin Roosevelt* (Washington, D.C.: Government Printing Office); (Hoover and Truman through Clinton) successive volumes of *The Public Papers of the Presidents* (Washington, D.C.: Government Printing Office).

Note: "Major speeches" are defined as live nationally televised and broadcast addresses to the country that preempt all major network programming. They include inaugural addresses, State of the Union messages, other addresses to joint sessions of Congress delivered during prime time, and prime time addresses to the nation.

[a] Excludes inaugural addresses and State of the Union messages.
[b] Includes full term from November 1963 to January 1969.
[c] 1993–1994 only.

Table 4-3   Major Presidential Speeches by Subject Category, Coolidge to Clinton

President	General N	General %	Foreign N	Foreign %	Economic N	Economic %	Domestic N	Domestic %	Total
Coolidge	12	50	2	8	4	17	6	25	24
Hoover	6	55	1	9	3	27	1	9	11
Roosevelt, I	4	33	0	0	5	42	3	25	12
Roosevelt, II	4	31	4	31	4	31	1	7	13
Roosevelt, III	5	26	11	58	2	10	1	5	19
Roosevelt, IV	1	100	—	—	—	—	—	—	1
Truman, I	4	24	5	29	5	29	3	18	17
Truman, II	4	27	7	47	2	13	2	13	15
Eisenhower, I	10	25	8	38	1	5	2	10	21
Eisenhower, II	5	25	12	60	0	0	3	15	20
Kennedy	5	33	6	40	1	7	3	20	15
Johnson[a]	10	43	4	17	3	13	6	26	23
Nixon, I	4	17	13	54	4	17	2	9	23
Nixon, II	3	23	2	15	5	38	3	23	13
Ford	5	42	1	8	5	42	1	8	12
Carter	6	35	6	35	5	29	0	0	17
Reagan, I	4	20	8	40	8	40	0	0	20
Reagan, II	6	22	14	52	2	7	5	19	27
Bush	5	28	6	35	1	5	5	28	17
Clinton[b]	3	33	3	33	3	22	1	11	9
Total	106		113		63		48		330
Average percent		32		34		19		15	

Sources: Coded and calculated by the author from (Coolidge) H. Quint and R. Farrell, *The Talkative President* (Amherst: University of Massachusetts Press, 1964), and various issues of the *New York Times*; (Roosevelt) successive volumes of *The Public Papers of Franklin Roosevelt* (Washington, D.C.: Government Printing Office); (Hoover and Truman through Clinton) successive volumes of *The Public Papers of the Presidents* (Washington, D.C.: Government Printing Office).

Note: Foreign policy subjects include diplomacy, summitry, treaties, and war. Economic policy includes the economy and energy. Domestic policy involves civil rights, civil protests, riots, social welfare, education, agriculture, and domestic political matters such as Watergate. General policy encompasses two or more of the three types.

[a] Includes full term from November 1963 to January 1969.
[b] 1993–1994 only.

Table 4-4   Presidential News Conferences by Year, Coolidge to Clinton

Coolidge			Truman, I	
1924	92		1945	36
1925	88		1946	46
1926	79		1947	33
1927	80		1948	27
1928	68		Total	142
Total	407		Yearly average	36
Yearly average	81		Monthly average	3.0
Monthly average	6.8			
			Truman, II	
Hoover			1949	47
1929	78		1950	39
1930	86		1951	39
1931	62		1952	35
1932–33	42		Total	160
Total	268		Yearly average	40
Yearly average	67		Monthly average	3.3
Monthly average	5.6			
			Eisenhower, I	
Roosevelt, I			1953	23
1933	81		1954	33
1934	73		1955	19
1935	59		1956	24
1936	67		Total	99
Total	280		Yearly average	25
Yearly average	70		Monthly average	2.1
Monthly average	5.8			
			Eisenhower, II	
Roosevelt, II			1957	26
1937	73		1958	21
1938	86		1959	31
1939	84		1960	16
1940	89		Total	94
Total	332		Yearly average	24
Yearly average	83		Monthly average	2.0
Monthly average	6.9			
			Kennedy	
Roosevelt, III			1961	19
1941	78		1962	27
1942	66		1963	19
1943	58		Total	65
1944	54		Yearly average	22
Total	256		Monthly average	1.9
Yearly average	64			
Monthly average	5.3		Johnson[a]	
			1963–64	33
Roosevelt, IV			1965	17
1945	13		1966	41
Total	13		1967	22
Yearly average	—		1968	19
Monthly average	3.1		Total	132

(Table continues)

Table 4-4 *(Continued)*

Johnson (continued)		Reagan, I	
Yearly average	26	1981	6
Monthly average	2.1	1982	6
		1983	7
Nixon, I		1984	4
1969	8	Total	23
1970	6	Yearly average	6
1971	9	Monthly average	0.5
1972	7		
Total	30	Reagan, II	
Yearly average	8	1985	5
Monthly average	0.6	1986	7
		1987	3
Nixon, II		1988	4
1973	7	Total	19
1974	2	Yearly average	5
Total	9	Monthly average	0.4
Yearly average	5		
Monthly average	0.5	Bush	
		1989	31
Ford		1990	31
1974	7	1991	47
1975	19	1992	22
1976	15	Total	131
Total	41	Yearly average	33
Yearly average	19	Monthly average	2.7
Monthly average	1.4		
		Clinton[b]	
Carter		1993	28
1977	22	1994	44
1978	19	Total	72
1979	12	Yearly average	36
1980	6	Monthly average	3
Total	59		
Yearly average	15		
Monthly average	1.2		

Source: Coded and calculated by the author from successive volumes of *Public Papers of the Presidents* (Washington, D.C.: Government Printing Office).

Note: Excludes interviews, call-ins, and informal remarks made to mark trip arrivals and departures.

[a] Includes full term from November 1963 to January 1969.
[b] 1993–1994 only.

Table 4-5   President Press Secretaries, Hoover to Clinton

Press secretary	President	Years	Background
George Akerson	Hoover	1929–31	Reporter
Theodore G. Joslin	Hoover	1931–33	AP reporter
Stephen T. Early	Roosevelt	1933–45	AP, UPI reporter
Charles Ross	Truman	1945–50	Reporter
Joseph H. Short	Truman	1950–52	Reporter
Roger Tubby	Truman	1952–53	Journalist
James C. Hagerty	Eisenhower	1953–61	Reporter
Pierre E. Salinger	Kennedy	1961–63	Investigative writer
Pierre E. Salinger	Johnson	1963–64	Investigative writer
George Reedy	Johnson	1964–65	UPI reporter
Bill Moyers	Johnson	1965–67	Associate director of Peace Corps
George Christian	Johnson	1967–69	Reporter
Ronald L. Ziegler	Nixon	1969–74	Advertising
Jerald F. terHorst	Ford	1974	Bureau chief, newspaper
Ron H. Nessen	Ford	1974–77	Journalist
Jody L. Powell	Carter	1977–81	Advertising
James Brady[a]	Reagan	1981–89	Campaign aide
Larry Speakes	Reagan	1981–87	Reporter
Marlin Fitzwater	Reagan	1987–89	Government information aide
Marlin Fitzwater	Bush	1989–92	Government information aide
Dee Dee Myers	Clinton	1993–94	Campaign aide
Michael McCurry	Clinton	1994–	State Department press aide

Source: Congressional Quarterly's Guide to the Presidency, ed. Michael Nelson (Washington, D.C.: Congressional Quarterly, 1989), 733; updated by the author.

[a] Although Brady was severely wounded in the 1981 presidential assassination attempt, his title remained press secretary until 1989. Speakes's title was assistant to the president and principal deputy press secretary, while Fitzwater's was assistant to the president for press relations. He became White House press secretary in the Bush administration.

Table 4-6 Foreign Appearances by President, Truman to Clinton

President	Days of travel	Number of appearances	Yearly average	
			Days	Appearances
Truman, I	10	7	3	2
Truman, II	0	0	0	0
Eisenhower, I	3	7	1	2
Eisenhower, II	50	115	13	29
Kennedy	28	77	9	26
Johnson[a]	29	55	6	11
Nixon, I	35	108	9	27
Nixon, II	17	25	9	14
Ford	30	63	14	29
Carter	52	69	13	17
Reagan, I	36	82	9	21
Reagan, II	48	51	12	13
Bush	86	113	24	29
Clinton[b]	38	62	31	2.6

Source: Coded and calculated by the author from successive volumes of *Public Papers of the Presidents* (Washington, D.C.: Government Printing Office).

Note: Foreign appearances are defined as the total number of appearances made by a president during travel outside the United States. An appearance includes formal remarks, toasts to other heads of state, airport greetings, remarks to reporters, and remarks to American citizens who reside in the host country.

[a] Includes full term from November 1963 to January 1969.
[b] 1993–1994 only.

Table 4-7   Minor Presidential Speeches by Year, Truman to Clinton

Truman, I		Nixon, I	
1945	4	1969	5
1946	0	1970	6
1947	1	1971	10
1948	0	1972	4
Total	5	Total	25
Yearly average	1	Yearly average	6
Monthly average	0.1	Monthly average	0.5
Truman, II		Nixon, II	
1949	8	1973	12
1950	13	1974	10
1951	9	Total	22
1952	9	Yearly average	12
Total	39	Monthly average	1.1
Yearly average	10		
Monthly average	0.8	Ford	
Eisenhower, I		1974	5
1953	5	1975	36
1954	2	1976	36
1955	2	Total	77
1956	2	Yearly average	35
Total	11	Monthly average	2.7
Yearly average	3		
Monthly average	0.2	Carter	
Eisenhower, II		1977	21
1957	5	1978	15
1958	7	1979	22
1959	2	1980	24
1960	4	Total	82
Total	18	Yearly average	21
Yearly average	5	Monthly average	1.7
Monthly average	0.4		
Kennedy		Reagan, I	
1961	6	1981	11
1962	7	1982	27
1963	17	1983	19
Total	30	1984	21
Yearly average	10	Total	78
Monthly average	0.9	Yearly average	20
Johnson[a]		Monthly average	1.6
1963–64	11	Reagan, II	
1965	9	1985	6
1966	11	1986	2
1967	4	1987	7
1968	14	1988	1
Total	49	Total	16
Yearly average	10	Yearly average	4
Monthly average	0.8	Monthly average	0.3

(Table continues)

Table 4-7   *(Continued)*

Bush		Clinton[b]	
1989	9	1993	26
1990	2	1994	23
1991	7	Total	49
1992	2	Yearly average	24.5
Total	20	Monthly average	2.0
Yearly average	5		
Monthly average	0.4		

Source: Coded and calculated by the author from successive volumes of *Public Papers of the Presidents* (Washington, D.C.: Government Printing Office).

[a] Includes full term from November 1963 to January 1969.
[b] 1993–1994 only.

Table 4-8   Public Appearances in Washington, D.C., by Year,
Truman to Clinton

Truman, I			Nixon, I	
1945	5		1969	146
1946	14		1970	99
1947	12		1971	76
1948	8		1972	47
Total	39		Total	368
Yearly average	10		Yearly average	92
Monthly average	0.8		Monthly average	7.7
Truman, II			Nixon, II	
1949	63		1973	88
1950	34		1974	34
1951	87		Total	122
1952	69		Yearly average	68
Total	253		Monthly average	6.1
Yearly average	63			
Monthly average	5.3		Ford	
Eisenhower, I			1974	68
1953	31		1975	173
1954	45		1976	202
1955	28		Total	443
1956	20		Yearly average	201
Total	124		Monthly average	15.3
Yearly average	31			
Monthly average	2.6		Carter	
Eisenhower, II			1977	204
1957	34		1978	168
1958	28		1979	156
1959	57		1980	189
1960	44		Total	717
Total	163		Yearly average	179
Yearly average	41		Monthly average	15.0
Monthly average	3.4			
Kennedy			Reagan, I	
1961	110		1981	170
1962	168		1982	185
1963	139		1983	252
Total	417		1984	206
Yearly average	139		Total	813
Monthly average	11.9		Yearly average	203
Johnson[a]			Monthly average	17.0
1963–64	273		Reagan, II	
1965	192		1985	139
1966	177		1986	137
1967	197		1987	182
1968	199		1988	175
Total	1,038		Total	633
Yearly average	208		Yearly average	158
Monthly average	17.0		Monthly average	13.2

(Table continues)

Table 4-8   *(Continued)*

Bush		Clinton[b]	
1989	181	1993	184
1990	189	1994	209
1991	218	Total	493
1992	145	Yearly average	247
Total	733	Monthly average	20.5
Yearly average	183		
Monthly average	15.3		

Source: Coded and calculated by the author from successive volumes of *Public Papers of the Presidents* (Washington, D.C.: Government Printing Office).

[a] Includes full term from November 1963 to January 1969.
[b] 1993–1994 only.

Table 4-9   U.S. Public Appearances by Year, Truman to Clinton

Truman, I			Nixon, I	
1945	5		1969	39
1946	7		1970	46
1947	6		1971	61
1948	17		1972	20
Total	35		Total	166
Yearly average	9		Yearly average	42
Monthly average	0.7		Monthly average	3.5
Truman, II			Nixon, II	
1949	8		1973	19
1950	26		1974	19
1951	9		Total	38
1952	10		Yearly average	21
Total	53		Monthly average	1.9
Yearly average	13			
Monthly average	1.1		Ford	
			1974	20
Eisenhower, I			1975	77
1953	16		1976	86
1954	30		Total	183
1955	22		Yearly average	83
1956	7		Monthly average	6.3
Total	75			
Yearly average	19		Carter[b]	
Monthly average	1.6		1977	35
			1978	42
Eisenhower, II			1979	40
1957	7		1980	55
1958	10		Total	172
1959	5		Yearly average	43
1960	21		Monthly average	3.6
Total	43			
Yearly average	11		Reagan, I	
Monthly average	0.9		1981	19
			1982	65
Kennedy			1983	103
1961	15		1984	73
1962	41		Total	260
1963	41		Yearly average	65
Total	97		Monthly average	5.4
Yearly average	32			
Monthly average	2.8		Reagan, II	
Johnson[a]			1985	33
1963–64	83		1986	20
1965	31		1987	45
1966	56		1988	35
1967	32		Total	133
1968	36		Yearly average	33
Total	244		Monthly average	2.7
Yearly average	49			
Monthly average	3.9			

(Table continues)

Table 4-9   *(Continued)*

Bush		Clinton[c]	
1989	69	1993	80
1990	58	1994	108
1991	70	Total	188
1992	58	Yearly average	94
Total	255	Monthly average	7.8
Yearly average	64		
Monthly average	5.3		

Source: Coded and calculated by the author from successive volumes of *Public Papers of the Presidents* (Washington, D.C.: Government Printing Office).

[a] Includes full term from November 1963 to January 1969.
[b] Does not include series of "town meetings" begun early in term.
[c] 1993–1994 only.

Table 4-10   Political Appearances by Year, Truman to Clinton

Truman, I		1972	46
1945	0	Total	102
1946	2		
1947	1	Nixon, II	
1948	82	1973	2
Total	85	1974	9
		Total	11
Truman, II			
1949	14	Ford	
1950	6	1974	34
1951	6	1975	44
1952	62	1976	331
Total	88	Total	409
Eisenhower, I		Carter	
1953	8	1977	13
1954	17	1978	51
1955	5	1979	21
1956	36	1980	149
Total	66	Total	234
Eisenhower, II		Reagan, I	
1957	3	1981	23
1958	16	1982	35
1959	2	1983	22
1960	24	1984	126
Total	45	Total	206
Kennedy		Reagan, II	
1961	7	1985	17
1962	33	1986	48
1963	9	1987	9
Total	49	1988	49
		Total	123
Johnson[a]			
1963–64	98	Bush	
1965	4	1989	21
1966	8	1990	73
1967	7	1991	14
1968	14	1992	250
Total	131	Total	358
Nixon, I		Clinton[b]	
1969	12	1993	11
1970	39	1994	47
1971	5	Total	58

Source: Coded and calculated by the author from successive volumes of *Public Papers of the Presidents* (Washington, D.C.: Government Printing Office).

[a] Includes full term from November 1963 to January 1969.
[b] 1993–1994 only.

Table 4-11 Political Appearances in Election and Nonelection Years, Truman to Clinton

President	Total	Election year[a]	Nonelection year
Truman, I	85	84	1
Truman, II	88	68	20
Eisenhower, I	66	53	13
Eisenhower, II	45	40	5
Kennedy	49	33	16
Johnson[b]	131	120	11
Nixon, I	102	85	17
Nixon, II	11	9	2
Ford	409	365	44
Carter	234	200	34
Reagan, I	206	161	45
Reagan, II	123	97	26
Bush	358	323	35
Clinton[c]	58	47	11

Source: Coded and calculated by the author from successive volumes of *Public Papers of the Presidents* (Washington, D.C.: Government Printing Office).

Note: A political appearance is defined as any appearance before an expressly partisan political group or for an expressly partisan purpose.

[a] Average of midterm congressional election years and presidential election year.
[b] Includes full term from November 1963 to January 1969.
[c] 1993–1994 only.

Table 4-12   Level of Public Activities of Presidents, Truman to Clinton

President	Total activities	Yearly average	Monthly average
Truman, I	248	62	5.2
Truman, II	520	130	10.8
Eisenhower, I	330	83	6.9
Eisenhower, II	338	85	7.0
Kennedy	658	219	18.8
Johnson[a]	1,463	293	24.0
Nixon, I	634	159	13.2
Nixon, II	204	113	10.2
Ford	756	344	26.0
Carter	1,047	262	22.0
Reagan, I	1,194	299	24.9
Reagan, II	852	213	18.0
Bush	1,244	311	26.0
Clinton[b]	713	357	29.7

Source: Coded and calculated by the author from successive volumes of *Public Papers of the Presidents* (Washington, D.C.: Government Printing Office).

Note: Public activities are defined as including all domestic public appearances by a president, including major speeches, news conferences, minor speeches, Washington appearances, and U.S. appearances but not political appearances.

[a] Includes full term from November 1963 to January 1969.
[b] 1993–1994 only.

180

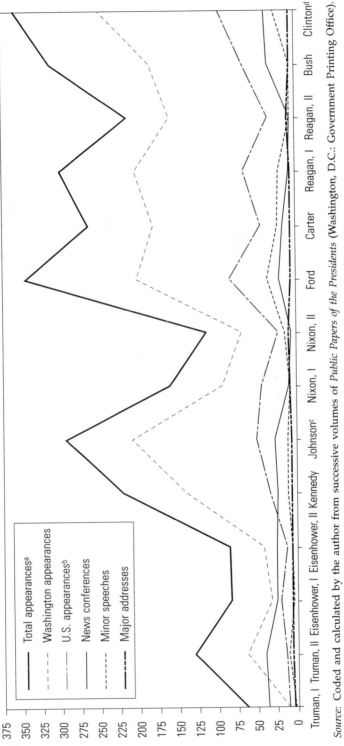

Figure 4-1 Number of Domestic Public Appearances by President, Truman to Clinton (yearly averages)

Source: Coded and calculated by the author from successive volumes of *Public Papers of the Presidents* (Washington, D.C.: Government Printing Office).

a Includes major addresses, news conferences, minor speeches, Washington appearances, and U.S. appearances, but not political appearances.

b Nonpartisan appearances before groups outside the vicinity of Washington, D.C.

c Includes full term from November 1963 to January 1969.

d 1993–1994 only.

5

Public Opinions

The previous chapter analyzed how presidents' public appearances form one type of institutional behavior. This chapter poses another critical test of the extent to which the presidency is an institution: How does the public evaluate the performances of individual presidents? If these public evaluations are president-specific, that is, if they respond uniquely to the decisions of the president and the events that occur during his term, then relations between the president and the public do not have a significant institutional component. Americans surely wish to believe that their evaluations of presidents are uniquely personal, both with respect to the individual making the judgment and to the particular president who is being judged. But when public evaluations reveal identifiable patterns across presidents, with the public responding alike to similar types of presidential activities and environmental circumstances, then they in fact constitute another form of institutional behavior.

This chapter is divided into three parts. First, it analyzes presidential approval over time; second, it considers approval among various political, demographic, and economic clusters of people within the population; and, finally, it compares public evaluations of presidents on domestic policy with evaluations of presidents on foreign policy.[1] The corresponding data help determine the type of institutional behavior patterns that may be observable within the public.

Approval Over Time

Presidential popularity or approval is the longest available time series on American public opinion. Since the 1940s the Gallup poll organization has asked scientifically selected samples of Americans the question, "Do you approve or disapprove of the way [the incumbent] is handling his job as president?" Critics have rightly raised concerns about the question's wording. It is unclear how people respond to the term *job*. What elements of the president's job are they judging? Are they actually judging the job itself or personal characteristics of the president that they use as a substitute barometer for job performance? Despite these legitimate complaints, the poll results are considered to be among the very few reliable political "facts" known about presidents. The president's popularity rating is one number that national politicians know without hesitation. When presidential popularity rises (or drops) abruptly, the shift is widely reported in the news media, discussed in Washington, and applauded (or lamented) at the White House.

As shown in Tables 5-1 through 5-3, presidential popularity since Harry S. Truman follows a strikingly uniform time trend: popularity starts high, drops, and then moves up slightly toward the end of the term (Stimson, 1976; Brace and Hinckley, 1992). Only two presidents since Truman have escaped this pattern: Dwight D. Eisenhower, whose first-term popularity started high and stayed high, and George Bush, whose popularity started moderately high, soared, and then plummeted. Presidents typically arrive at the White House with relatively high levels of approval. Table 5-3 shows that Presidents Truman, Eisenhower, Lyndon Johnson, and Gerald Ford received the highest approval rating for their entire terms during their first month in office. Presidents John F. Kennedy, Richard Nixon, Jimmy Carter, and Ronald Reagan all found their high point within their first four months in office. Thus, although these presidents varied considerably in the activities they undertook at the outset of their terms and later, public approval nevertheless followed a similar course for each president.

Figure 5-1 examines presidential popularity over time in greater detail. There are three phases to the overall pattern: the honeymoon, disillusionment, and forgiveness. A honeymoon of relatively high public approval characterizes the first phase, typically lasting six months to one year. During this time, the public explores the personal profiles of the presidents and their families. This is also the time during which presidents may announce major policy initiatives without having yet begun the battles on Capitol Hill to bring their proposals to fruition, battles that they may not win. During this phase presidents come closest to matching the single executive image—the image of the president as a powerful, unique, important, and visible official, and the one who is in charge of government.

Honeymoons are of varying durations. Ford's honeymoon ended after three months when he pardoned Nixon. His approval ratings plummeted twenty-one points, from 71 percent upon taking office to just 50 percent in October 1974. Bill Clinton's honeymoon may have actually ended even before his inauguration. Controversies surrounding his promise to lift the ban on gays in the military and his nominee for attorney general, Zoë Baird, dampened the public's approval of the president-elect. Other honeymoons end more gradually. Johnson's popularity eroded slowly as pessimism about Vietnam grew. His popularity averaged 63 percent during 1965, but by May 1966 had dipped to the 50 percent mark.

The disillusionment phase emerges as a gap between public expectations and presidential performance arises (Sigelman and Knight, 1983). Presidents are judged on how well they have lived up to expectations people associate with the presidency, the performance of past presidents, and the promises made during the election campaign. Reagan, dubbed by the press the "Teflon President" because problems encountered by his administration never seemed to stick to him personally, was perceived as able to satisfy public expectations to an extent that other presidents had not been able to match. Reagan's honeymoon seemed never to completely end. Yet, as Figure 5-2 reveals, Reagan did not escape the disillusionment phase. Reagan's popularity during his first three years in office was nearly identical to Carter's. Both Carter and Reagan saw their honeymoons fade toward the end of their first year; both faced disillusionment over the next two years with deepening economic woes—Carter's primarily inflation, Reagan's primarily unemployment. Although Reagan may have projected a more comfortable image than Carter, he was no more a "Teflon President" than was his predecessor.

Forgiveness may occur in the fourth year of the term as presidents enjoy slight increases in popularity. People respond to the upcoming election and discover that the president's opponent is mortal, too. Or, if the president is leaving office, people conclude that he was not so bad after all. Table 5-3 reveals that even Presidents Carter and Bush, who actually lost their reelection bids, saw their approval ratings rise slightly in the months nearing or even after the election. For example, Bush's approval rating reached its lowest point, 32 percent, in July 1992, but his popularity rebounded to 43 percent in November 1992 after he had been defeated for reelection.

These data provide evidence of institutional behavior in the way the public judges presidents. Certainly it is difficult to conceptualize the public as a part of an institution behaving in ways specific to that institution. Despite writers' use of the term *the public* as a proper noun, they are, in fact, referring to an unwieldly mixture of millions of people of varied background who all think differently. Yet the breadth of these differences is actually compelling evidence that public opinion is a form of institutional behavior. This vast array of people, with little in common, all evaluate presidents favorably early in the term, increasingly less favorably as the term progresses, and then with an upswing in opinion at term's end. This holds true even among very different categories of individuals within the population. The expectations that people have of presidents, drawn in large measure from the single executive image, become the centerpiece of this institutional behavior—the glue, as it were, that holds millions of opinions together.

The Carter-Reagan comparison in Figure 5-2 offers a good example of the public's institutional behavior. Despite differences in personal styles, specific events, and ongoing conditions that unfolded during their first three years in office, popularity ratings for Carter and Reagan evolved in a very similar way. Even President Bush's exceptional approval ratings held some elements of the overall institutional pattern. His term began with 57 percent approval (one percentage point less than the inaugural rating for President Clinton). It then peaked at 89 percent at the end of the Persian Gulf War in February 1991—the highest figure ever recorded for an American president. After the war, however, Bush's approval more nearly followed the familiar downward trend. His approval dropped fifty-eight percentage points in a single year to 41 percent by February 1992, and then rose slightly at the close of his term to 49 percent approval.

Social Categories and Presidential Approval

Attention to presidents' overall approval ratings presents a picture of national public opinion that can be decidedly misleading. Too often press commentaries on the latest poll results and scholarly studies of presidential approval treat the nation as a monolith. Yet various segments of the population are not likely to uniformly approve of a president. The analysis below permits an examination of variations across political, demographic, and economic breakdowns of the population on the basis of party identification, region, income, race, gender, age, and education.

Party, Region, and Income Differences

Tables 5-4 and 5-5 present a breakdown of public approval by party identification, region, and income on a quarterly basis and averaged over a term, respectively. Not surprisingly, the tables show that citizens are far more likely to approve of a president of their own party than one of the other party. Indeed, this generalization holds on average for every quarter since 1953. In addition, unlike the public's general attachment to party, this partisan aspect of presidential approval has not weakened over time. The split in party approval has been most substantial under Presidents Reagan and Clinton—in both cases a difference of some fifty percentage points between Democrats and Republicans. However, an average difference of thirty-five percentage points for the remaining presidents is not inconsequential.

It is also apparent that Republican presidents generally command higher approval among their partisans than do Democratic presidents. The natural advantage that Democratic presidents have that is the result of larger numbers of Democratic party identifiers in the population may be partly canceled by Republicans' stronger approval for their party's presidents. These party differences are an indicator of the ambivalence toward parties that confront American presidents. Although they may disparage parties as ugly roadblocks to national progress, Americans nonetheless use party affiliation as a convenient and powerful device by which to evaluate presidents' performances.

Tables 5-4 and 5-5 also reveal that regional variation in presidential approval is far less striking than party differences. The principal contrast appears to be between the South and the other regions of the country. Three Republican presidents, Nixon, Reagan, and Bush, generally received stronger approval in the South than in the rest of the nation. Each developed a "southern strategy," an approach originated by Nixon to gain Republican inroads in the predominantly Democratic South. The South is now a much more competitive, increasingly Republican, region. Carter, a southerner, did as well as Nixon in the region; Clinton, another southerner, did not.

The two tables show that Democratic presidents receive higher approval ratings from the poor than from the wealthy; for Republican presidents, the pattern is reversed. For most quarters and all presidents, this differences is quite noticeable. The income gap was largest during Reagan's term.

Demographic and Education Differences

Tables 5-6 through 5-9 consider differences based on three key demographic categories—race, gender, and age. In addition, Tables 5-8 and 5-9 examine approval across different levels of education. Democratic presidents, especially Clinton, have received much higher approval from nonwhites than Republican presidents. Nonwhites gave especially low marks to Presidents Nixon and Reagan. The so-called gender gap is much less distinct. The results show no evidence of systematic differences between men and women in presidents' approval ratings. However, they do show a dramatic difference in men's and women's ratings of Reagan. Men's approval of Reagan was on average nine percentage points higher than women's in his first term and eight percentage points higher in his second term.

Tables 5-8 and 5-9 examine public approval broken down by age and education. Age differences were most distinct for Kennedy, Reagan (in his second term), and Bush, all of whom were favored more by younger people than older people. The data dispel two common impressions about young Americans' views of presidents: despite Vietnam, Johnson was not disliked by younger Americans, and only during his second term was Reagan more popular with younger people than older people. Among the young, Reagan's first term approval rating of 50 percent equaled that for

Carter and Ford and was lower than the 53 percent received by Clinton. Age differences were far less distinct than education differences. Approval of Republican presidents generally increased from the lowest to the highest levels of education. Three Democratic presidents—Kennedy, Johnson, and Carter—showed very slight differences in the opposite direction. They were somewhat more popular among those with limited education than those with at least some college training.

Social Groups and Approval Over Time

The tables not only permit an analysis of the differences among political, demographic, and economic categories in the population, they also reveal the overall time trend of declining presidential popularity over the course of a term observed for the nation as a whole. This is acutely evident across each of the several social category breakdowns—party, region, income, race, gender, age, and education. Although levels of approval vary sharply across subgroups, the overall direction of approval starts as high as it is ever likely to be, falls, and then rebounds slightly at the end of a president's term.

Policy and Office Approval

Public approval measures are a generic barometer of public reactions to presidents. They do not capture any specific judgments citizens may have about the way in which a president handles certain policy areas or their impressions of the office of the presidency. Table 5-10 presents public approval of presidents' handling of the economy and foreign policy since the 1970s. Americans judged Reagan and Clinton equally competent in the two areas, while Carter and Bush were rated more highly in foreign affairs than on the economy. The data are not sufficient, however, to indicate a distinction between two types of presidencies—one foreign, the other domestic—a distinction that has long been debated in studies of presidents' relations with Congress.

In survey answers respondents have identified what they believed to be the most important national problem for each year since 1935 (Table 5-11). These national problems, which have primarily involved war and economic difficulties, are usually ones that presidents are expected to solve. Since 1945, citizens have also been asked which political party they believed would best be able to handle the national problem they identified in these surveys. Table 5-12 shows that respondents have tended to place their faith more heavily in Democrats, regardless of whether they held the White House or not. These patterns are seemingly related to partisanship in the citizenry. The larger percentage of people who identify with the

Democratic party may be positively predisposed toward believing that that party will better be able to solve the nation's problems.

The final table in the chapter, Table 5-13, reveals the low level of confidence people have in the presidency as an office. Confidence in the White House dropped significantly in the wake of the Watergate scandal. Indeed, the percentage of the public having a great deal of confidence in the White House did not rise above 20 percent until the election of Carter. Public confidence dropped again during the latter part of Carter's term. Not surprisingly, confidence was renewed at the time of the Persian Gulf War, but declined to more typical levels thereafter. Compared with other institutions in American society, the White House generally enjoys less of the public's confidence than the Supreme Court, though usually more than Congress. This, too, is a behavioral component of the institution that may account for the predictable drop in presidents' approval ratings.

Conclusion

Presidents' popularity with the public as a whole and among key demographic and political groups exhibits an inexorable downward trend over the course of a term. Presidents come into office enjoying their highest levels of popularity, but that popularity quickly erodes. This has been true of presidents who presided over robust economies, had dramatic successes in international diplomacy, conducted popular military interventions, and won reelection. This decline is evident even amongst a president's most ardent supporters. Presidents can engage in activities to temporarily boost their popularity—major national addresses, legislative victories, and dramatic foreign policy successes (Ragsdale, 1984; Brace and Hinckley, 1992). But the time trend does not alter, and is certainly an institutional pattern of the presidency. The clash between presidents' institutional behavior, in the form of public appearances, and the public's institutional response means that large numbers of public appearances will not ensure a high level of popularity.

The downward trend in approval constrains the behavior of presidents. It sets off a stopwatch that presidents must heed. They know that they can count on the benefit of public approval with any degree of certainty only during their first year in office. Thereafter, national and international events, over which presidents may or may not have some control, and presidents' own accomplishments may boost their support, but only temporarily.

Approval may also constrain presidential behavior in another way. Presidents may consciously design certain policy decisions or the timing of decisions with approval ratings in mind (Brace and Hinckley, 1992). Thus, they juggle the demands of government with their level of popularity.

There is no evidence, however, that this type of manipulation has paid off, as presidents' popularity still starts high and finishes low. Since presidents cannot ever fully live up to the single executive image, no matter how they frame and time their decisions, the erosion of popularity is all but inevitable.

The social category differences that are observed across presidents are undergirded by party. People typically found in Democratic electoral coalitions—nonwhites, the poor, the less-educated—continue to be relatively strong supporters of Democratic presidents throughout their terms in office. Similarly, people who are typically part of Republican electoral coalitions—whites, those with higher incomes, and the better-educated—continue to support Republican presidents throughout their terms in office. Part of the institutional profile of the presidency is its partisan nature and the polarizing effects of that partisanship. This is not only revealed in these data and the electoral data from Chapters 2 and 3, but will also be evident in Chapter 8, which examines presidential relations with Congress. Although presidents like to portray themselves as presidents of all of the people, these data reveal how difficult it is for a president to convert people who are not among the electoral supporters of the chief executive's party.

Separate from the interplay of party and social categories, one incumbent-specific portrait of polarization stands out. Across each of the social category breakdowns examined in these data—party, income, race, gender, age, and education—Reagan's approval is consistently at the extremes for opposing subpopulations—high for whites, low for nonwhites, high for the wealthy, low for the poor. There seems to be little middle ground in Reagan's approval patterns, and this accentuates the typical party differences that other presidents encounter. For Reagan, polarization was not simply a feature of party, but also a matter of his own political agenda and people's reactions to it.

Individual presidents may make some degree of difference in their dealings with the public, but such independent efforts are largely overshadowed by the time trend and social category differences that do not depend on who the president is, but rather at what point he is in his term and what party affiliation he holds.

Note

1. National presidential popularity is presented here since Truman. Although the Gallup time series begins with Franklin Roosevelt, the polls were taken very sporadically during his time in office. Demographic and political breakdowns in approval are available only since Eisenhower. Data on economic and foreign policy approval are available beginning with Nixon.

Table 5-1 Presidential Approval by Month Since Inauguration, Truman to Clinton (percent)

Month	Truman[b]	Eisenhower	Kennedy	Johnson	Nixon	Ford	Carter	Reagan	Bush	Clinton[c]
					Percentage approving[a]					
1st month	—	—	—	—	59	71	—	51	57	58
2nd month	—	68	—	79	61	50	71	55	63	59
3rd month	—	59	73	80	63	55	72	60	56	52
4th month	87	74	83	75	61	48	63	67	58	55
5th month	—	74	76	73	65	42	64	68	56	44
6th month	—	—	74	77	63	39	63	58	70	46
7th month	75	71	71	75	65	39	67	60	66	44
8th month	—	—	73	74	62	37	66	60	69	56
9th month	—	75	75	—	58	39	59	52	70	48
10th month	—	65	76	—	56	51	51	56	68	48
11th month	63	—	77	—	68	52	56	54	70	54
12th month	—	60	78	—	59	—	57	49	71	58
13th month	50	68	77	69	61	46	52	47	80	53
14th month	—	71	78	69	56	47	50	47	73	51
15th month	—	68	79	71	53	44	48	46	74	48
16th month	43	—	77	—	56	41	41	44	67	51
17th month	—	64	73	69	59	39	43	45	65	46
18th month	—	61	71	67	55	46	42	44	69	43
19th month	32	—	69	64	55	48	39	41	63	41
20th month	—	71	66	70	56	50	43	42	76	42
21st month	—	65	67	69	—	48	48	42	67	44
22nd month	35	64	62	65	58	47	49	42	54	45
23rd month	48	57	—	65	57	45	50	43	54	41
24th month	60	63	74	63	52	—	51	41	63	47
25th month	—	69	76	64	56	—	43	35	83	—

(Table continues)

Table 5-1   (Continued)

Month	Truman[b]	Eisenhower	Kennedy	Johnson	Nixon	Ford	Carter	Reagan	Bush	Clinton[c]
				Percentage approving[a]						
26th month	—	71	70	63	50	—	37	40	80	—
27th month	54	66	67	61	50	—	42	41	82	—
28th month	—	68	66	56	50	—	40	41	82	—
29th month	55	69	64	57	49	53	32	46	76	—
30th month	—	—	61	54	48	—	29	47	76	—
31st month	—	72	61	51	50	—	29	42	72	—
32nd month	—	71	63	48	49	—	32	43	71	—
33rd month	—	—	56	56	—	—	30	48	74	—
34th month	—	—	58	47	52	—	31	46	66	—
35th month	—	77	58	46	49	—	38	53	65	—
36th month	—	75	—	44	50	—	54	54	52	—
37th month	36	77	—	49	50	—	58	55	50	—
38th month	—	76	—	44	52	—	55	55	46	—
39th month	39	72	—	46	53	—	39	54	41	—
40th month	—	69	—	45	—	—	39	52	42	—
41st month	—	—	—	45	62	—	38	54	42	—
42nd month	—	—	—	49	57	—	31	54	41	—
43rd month	—	69	—	45	—	—	21	52	38	—
44th month	—	67	—	51	—	—	32	54	32	—
45th month	69	—	—	47	—	—	—	57	40	—
46th month	—	—	—	39	—	—	—	58	36	—
47th month[d]	57	75	—	38	62	—	—	61	34	—
48th month	—	79	—	38	59	—	34	59	43	—
49th month	—	73	—	42	67	—	—	64	49	—
50th month	—	72	—	46	65	—	—	60	56	—
51st month	57	72	—	49	—	—	—	56	—	—

52nd month	—	67	—	—	41	48	—	—	52	—	—
53rd month	—	62	—	—	—	44	—	—	55	—	—
54th month	51	—	—	—	50	44	—	—	58	—	—
55th month	—	63	—	—	41	39	—	—	63	—	—
56th month	—	—	—	—	43	36	—	—	65	—	—
57th month	45	59	—	—	40	33	—	—	60	—	—
58th month	—	57	—	—	35	27	—	—	63	—	—
59th month	—	—	—	—	—	27	—	—	65	—	—
60th month	—	—	—	—	42	29	—	—	63	—	—
61st month	37	58	—	—	43	26	—	—	64	—	—
62nd month	37	54	—	—	44	27	—	—	—	—	—
63rd month	43	50	—	—	49	26	—	—	63	—	—
64th month	—	54	—	—	—	26	—	—	62	—	—
65th month	39	54	—	—	—	26	—	—	68	—	—
66th month	—	—	—	—	—	28	—	—	64	—	—
67th month	—	58	—	—	—	26	—	—	63	—	—
68th month	36	56	—	—	—	24	—	—	61	—	—
69th month	26	56	—	—	—	23	—	—	61	—	—
70th month	28	58	—	—	—	—	—	—	63	—	—
71st month	—	52	—	—	—	—	—	—	—	—	—
72nd month	24	57	—	—	—	—	—	—	47	—	—
73rd month	25	57	—	—	—	—	—	—	48	—	—
74th month	29	59	—	—	—	—	—	—	40	—	—
75th month	31	58	—	—	—	—	—	—	47	—	—
76th month	32	60	—	—	—	—	—	—	48	—	—
77th month	29	64	—	—	—	—	—	—	—	—	—
78th month	23	60	—	—	—	—	—	—	53	—	—
79th month	—	61	—	—	—	—	—	—	49	—	—
80th month	—	66	—	—	—	—	—	—	49	—	—
81st month	26	66	—	—	—	—	—	—	—	—	—
82nd month	25	66	—	—	—	—	—	—	—	—	—

(Table continues)

Table 5-1 (*Continued*)

Month		Percentage approving[a]									
	Truman[b]	Eisenhower	Kennedy	Johnson	Nixon	Ford	Carter	Reagan	Bush	Clinton[c]
83rd month	—	64	—	—	—	—	—	—	—	—
84th month	28	76	—	—	—	—	—	49	—	—
85th month	28	66	—	—	—	—	—	49	—	—
86th month	32	64	—	—	—	—	—	51	—	—
87th month	—	65	—	—	—	—	—	50	—	—
88th month	—	62	—	—	—	—	—	48	—	—
89th month	—	57	—	—	—	—	—	51	—	—
90th month	32	63	—	—	—	—	—	54	—	—
91st month	—	61	—	—	—	—	—	53	—	—
92nd month	—	58	—	—	—	—	—	54	—	—
93rd month	—	58	—	—	—	—	—	51	—	—
94th month	—	59	—	—	—	—	—	57	—	—
95th month	—	59	—	—	—	—	—	63	—	—
96th month	—	—	—	—	—	—	—	—	—	—
Average	41	65	70	55	52	47	46	53	61	49

Source: Adapted from *Public Opinion*, February/March 1986, 37–38, and updated from successive volumes of *Gallup Poll Monthly*. Reprinted with the permission of the American Enterprise Institute for Public Policy Research, Washington, D.C.

Note: The question was: "Do you approve or disapprove of the way [the incumbent] is handling his job as president?"

[a] In months in which more than one approval poll was conducted, the last results of the month are presented.
[b] Beginning in 1945.
[c] 1993–1994 only.
[d] End of first term for those presidents elected to office.

Table 5-2 Presidential Approval Average by Year of Term, Truman to Clinton (percent)

Year	Truman	Eisenhower	Kennedy	Johnson	Nixon	Ford	Carter	Reagan	Bush	Clinton[a]
(First rating)	87	68	73	79	59	71	71	51	57	58
1st	78	68	76	75	61	47	61	57	65	52
2nd	45	66	71	66	54	43	46	44	67	47
3rd	55	73	62	50	49	—	39	45	73	
4th	38	72	—	44	62	—	36	56	49	
5th	59	62	—	42	40	—	—	60	—	
6th	41	58	—	—	26	—	—	60	—	
7th	28	64	—	—	—	—	—	47	—	
8th	29	61	—	—	—	—	—	52	—	
(Last rating)	32	59	58	49	26	53	34	63	56	

Source: Adapted from *Public Opinion*, February/March 1986, 37–38, and updated from successive volumes of *Gallup Poll Monthly*. Reprinted with the permission of the American Enterprise Institute for Public Policy Research, Washington, D.C.

[a] 1993–1994 only.

Table 5-3   Aggregate Public Approval, Truman to Clinton (percent)

President/date	Approve	Disapprove	No opinion
Truman, I			
May 1945	87	3	10
October 1945	82	9	9
November 1945	75	14	11
January 1946	63	22	15
March 1946	50	36	14
June 1946	43	45	12
September 1946	32	53	15
December 1946	35	47	18
January 1947	48	39	13
March 1947	60	23	17
April 1947	57	28	15
June 1947	54	33	13
September 1947	55	29	16
April 1948	36	50	14
May 1948	39	47	14
Truman, II			
January 7, 1949	69	17	14
March 6, 1949	57	24	19
June 11, 1949	57	26	17
September 25, 1949	51	31	18
January 8, 1950	45	40	15
February 26, 1950	37	44	19
Late April 1950	37	44	19
June 1950	37	45	18
July 1950	46	37	17
Late July 1950	40	40	20
August 20, 1950	43	32	25
October 1950	39	42	19
January 8, 1951	36	49	1
February 4, 1951	26	57	17
March 26, 1951	28	57	15
May 19, 1951	24	61	15
June 16, 1951	25	59	16
July 8, 1951	29	54	17
August 3, 1951	31	57	12
September 21, 1951	32	54	14
October 14, 1951	29	55	16
November 11, 1951	23	58	19
January 20, 1952	26	62	13
February 9, 1952	25	62	13
April 13, 1952	28	59	13
May 1952	28	59	13
June 15, 1952	32	58	10
October 9, 1952	32	55	13
December 6, 1952	31	56	13
Eisenhower, I			
January 11, 1953	78	4	18
February 1, 1953	68	7	25
February 22, 1953	67	8	25
March 28, 1953	74	8	18
April 1953	74	10	16

Table 5-3   *(Continued)*

President/date	Approve	Disapprove	No opinion
Eisenhower, I (continued)			
May 9, 1953	74	10	16
July 4, 1953	71	15	14
Late July 1953	73	13	14
August 1953	74	14	12
September 12, 1953	75	14	12
October 9, 1953	66	20	14
Early November 1953	61	26	13
Late November 1953	58	25	17
December 11, 1953	66	20	14
January 9, 1954	71	19	10
January 1954	70	17	13
February 25, 1954	68	19	13
March 1954	65	22	13
April 1954	68	21	11
May 2, 1954	60	22	18
Late May 1954	61	23	16
June 12, 1954	62	24	14
Early July 1954	64	22	14
Late July 1954	75	11	14
August 5, 1954	68	20	12
August 26, 1954	62	23	15
September 1954	66	21	13
October 1954	61	26	13
November 1954	57	23	20
December 2, 1954	68	23	9
January 1, 1955	70	18	12
Late January 1955	70	17	13
February 10, 1955	71	16	13
Early March 1955	70	19	11
Late March 1955	66	21	13
April 14, 1955	68	18	14
May 12, 1955	69	16	15
July 1955	72	18	10
August 3, 1955	76	11	13
August 25, 1955	71	16	13
November 1955	77	13	10
December 8, 1955	75	13	12
Early January 1956	76	12	12
Late January 1956	77	14	9
February 16, 1956	76	14	10
March 1956	72	18	10
March 1956	73	18	9
April 19, 1956	69	19	12
July 12, 1956	69	21	12
August 3, 1956	67	20	13
November 22, 1956	75	15	10
December 1956	79	11	10
Eisenhower, II			
January 17, 1957	73	14	13
February 1957	72	16	12

(Table continues)

Table 5-3   *(Continued)*

President/date	Approve	Disapprove	No opinion
Eisenhower, II (continued)			
February 28, 1957	72	18	10
Early April 1957	66	21	13
April 25, 1957	67	21	12
May 1957	62	23	15
June 6, 1957	62	23	15
June 27, 1957	63	23	15
Late August 1957	59	23	18
September 1957	59	26	15
October 10, 1957	57	27	16
January 3, 1958	60	30	10
Late January 1958	58	27	15
February 14, 1958	54	32	14
March 6, 1958	50	34	16
Late March 1958	48	36	16
April 16, 1958	54	31	15
May 1958	53	32	15
Late May 1958	54	31	15
July 1958	52	32	16
July 1958	58	27	15
August 1958	56	27	15
September 10, 1958	56	29	15
October 1958	58	25	17
November 7, 1958	52	30	18
December 3, 1958	57	32	11
January 7, 1959	57	27	16
February 4, 1959	59	26	15
March 1959	58	26	16
April 2, 1959	62	22	16
April 29, 1959	60	24	16
May 29, 1959	64	21	15
June 25, 1959	60	24	16
July 23, 1959	61	26	13
August 20, 1959	66	20	14
September 18, 1959	66	19	15
October 16, 1959	66	19	15
November 1959	64	22	14
Middle December 1959	76	15	9
January 6, 1960	66	18	16
February 1960	64	21	15
March 1960	64	22	14
March 30, 1960	65	22	13
Late April 1960	62	22	16
May 26, 1960	65	22	13
June 1960	61	24	15
Late June 1960	57	26	17
July 1960	49	33	18
Late July 1960	63	26	11
Early August 1960	63	24	13
Late August 1960	61	28	11
September 1960	58	28	14
October 18, 1960	58	31	11
November 1960	59	26	15
December 1960	59	27	14

Table 5-3   *(Continued)*

President/date	Approve	Disapprove	No opinion
Kennedy			
February 10, 1961	72	6	22
March 10, 1961	73	7	20
April 1961	78	6	16
April 28, 1961	83	5	12
Early May 1961	77	9	14
Middle May 1961	75	10	15
May 28, 1961	74	11	15
June 23, 1961	71	14	15
July 27, 1961	74	12	14
August 1961	75	12	13
September 21, 1961	79	10	11
October 17, 1961	77	12	11
November 1961	79	9	12
December 1961	77	11	12
January 11, 1962	78	9	13
February 18, 1962	78	11	11
March 8, 1962	79	12	9
April 1962	77	13	10
May 3, 1962	74	16	10
May 31, 1962	71	19	10
Late June 1962	69	19	12
July 26, 1962	66	23	11
August 23, 1962	67	20	13
September 20, 1962	62	22	16
October 1962	61	24	15
November 16, 1962	73	14	13
December 1962	76	13	11
January 11, 1963	74	14	12
February 7, 1963	70	18	12
March 8, 1963	67	20	13
April 4, 1963	66	21	13
May 8, 1963	64	25	11
Middle May 1963	65	23	12
Late May 1963	64	24	12
June 21, 1963	61	26	13
July 1963	61	27	12
August 15, 1963	62	26	13
September 12, 1963	56	29	15
October 11, 1963	58	29	13
November 1963	58	30	12
Johnson[a]			
Early December 1963	78	2	20
December 12, 1963	79	3	18
January 2, 1964	80	5	15
February 1, 1964	75	8	17
Middle February 1964	73	9	18
February 28, 1964	79	9	12
Middle March 1964	77	9	14
March 27, 1964	75	12	13
April 1964	75	11	15

(Table continues)

Table 5-3 *(Continued)*

President/date	Approve	Disapprove	No opinion
Johnson (continued)			
May 6, 1964	75	11	14
Late May 1964	74	13	13
June 4, 1964	74	12	14
Middle June 1964	74	14	12
Late June 1964	74	15	11
November 1964	69	18	13
December 11, 1964	69	18	13
January 7, 1965	71	15	14
Late January 1965	71	16	13
February 1965	68	18	14
Early March 1965	69	21	10
Late March 1965	69	21	10
Early April 1965	67	22	11
April 23, 1965	64	22	14
May 13, 1965	70	18	12
June 4, 1965	69	19	12
June 24, 1965	65	21	14
July 16, 1965	65	20	15
Early August 1965	65	22	13
August 27, 1965	64	25	13
September 16, 1965	63	24	13
October 1965	66	21	13
October 19, 1965	64	22	14
November 18, 1965	62	22	16
December 11, 1965	63	26	11
Early January 1966	59	24	17
January 21, 1966	61	27	12
February 10, 1966	56	34	10
March 3, 1966	58	28	14
March 24, 1966	57	28	15
April 1966	54	33	13
May 5, 1966	46	34	20
May 19, 1966	50	33	17
June 1966	48	39	13
July 8, 1966	56	30	14
July 29, 1966	51	38	11
August 1966	48	38	14
September 8, 1966	46	39	15
Early October 1966	44	42	14
Late October 1966	44	41	15
November 10, 1966	48	37	15
December 1966	44	47	9
Early January 1967	47	37	16
January 26, 1967	46	38	16
February 1967	45	42	13
March 1967	45	41	14
Late March 1967	46	38	16
April 19, 1967	48	37	15
May 1967	45	39	16
June 2, 1967	44	40	16
June 22, 1967	52	35	13
July 1967	47	39	14

Table 5-3   *(Continued)*

President/date	Approve	Disapprove	No opinion
Johnson (continued)			
Early August 1967	40	48	12
August 24, 1967	39	48	13
September 1967	38	47	15
October 1967	38	50	12
October 27, 1967	41	49	10
December 7, 1967	46	41	13
January 4, 1968	48	39	13
February 1, 1968	41	47	12
Late February 1968	41	48	11
March 15, 1968	36	52	12
April 4, 1968	42	47	11
Early May 1968	46	43	11
Late May 1968	41	45	14
Early June 1968	42	45	13
Late June 1968	40	47	13
July 1968	40	47	13
August 7, 1968	35	52	13
September 26, 1968	42	51	7
November 9, 1968	43	44	13
December 1968	44	43	13
January 1, 1969	49	37	14
Nixon, I			
January 23, 1969	59	5	36
February 20, 1969	60	6	34
March 12, 1969	65	9	26
Late March 1969	63	10	27
April 10, 1969	61	12	27
Early May 1969	62	15	23
May 15, 1969	65	12	23
Late May 1969	62	15	23
June 1969	63	16	21
July 19, 1969	58	22	20
August 14, 1969	65	20	15
September 11, 1969	60	24	16
September 19, 1969	58	23	19
October 3, 1969	57	24	19
Late October 1969	56	29	15
November 12, 1969	67	19	14
December 1969	59	23	18
January 2, 1970	61	22	17
Middle January 1970	63	23	14
January 30, 1970	64	24	12
Late February 1970	56	27	17
March 18, 1970	53	30	17
March 27, 1970	54	34	12
April 17, 1970	56	31	13
April 29, 1970	57	32	11
May 21, 1970	59	29	12
June 13, 1970	55	31	14
July 9, 1970	61	28	11

(Table continues)

Table 5-3 *(Continued)*

President/date	Approve	Disapprove	No opinion
Nixon, I (continued)			
July 31, 1970	55	32	13
August 25, 1970	55	31	14
Early September 1970	57	30	13
Late September 1970	51	31	18
October 9, 1970	58	27	15
November 13, 1970	57	30	13
December 3, 1970	52	34	14
January 1971	56	33	11
February 19, 1971	49	37	14
March 3, 1971	56	32	12
March 11, 1971	50	37	13
Early April 1971	49	38	13
April 23, 1971	50	38	12
May 1971	50	35	15
June 4, 1971	48	37	15
Middle June 1971	48	37	15
June 25, 1971	48	39	13
July 1971	50	37	13
Middle August 1971	50	38	12
October 8, 1971	52	37	11
October 29, 1971	49	37	14
November 19, 1971	50	37	13
December 16, 1971	49	37	14
January 7, 1972	49	39	12
February 4, 1972	52	36	12
March 3, 1972	56	32	12
March 24, 1972	53	36	11
May 26, 1972	62	30	8
June 16, 1972	59	30	11
June 23, 1972	56	33	11
November 1972	62	28	10
December 8, 1972	59	30	11
Nixon, II			
January 12, 1973	51	37	12
January 26, 1973	67	25	8
February 26, 1973	67	25	10
March 30, 1973	57	33	10
April 6, 1973	54	36	10
April 27, 1973	48	40	12
May 4, 1973	45	42	13
May 11, 1973	44	45	11
June 1, 1973	44	44	12
June 22, 1973	44	45	11
July 6, 1973	39	49	12
August 3, 1973	31	58	11
August 17, 1973	36	54	10
September 7, 1973	34	56	10
September 21, 1973	33	59	8
October 5, 1973	30	57	13
October 19, 1973	27	60	13
November 2, 1973	27	63	10
November 30, 1973	31	59	10

Table 5-3   *(Continued)*

President/date	Approve	Disapprove	No opinion
Nixon, II (continued)			
December 7, 1973	29	60	11
January 4, 1974	27	63	10
January 18, 1974	26	64	10
February 1, 1974	28	59	13
February 8, 1974	27	63	10
February 22, 1974	25	64	11
March 8, 1974	26	62	12
March 29, 1974	26	65	9
April 12, 1974	25	62	13
Late April 1974	26	60	14
May 10, 1974	25	61	14
May 31, 1974	28	61	11
June 21, 1974	26	61	13
July 12, 1974	24	63	13
August 12, 1974	23	66	10
Ford			
August 16, 1974	71	3	26
Early September 1974	66	13	21
September 27, 1974	50	28	22
Early October 1974	52	29	19
October 18, 1974	55	28	17
November 8, 1974	47	33	20
November 15, 1974	48	32	20
December 6, 1974	42	41	17
January 10, 1975	37	39	24
January 31, 1975	39	43	18
February 28, 1975	39	45	16
March 28, 1975	37	43	20
April 4, 1975	44	37	19
April 18, 1975	39	46	15
May 2, 1975	40	43	17
May 30, 1975	51	33	16
June 27, 1975	52	33	15
August 1, 1975	45	37	18
August 15, 1975	46	37	17
September 12, 1975	47	36	17
October 3, 1975	47	37	16
October 17, 1975	47	40	13
October 31, 1975	44	44	12
November 21, 1975	41	46	13
December 5, 1975	46	37	17
December 12, 1975	39	46	15
January 2, 1976	46	42	12
January 23, 1976	45	45	10
January 30, 1976	46	40	14
February 27, 1976	48	38	14
March 19, 1976	50	36	14
April 9, 1976	48	41	11
May 21, 1976	47	38	15
June 11, 1976	45	40	15
December 10, 1976	53	32	15

(Table continues)

Table 5-3   *(Continued)*

President/date	Approve	Disapprove	No opinion
Carter			
January 1, 1977	66	8	26
March 1, 1977	70	9	20
March 15, 1977	75	9	16
March 22, 1977	72	10	18
March 29, 1977	67	14	19
April 12, 1977	63	18	19
April 26, 1977	63	18	18
May 3, 1977	66	19	16
May 17, 1977	64	19	18
May 31, 1977	62	19	18
June 14, 1977	63	18	19
July 5, 1977	62	22	16
July 19, 1977	67	17	16
August 2, 1977	60	23	17
August 16, 1977	66	16	18
September 6, 1977	54	29	17
September 27, 1977	59	23	17
October 11, 1977	55	29	16
October 18, 1977	54	30	16
October 25, 1977	51	30	18
November 1, 1977	55	30	15
November 15, 1977	56	30	14
December 16, 1977	57	27	16
January 3, 1978	55	27	18
January 17, 1978	52	29	20
February 8, 1978	47	35	19
February 21, 1978	50	33	16
March 1, 1978	49	33	18
March 7, 1978	50	35	16
March 28, 1978	47	39	13
April 11, 1978	40	44	16
April 25, 1978	41	42	17
May 3, 1978	41	43	16
May 16, 1978	43	43	14
May 30, 1978	44	41	16
June 13, 1978	42	42	15
July 5, 1978	40	41	19
July 18, 1978	39	44	17
August 1, 1978	39	44	17
August 8, 1978	40	43	17
August 15, 1978	43	41	16
September 5, 1978	42	42	16
September 11, 1978	45	40	15
September 19, 1978	48	34	18
October 29, 1978	49	36	15
December 5, 1978	51	33	15
January 2, 1979	50	36	14
January 16, 1979	43	41	16
January 30, 1979	42	42	16
February 20, 1979	37	46	16
February 27, 1979	39	48	13
March 13, 1979	47	40	14
March 20, 1979	43	44	14

Table 5-3 *(Continued)*

President/date	Approve	Disapprove	No opinion
Carter (continued)			
April 3, 1979	40	46	14
May 1, 1979	37	49	14
May 15, 1979	32	53	15
May 29, 1979	29	56	15
June 19, 1979	29	57	14
June 26, 1979	28	59	13
July 10, 1979	29	58	13
July 30, 1979	32	53	14
July 31, 1979	32	53	15
August 7, 1979	34	55	12
August 14, 1979	32	54	14
September 4, 1979	30	56	15
October 2, 1979	29	59	13
October 14, 1979	31	55	13
November 13, 1979	38	50	13
November 27, 1979	52	37	12
December 4, 1979	54	35	11
January 2, 1980	56	33	10
January 22, 1980	58	32	10
January 29, 1980	55	36	9
February 26, 1980	52	38	10
March 4, 1980	43	45	12
March 24, 1980	50	49	1
April 8, 1980	40	50	11
April 29, 1980	43	47	10
May 13, 1980	38	51	11
May 27, 1980	38	51	10
June 10, 1980	32	56	12
June 24, 1980	31	58	11
July 8, 1980	33	55	12
August 12, 1980	32	55	13
September 9, 1980	37	55	8
November 18, 1980	31	56	13
December 3, 1980	34	55	11
Reagan, I			
January 27, 1981	57	14	36
February 20, 1981	55	18	27
March 10, 1981	59	24	16
March 31, 1981	67	18	15
April 7, 1981	67	19	14
May 5, 1981	68	21	12
June 2, 1981	59	28	13
June 16, 1981	59	29	13
June 23, 1981	58	30	12
July 21, 1981	56	30	14
July 28, 1981	59	28	12
August 11, 1981	60	30	11
September 15, 1981	52	37	11
September 29, 1981	56	35	9
October 27, 1981	54	34	11

(Table continues)

Table 5-3　*(Continued)*

President/date	Approve	Disapprove	No opinion
Reagan, I (continued)			
November 10, 1981	49	40	11
November 17, 1981	55	37	9
December 8, 1981	49	41	10
January 9, 1982	49	40	11
January 23, 1982	47	41	11
February 7, 1982	47	43	10
March 14, 1982	46	45	9
April 4, 1982	45	46	9
April 25, 1982	43	47	10
May 2, 1982	44	46	10
May 16, 1982	45	44	11
June 13, 1982	45	45	10
June 27, 1982	44	46	10
July 25, 1982	42	46	11
August 1, 1982	41	47	12
August 15, 1982	41	49	10
August 29, 1982	42	46	12
September 19, 1982	42	48	10
October 17, 1982	42	48	10
November 7, 1982	43	47	10
November 21, 1982	43	47	10
December 21, 1982	41	50	8
January 16, 1983	37	54	9
January 25, 1983	37	53	10
January 30, 1983	35	56	9
February 27, 1983	40	50	10
March 13, 1983	41	49	10
April 17, 1983	41	49	10
May 1, 1983	43	46	11
May 15, 1983	43	45	12
May 22, 1983	46	43	12
June 12, 1983	43	45	11
June 26, 1983	47	44	9
July 24, 1983	42	47	11
August 1, 1983	44	42	14
August 7, 1983	43	47	10
August 14, 1983	43	45	12
August 21, 1983	43	46	11
September 11, 1983	47	42	11
September 18, 1983	47	43	10
October 10, 1983	45	44	11
October 23, 1983	49	41	10
November 20, 1983	53	37	11
December 11, 1983	54	38	8
January 15, 1984	52	38	10
January 28, 1984	55	36	8
February 11, 1984	56	36	9
March 17, 1984	54	39	8
April 7, 1984	54	37	9
May 19, 1984	53	38	8
June 23, 1984	54	36	10
July 1, 1984	53	37	10
July 7, 1984	53	36	11

Table 5-3   *(Continued)*

President/date	Approve	Disapprove	No opinion
Reagan, I (continued)			
July 28, 1984	52	37	11
September 4, 1984	57	36	7
September 18, 1984	57	37	7
September 25, 1984	54	35	11
October 27, 1984	58	33	9
November 19, 1984	61	31	8
December 1, 1984	62	30	8
December 9, 1984	59	32	9
Reagan, II			
January 11, 1985	62	29	9
January 13, 1985	62	30	9
January 25, 1985	64	28	8
February 15, 1985	60	31	9
March 8, 1985	56	37	7
April 12, 1985	52	37	11
May 17, 1985	55	37	8
June 7, 1985	58	32	10
July 12, 1985	63	28	9
August 13, 1985	65	26	9
September 13, 1985	60	30	10
October 11, 1985	63	29	8
November 1, 1985	62	28	10
November 11, 1985	65	24	11
December 6, 1985	63	29	8
January 10, 1986	64	27	9
March 7, 1986	63	26	11
April 11, 1986	62	29	9
May 16, 1986	68	23	9
June 6, 1986	61	29	10
June 9, 1986	64	26	10
July 11, 1986	63	28	9
August 8, 1986	61	27	12
September 12, 1986	61	25	14
October 24, 1986	63	29	8
December 4, 1986	47	44	9
January 16, 1987	48	43	9
February 27, 1987	40	53	7
March 5, 1987	46	46	8
March 14, 1987	47	44	9
April 10, 1987	48	43	9
June 8, 1987	53	40	7
July 10, 1987	49	43	8
August 24, 1987	49	42	9
December 4, 1987	49	41	10
January 22, 1988	49	40	11
March 9, 1988	51	37	11
April 8, 1988	50	39	11
May 13, 1988	48	43	9
June 10, 1988	51	39	10
July 15,1988	54	36	10

(Table continues)

Table 5-3   *(Continued)*

President/date	Approve	Disapprove	No opinion
Reagan, II (continued)			
August 19, 1988	53	37	11
September 25, 1988	54	37	9
October 21, 1988	51	38	11
November 11, 1988	57	35	8
December 27, 1988	63	29	8
Bush			
January 24, 1989	57	6	43
February 28, 1989	63	13	24
March 10, 1989	56	16	28
April 10, 1989	58	16	26
May 4, 1989	56	22	22
June 8, 1989	70	14	16
July 6, 1989	66	19	15
August 10, 1989	69	19	12
September 7, 1989	70	17	13
October 5, 1989	68	20	12
November 2, 1989	70	17	13
December 7, 1989	71	20	9
January 4, 1990	80	11	11
February 8, 1990	73	16	11
February 15, 1990	73	16	11
March 8, 1990	68	18	14
March 15, 1990	74	15	11
April 5, 1990	68	16	16
April 19, 1990	67	17	16
May 17, 1990	65	20	15
June 7, 1990	67	18	15
June 15, 1990	69	17	14
July 6, 1990	63	24	13
July 19, 1990	63	24	13
August 9, 1990	74	16	10
August 16, 1990	75	16	9
August 23, 1990	76	16	8
August 30, 1990	74	17	9
September 10, 1990	76	16	8
September 14, 1990	73	17	10
September 27, 1990	67	20	13
October 3, 1990	66	25	9
October 11, 1990	56	33	11
October 18, 1990	53	37	10
October 25, 1990	54	36	10
November 1, 1990	58	32	10
November 8, 1990	58	34	8
November 15, 1990	54	33	13
November 29, 1990	61	29	10
December 6, 1990	58	33	9
December 13, 1990	63	30	7
January 3, 1991	58	31	11
January 11, 1991	64	25	11
January 17, 1991	82	12	6
January 19, 1991	80	14	6
January 23, 1991	83	13	4

Table 5-3   *(Continued)*

President/date	Approve	Disapprove	No opinion
Bush (continued)			
January 30, 1991	82	15	3
February 7, 1991	79	18	3
February 14, 1991	80	14	6
February 21, 1991	80	13	7
February 28, 1991	89	8	3
March 7, 1991	87	8	5
March 14, 1991	86	9	5
March 21, 1991	84	10	6
March 28, 1991	82	11	7
April 4, 1991	83	12	5
April 11, 1991	77	13	10
April 25, 1991	76	15	9
May 2, 1991	74	19	7
May 16, 1991	77	15	8
May 23, 1991	76	16	8
May 30, 1991	74	17	9
June 13, 1991	71	19	10
June 27, 1991	72	22	6
July 11, 1991	72	21	7
July 18, 1991	70	21	9
July 25, 1991	71	21	8
August 8, 1991	71	22	7
August 23, 1991	74	18	8
August 29, 1991	69	22	9
September 5, 1991	70	21	9
September 13, 1991	68	22	10
September 26, 1991	66	25	9
October 3, 1991	65	27	8
October 10, 1991	66	28	6
October 17, 1991	66	26	8
October 24, 1991	62	29	9
October 31, 1991	59	33	8
November 7, 1991	56	36	8
November 14, 1991	56	36	8
November 21, 1991	52	39	9
December 5, 1991	52	42	6
December 12, 1991	50	41	9
January 3, 1992	46	47	7
January 16, 1992	46	48	6
January 31, 1992	47	48	5
February 6, 1992	44	48	8
February 19, 1992	39	47	14
February 28, 1992	41	53	6
March 11, 1992	41	47	12
March 20, 1992	41	49	10
March 26, 1992	42	51	7
April 9, 1992	39	54	7
April 20, 1992	42	48	10
May 18, 1992	41	52	7
June 4, 1992	37	56	7
June 12, 1992	37	55	8

(Table continues)

Table 5-3   *(Continued)*

President/date	Approve	Disapprove	No opinion
Bush (continued)			
June 26, 1992	38	55	7
July 24, 1992	32	59	9
July 31, 1992	39	54	7
August 8, 1992	35	58	7
August 21, 1992	40	54	6
August 31, 1992	39	54	7
September 17, 1992	36	54	10
September 11, 1992	39	55	6
September 17, 1992	36	54	10
October 12, 1992	34	56	10
November 20, 1992	43	46	11
December 4, 1992	49	47	4
December 18, 1992	49	41	10
January 8, 1993	56	37	7
Clinton[b]			
January 24, 1993	58	20	22
January 29, 1993	54	30	16
February 12, 1993	51	34	15
February 26, 1993	59	29	12
March 12, 1993	53	34	15
March 29, 1993	52	37	11
April 22, 1993	55	37	8
May 10, 1993	45	44	11
May 21, 1993	44	46	10
June 5, 1993	38	49	14
June 18, 1993	39	50	11
June 29, 1993	46	47	7
July 19, 1993	41	49	10
August 8, 1993	44	48	8
August 23, 1993	44	47	9
September 10, 1993	47	42	11
September 13, 1993	46	43	11
September 24, 1993	56	36	8
October 8, 1993	50	42	8
October 13, 1993	47	44	8
October 28, 1993	48	45	7
November 2, 1993	48	45	7
November 15, 1993	50	43	7
November 19, 1993	48	43	9
December 4, 1993	52	38	10
December 17, 1993	54	40	8
January 6, 1994	54	38	8
January 15, 1994	54	38	8
January 28, 1994	58	35	7
February 26, 1994	53	41	6
March 7, 1994	50	42	8
March 11, 1994	50	41	9
March 25, 1994	52	41	7
March 28, 1994	51	42	7
April 16, 1994	51	41	8
April 22, 1994	48	44	8

Table 5-3   *(Continued)*

President/date	Approve	Disapprove	No opinion
Clinton (continued)			
May 20, 1994	51	42	7
June 3, 1994	46	47	7
June 11, 1994	49	44	7
June 25, 1994	44	47	9
July 1, 1994	43	48	9
July 15, 1994	42	49	9
August 8, 1994	43	48	9
August 15, 1994	39	52	9
September 6, 1994	39	54	7
September 16, 1994	42	50	8
September 23, 1994	44	51	5
October 7, 1994	42	52	6
October 18, 1994	41	52	7
October 22, 1994	48	46	6
November 2, 1994	46	46	8
November 28, 1994	43	49	8
December 2, 1994	42	50	8
December 16, 1994	42	53	5
December 28, 1994	40	52	8

Source: (1945–1976) Adapted from *The Gallup Opinion Index*, Report 182, October–November 1980, 13–59; (1977–1984) calculated from original Gallup survey data; (1985–1994) calculated from successive volumes of *Gallup Poll Monthly*.

[a] Includes full term from November 1963 to January 1969.
[b] 1993–1994 only.

210

Figure 5-1 Popularity Trends, Truman to Clinton

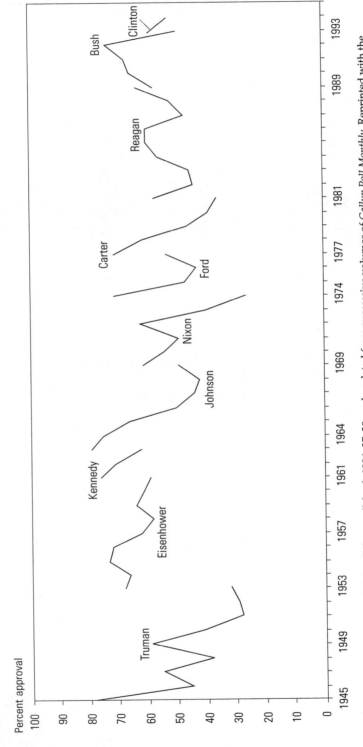

Source: Adapted from *Public Opinion*, February/March 1986, 37–38, and updated from successive volumes of *Gallup Poll Monthly*. Reprinted with the permission of the American Enterprise Institute for Public Policy Research, Washington, D.C.

211

Figure 5-2 Comparison of Carter's and Reagan's Popularity

Percent approval

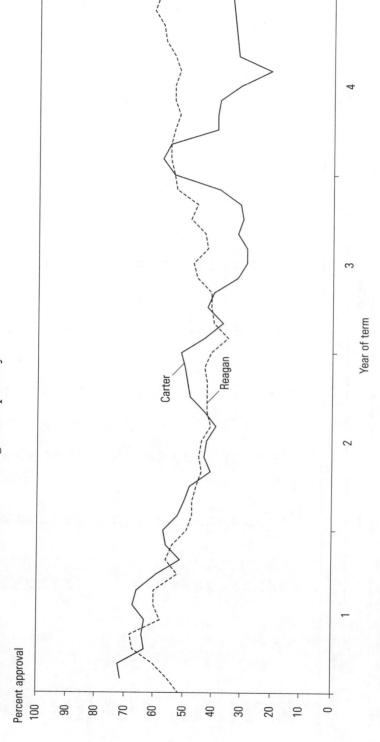

Source: Original Gallup data made available by the Roper Center, Storrs, Connecticut.

Table 5-4 Quarterly Presidential Approval by Party, Region, and Income, Eisenhower to Clinton (average percent per quarter)

President/year/quarter	Party			Region				Income[a, b]		
	Rep.	Dem.	Ind.	East	Midwest	South	West	High	Middle	Low
Eisenhower, I										
1953/1	85	60	69	71	70	70	69	—	—	—
1953/2	88	64	74	73	74	74	74	—	—	—
1953/3	88	57	68	70	70	66	73	—	—	—
1953/4	87	47	64	66	64	61	64	—	—	—
1954/1	90	53	72	67	70	70	69	—	—	—
1954/2	86	46	66	63	63	61	69	—	—	—
1954/3	87	51	70	67	69	64	70	—	—	—
1954/4	87	50	68	64	64	65	66	—	—	—
1955/1	90	55	73	68	70	68	75	—	—	—
1955/2	90	54	70	67	70	66	74	—	—	—
1955/3	90	57	76	74	73	67	77	—	—	—
1955/4	92	62	80	80	79	69	79	—	—	—
1956/1	94	58	78	78	74	69	76	—	—	—
1956/2	92	53	73	76	71	65	69	—	—	—
1956/3	92	49	73	73	67	65	70	—	—	—
1956/4	95	62	80	80	79	69	79	—	—	—
Eisenhower, II										
1957/1	90	55	75	75	71	67	71	—	—	—
1957/2	85	47	65	68	64	58	65	—	—	—
1957/3	84	44	65	68	64	58	65	—	—	—
1957/4	84	40	59	65	62	54	62	—	—	—
1958/1	83	36	56	59	57	47	54	—	—	—
1958/2	81	34	55	59	56	44	56	—	—	—
1958/3	82	39	57	59	56	49	58	—	—	—

1958/4	84	36	56	61	59	42	57	—	—	—
1959/1	85	42	60	63	60	50	60	—	—	—
1959/2	88	47	64	65	63	56	66	—	—	—
1959/3	88	49	68	68	67	58	66	—	—	—
1959/4	90	55	71	70	68	66	74	—	—	—
1960/1	90	48	68	68	66	59	67	—	—	—
1960/2	87	45	67	67	65	53	61	—	—	—
1960/3	86	41	64	62	60	54	59	—	—	—
1960/4	89	40	58	61	60	56	60	—	—	—
Kennedy										
1961/1	56	85	68	74	72	70	75	—	—	—
1961/2	59	88	72	79	78	70	77	—	—	—
1961/3	60	87	73	79	78	70	79	—	—	—
1961/4	59	88	76	80	80	74	78	—	—	—
1962/1	63	90	75	79	81	77	78	—	—	—
1962/2	50	86	71	76	74	68	75	—	—	—
1962/3	39	82	63	68	65	59	67	—	—	—
1962/4	46	87	67	75	73	62	72	—	—	—
1963/1	48	84	68	76	72	63	69	—	—	—
1963/2	40	80	59	71	67	52	65	—	—	—
1963/3	39	75	54	69	63	43	64	—	—	—
1963/4	31	79	55	68	61	45	59	—	—	—
Johnson[c]										
1963/4	73	80	71	76	79	71	80	—	—	—
1964/1	67	84	72	80	78	72	76	—	—	—
1964/2	61	84	68	81	77	65	73	—	—	—
1964/3	—	—	—	—	—	—	—	—	—	—
1964/4	47	85	63	80	72	58	71	—	—	—
1965/1	60	79	72	76	74	64	68	68	76	70
1965/2	51	77	62	79	70	52	63	65	71	67
1965/3	50	77	57	71	67	60	66	64	68	67

(Table continues)

Table 5-4 (Continued)

President/year/quarter	Party			Region				Income[a,b]		
	Rep.	Dem.	Ind.	East	Midwest	South	West	High	Middle	Low
Johnson (continued)										
1965/4	46	76	60	75	64	51	59	65	66	64
1966/1	40	73	47	66	59	45	61	58	59	53
1966/2	33	65	44	59	51	43	48	48	54	52
1966/3	32	67	47	61	51	43	50	52	54	49
1966/4	28	66	40	62	46	40	43	47	48	53
1967/1	25	62	40	55	46	40	42	43	46	49
1967/2	29	61	41	52	46	39	49	46	46	47
1967/3	25	56	37	48	42	34	43	41	42	41
1967/4	25	60	35	49	39	35	44	41	42	41
1968/1	26	57	31	46	39	38	44	38	45	46
1968/2	32	61	39	55	46	39	43	46	49	44
1968/3	24	51	31	43	37	32	36	34	38	45
1968/4	29	59	35	50	43	33	43	41	45	42
Nixon, I										
1969/1	80	51	60	56	64	63	63	67	62	57
1969/2	83	49	58	63	60	63	64	66	64	58
1969/3	82	49	61	60	62	64	62	63	63	57
1969/4	83	49	63	59	64	66	60	67	60	59
1970/1	84	42	62	56	59	64	58	67	60	56
1970/2	81	42	61	55	55	63	59	64	56	53
1970/3	82	40	56	53	55	55	58	58	53	52
1970/4	82	39	55	55	52	61	55	60	55	49
1971/1	80	37	54	52	51	54	49	59	52	43
1971/2	80	34	48	48	48	53	46	52	50	43
1971/3	81	38	49	52	51	54	47	58	53	46
1971/4	85	34	45	52	45	52	47	54	48	43
1972/1	81	35	53	50	50	57	49	56	51	45

1972/2	88	43	62	59	56	68	51	63	59	53
1972/3	88	43	61	58	58	66	50	64	58	59
1972/4	88	44	60	57	60	65	50	66	58	56
Nixon, II										
1973/1	90	49	70	64	65	71	62	71	66	58
1973/2	75	29	47	41	45	51	42	52	42	39
1973/3	63	20	36	36	35	39	33	52	46	39
1973/4	54	17	27	24	29	36	28	31	27	27
1974/1	54	13	26	21	28	32	23	27	25	25
1974/2	51	14	26	22	26	31	27	30	24	25
1974/3	50	13	22	20	21	30	25	27	23	23
Ford										
1974/3	71	56	61	67	76	68	72	76	69	65
1974/4	68	37	49	46	50	47	48	53	47	42
1975/1	61	29	37	35	40	39	38	42	38	33
1975/2	66	37	51	47	47	48	48	54	47	33
1975/3	65	37	46	44	48	45	47	54	42	40
1975/4	63	31	43	39	47	42	41	46	41	35
1976/1	66	35	50	40	47	47	51	51	44	38
1976/2	68	35	49	41	49	50	49	52	42	42
1976/3	74	37	52	45	54	52	50	—	—	—
1976/4	80	40	54	49	58	54	51	—	—	—
Carter										
1977/1	56	81	70	67	67	72	63	73	72	66
1977/2	48	72	62	65	62	63	65	64	62	62
1977/3	47	73	61	63	64	63	60	64	62	60
1977/4	40	66	53	55	54	58	56	56	56	56
1978/1	34	60	53	53	55	55	47	48	51	54
1978/2	25	53	38	43	39	44	37	33	43	44
1978/3	20	52	36	40	38	40	44	40	47	52
1978/4	31	63	52	52	53	54	50	51	51	60

(Table continues)

Table 5-4 (*Continued*)

President/year/quarter	Party			Region				Income[a, b]		
	Rep.	Dem.	Ind.	East	Midwest	South	West	High	Middle	Low
Carter (continued)										
1979/1	24	55	43	47	38	46	42	44	43	41
1979/2	20	43	33	33	33	38	34	30	36	38
1979/3	19	36	24	25	25	34	26	25	28	31
1979/4	28	48	36	—	—	—	—	—	—	—
1980/1	42	65	50	56	55	63	47	54	55	57
1980/2	28	57	35	42	43	53	36	52	44	48
1980/3	14	48	20	28	30	42	25	50	33	38
1980/4	14	49	30	28	35	38	36	33	31	43
Reagan, I										
1981/1	80	39	57	52	56	57	55	65	54	39
1981/2	89	49	66	62	66	66	64	74	64	47
1981/3	85	42	60	55	60	60	60	72	58	40
1981/4	84	33	53	50	53	52	51	61	47	31
1982/1	82	27	50	45	48	48	49	57	45	32
1982/2	79	24	47	44	46	44	45	56	43	30
1982/3	76	21	44	42	44	39	42	55	41	28
1982/4	79	22	44	39	44	40	48	55	41	29
1983/1	67	19	41	37	39	35	38	48	37	27
1983/2	78	26	49	45	44	45	50	57	46	29
1983/3	83	30	52	48	50	50	50	61	54	37
1983/4	87	33	54	50	55	55	51	64	61	44
1984/1	86	33	56	52	54	61	53	70	66	43
1984/2	85	32	58	52	51	54	59	71	58	45
1984/4	92	32	63	56	60	65	52	70	62	43
Reagan, II										
1985/1	88	39	61	57	64	64	63	71	68	51
1985/2	87	24	55	50	54	57	59	65	59	44

Period										
1985/3	53	70	74	56	72	67	63	68	39	90
1985/4	56	66	70	66	62	55	67	63	39	90
1986/1	56	65	73	65	65	61	61	60	40	88
1986/2	56	70	78	67	68	67	69	70	51	88
1986/3	54	67	69	64	64	61	66	65	44	88
1986/4	—	—	—	50	47	48	45	45	24	74
1987/1	34	50	59	50	48	47	49	49	23	80
1987/2	41	49	53	45	54	48	44	50	24	76
1987/3	36	45	58	45	50	50	50	48	28	78
1987/4	36	48	57	50	54	47	43	51	21	78
1988/1	—	—	—	50	57	51	46	51	28	81
1988/2	—	—	—	—	—	—	—	—	—	—
1988/3	48	47	56	59	54	48	49	49	29	78
1988/4	42	54	63	49	58	54	51	55	24	87
Bush										
1989/1	48	44	56	53	57	48	47	47	38	69
1989/2	50	55	65	50	62	60	58	51	42	81
1989/3	66	68	73	67	71	72	66	66	59	83
1989/4	61	72	74	69	70	63	68	66	49	87
1990/1	71	78	85	76	81	77	75	75	64	93
1990/2	60	60	71	64	71	66	59	63	51	86
1990/3	61	71	78	66	73	68	69	66	58	86
1990/4	—	—	—	—	—	—	—	—	—	—
1991/1	77	86	87	83	84	82	80	80	72	95
1991/2	65	80	85	75	83	75	72	74	63	94
1991/3	67	72	79	73	70	72	69	66	61	88
1991/4	52	62	67	57	67	58	57	57	37	80
1992/1	36	44	50	42	46	41	42	38	21	71
1992/2	38	42	42	42	43	40	38	36	18	68
1992/3	32	36	42	40	37	35	32	30	13	70
1992/4	34	44	49	39	45	43	40	38	19	75

(Table continues)

218

Table 5-4 (Continued)

President/year/quarter	Party			Region				Income[a, b]		
	Rep.	Dem.	Ind.	East	Midwest	South	West	High	Middle	Low
Clinton[d]										
1993/1	28	82	51	63	53	51	57	52	53	61
1993/2	23	75	35	50	52	45	47	44	49	53
1993/3	24	73	43	53	50	44	42	41	48	52
1993/4	24	77	46	54	51	46	50	47	49	52
1994/1	28	78	54	59	54	51	54	48	55	59
1994/2	24	77	46	59	47	47	48	49	52	50
1994/3	17	76	40	47	48	39	42	35	45	47
1994/4	14	77	46	55	48	44	46	38	45	52

Source: (1953–1964) George Edwards III and George Gallup, Presidential Approval (Baltimore: John Hopkins University Press, 1989), reprinted by permission of the Johns Hopkins University Press; (1965–1976) compiled from The Gallup Public Opinion Index, periodic volumes; (1977–1984) from the author's analysis of original Gallup surveys; (1988–1994) from Gallup Poll Monthly, successive volumes.

Note: Each number is the average of all Gallup Polls for which the breakdowns were reported for that quarter. "—" indicates not available.

[a] Gallup provides respondents with a series of family income categories for self-placement. These have been collapsed into three broad classifications of low, middle, and high income. The income categories reported by Gallup that were at or below the family poverty line, as taken from census data, constitutes the low-income category. Gallup breakdowns that ranged around the national mean income, again as reported by the census, represent the middle-income classification. Finally, incomes that fell into the highest brackets specified by Gallup make up the high-income category.

[b] Data on income from 1953–1964 are not available.

[c] Includes full term from November 1963 to January 1969.

[d] 1993–1994 only.

Table 5-5 Party, Regional, and Income Differences in Presidential Approval by Term, Eisenhower to Clinton (average percent approving per term)

President	Party			Region			Income[a, b]		
	Republicans	Democrats	Differences	Non-South	South	Difference	High	Low	Difference
Eisenhower, I	90	55	35	71	67	4	—	—	—
Eisenhower, II	86	44	42	63	54	9	—	—	—
Kennedy	49	84	−35	73	63	10	—	—	—
Johnson	40	69	−29	58	48	10	50	52	−2
Nixon, I	83	39	44	55	61	−6	62	52	10
Nixon, II	62	22	40	34	41	−7	41	34	7
Ford	68	37	31	49	49	0	54	41	13
Carter	29	55	−26	43	48	−6	45	47	−2
Reagan, I	77	29	48	47	48	−1	59	34	25
Reagan, II	83	32	51	55	58	−3	65	47	18
Bush	77	44	33	59	64	−5	67	55	12
Clinton[c]	23	77	−54	51	46	5	44	53	−8

Source: (Eisenhower and Kennedy) George Edwards III and George Gallup, *Presidential Approval* (Baltimore: Johns Hopkins University Press, 1989), reprinted by permission of the Johns Hopkins University Press; (Johnson through Ford) compiled from *The Gallup Public Opinion Index*, periodic volumes; (Carter through Reagan, II) from author analysis of original Gallup surveys; (Bush and Clinton) from *Gallup Poll Monthly*, successive volumes.

[a] Gallup provides respondents with a series of family income categories for self-placement. These have been collapsed into three broad classifications of low, middle, and high income. The income categories reported by Gallup that were at or below the family poverty line, as taken from census data, constitutes the low-income category. Gallup breakdowns that ranged around the national mean income, again as reported by the census, represent the middle-income classification. Finally, incomes that fell into the highest brackets specified by Gallup make up the high-income category.

[b] Data on income from 1953 to 1964 (Eisenhower through Kennedy) are not available.

[c] 1993–1994 only.

Table 5-6   Quarterly Presidential Approval by Race and Gender, Eisenhower to Clinton (average percent per quarter)

President/year/quarter	Race		Gender	
	White	Nonwhite[a]	Men	Women
Eisenhower, I				
1953/1	71	56	71	69
1953/2	75	57	74	73
1953/3	69	56	68	70
1953/4	65	49	62	65
1954/1	70	54	69	69
1954/2	65	48	62	64
1954/3	68	56	67	68
1954/4	65	56	65	64
1955/1	71	58	70	70
1955/2	69	63	70	68
1955/3	73	64	73	72
1955/4	77	71	75	78
1956/1	76	65	74	75
1956/2	72	60	70	72
1956/3	70	60	68	70
1956/4	77	73	78	76
Eisenhower, II				
1957/1	72	60	70	72
1957/2	63	55	63	64
1957/3	62	55	60	63
1957/4	56	68	59	56
1958/1	54	54	52	56
1958/2	54	50	51	56
1958/3	56	50	54	57
1958/4	56	46	54	56
1959/1	59	48	58	59
1959/2	64	50	62	60
1959/3	65	60	64	66
1959/4	70	61	68	70
1960/1	66	56	63	67
1960/2	64	47	61	62
1960/3	62	50	58	62
1960/4	61	44	58	60
Kennedy				
1961/1	72	77	73	72
1961/2	74	80	76	75
1961/3	76	80	79	75
1961/4	77	84	80	76
1962/1	79	82	78	80
1962/2	71	86	73	73
1962/3	64	86	66	65
1962/4	69	85	71	70
1963/1	68	85	70	70
1963/2	61	85	63	65
1963/3	56	87	57	62
1963/4	54	87	57	60

Table 5-6   *(Continued)*

President/year/quarter	Race		Gender	
	White	Nonwhite[a]	Men	Women
Johnson[b]				
1963/4	76	76	77	75
1964/1	76	81	77	76
1964/2	72	86	75	73
1964/3	—	—	—	—
1964/4	68	95	72	68
1965/1	67	89	70	69
1965/2	65	86	68	66
1965/3	61	90	65	64
1965/4	60	85	64	62
1966/1	55	82	59	57
1966/2	48	74	51	48
1966/3	47	78	52	48
1966/4	43	71	47	44
1967/1	43	66	48	44
1967/2	46	66	49	46
1967/3	39	67	41	40
1967/4	40	61	44	41
1968/1	41	63	41	42
1968/2	42	60	45	43
1968/3	35	58	39	38
1968/4	42	71	45	43
Nixon, I				
1969/1	60	50	60	58
1969/2	66	38	64	62
1969/3	63	42	62	60
1969/4	62	33	63	57
1970/1	64	30	62	56
1970/2	60	26	60	54
1970/3	59	27	57	55
1970/4	58	29	59	52
1971/1	54	31	55	49
1971/2	52	25	50	48
1971/3	53	26	49	50
1971/4	53	23	52	49
1972/1	56	25	55	51
1972/2	61	34	60	56
1972/3	—	—	—	—
1972/4	66	27	64	59
Nixon, II				
1973/1	64	31	62	59
1973/2	51	20	47	47
1973/3	37	14	35	34
1973/4	31	12	29	28
1974/1	29	9	27	26
1974/2	29	11	27	26
1974/3	26	9	25	23

(Table continues)

Table 5-6   *(Continued)*

President/year/quarter	Race		Gender	
	White	Nonwhite[a]	Men	Women
Ford				
1974/3	64	51	62	63
1974/4	51	30	47	50
1975/1	41	22	37	39
1975/2	48	25	45	45
1975/3	47	29	44	46
1975/4	46	25	44	44
1976/1	49	30	48	47
1976/2	49	33	46	47
1976/3	—	—	—	—
1976/4	58	27	53	54
Carter				
1977/1	70	76	71	70
1977/2	64	66	64	64
1977/3	61	66	63	60
1977/4	54	62	55	55
1978/1	49	58	50	50
1978/2	41	54	42	42
1978/3	41	52	42	42
1978/4	49	61	50	54
1979/1	42	51	43	43
1979/2	32	41	31	34
1979/3	37	39	31	32
1979/4	39	45	39	40
1980/1	50	56	50	51
1980/2	37	39	35	39
1980/3	31	51	32	36
1980/4	30	55	29	36
Reagan, I				
1981/1	60	22	59	52
1981/2	69	23	67	59
1981/3	63	19	63	52
1981/4	58	18	57	48
1982/1	53	13	57	44
1982/2	50	15	49	40
1982/3	46	14	46	37
1982/4	47	14	47	39
1983/1	42	13	42	34
1983/2	48	18	48	34
1983/3	50	14	50	39
1983/4	55	18	56	46
1984/1	59	19	59	50
1984/2	58	21	58	50
1984/3	60	18	59	51
1984/4	66	24	64	57
Reagan, II				
1985/1	65	32	63	58
1985/2	60	23	58	51
1985/3	65	34	66	58
1985/4	67	35	67	60

Table 5-6   *(Continued)*

President/year/quarter	Race		Gender	
	White	Nonwhite[a]	Men	Women
Reagan, II (continued)				
1986/1	67	35	68	60
1986/2	67	37	70	58
1986/3	66	36	65	59
1986/4	55	32	56	50
1987/1	50	21	49	43
1987/2	53	24	53	46
1987/3	51	21	54	42
1987/4	53	23	55	45
1988/1	53	23	56	44
1988/2	53	25	54	45
1988/3	57	25	59	48
1988/4	61	29	62	52
Bush				
1989/1	58	50	60	54
1989/2	63	49	64	59
1989/3	71	57	75	66
1989/4	72	57	71	67
1990/1	78	62	79	72
1990/2	69	58	69	66
1990/3	71	45	73	63
1990/4	61	28	62	53
1991/1	82	55	86	78
1991/2	77	53	77	72
1991/3	73	55	72	68
1991/4	53	40	56	46
1992/1	45	29	45	41
1992/2	43	25	39	42
1992/3	38	19	39	33
1992/4	45	23	44	40
Clinton[c]				
1993/1	53	77	55	56
1993/2	45	73	44	51
1993/3	45	65	45	49
1993/4	46	73	47	52
1994/1	51	71	53	55
1994/2	46	71	50	50
1994/3	41	64	42	45
1994/4	44	72	48	47

Source: (1953–1988) George Edwards III and George Gallup, *Presidential Approval* (Baltimore: Johns Hopkins University Press, 1989), reprinted by permission of the Johns Hopkins University Press; (1989–1994) data taken from successive volumes of *Gallup Poll Monthly*.

Note: Each number is the average of all Gallup polls for which the breakdowns were reported for that quarter. "—" indicates not available.

[a] Includes African-Americans, Mexican-Americans, Native Americans, and Asian-Americans.
[b] Includes full term from November 1963 to January 1969.
[c] 1993–1994 only.

Table 5-7   Race and Gender Differences in Presidential
Approval by Term, Eisenhower to Clinton
(average percent approving per term)

President	Race			Gender		
	White	Nonwhite[a]	Difference	Men	Women	Difference
Eisenhower, I	71	59	12	70	70	0
Eisenhower, II	62	53	9	60	62	2
Kennedy	68	84	−16	70	70	0
Johnson[b]	53	75	−22	57	54	−3
Nixon, I	59	31	28	58	54	−4
Nixon, II	38	15	23	36	35	−1
Ford	50	30	20	45	46	1
Carter	45	55	−10	46	47	1
Reagan, I	55	18	37	55	46	−9
Reagan, II	59	28	31	60	52	−8
Bush	62	44	18	63	58	−5
Clinton[c]	46	71	−25	51	48	−3

Sources: (Eisenhower through Reagan) George Edwards III and George Gallup, *Presidential Approval* (Baltimore: Johns Hopkins University Press, 1989), reprinted by permission of the Johns Hopkins University Press; (Bush and Clinton) data taken from successive volumes of *Gallup Poll Monthly.*

[a] Includes African-Americans, Mexican-Americans, Native Americans, and Asian-Americans.
[b] Includes full term from November 1963 to January 1969.
[c] 1993–1994 only.

Table 5-8 Quarterly Presidential Approval by Age and Education Level, Eisenhower to Clinton (average percent per quarter)

President/ Year/quarter	Age			Education		
	18–29	30–49	50 and over	Grade School	High School	College
Eisenhower, I						
1953/1	71	68	71	64	72	78
1953/2	73	73	74	66	76	85
1953/3	71	69	69	62	72	72
1953/4	65	63	64	57	65	70
1954/1	70	66	71	63	69	76
1954/2	62	61	67	57	65	72
1954/3	67	66	69	65	68	74
1954/4	64	63	67	58	66	72
1955/1	69	69	71	63	71	79
1955/2	67	68	71	65	69	77
1955/3	73	72	73	66	74	81
1955/4	78	76	78	73	78	80
1956/1	76	73	75	69	76	81
1956/2	73	70	72	66	72	78
1956/3	72	68	69	64	69	75
1956/4	79	76	78	73	79	79
Eisenhower, II						
1957/1	73	71	69	66	72	74
1957/2	69	64	61	60	65	68
1957/3	65	61	60	57	62	68
1957/4	61	57	58	53	58	64
1958/1	58	53	55	60	55	59
1958/2	56	52	54	47	54	61
1958/3	57	54	56	53	56	61

(Table continues)

Table 5-8 (*Continued*)

President/ Year/quarter	Age			Education		
	18–29	30–49	50 and over	Grade School	High School	College
Eisenhower, II (continued)						
1958/4	59	56	54	52	56	60
1959/1	61	56	61	53	59	66
1959/2	64	61	63	56	64	69
1959/3	68	64	64	57	67	73
1959/4	71	68	69	62	71	77
1960/1	69	64	65	57	68	72
1960/2	63	62	61	58	63	67
1960/3	62	59	62	58	61	64
1960/4	62	57	60	54	61	63
Kennedy						
1961/1	77	75	68	71	72	76
1961/2	79	78	70	73	77	72
1961/3	80	79	72	75	78	73
1961/4	82	80	74	77	81	76
1962/1	87	80	74	77	81	76
1962/2	81	76	67	74	75	66
1962/3	77	69	58	65	67	62
1962/4	78	73	65	69	74	64
1963/1	79	74	63	68	73	67
1963/2	71	67	57	63	67	59
1963/3	67	62	54	60	61	57
1963/4	69	61	53	59	60	53
Johnson[a]						
1963/4	77	75	68	69	72	66
1964/1	81	76	76	75	77	79

	74	75	73	72	76	76
1964/2	—	—	—	—	—	—
1964/3	—	—	—	—	—	—
1964/4	65	71	74	68	73	68
1965/1	66	72	69	68	71	71
1965/2	66	68	66	65	69	70
1965/3	61	67	64	62	64	72
1965/4	60	64	63	59	65	68
1966/1	54	58	60	56	59	61
1966/2	48	50	51	46	52	54
1966/3	48	51	51	46	52	55
1966/4	38	46	49	46	44	48
1967/1	43	46	47	46	45	45
1967/2	48	48	45	40	48	49
1967/3	39	41	41	41	41	43
1967/4	40	44	40	44	44	40
1968/1	36	42	46	44	41	36
1968/2	44	44	44	40	45	42
1968/3	36	38	42	45	38	36
1968/4	36	45	47		43	44
Nixon, I						
1969/1	64	60	53	58	59	61
1969/2	70	63	57	62	63	65
1969/3	65	63	53	59	61	64
1969/4	66	61	52	61	59	61
1970/1	67	59	51	59	59	59
1970/2	65	57	48	55	58	58
1970/3	58	56	52	57	57	53
1970/4	57	57	51	57	56	53
1971/1	59	51	45	53	51	50
1971/2	50	50	46	50	51	45
1971/3	53	50	48	54	49	45
1971/4	57	50	42	52	52	47

(Table continues)

Table 5-8 (*Continued*)

President/ Year/quarter	Age			Education		
	18–29	30–49	50 and over	Grade School	High School	College
Nixon, I (continued)						
1972/1	49	55	54	44	53	60
1972/2	54	56	59	54	58	61
1972/3	—	—	—	—	—	—
1972/4	56	61	64	59	62	62
Nixon, II						
1973/1	55	62	64	55	62	61
1973/2	43	49	47	42	48	48
1973/3	32	33	38	31	35	38
1973/4	24	28	39	34	33	35
1974/1	23	25	30	27	26	27
1974/2	22	26	30	27	26	28
1974/3	20	24	26	21	24	26
Ford						
1974/3	64	61	62	58	60	70
1974/4	51	48	47	42	49	53
1975/1	40	38	37	29	37	46
1975/2	45	45	44	37	44	54
1975/3	50	46	41	32	44	58
1975/4	48	46	39	35	44	50
1976/1	50	46	46	40	47	52
1976/2	50	48	45	40	46	52
1976/3	—	—	—	—	—	—
1976/4	56	47	56	45	52	59
Carter						
1977/1	75	71	67	67	71	73

1977/2	69	65	60	60	62	71
1977/3	67	62	56	55	60	67
1977/4	60	55	50	52	54	57
1978/1	55	50	47	52	49	49
1978/2	48	40	39	45	41	41
1978/3	46	40	41	46	42	39
1978/4	53	50	51	56	51	49
1979/1	53	49	47	51	49	52
1979/2	37	31	31	35	32	35
1979/3	33	31	31	34	31	31
1979/4	41	37	40	42	39	39
1980/1	52	49	51	53	50	50
1980/2	40	34	37	40	37	35
1980/3	37	31	35	41	35	29
1980/4	38	28	33	38	35	26
Reagan, I						
1981/1	54	58	54	36	57	62
1981/2	62	66	72	47	63	71
1981/3	57	60	56	41	57	66
1981/4	52	54	51	38	52	60
1982/1	47	49	47	32	47	55
1982/2	44	46	44	35	42	54
1982/3	43	42	40	32	40	50
1982/4	41	43	43	29	41	51
1983/1	40	39	43	24	37	48
1983/2	42	46	43	32	42	53
1983/3	46	45	43	31	42	54
1983/4	49	52	50	40	48	56
1984/1	55	56	52	40	52	61
1984/2	56	56	51	36	51	62
1984/3	55	57	52	41	52	61
1984/4	62	60	59	45	57	65

(Table continues)

Table 5-8 (Continued)

President/ Year/quarter	Age			Education		
	18–29	30–49	50 and over	Grade School	High School	College
Reagan, II						
1985/1	66	59	57	43	59	66
1985/2	58	57	50	36	51	63
1985/3	65	63	57	42	60	67
1985/4	66	64	60	47	62	69
1986/1	67	66	59	51	61	69
1986/2	68	67	58	44	63	69
1986/3	69	65	54	44	61	67
1986/4	56	54	48	48	54	59
1987/1	50	48	41	35	44	50
1987/2	53	52	48	40	49	51
1987/3	52	49	42	37	44	53
1987/4	55	51	45	44	48	53
1988/1	54	49	48	41	49	53
1988/2	54	48	47	43	48	51
1988/3	60	53	48	41	52	56
1988/4	59	58	54	50	55	59
Bush						
1989/1	54	50	50	41	53	58
1989/2	63	60	49	41	56	62
1989/3	70	70	68	64	70	74
1989/4	70	72	72	68	71	71
1990/1	73	75	71	63	74	78
1990/2	68	68	62	57	67	71
1990/3	63	66	53	46	61	70

1990/4	53	63	46	45	52	61
1991/1	73	74	76	75	76	70
1991/2	84	84	78	72	83	84
1991/3	73	74	66	64	75	68
1991/4	60	54	37	50	50	47
1992/1	54	41	35	34	42	46
1992/2	46	43	37	39	40	43
1992/3	39	31	28	27	35	40
1992/4	44	43	43	36	39	50
Clinton[b]						
1993/1	60	54	54	c	56	57
1993/2	55	48	45	c	50	47
1993/3	47	48	49	c	48	49
1993/4	51	49	50	c	50	54
1994/1	54	54	53	c	50	57
1994/2	50	51	49	c	51	49
1994/3	46	43	44	c	42	46
1994/4	50	47	48	c	51	48

Sources: (1953–1988) George Edwards III and George Gallup, *Presidential Approval* (Baltimore: Johns Hopkins University Press, 1989), reprinted by permission of Johns Hopkins University Press; (1989–1994) data taken from successive volumes of *Gallup Poll Monthly*.

Note: Figures are the average of all Gallup polls for which the breakdowns were reported for that quarter. "—" indicates not available.

[a] Includes full term from November 1963 to January 1969.

[b] 1993–1994 only.

[c] Due to a change in Gallup survey techniques, grade school data not available.

Table 5-9 Age and Education Differences in Presidential Approval by Term, Eisenhower to Clinton (average percent approving per term)

President	Age			Education		
	18–29	50 and over	Difference	Grade school	College	Difference
Eisenhower, I	71	71	0	64	77	–13
Eisenhower, II	64	61	3	56	67	–11
Kennedy	77	65	12	69	67	2
Johnson[a]	57	54	3	56	52	4
Nixon, I	55	57	–2	50	61	–11
Nixon, II	31	39	–8	34	38	–4
Ford	50	46	4	40	55	–15
Carter	50	45	5	48	46	2
Reagan, I	50	50	0	36	58	–22
Reagan, II	60	51	9	43	60	–17
Bush	62	54	8	51	62	–11
Clinton[b]	52	49	3	c	51	—

Sources: (Eisenhower through Reagan) George Edward III and George Gallup, *Presidential Approval* (Johns Hopkins University Press, 1989), reprinted by permission of the Johns Hopkins University Press; (Bush and Clinton) data taken from successive volumes of *Gallup Poll Monthly.*

[a] Includes full term from November 1963 to January 1969.
[b] 1993–1994 only.
[c] Due to a change in Gallup survey techniques, grade school data not available.

Table 5-10 Public Approval of Presidents' Handling of the Economy and Foreign Policy, Nixon to Clinton (percent)

President/date	Economy[a]			Foreign policy[b]		
	Approve	Disapprove	Don't know/ no opinion	Approve	Disapprove	Don't know/ no opinion
Nixon[c]						
June 21, 1974	—	—	—	54	32	14
Ford[c]						
November 8, 1974	32	48	20	—	—	—
January 31, 1975	29	57	14	—	—	—
April 18, 1975	30	59	11	—	—	—
Average approval	30					
Carter[c]						
May 1977	47	53	—	—	—	—
June 1977	44	56	—	—	—	—
July 1977	41	59	—	48	52	—
August 1977	39	61	—	—	—	—
September 1977	35	65	—	32	68	—
October 1977	32	68	—	38	62	—
November 1977	33	67	—	38	62	—
December 1977	34	66	—	42	58	—
January 1978	28	72	—	43	57	—
February 1978	27	73	—	38	62	—
April 1978	22	78	—	29	71	—
June 1978	21	79	—	25	75	—
July 1978	16	84	—	22	78	—
August 1978	16	84	—	22	78	—
September 1978	22	78	—	56	44	—

(Table continues)

Table 5-10 (Continued)

President/date	Economy[a]			Foreign policy[b]		
	Approve	Disapprove	Don't know/ no opinion	Approve	Disapprove	Don't know/ no opinion
Carter (continued)						
November 1978	23	77	—	47	53	—
December 1978	27	73	—	46	54	—
February 1979	22	78	—	37	63	—
March 1979	16	84	—	45	55	—
Average approval	29			38		
Reagan, I						
February 13, 1981	—	—	—	51	16	33
March 13, 1981	56	32	12	53	29	18
April 10, 1981	60	29	11	—	—	—
May 8, 1981	58	31	11	—	—	—
June 26, 1981	51	40	9	—	—	—
August 14, 1981	53	35	12	—	—	—
September 25, 1981	59	34	7	—	—	—
October 1, 1981	53	37	9	—	—	—
October 9, 1981	—	—	—	63	30	7
October 30, 1981	45	43	12	—	—	—
November 13, 1981	40	50	10	—	—	—
November 17, 1981	46	46	8	—	—	—
December 11, 1981	41	50	9	—	—	—
January 8, 1982	41	51	8	—	—	—
January 22, 1982	46	46	8	52	33	15
February 5, 1982	38	53	9	44	38	18
February 17, 1982	38	57	5	40	41	19

March 3, 1982	42	53	5	45	43	12
March 12, 1982	56	32	12	36	44	20
March 18, 1982	43	52	5	43	45	12
April 2, 1982	38	56	6	36	45	19
April 21, 1982	44	51	5	53	34	14
April 30, 1982	37	55	8	43	37	20
May 24, 1982	40	53	7	46	35	19
June 11, 1982	35	58	7	45	36	19
August 17, 1982	40	55	5	—	—	—
September 9, 1982	41	52	7	50	35	15
September 24, 1982	40	55	5	43	45	13
October 5, 1982	41	51	9	44	39	17
October 15, 1982	36	56	8	38	39	23
December 7, 1982	38	58	5	45	33	22
January 14, 1983	29	64	7	36	41	23
January 18, 1983	38	58	5	45	33	22
February 25, 1983	43	54	3	—	—	—
April 8, 1983	42	54	4	—	—	—
April 15, 1983	29	64	7	32	44	24
August 19, 1983	37	54	9	31	46	23
November 18, 1983	48	46	6	46	41	13
January 13, 1984	48	43	9	38	49	13
February 10, 1984	49	44	7	40	46	14
May 3, 1984	48	46	6	42	44	14
May 18, 1984	49	43	8	37	48	15
November 9, 1984	—	—	—	50	35	15
November 30, 1984	57	36	7	—	—	—
Average approval	44			44		
Reagan, II						
January 11, 1985	51	41	8	52	33	15
March 3, 1985	51	44	5	45	39	16

(Table continues)

Table 5-10 (*Continued*)

President/date	Economy[a] Approve	Economy[a] Disapprove	Economy[a] Don't know/ no opinion	Foreign policy[b] Approve	Foreign policy[b] Disapprove	Foreign policy[b] Don't know/ no opinion
Reagan, II (continued)						
May 17, 1985	47	47	8	43	45	12
July 12, 1985	53	39	8	50	37	13
October 11, 1985	48	44	8	—	—	16
January 10, 1986	53	38	9	50	34	13
April 11, 1986	50	40	10	52	35	14
July 11, 1986	49	43	8	51	35	9
December 4, 1986	50	45	5	34	57	10
January 16, 1987	—	—	—	33	57	10
April 10, 1987	42	53	5	33	57	6
June 8, 1987	48	49	3	37	57	9
August 24, 1987	46	49	5	34	57	11
March 8, 1988	40	53	7	41	48	11
July 1, 1988	43	51	6	54	35	
Average approval	48			44		
Bush						
March 10, 1989	52	27	21	62	15	23
November 2, 1989	40	51	9	65	21	14
July 6, 1990	40	53	7	62	26	12
October 11, 1990	30	65	5	61	29	10
March 7, 1991	37	—	—	79	—	—
March 28, 1991	37	56	7	79	11	10
June 27, 1991	36	58	6	64	28	8
July 25, 1991	34	59	7	71	19	10

August 8, 1991	36	59	5	74	20	6
August 23, 1991	36	—	—	74	—	—
September 13, 1991	32	—	—	70	—	—
October 3, 1991	29	64	7	70	25	5
October 24, 1991	28	—	—	68	—	—
December 5, 1991	22	73	—	64	30	—
January 3, 1992	24	—	—	64	—	—
January 31, 1992	22	—	—	65	—	—
February 28, 1992	21	—	—	55	—	—
May 7, 1992	20	—	—	52	—	—
Average approval	32	76	—	67	43	—
Clinton[d]						
February 12, 1993	45	35	20	53	22	25
March 29, 1993	49	42	9	55	30	15
April 22, 1993	43	50	7	53	34	13
May 21, 1993	35	59	6	44	43	12
June 18, 1993	36	56	8	48	36	16
June 29, 1993	35	59	6	56	33	11
July 9, 1993	34	60	6	49	38	13
August 8, 1993	38	57	5	46	44	10
August 23, 1993	38	53	9	48	39	13
September 10, 1993	39	50	11	46	36	18
September 24, 1993	47	45	8	55	32	13
October 8, 1993	43	48	9	40	52	8
November 2, 1993	37	57	6	34	57	9
November 19, 1993	43	50	7	41	49	10
December 4, 1993	47	46	7	45	44	11
January 6, 1994	49	45	6	45	43	12
January 15, 1994	46	47	7	54	36	10
January 28, 1994	53	40	7	52	37	11
February 26, 1994	48	48	4	51	40	9

(Table continues)

Table 5-10 *(Continued)*

President/date	Economy[a] Approve	Disapprove	Don't know / no opinion	Foreign policy[b] Approve	Disapprove	Don't know / no opinion
Clinton (continued)						
March 7, 1994	51	42	7	51	38	11
April 22, 1994	45	48	7	39	51	10
May 20, 1994	50	45	5	37	52	11
June 3, 1994	47	46	7	39	50	11
June 11, 1994	49	45	6	44	45	11
June 25, 1994	43	48	9	34	52	14
July 15, 1994	36	57	7	33	60	7
August 15, 1994	42	49	9	34	52	14
September 6, 1994	43	52	5	34	57	9
September 23, 1994	40	55	5	40	55	5
October 18, 1994	38	57	5	—	—	—
October 22, 1994	42	53	5	—	—	—
Average approval	43			45		

Sources: (Nixon and Ford) Data taken from various volumes of *Gallup Opinion Index*; (Carter through Clinton) adapted from various issues of the *Gallup Report* and *Gallup Poll Monthly*.

Note: "—" indicates question not asked.

[a] Question asked was: (Nixon and Carter) "How would you rate [incumbent] on his handling of the economy—excellent, pretty good, only fair, or poor?" (Reagan through Clinton) "Do you approve or disapprove of the way [incumbent] is handling the nation's economy?"

[b] Question asked was: (Nixon and Carter) "How would you rate [incumbent] on his handling of foreign policy—excellent, pretty good, only fair, or poor?" (Reagan through Clinton) "Do you approve or disapprove of the way [incumbent] is handling foreign affairs?"

[c] Approval is the percentage who rated [incumbent] excellent or pretty good in each policy area.

[d] 1993–1994 only.

Table 5-11   The Public's Most Important Problem, 1935–1994

Year	Problem
1935	Unemployment
1936	Unemployment
1937	Unemployment
1938	Keeping out of war
1939	Keeping out of war
1940	Keeping out of war
1941	Keeping out of war, winning war
1942	Winning war
1943	Winning war
1944	Winning war
1945	Winning war
1946	High cost of living
1947	High cost of living, labor unrest
1948	Keeping peace
1949	Labor unrest
1950	Labor unrest
1951	Korean War
1952	Korean War
1953	Keeping peace
1954	Keeping peace
1955	Keeping peace
1956	Keeping peace
1957	Race relations, keeping peace
1958	Unemployment, keeping peace
1959	Keeping peace
1960	Keeping peace
1961	Keeping peace
1962	Keeping peace
1963	Keeping peace, race relations
1964	Vietnam, race relations
1965	Vietnam, race relations
1966	Vietnam
1967	Vietnam, high cost of living
1968	Vietnam
1969	Vietnam
1970	Vietnam
1971	Vietnam, high cost of living
1972	Vietnam
1973	High cost of living, Watergate
1974	High cost of living, Watergate, energy crisis
1975	High cost of living, unemployment
1976	High cost of living, unemployment
1977	High cost of living, unemployment
1978	High cost of living, energy problems
1979	High cost of living, energy problems
1980	High cost of living, unemployment
1981	High cost of living, unemployment

(Table continues)

Table 5-11 *(Continued)*

Year	Problem
1982	Unemployment, high cost of living
1983	Unemployment, high cost of living
1984	Unemployment, fear of war
1985	Fear of war
1986	Unemployment
1987	Fear of war
1988	Economy in general
1989	Drugs
1990	Economy in general
1991	Economy in general
1992	Economy in general
1993	Economy in general
1994	Crime/violence

Sources: (1935–1984) Adapted from *Gallup Report*, October 1984, 22; (1985–1994) adapted from *Gallup Poll Monthly*, various issues.

Table 5-12   The Party Best Able to Handle the Most Important Problem, 1945–1994 (percent)

Year	Month	Republican	Democratic	Uncommitted
1945	August	23	48	29
1946	August	35	34	31
1948	April	32	28	40
1950	September	19	27	54
1956	October	33	25	42
1958	February	19	40	41
1958	March	23	39	38
1959	February	26	34	40
1959	March	26	41	33
1959	October	27	29	44
1960	March	24	32	44
1960	July	23	36	41
1960	August	35	36	29
1960	October	27	29	44
1962	April	16	40	44
1962	September	17	33	50
1963	April	17	36	47
1963	October	23	49	28
1964	March	16	39	45
1964	May	16	40	44
1964	July	25	38	37
1964	October	23	49	28
1965	June	16	37	47
1965	August	16	36	48
1965	October	17	34	49
1965	December	17	38	45
1966	May	22	29	49
1966	September	21	28	51
1967	November	30	28	42
1968	May	28	30	42
1968	July	31	27	42
1968	September	37	25	38
1968	October	34	29	37
1970	February	27	25	48
1970	August	19	31	50
1970	October	21	30	49
1971	June	20	30	50
1971	August	18	35	47
1971	December	22	32	46
1972	May	28	34	38
1972	October	39	29	32
1974	January	15	39	46
1974	June	16	38	46
1974	August	20	38	42
1974	September	13	39	48
1974	October	18	39	43

(Table continues)

Table 5-12   *(Continued)*

Year	Month	Republican	Democratic	Uncommitted
1975	February–March	14	42	44
1975	October	15	42	43
1976	January	18	40	42
1976	April	18	39	43
1976	October	23	43	34
1977	October	14	38	48
1978	February	19	35	46
1978	April	22	32	46
1978	July	19	33	48
1978	September	20	34	46
1978	October	21	31	48
1979	February	23	29	48
1979	March	23	29	48
1979	May	21	31	48
1979	August	20	30	50
1979	October	25	33	42
1980	January	21	34	45
1980	March	28	32	40
1980	July	30	27	43
1980	September	35	32	33
1980	October	40	31	29
1981	January–February	39	20	41
1981	May	36	21	43
1981	October	32	29	39
1982	January	30	34	36
1982	April	25	35	40
1982	June	28	35	37
1982	August	26	35	39
1982	October	29	41	30
1983	April	20	41	39
1983	July	24	38	38
1983	November	28	35	37
1984	February	30	32	38
1984	June	33	35	32
1985	January	39	29	24
1985	October	32	32	23
1986	July	33	36	21
1987	April	29	37	34
1988	September	38	33	29
1989	—	—	—	—
1990	October	30	29	41
1991	March	40	27	41
1992	March	34	40	26
1993	January	29	45	26
1993	September	31	37	32
1994	January	31	39	30

Sources: (1945–1984) Adapted from *Gallup Report,* July 1984, 21; (1985–1994) adapted from various issues of *Gallup Poll Monthly.*

Note: "—" indicates not available.

Table 5-13 Confidence in Leaders of Major Institutions, 1966–1994 (percent)

Date	Survey organization	Major institution									
		White House[a]	Congress	Supreme Court	Medicine	Education	Military	Organized religion	Companies	Press	Organized labor
February 1966	Harris	41	42	50	72	61	62	41	55	29	22
January 1967[b]	Harris	37	41	40	60	56	56	40	47	26	20
August 1971	Harris	23	19	23	61	37	27	27	27	18	14
October 1972[b]	Harris	27	21	28	48	33	36	29	27	18	15
March 1973	NORC	29	24	32	54	37	32	35	29	23	16
September 1973	Harris	19	30	33	58	44	40	36	30	30	20
December 1973	Harris	13	17	—	60	46	—	29	28	28	16
March 1974	NORC	14	17	33	60	49	40	44	31	26	18
August 1974	Harris	28	18	40	49	39	34	32	22	25	17
September 1974	Harris	18	16	35	48	39	31	32	16	26	18
March 1975	NORC	13	13	31	50	31	35	24	19	24	10
April 1975	Harris	13	14	29	43	36	24	32	20	26	14
August 1975	Harris	16	12	28	54	37	30	36	20	28	18
March 1976	Harris	16	18	32	—	—	36	—	22	21	—
March 1976	NORC	14	14	35	54	38	39	31	22	28	12
January 1977	Harris	23	16	29	42	37	28	29	20	18	14
March 1977	NORC	28	19	36	52	41	36	40	27	25	15
November 1977	Harris	23	15	31	55	41	31	34	23	19	15
March 1978	NORC	13	13	28	46	28	30	31	22	20	11
August 1978	Harris	14	10	29	42	41	29	34	22	23	15
February 1979	Harris	17	18	28	30	33	29	20	18	28	10
March 1980	NORC	12	9	25	52	30	28	35	27	22	15
November 1980	Harris	17	18	27	34	36	28	22	16	19	14
September 1981	Harris	24	16	29	37	34	28	22	16	16	12

(Table continues)

Table 5-13 (*Continued*)

Date	Survey organization	White House[a]	Congress	Supreme Court	Medicine	Education	Military	Organized religion	Companies	Press	Organized labor
							Major institution				
March 1982	NORC	19	13	31	45	33	31	32	23	18	12
November 1982	Harris	20	13	25	32	30	31	20	18	14	8
March 1983	NORC	13	10	27	52	29	29	28	24	13	8
November 1983	Harris	23	20	33	35	36	35	22	18	19	10
March 1984	NORC	19	13	35	52	29	37	32	32	17	9
November 1984	Harris	42	28	35	43	40	45	24	19	18	12
1985	Gallup	—	39	56	—	48	61	66	31	35	28
1986	Gallup	—	41	54	—	49	63	57	28	37	29
1987	Gallup	—	—	52	—	50	61	61	25	31	26
1988	Gallup	—	35	56	—	49	58	52	—	36	26
1989	Gallup	—	32	46	—	43	63	56	25	—	—
1990	Gallup	—	24	47	—	45	68	59	26	39	27
March 1991	Gallup	72	30	48	—	44	85	56	22	32	25
October 1991	Gallup	50	18	39	—	35	69	56	22	32	22
1993	Gallup	43	18	44	34	39	68	53	22	31	26
1994	Gallup	38	18	42	36	34	64	54	26	29	26

Sources: (1966–1984) Adapted from *Public Opinion*, April/May 1985, 8; (1985–1994) adapted from *Gallup Poll Monthly*, April 1994, 6. Reprinted with the permission of the American Enterprise Institute for Public Policy Research, Washington, D.C.

Note: NORC—National Opinion Research Center. The question for NORC and Harris was "As far as the people *running* various institutions are concerned, would you say you have a great deal of confidence, only some confidence, or hardly any confidence at all in them?" Figures are percentage of respondents answering "a great deal." The Gallup questions was "How much confidence do you have in [the institution]—a great deal, quite a lot, some, or very little." Figures are percentage of respondents answering "a great deal" and "quite a lot." "—" indicates question not asked.

[a] "White House" (Harris), "Executive Branch" (NORC), and "the presidency" (Gallup).
[b] Electoral participants only.

6

Presidential Organization and the Executive Branch

Chapters 2 and 3 considered elections as a structural element of the presidency. Chapters 4 and 5 analyzed public appearances and public opinion as behavioral elements of the institution. This chapter and the next examine the organizational aspects of the presidency. The current chapter details the size and shape of the organization, while Chapter 7 considers how the organization makes decision. There is perhaps no better or more tangible evidence of the institutional nature of the presidency than the large, ongoing, decentralized organization that surrounds presidents. Currently consisting of some 40 units, 1,600 people, and a budget of $100 million, its design clarifies the extent to which the institution has a life of its own and presidents are merely one, albeit important, player among many.

Presidents must respond to the dual problems of organization and administration in defining the executive office. Chief executives organize information and communication so that they can elicit the best advice possible for decision making. They also attempt to coordinate and control the activities of government and thereby administer the decisions that have been made. This chapter outlines three different strategies that presidents have used to address these challenges: (1) control of the bureaucratic administration surrounding the president, (2) cultivation of intimacy among the president's immediate advisers, and (3) attention to political representativeness in appointments to executive departments and agencies. Unhappily, data on the last two strategies are not as readily available as data on the first strategy. This imbalance in the empirical record does not imply any imbalance in the presidents' proportionate use of the three.

The Bureaucratic Administration

According to Max Weber, the first strategy involves "the exercise of control on the basis of knowledge" (1947, 339). The key words are *control*   **245** and *knowledge*. The advisory staff, put in place to obtain information, is also used to control subsequent decisions. The staff acts primarily on the basis of what Weber calls "rational-legal authority." Established, universal rules guide the behavior of individuals who occupy offices and gain their legitimized status from their official positions. This strategy suggests the need for a staff of experts who can act as both presidential advisers and administrative officers.

The first outlines of the bureaucratic administrative approach emerged as presidents sought advice and used the administrative skills of their cabinet members, who had specific spheres of competence and who occupied offices established by law (Fenno, 1959). However, the cabinet's role was always severely limited by its partisan character. Because of this, a full-fledged bureaucratic administrative strategy evolved in the White House beginning in the 1920s and was permanently fixed there in 1939 when three important changes in the makeup of the presidency as a collective office occurred: (1) the Executive Office of the President (EOP) was created, which serves as an official staff arm for presidents, (2) the Bureau of the Budget (BOB) was transferred from the Treasury Department to the executive office, and (3) White House Office (WHO) was formally organized within the EOP.

Each of these changes led to the establishment of "rational-legal" authority on impersonal terms—the offices and spheres of competence were present regardless of who worked within them and who was president. During the ensuing years, the organization of the executive office followed three central patterns of establishment.[1] First, boundaries were defined between the executive office as an organization and other executive departments and agencies. Second, the complexity of the organization increased as more functions became internally separated and more functions were added to the office. Third, universalistic and automatic modes of decision making were implemented within the EOP, especially at the BOB, which was reorganized and renamed the Office of Management and Budget (OMB) in 1970.

Organizational Boundaries

The organizational integrity of the executive office hinges on two key parameters: personnel size and budget resources. Table 6-1 and Figure 6-1 present data on the initial size of the executive staff, its expansion, and its eventual relative stability.[2] Tables 6-2 through 6-4 and Figure 6-2 examine the growth in expenditures for the White House organization.

Boundaries do not appear haphazardly but result from the various incentives and interests within the political institutions involved. Growth in the number of employees and in the budgets of the organizational presidency have had three main sources: presidential initiatives, congressional initiatives, and joint presidential-congressional efforts.

Presidential Initiatives. One of the principal sources of growth in the organizational presidency has been presidential efforts to develop and coordinate programs from the executive office. Presidents have used the executive office, and more narrowly the WHO, as visible organizational centers for their efforts. Presidents' initiatives are apparent in the statistics shown in Table 6-1 on the growth of the EOP and the units within it. Unevenness of growth over time, especially in the early period of these offices, stemmed partly from presidential responses to unpredictable changes in the political and policy environments. Franklin Roosevelt sought to coordinate both domestic and military efforts of American involvement in World War II through the EOP, which employed nearly 200,000 people in 1943 at the height of the war. The White House supervised various war establishment units, including the Office of War Mobilization, the Office for Emergency Management, the Board of Economic Warfare, the Office of Price Administration, and the Selective Service System.

Several other presidential initiatives were more the results of presidents' own interests rather than the vagaries of political events. Harry S. Truman dismantled the wartime executive office but increased the size of the WHO nearly fourfold. This increase was meant to provide a base for policy interests that Truman wished to pursue in the form of an annual presidential legislative program (Moe, 1985, 251; Hess, 1976, 44–58). "Responsiveness, however, can breed dependency" (Helmer, 1981, 63), and the size of the WHO never decreased after Truman's early expansion.

The next large increase in the size of the WHO occurred in 1971, when Richard Nixon attempted to control federal departments from the White House (Nathan, 1983). Contrary to popular belief about the dramatic growth of the office, Nixon's doubling of the number of employees in the WHO, while dramatic, was notably less than the fourfold increase by Truman. "It is [also] a common misconception to regard the current EOP as the legacy of the Nixon period" (Helmer, 1981, 61). In fact, as the figures in Table 6-1 make clear, the greatest expansion of the total EOP in the post-World War II period occurred in 1958 under Dwight D. Eisenhower and in 1966 under Lyndon B. Johnson. Eisenhower pursued some restructuring and additions to the management responsibilities of the EOP (Berman, 1979, 58–63). Johnson tried to centralize programs of the Great Society in the White House (Moe, 1985, 253–254). The executive office under Nixon was on average no larger than it was under Johnson after 1966.

The size of the executive office was reduced only once in the postwar period. In the aftermath of Watergate, Gerald Ford decreased the EOP by

67 percent, eliminating some of the agencies and councils established during the Nixon years. In the process, he did not reduce the size of the WHO or the OMB. Indeed, both increased slightly by comparison with their counterparts during the Nixon administration. Although presidents since Ford have proclaimed that they will cut the size of the White House, as an example for the rest of the government, they have been only marginally successful in their efforts. The size of the EOP has been roughly stable since Ford. It decreased only 7 percent from the Ford to the Carter administrations and another 7 percent from the Carter to the Reagan administration. The size of the EOP during the Bush administration and the first year of Bill Clinton's term returned to where it stood under Jimmy Carter.

Presidential initiatives need not be as dramatic as the large staff increases and decreases noted above. As Table 6-1 shows, increases in the BOB/OMB were consistently incremental after boosts by Franklin Roosevelt, who added 453 staff members to this office in the 1939–1943 period. Although presidential scholars often note that the OMB was reorganized and enlarged after 1970 (Moe, 1985, 256), the analysis here indicates that personnel increased only 17 percent from 1970 to 1971, considerably less than the largest increase of 96 percent from 1940 to 1941.

Congressional initiatives. Despite its name, many units of the EOP were the creation of Congress and were either not sought by presidents or actually opposed by them. Congress contributed to the growth of the office because it desired policy coordination from a central agency. Efforts by Congress to enlarge and consolidate the executive office are evident from the data in Table 6-1. The Council of Economic Advisers (CEA) was created by congressional passage of the Employment Act of 1946, which gave the president the responsibility to "use all practicable means . . . to promote maximum employment, production, and purchasing power" (60 U.S. Statutes 24, February 20, 1946). The CEA has remained roughly the same size since it was founded (37 people in 1949, 31 people in 1993). The National Security Act of 1947, which gave presidents responsibility for coordinating national defense and foreign policy, also gave presidents a committee of advisers—the National Security Council (NSC). Unlike the CEA, the NSC has increased in size as a result of presidential initiative. Most notably, for a short period under Eisenhower (1958–1960) policy formation and implementation were separated into two boards in the NSC staff system, and hence the council size increased. A second increase occurred in 1970 when Nixon instructed Henry Kissinger, his newly named head of the NSC, to reestablish an "Eisenhower NSC system" (Kissinger, 1979).

Presidents, however, have not always appreciated congressional initiatives taken to enlarge the executive office. The Council on Environmental

Quality, established by Congress in 1970, was actively resisted by Nixon, even though he later called it one of his accomplishments (Hess, 1976, 124).

Congress, of course, is at a disadvantage in establishing presidential agencies. Congressional initiatives are ultimately translated by presidents as they see fit, and chief executives have considerable flexibility in making as much or as little as they desire of the offices provided. In addition, Congress is usually unable to reclaim authority in a policy area once it has established the executive apparatus.

Joint Efforts of Presidents and Congress.   Presidents and Congress have also combined efforts to establish firmer boundaries for the executive office and units within it. In addition to creating more units with more personnel, the two branches have increased the budgets for the existing organizational units. Table 6-2 shows the average expenditures of the executive office and selected units within it. Table 6-3 presents annual appropriation and expenditure figures for the WHO and the total executive office. Table 6-4 lists similar figures for other key units of the EOP.

A comparison of Table 6-1 with Tables 6-2 through 6-4 shows that the number of personnel assigned to the executive offices and the amounts of money spent in running these offices are quite different. The staff of the EOP has grown only 30 percent in the period since 1949, whereas expenditures have increased nearly thirteen times during the same years. Even calculated in constant dollars, the executive office budget shows a 200 percent increase. This growth is largely explained by budget increases in just two units—the WHO and the BOB/OMB. The budget of the former increased eighteen times in current dollars (and doubled in constant dollars) since 1949, though its staff size grew by a relatively moderate 63 percent. As Table 6-4 indicates, the budget of the latter grew eleven times in current dollars (and nearly doubled in constant dollars), with only a 7 percent increase in staff over the same period. The budget growth of these two units helps to illuminate some of the anomalies between the two sets of figures. Johnson's efforts to coordinate the Great Society, for instance, left the expenditures of the EOP virtually unchanged but increased the money spent by the BOB. Ford's personnel cutbacks in 1975 were countered by increases in expenditures during 1975 and 1976, with the largest increases observed in monies for the WHO and the OMB. The budget figures presented in Table 6-4 also show that the reorganization of the OMB was accompanied by budgetary expansion (a 58 percent increase from 1970 to 1972), though not personnel expansion.

Perhaps most intriguing, these budgetary figures indicate that relatively few attempts were made by presidents since Johnson to work with less money. Figure 6-2 displays the budget growth in real dollars for the total executive office, the WHO, and the BOB/OMB since 1924. Presidents may reduce the number of personnel for the total executive office, as Ford did, or for any one agency in the executive office, but they do not tamper with the overall budgets of these units. Carter and Ronald Reagan achieved very modest decreases in the budgets for the three offices, which were reversed during the Bush administration and the first year of the Clinton administration.

Presidents and Congresses by and large accept the work of their predecessors, which is etched in the institutional history of the organization. A rare case in which a president actually attempted to dismantle an organization occurred when Reagan attempted to curtail funds for the Council on Environmental Quality. Yet, with pressure from Congress and citizens' groups, Reagan's efforts at budget-cutting were not fully successful. During his term of office, as Table 6-4 reveals, there was a tug-of-war between congressional appropriations and presidential expenditures for the council. Congress from 1981 to 1984 authorized more money than the council actually spent. Ironically, in 1985, the council's expenditures more than quadrupled, although its budget authority was somewhat curtailed by Reagan.

Organizational Complexity

Greater size typically means greater complexity. The larger an organization, the more likely internal differentiation will occur. In many ways the internal complexity of an office reflects the complexity of the environment. Presidents attempt to satisfy disparate policy goals and policy groups by creating special offices or councils within the EOP. These special offices need not last long to allow presidents to exhibit their concern about a particular problem or group. Table 6-5 depicts the organizational units of the executive office since its creation in 1939. Although the core of offices in the EOP remains well established today, other units, such as the Permanent Advisory Committee on Government Organizations (1953–1961), have come and gone within and across presidential administrations. Not surprisingly, every president wants to put his own stamp on the EOP, either by adding, subtracting, or renaming units. Another indicator of complexity is depicted in Table 6-6, which lists the current Clinton administration roster of fifteen offices in the EOP. Table 6-7 lists the twenty-four units of the WHO. The level of specialization, especially in the WHO, is striking.

Another way of examining complexity is to consider the way in which members of the WHO moved from generalist to specialist positions over time. Table 6-8 shows that the number of White House staff members who held explicit roles has increased dramatically since 1939. From 1939 to 1943, more than 90 percent of the staff had no functional title. By the late 1970s and the 1980s, more than 90 percent of the staff had functional roles. The final column of the table reports the number of self-identified subunits in the WHO. The number jumped sharply in 1975, from six to thirty where it has remained relatively stable.

Automatic Decisions

The OMB engages in five types of automatic procedures in handling the high volume of presidential business: budget clearance, adopted in 1924; executive order clearance, adopted in 1936; legislative clearance, adopted in 1924; enrolled bill clearance, adopted in 1938; and a relatively recent innovation: administrative clearance, adopted in 1981. (These procedures are discussed in more detail in Chapters 7 and 8.)

Budget clearance procedures require all departments and agencies of the federal government to submit their budget requests to the OMB for approval. Similarly, legislative clearance procedures require departments and agencies to submit their legislative proposals to the OMB. All department or agency initiatives must be "in accord with the president's program" before they are sent to Capitol Hill. The OMB also screens executive orders, many of which are submitted to the White House by departments and agencies, before presidents sign them.

Enrolled bill procedures involve the OMB's examination of legislation that has passed Congress and awaits the president's signature. Given that some nine hundred pieces of legislation are passed by Congress each year, presidents are unlikely to be familiar with very many of them. Departments in the executive branch make recommendations to the OMB, which in turn advises the White House as to whether the president should sign a given bill; presidents only involve themselves in the process when most of the work has already been done.

Administrative clearance involves a system by which the OMB reviews administrative rule making. The clearance process arose from precedents set by Nixon, Ford, and Carter and was formally codified by Reagan in Executive Order No. 12291. The Office of Information and Regulatory Affairs within the OMB screens various rules and regulations drafted by departments and agencies. Each agency must provide a "regulatory impact analysis" of final regulations, justifying costs, benefits, and possible alternatives (West and Cooper, 1985). The OMB then determines, on the basis of these analyses, whether the rules are consistent with the White House criteria. If they are not, the rules are returned to the appropriate agency for modification. Table 6-9 summarizes OMB action on these administrative rules. Although most of the regulations are approved by the OMB, any intervention by the office is significant. The increasing organizational diffusion and standard operating procedures of the OMB are reflected in its budgeting, as well as its legislative and rule-making tasks.

Size and Permanence

The most significant outcome of the bureaucratic administration strategy is the magnitude and scope of the presidential entourage. This feature produces considerable institutional continuity across presidential administrations. Presidents find dismantling entrenched organizational/administrative units quite difficult, and it is usually either not worth the effort or not in their best interest to do so.

Presidents' Intimates

A second strategy by which presidents may gain knowledge and control involves personal intimacy—engaging with those whom the executives are familiar. This strategy reflects a desire among all heads of state, not just American presidents, to surround themselves with individuals who are personally loyal. As Aristotle wrote, "It is already the practice of kings to make themselves many eyes and ears and hands and feet. For they make colleagues of those who are friends of themselves and their governments" (1943, 165). Thus, the knowledge is not expertise, as it is in the bureaucratic administration approach, but intimacy. As Frederic Malek, an adviser on personnel for Nixon has commented, "You don't get the best people. You get the people you know" (1978, 64).

Apart from the broad organizational units, presidents have always relied on small groups of loyal advisers. This partly reflects presidents' inability to interact easily with the large White House staff and their desire to seek advice on key decisions from a manageable group of loyalists. These personal advisers often reflect idiosyncrasies associated with a given president, in contrast to the established procedures and organizations within the executive office that extend from one president to the next.

An examination of the backgrounds of presidents' immediate advisers reveal that there are many similarities between presidents and their advisers. People nicknamed John F. Kennedy's intimates the "Irish mafia"; they included Kenneth O'Donnell, Lawrence O'Brien, and Robert Kennedy. Johnson brought Texans Walter Jenkins, Bill Moyers, and Jack Valenti to the White House. Nixon invited Californians H. R. Haldeman and John Ehrlichman and longtime friend John Mitchell. Ford relied on many former colleagues in Congress, including Sen. Robert Griffin of Michigan, former Wisconsin representative Melvin Laird, and Rep. Richard Cheney of Wyoming. Carter was identified with a contingent of Georgians who came to Washington, including Bert Lance, Charles Kirbo, and Hamilton Jordan. Reagan looked to longtime friends and Californians such as William French Smith, William Clark, Edwin Meese, and Michael Deaver. George Bush relied on friends from the presidential campaign—John Sununu, governor of New Hampshire, and James Baker, a member of the Reagan administration. Clinton's so-called "Arkansas Mafia" included boyhood friend and first chief of staff Thomas "Mac" McLarty, Deputy White House Counsel Vincent Foster, and senior adviser Bruce Lindsay.

Table 6-10 lists the people who have held the position of White House chief of staff since 1932.

In outlook and values presidents' advisers are likely to differ from members of the larger executive office. Presidents and their intimates often make decisions on long-range plans and more crisis-oriented issues concerning domestic, foreign, and military affairs. Yet, scholars too often concentrate on the decisions made by this small group, as though this was the only decision-making group worthy of study. They overlook that many of the decisions of the president and his closest advisers depend on information, positions, and decisions provided by the larger presidential organization. In addition, the organizational apparatus that surrounds each president and his advisers makes thousands of decisions that are attributed to the president, although he and his advisers know little about them.

Political Representation and the Executive Branch

Presidents also pursue a third strategy: political representativeness. Individuals are chosen on the basis of their political backgrounds—their partisan affiliations or ties to specific social groups. These presidential appointees are of a different sort from those chosen through the intimacy strategy. Most obviously, presidents reward members of their own party with positions in the government, or presidents select enthusiasts with a policy outlook similar to their own. Presidents also select as appointees representatives from particular social groups, including women, racial and ethnic minorities, and people from specific geographic regions.

Presidents most often invoke this option in the appointment of people to key policy-making positions in the executive departments and agencies. Presidents are nominally "in charge" of the executive branch, but they do *not* control it. Tables 6-11 and 6-12 make clear why contemporary presidents find it so difficult to wield any real clout over executive departments and why "infiltration" of departments with party supporters is not easily accomplished. Table 6-11 details the size of executive departments. Table 6-12 gives employment figures for the independent agencies of the government.

Since the "spoils system" appointments made by Andrew Jackson, presidents have appointed numerous individuals on the basis of partisan or ideological persuasion as a way of leaving their imprint "on the vast executive apparatus upon which the effective management of [their] programs depends" (Brown 1982, 282). Table 6-13 shows the full scope of appointments presidents make that require Senate approval. Most of them involve the commissioning of officers in the armed services, which are not only pro forma appointments but also pro forma confirmations. Of the approximately sixty thousand recommendations that presidents since

Truman have sent to the Senate each year, only about two thousand are political appointments (MacKenzie, 1981, 4–5). Of these, the number that
represents highly placed policy executives is smaller still. As Table 6-14
shows, presidents since Kennedy have on average made fewer than seven
hundred major appointments to such positions as department secretaries,
undersecretaries, assistant secretaries, agency heads, and ambassadors.

Presidents do have considerable leeway in making cabinet appointments, as Table 6-15 shows. The Senate rarely rejects a cabinet nomination.
However, this leeway cannot be equated with control of the appointment
process. Presidents cannot know whom to appoint to all positions. And
their reliance on party and ideology as qualifications for employment
offers no guarantee that the right person will be found for the job.
Table 6-16 traces the appointment of party people to departmental posts
for Presidents Kennedy through Reagan. It shows that presidential appointments to the so-called political departments—those with clientele
groups such as Agriculture, Commerce, Housing and Urban Development,
and Labor—are quite partisan. Other departments, requiring more traditionally specialized backgrounds, such as Defense and State, have fewer
partisan appointments. Reagan's attempt to place as many party stalwarts
as possible in federal departments is evidenced in this table: he made more
partisan appointments than any other president. Indeed, Reagan has the
highest overall percentage of party appointments of any president since
Franklin Roosevelt. An early study, using data somewhat different from
those presented here, examined appointees by Presidents Franklin Roosevelt through Eisenhower and found that fully 89 percent of Roosevelt's, 84
percent of Truman's, and 76 percent of Eisenhower's appointees were partisan (Stanley, Mann, and Doig, 1967). Beyond the problem of knowing
those hired, presidents face another difficulty in controlling their administrations: political executives, whether or not they come from the president's party, tend not to stay in government very long. Calvin MacKenzie
reports that from 1945 through 1977 the median term of service for a cabinet secretary was only 2.1 years, with 40 percent staying less than 2 years
(1981, 7–8). Turnover at the subcabinet level is comparable.

Conclusion

The three strategies—bureaucratic administration, personal intimacy,
and political representation—are distinct yet often overlap. In the simplest
terms, the bureaucratic strategy says, "Get the best people possible," the
intimacy strategy says, "Get the people you know best," and the representation approach says, "Get people from the party and interest groups."
The people presidents select following each of the three strategies may be
the same—for instance, the president may appoint as national security ad-

viser a party stalwart who is a longtime friend and an expert on foreign policy. In addition, the goal of each strategy is identical: to centralize organizational and administrative control in the White House. Separately and together, however, the strategies result in wholly decentralized mechanisms for decision making. Appointees to departments and agencies are both physically and bureaucratically distant from presidents. Experts on the White House staff are not much closer. Even personal intimates of presidents sometimes feign ignorance of presidential involvement or their own involvement in controversial decisions and give the impression that decisions were made elsewhere.

Chief executives are confronted with a keen dilemma. They seek *singular* control of information and policy decisions but are forced to work through a *collective* apparatus. The pastiche of staffs, interests, and loyalties makes it difficult for presidents to gain either the information or the control they seek. The problem presidents face is that they do not control the collective organization, although the collectivity has considerable control over many of their decisions. "When those subject to bureaucratic control seek to escape the influence of the existing bureaucratic apparatus, this is normally possible only by creating an organization of their own which is equally subject to the process of bureaucratization" (Weber, 1947, 338).

The WHO, as a specific unit within the larger executive office, thus symbolizes presidents' power. It was established to give presidents immediate information and advice on pressing national problems that could not readily be obtained from the larger executive office. But this immediacy has vanished with the emergence of a bureaucracy of over four hundred people. In common parlance, presidents "have administrations," but they, in fact, administer much less than does the broad organizational unit of the executive office. Through the organizational diffusion of the presidency, "the president" and "his administration" have become more independent from each other and less interdependent.

The problem of control seems inherently unsolvable. Presidents could not control cabinet departments, so they increased the size of the EOP. Because the EOP was itself too big and too diverse to control, presidents then expanded the WHO. The single individual in the Oval Office can personally supervise only a limited number of people, organizations, offices, agencies, goals, desires, plans, and programs, and this number cannot be expanded by reorganization or reallocation of control. The growth of the executive office (or any office) adds an inertial feature to the institution, emphasizing its separateness from other, already established organizations. The unit soon adopts rules and patterns of behavior that define the autonomy of the group and the regularity of its operation. As Terry Moe has noted, "organizations have their own routines, their own agendas, their own norms, their own ways of coding and interpreting the world" (1985, 240). Presidents, too, must learn to play by these organizational rules.

Notes

1. This discussion is adapted from Polsby (1968, 144–168). Polsby uses the term *institutionalization* to denote the process of establishing fixed procedures for decision making, routines and sanctions for hiring and firing, and the establishment of official positions within an organization. Because this book describes the institution of the presidency and not just the institutionalization of its administrative component, the term is avoided here.
2. Tables 6-1 through 6-4 and Figures 6-1 and 6-2 begin with President Coolidge since his is the first full term with available data from the budget of the United States on presidential staff expenditures. Note also that, although the White House staff was formally designated the White House Office in 1939, Tables 6-2 through 6-4 use this term for all presidents listed.

Table 6-1 Size of Executive Office of the President, Coolidge to Clinton

President/year	Number of units	Total executive staff	White House Office	Bureau of Budget/OMB	National Security Council	Council of Economic Advisers	Council of Environmental Quality	All others
Coolidge								
1924	1	133	38	—	—	—	—	—
1925	1	133	38	—	—	—	—	—
1926	1	137	37	—	—	—	—	—
1927	1	141	37	—	—	—	—	—
1928	1	135	37	—	—	—	—	—
Average for term		136	37					
Hoover								
1929	1	131	36	—	—	—	—	—
1930	1	139	36	—	—	—	—	—
1931	1	114	37	—	—	—	—	—
1932	1	109	37	—	—	—	—	—
Average for term		123	37					
Roosevelt, I								
1933	1	110	50	—	—	—	—	60
1934	1	107	49	—	—	—	—	58
1935	1	97	44	—	—	—	—	53
1936	1	98	44	—	—	—	—	54
Average for term		103	47					56
Roosevelt, II								
1937	1	100	45	—	—	—	—	55
1938	1	105	45	—	—	—	—	60
1939	6	631	45	103	—	—	—	483
1940	6	647	63	156	—	—	—	428
Average for term		371	47	130				257

(Table continues)

Table 6-1 (Continued)

President/year	Number of units	Total executive staff	White House Office	Bureau of Budget/ OMB	National Security Council	Council of Economic Advisers	Council of Environmental Quality	All others
Roosevelt, III								
1941	6	21,428	53	305	—	—	—	21,070[a]
1942	5	86,817	49	459	—	—	—	86,309[a]
1943	4	194,194	51	556	—	—	—	193,587[a]
1944	4	182,833	50	546	—	—	—	182,237[a]
Average for term		121,318	51	467	—	—	—	120,801[a]
Roosevelt/Truman								
1945	3	174,138	61	565	—	—	—	173,512[a]
Truman, I								
1946	4	95,068	61	718	—	—	—	94,289[a]
1947	6	43,232	293	562	—	—	—	42,377[a]
1948	6	1,118	210	561	19	43	—	285[a]
Average for term		46,472	188	614				45,650[a]
Truman, II								
1949	6	1,167	223	512	17	37	—	381
1950	6	1,256	295	520	17	36	—	388
1951	8	1,219	259	522	19	41	—	378
1952	9	1,434	245	498	23	34	—	634
Average for term		1,269	256	513	19	37	—	445
Eisenhower, I								
1953	9	1,376	248	457	24	34	—	613
1954	7	1,175	266	419	28	26	—	436
1955	7	1,167	290	438	28	35	—	370

1956	8	1,196	374	27	31	—	334
Average for term		1,229	295	27	32	—	438
Eisenhower, II							
1957	8	1,218	387	26	31	—	332
1958	10	2,660	394	64	28	—	1,734
1959	9	2,631	405	65	34	—	1,696
1960	9	2,919	446	65	32	—	1,942
Average for term		2,357	408	55	31	—	1,426
Kennedy							
1961	7	2,838	411	56	35	—	1,851
1962	8	1,676	467	44	44	—	626
1963	9	1,659	388	39	38	—	684
Average for term		2,058	422	46	39	—	1,054
Johnson[b]							
1964	10	1,542	349	43	42	—	588
1965	11	2,849	333	38	46	—	1,908
1966	12	4,683	295	37	53	—	3,672
1967	12	4,813	272	38	55	—	3,795
1968	12	5,306	273	35	78	—	4,326
Average for term		3,839	304	38	55	—	2,858
Nixon							
1969	14	5,167	344	46	53	—	4,142
1970	15	4,742	311	75	59	32	3,632
1971	17	5,360	660	83	59	54	3,777
1972	17	5,639	596	81	70	57	4,132
1973	15	4,804	542	82	53	56	3,434
Average for term		5,142	491	73	59	50	3,823
Nixon/Ford							
1974	15	5,751	583	85	42	61	4,292

(Table continues)

Table 6-1 (Continued)

President/year	Number of units	Total executive staff	White House Office	Bureau of Budget/OMB	National Security Council	Council of Economic Advisers	Council of Environmental Quality	All others
Ford								
1975	13	1,910	625	699	89	40	61	422
1976	15	1,899	541	724	95	39	69	431
Average for term		1,905	583	712	92	40	65	427
Carter								
1977	12	1,716	464	709	73	38	49	383
1978	11	1,613	371	602	74	33	49	484
1979	11	1,818	408	637	74	23	48	646
1980	11	1,886	406	616	69	35	49	711
Average for term		1,758	412	641	73	82	49	556
Reagan, I								
1981	11	1,683	394	677	67	34	16	495
1982	11	1,596	366	612	60	40	12	506
1983	11	1,621	384	611	60	33	11	522
1984	12	1,595	374	603	64	29	13	512
Average for term		1,624	380	626	63	34	13	509
Reagan, II								
1985	12	1,549	362	569	61	32	11	514
1986	12	1,519	363	543	67	33	11	502
1987	12	1,514	361	513	67	35	11	527
1988	12	1,645	362	532	61	33	12	645
Average for term		1,557	362	539	64	33	11	547
Bush								
1989	12	1,589	363	527	66	33	10	590
1990	14	1,680	374	515	68	40	15	668

1991	14	1,782	384	548	65	33	23	729
1992	14	1,855	400	561	54	31	27	782
Average for term		1,727	380	538	63	34	19	692
Clinton								
1993	14	1,776	445	561	51	31	22	666
1994c	14	1,637	400	556	60	35	3	583
1995c	14	1,631	400	542	60	35	10	584
Average		1,683	415	553	57	34	12	611

Sources: U. S. Department of Commerce, *Statistical Abstract of the United States 1924–1987* (Washington, D.C.: Government Printing Office, 1924–1987); U. S. Executive Office of the President, *The Budget of the United States 1924–1995* (Washington, D.C.: Government Printing Office, 1924–1995).

Note: The Bueau of Budget moved to the executive office from the Treasury Department in 1939 and was reorganized and renamed the Office of Management and Budget in 1970. The National Security Council was created in 1947; the Council of Economic Advisers in 1946; the Council of Environmental Quality in 1969. The "All others" category includes personnel for Maintenance and Grounds, which ranges from sixty people in the 1930s to eighty people in the 1980s. Remaining employees have some tie to White House policy units.

[a] Includes war establishment units.
[b] Includes full term from November 1963 to January 1969.
[c] Estimates.

Figure 6-1 Number of Employees in the Executive Office of the President, Office of Management and Budget, and White House Office, Coolidge to Clinton

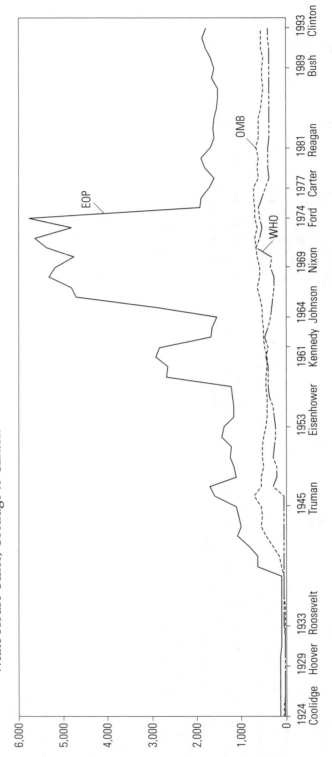

Source: Lyn Ragsdale and John J. Theis, "The Institutionalization of the American Presidency, 1924–1992" (Paper presented at the annual meeting of the Midwest Political Science Association, Chicago, April, 1994).

Note: Employees in war establishment units from 1941 to 1946 have been excluded. Prior to 1970, the Office of Management and Budget was known as the Bureau of the Budget.

Table 6-2 Average Expenditures for Selected Units in Executive Office of the President by Term, Coolidge to Clinton (in thousands of current dollars)

President	Executive office total	White House Office	Bureau of Budget/OMB	National Security Council	Council of Economic Advisers	Council of Environmental Quality
Coolidge	501	391	—	—	—	—
Hoover	506	317	—	—	—	—
Roosevelt, I	403	264	—	—	—	—
Roosevelt, II	1,503	291	519	—	—	—
Roosevelt, III/IV	1,465,980	407	2,007	—	—	—
Truman, I	196,030	969	3,403	—	230	—
Truman, II	8,556	1,537	3,338	105	308	—
Eisenhower, I	9,226	2,121	3,398	203	277	—
Eisenhower, II	49,216	3,541	4,314	595	361	—
Kennedy	40,383	3,854	5,463	594	534	—
Johnson[a]	26,120	3,882	7,888	619	693	—
Nixon, I	42,115	7,660	14,123	1,620	1,152	1,635
Nixon, II	57,614	11,458	19,491	2,485	1,462	2,334
Ford	86,024	15,792	23,457	2,907	1,522	2,958
Carter	80,733	17,309	29,632	3,246	1,956	3,750
Reagan, I	101,593	19,421	34,841	3,618	2,068	301
Reagan, II	112,328	24,483	38,637	4,450	2,329	1,147
Bush[b]	164,966	31,033	47,635	5,209	2,915	1,875
Clinton[b]	190,679	39,812	55,915	6,411	3,343	1,337

Source: U. S. Executive Office of the President, *The Budget of the United States 1924–1995* (Washington, D.C.: Government Printing Office, 1924–1995).

Note: The Bureau of the Budget moved to the executive office from the Treasury Department in 1939 and was reorganized and renamed the Office of Management and Budget in 1970. The National Security Council was created in 1947, the Council of Economic Advisers in 1946, and the Council of Environmental Quality in 1969.

[a] Includes full term from November 1963 to January 1969.
[b] Clinton figures average the actual outlays for 1993 with estimated values for 1994 and 1995.

Table 6-3   Budget Allocations and Expenditures for White House Staff, Coolidge to Clinton (in thousands of current dollars)

President/year	Total executive office		White House Office	
	Appropriations	Expenditures	Appropriations	Expenditures
Coolidge				
1924	574	451	475	324
1925	657	412	558	311
1926	502	439	452	333
1927	819	613	709	496
1928	438	590	334	489
Hoover				
1929	437	487	335	360
1930	653	605	487	289
1931	425	507	290	331
1932	475	425	290	288
Roosevelt, I				
1933	392	369	267	255
1934	369	359	249	248
1935	442	458	268	279
1936	437	425	294	275
Roosevelt, II				
1937	515	502	294	278
1938	511	479	301	293
1939	2,531	2,371	304	287
1940	2,810	2,661	402	304
Roosevelt, III				
1941	3,896	10,219	396	343
1942	440,762	239,019	398	366
1943	1,722,539	1,646,903	399	416
1944	2,970,258	2,760,787	377	437
Roosevelt/Truman				
1945	1,223,701	2,672,974	429	473
Truman, I				
1946	657,022	446,364	418	507
1947	133,573	133,400	959	915
1948	6,692	8,327	1,028	1,486
Truman, II				
1949	9,948	7,997	1,245	1,271
1950	10,736	8,407	1,525	1,495
1951	9,339	8,710	1,736	1,587
1952	9,817	9,108	2,034	1,795
Eisenhower, I				
1953	9,350	8,936	2,108	1,860
1954	9,395	9,493	1,950	1,780
1955	8,533	8,535	2,045	1,957
1956	10,395	9,938	3,283	2,885

Table 6-3   *(Continued)*

| President/year | Total executive office | | White House Office | |
	Appropriations	Expenditures	Appropriations	Expenditures
Eisenhower, II				
1957	10,715	10,399	3,525	3,370
1958	51,029	75,074	3,583	3,535
1959	55,297	55,788	3,702	3,672
1960	63,140	55,604	2,521	3,585
Kennedy				
1961	71,780	69,042	3,906	3,864
1962	26,507	28,993	4,145	4,007
1963	23,601	23,113	4,195	3,691
Johnson[a]				
1964	24,972	22,904	4,380	4,067
1965	26,444	24,018	4,380	4,112
1966	26,282	27,416	4,505	3,786
1967	29,307	27,767	4,605	3,671
1968	31,011	28,495	4,659	3,722
Nixon				
1969	32,066	30,889	4,924	4,577
1970	38,403	36,355	6,690	6,468
1971	49,958	47,127	10,109	8,623
1972	60,113	54,087	11,092	10,971
1973	93,369	49,164	11,517	11,635
Nixon/Ford				
1974	97,252	66,064	11,924	11,280
Ford				
1975	75,646	92,823	16,617	15,543
1976[b]	69,258	79,224	17,013	16,041
Carter				
1977	78,149	73,387	17,412	17,236
1978	77,687	74,568	16,665	16,822
1979	81,763	79,590	17,413	16,159
1980	100,334	95,386	19,191	19,017
Reagan, I				
1981	103,121	95,635	21,528	21,078
1982	92,817	94,675	19,902	19,953
1983	101,371	94,186	22,115	20,766
1984	109,064	95,317	23,436	15,885
Reagan, II				
1985	115,715	111,261	25,439	24,306
1986	107,736	107,345	23,835	23,192
1987	117,999	109,422	24,824	25,059
1988	125,093	121,282	26,426	25,374

(Table continues)

Table 6-3   *(Continued)*

President/year	Total executive office		White House Office	
	Appropriations	Expenditures	Appropriations	Expenditures
Bush				
1989	128,976	123,980	27,950	27,276
1990	292,351	157,406	30,232	29,329
1991	190,000	193,000	33,000	32,000
1992	226,000	185,478	35,000	35,527
Clinton				
1993	242,582	195,400	42,795	40,186
1994[c]	184,799	192,303	38,754	38,754
1995[c]	190,187	188,068	41,822	40,497

Source: U. S. Executive Office of the President, *The Budget of the United States 1924–1995* (Washington, D. C.: Government Printing Office, 1924–1995).

Note: Figures for the White House office include the salaries of the president and vice president. Figures for the total executive office include the budget for the White House mansion and grounds. All funds are those allocated and spent during the fiscal year ending June 30.

[a] Includes full term from November 1963 to January 1969.
[b] Transition quarter excluded from figures for this year. In 1976 the beginning of the fiscal year was changed from July 1 to October 1. A transition quarter (July 1–September 30, 1976) was used. It belonged to neither fiscal year 1976 nor fiscal 1977.
[c] Estimates.

Table 6-4 Budget Appropriations and Expenditures for Key Executive Office Units, Franklin Roosevelt to Clinton (in thousands of current dollars)

President/year	Bureau of Budget/OMB		National Security Council		Council of Economic Advisers		Council on Environmental Quality	
	BA	E	BA	E	BA	E	BA	E
F. Roosevelt, II								
1939	481	397	—	—	—	—	—	—
1940	671	640	—	—	—	—	—	—
F. Roosevelt, III								
1941	836	945	—	—	—	—	—	—
1942	1,315	1,512	—	—	—	—	—	—
1943	1,982	2,126	—	—	—	—	—	—
1944	2,601	2,818	—	—	—	—	—	—
F. Roosevelt/Truman								
1945	2,956	2,633	—	—	—	—	—	—
Truman, I								
1946	3,037	3,278	—	—	—	—	—	—
1947	3,762	3,598	—	—	275	148	—	—
1948	3,377	3,334	—	52	350	311	—	—
Truman II								
1949	3,281	3,261	200	113	310	319	—	—
1950	3,300	3,191	200	99	300	283	—	—
1951	3,377	3,225	160	121	300	286	—	—
1952	3,608	3,676	160	139	342	345	—	—

(Table continues)

Table 6-4 (*Continued*)

President/year	Bureau of Budget/OMB		National Security Council		Council of Economic Advisers		Council on Environmental Quality	
	BA	E	BA	E	BA	E	BA	E
Eisenhower, I								
1953	3,461	3,442	155	154	225	243	—	—
1954	3,412	3,260	220	202	302	234	—	—
1955	3,889	3,310	215	204	341	304	—	—
1956	3,559	3,580	244	253	329	328	—	—
Eisenhower, II								
1957	3,935	3,853	248	252	366	340	—	—
1958	4,340	4,157	711	613	375	339	—	—
1959	4,551	4,615	759	767	393	383	—	—
1960	4,665	4,632	792	746	395	382	—	—
Kennedy								
1961	5,426	5,260	817	794	436	421	—	—
1962	5,517	5,304	554	503	584	506	—	—
1963	5,872	5,825	550	485	601	675	—	—
Johnson[a]								
1964	6,500	6,636	575	515	615	613	—	—
1965	7,307	7,089	627	608	697	655	—	—
1966	8,104	7,627	738	731	675	613	—	—
1967	8,913	9,063	664	601	790	731	—	—
1968	9,500	9,024	664	639	858	854	—	—
Nixon								
1969	9,674	10,050	811	668	1,130	1,020	—	—
1970	11,676	12,141	1,860	1,418	1,187	1,188	350	—

1971	14,785	15,100	2,182	2,171	1,233	1,234	1,500	1,378
1972	18,311	19,200	2,424	2,221	2,112	1,166	2,300	1,891
1973	18,544	19,581	2,762	2,437	1,369	1,498	2,550	2,310
Nixon/Ford								
1974	18,271	19,400	2,802	2,532	1,414	1,425	2,466	2,358
Ford								
1975	21,735	21,910	2,900	2,621	1,600	1,468	2,500	2,735
1976[b]	23,592	25,004	3,052	3,192	1,621	1,575	3,236	3,181
Carter								
1977	29,153	26,536	3,270	2,965	1,873	1,833	3,300	3,780
1978	30,371	29,299	3,315	3,039	2,018	2,024	2,854	1,267
1979	31,919	29,788	3,525	3,451	2,042	1,822	3,026	4,251
1980	33,431	32,907	3,645	3,527	2,102	2,145	3,126	5,702
Reagan, I								
1981	36,022	35,123	3,839	3,268	2,205	1,975	2,542	-906
1982	35,896	36,722	3,557	3,488	1,985	2,103	1,957	936
1983	34,987	32,531	4,064	3,852	2,177	2,048	926	827
1984	37,311	34,987	4,497	3,864	2,464	2,144	1,475	348
Reagan, II								
1985	38,852	39,754	4,605	4,454	2,560	2,170	700	1,830
1986	37,237	36,810	4,428	4,235	2,202	2,306	670	1,159
1987	39,033	37,306	4,612	4,369	2,370	2,375	803	408
1988	41,300	40,676	5,000	4,743	2,500	2,463	826	1,191
Bush								
1989	41,993	41,871	5,100	4,959	2,787	2,715	850	769
1990	46,943	44,372	5,335	5,352	2,865	2,834	1,465	1,175
1991	51,000	53,000	6,000	5,000	3,000	3,000	2,000	3,000
1992	55,000	51,297	6,185	5,523	3,345	3,109	2,525	2,554

(Table continues)

Table 6-4 (*Continued*)

President/year	Bureau of Budget/OMB		National Security Council		Council of Economic Advisers		Council on Environmental Quality	
	BA	E	BA	E	BA	E	BA	E
Clinton								
1993	56,039	54,753	6,118	6,173	3,428	3,323	2,560	2,148
1994[c]	56,539	56,489	6,648	6,411	3,420	3,237	375	501
1995[c]	56,499	56,503	6,872	6,650	3,474	3,469	1,000	937

Source: U. S. Executive Office of the President, *The Budget of the United States 1939–1995* (Washington, D.C.: Government Printing Office 1939–1995).

Note: The Bureau of the Budget was moved to the White House from the Treasury Department in 1939. It was reorganized and renamed the Office of Management and Budget in 1970. The Council of Economic Advisers was designated in 1946, with funding beginning in 1947. The National Security Council, authorized in 1947, did not expend funds until 1948. The Council of Environmental Quality began in 1970. BA = budget appropriations. E = expenditures.

[a] Includes full term from November 1963 to January 1969.
[b] Transition quarter excluded from figures for the year. In 1976 the beginning of the fiscal year was changed from July 1 to October 1. A transition quarter (July 1–September 30, 1976) was used. It belonged to neither fiscal 1976 nor fiscal 1977.
[c] Estimates.

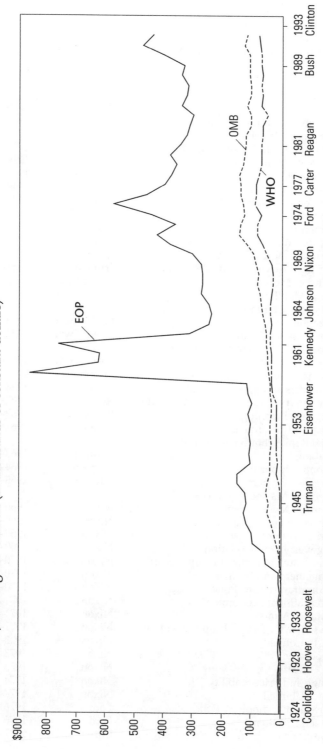

Figure 6-2 Expenditures by the Executive Office of the President, Office of Management and Budget, and White House Office, Coolidge to Clinton (in thousands of constant dollars)

Source: Lyn Ragsdale and John J. Theis, "The Institutionalization of the American Presidency, 1924–1992" (Paper presented at the annual meeting of the Midwest Political Science Association, Chicago, April, 1994).

Notes: Data calculated in constant (real) dollars using 1967 as the base. This procedure takes into account the inflation rate for the periods, thereby discounting the budget figures. To obtain the constant dollar figures, the budget values are divided by the consumer price index for the period. Expenditures for war establishment units from 1941 to 1946 have been excluded. Prior to 1970, the Office of Management and Budget was known as the Bureau of the Budget.

271

Table 6-5   Units in the Executive Office of the President, 1939–1993

Unit	President	Duration
White House Office[a]	Roosevelt	1939–
Council on Personnel Administration	Roosevelt	1939–1940
Office of Government Reports	Roosevelt	1939–1942
Liaison Office for Personnel Management	Roosevelt	1939–1943
National Resources Planning Board	Roosevelt	1939–1943
Bureau of the Budget[a]	Roosevelt	1939–1970
Office of Emergency Management	Roosevelt	1940–1954
Committee for Congested Production Areas	Roosevelt	1943–1944
War Refugee Board	Roosevelt	1944–1945
Council of Economic Advisers	Truman	1946–
Natitonal Security Council	Truman	1947–
National Security Resources Board	Truman	1947–1953
Telecommunications Adviser to the President	Truman	1951–1953
Office of Director of Mutual Security	Truman	1951–1954
Office of Defense Mobilization	Truman	1952–1959
Permanent Advisory Committee on Government Organizations	Eisenhower	1953–1961
Operations Coordinating Board	Eisenhower	1953–1961
President's Board of Consultants on Foreign Intelligence Activities	Eisenhower	1956–1961
Office of Civil and Defense Mobilization	Eisenhower	1958–1962
National Aeronautics and Space Council	Eisenhower	1958–1973
President's Foreign Intelligence Advisory Board	Kennedy	1961–1977
Office of Emergency Planning	Kennedy	1962–1969
Office of Science and Technology	Kennedy	1962–1973
Office of Special Representative for Trade Negotiations	Kennedy	1963–
Office of Economic Opportunity	Johnson	1964–1975
Office of Emergency Preparedness	Johnson	1965–1973
National Council on Marine Resources and Engineering Development	Johnson	1966–1971
Council on Environmental Quality	Nixon	1969–
Council for Urban Affairs	Nixon	1969–1970
Office of Intergovernmental Relations	Nixon	1969–1973
Domestic Policy Council/Domestic Policy Staff[b]	Nixon	1970–1978
Office of Management and Budget	Nixon	1970–
Office of Telecommunications Policy	Nixon	1970–1977
Council on International Economic Policy	Nixon	1971–1977
Office of Consumer Affairs	Nixon	1971–1973
Special Action Office for Drug Abuse Prevention	Nixon	1971–1975
Federal Property Council	Nixon	1973–1977
Council on Economic Policy	Nixon	1973–1974
Energy Policy Office	Nixon	1973–1974
Council on Wage and Price Stability	Nixon	1974–1981
Energy Resource Council	Nixon	1974–1977
Office of Science and Technology Policy	Ford	1976–
Intelligence Oversight Board	Ford	1976–
Office of Administration	Carter	1977–

Table 6-5 *(Continued)*

Unit	President	Duration
Office of Drug Abuse Policy	Carter	1977–1978
Office of Policy Development	Carter	1978–
Office of Private Sector Initiatives	Reagan	1981–1989
National Critical Materials Council	Reagan	1984–1993
Office of National Drug Control Policy	Bush	1989–
Office of National Service	Bush	1989–
National Space Council	Bush	1990–1993
Points of Light Foundation	Bush	1990–1993
National Economic Council	Clinton	1993–
President's Council on Sustainable Development	Clinton	1993–
National Partnership Council	Clinton	1993–

Source: Adapted from Thomas Cronin, *The State of the Presidency,* 2d ed. (Boston: Little, Brown, 1980), Table A.3, 386; updated by the author.

Note: This list does not include short-term advisory commissions, study councils, and cabinet-level coordinating committees. Also excluded is the Central Intelligency Agency, which since 1947 has been formally part of the Executive Office of the President but in practice operates as an independent agency.

[a] Unit currently in operation as Office of Management and Budget.
[b] Unit currently in operation as Office of Policy Development.

Table 6-6   Executive Office of the President, Clinton

White House Office
Office of Administration
Council of Economic Advisers
Council on Environmental Quality
Domestic Policy Council
National Critical Materials Council[a]
National Security Council
National Space Council[a]
Office of Management and Budget
Office of National Drug Control Policy
Office of Policy Development
Regulatory Information Service Center
Office of Science and Technology Policy
Office of U. S. Trade Representation
Office of the Vice President

Source: 1992/3 Federal Staff Directory (Mt. Vernon, Va.: Staff Directories, Ltd, 1992), vii–36.

[a] Dissolved in FY 1993.

Table 6-7   Units of the White House Office, Clinton

Office of the Chief of Staff
Office of the Staff Secretary
Office of National Security Affairs
Office of the Counsel
Office of Communications
Office of Speechwriting
Office of Research
Office of Public Liaison
Office of Media Affairs
Office of Media Relations
Office of Public Affairs
Press Secretary
Office of Legislative Affairs (formerly Office of Congressional Relations)
Office of Management and Administration
Office of Intergovernmental Affairs
Office of Policy Planning
Office of National Service
Office of Special Activities and Initiatives (Advance Office)
Office of Political Affairs
Office of the Cabinet Secretary
Presidential Personnel Office
White House Military Office
Office of the First Lady

Source: 1992/3 Federal Staff Directory (Mt. Vernon, Va.: Staff Directories, Ltd, 1992), vii–36.

Table 6-8   Top Level Staff Not Assigned to Specific White House
Office Subunits, 1939–1992

Year	Total staff listed[a]	Total number unassigned[b]	Percent unassigned	Number of subunits[c]
1939	8	7	87.5	1
1940	9	7	77.8	1
1941	9	7	77.8	1
1942	11	9	81.8	1
1943	13	11	84.6	1
1944	13	10	76.9	2
1945	14	9	64.2	3
1946	17	11	64.6	5
1947	16	8	50.0	6
1948	—	—	—	—
1949	—	—	—	—
1950	18	10	55.6	6
1951	17	9	52.9	6
1952	18	10	55.6	6
1953	29	14	48.3	11
1954	32	13	40.6	12
1955	41	23	56.1	15
1956	—	—	—	—
1957	47	25	53.2	13
1958	45	24	53.3	13
1959	49	22	44.9	13
1960	49	22	44.9	13
1961	26	11	42.3	9
1962	29	14	48.3	6
1963	28	13	46.4	9
1964	29	14	48.3	8
1965	25	12	48.0	9
1966	26	13	50.0	7
1967	26	11	42.3	8
1968	27	12	44.9	6
1969	46	21	45.6	11
1970	57	28	49.1	15
1971	49	23	46.9	14
1972	52	25	48.1	13
1973	40	22	55.0	5
1974	47	32	68.1	6
1975	64	9	14.1	30
1976	60	8	13.3	30
1977	80	4	5.0	34
1978	75	7	9.3	31
1979	78	8	10.3	29
1980	84	9	10.7	31
1981	58	7	12.1	19
1982	78	6	7.7	28

(Table continues)

Table 6-8   *(Continued)*

Year	Total staff listed[a]	Total number unassigned[b]	Percent unassigned	Number of subunits[c]
1983	92	6	6.5	28
1984	90	6	6.7	30
1985	79	3	3.8	32
1986	84	4	4.8	33
1987	82	5	6.1	35
1988	82	4	4.9	34
1989	84	4	4.8	36
1990	87	5	5.7	35
1991	86	4	4.7	35
1992	90	4	4.4	36

Sources: Lyn Ragsdale and John J. Theis, "The Institutionalization of the American Presidency, 1924–1992" (Paper presented at the annual meeting of the Midwest Political Sciences Association, Chicago, April 1994).

Note: "—" indicates not available.

[a] Total number of individuals listed under the heading of White House Office.
[b] Refers to those individuals listed with the title Special Assistant to the President, Deputy Assistant to the President, Assistant to the President, Counselor to the President, or Special Consultant to the President. These individuals have no specific functional area linked to their title.
[c] Refers to the number of subunits, as reported by the White House.

Table 6-9 Office of Management and Budget Review of Agency Rules, 1981–1991

OMB decision[a]	1981	1982	1983	1984	1985	1986	1987	1988	1989	1990	1991[b]
Consistent without change											
Number	2,447	2,214	2,044	1,641	1,564	1,370	1,631	1,674	1,638	1,535	1,594
Percentage	87.1	84.1	82.3	78.0	70.7	68.5	70.6	71.0	73.8	71.8	63.2
Consistent with change											
Number	136	271	316	319	510	459	549	518	431	412	685
Percentage	4.9	10.3	12.7	15.2	23.1	23.0	23.8	22.0	19.4	19.3	27.2
Withdrawn by agency											
Number	50	32	40	52	69	56	59	57	61	54	70
Percentage	1.8	1.2	1.6	2.5	3.1	2.8	2.5	2.4	2.7	2.5	2.8
Returned for consideration											
Number	133	79	32	57	41	29	10	29	29	21	28
Percentage	4.7	3.0	1.3	2.7	1.8	1.5	.4	1.2	1.3	1.0	1.1
Suspended											
Number	—	—	—	—	—	—	—	—	15	58	69
Percentage	—	—	—	—	—	—	—	—	0.7	2.7	2.7
Emergency, statutory, or judicial deadline											
Number	39	37	50	35	17	86	60	81	45	54	75
Percentage	1.4	1.4	2.0	1.7	1.2	4.3	2.6	3.4	2.0	2.6	3.0
Total regulations	2,803	2,633	2,482	2,104	2,211	2,000	2,309	2,359	2,219	2,134	2,523

Source: U. S. Executive Office of the President, Office of Management and Budget, *Regulatory Programs of the United States* (Washington, D.C.: Government Printing Office, successive years).

Note: " — " indicates not available.

[a] OMB decides whether a particular rule is consistent with Executive Order 12291. The order mandates that all agencies and departments must supply proper justification of the cost and necessity for their rules.
[b] Latest year data available.

Table 6-10   Chiefs of Staff, 1932–1994

President	Chief of Staff	Years
Roosevelt	None	—
Truman	John R. Stedman[a]	1946–1952
Eisenhower	Sherman Adams[a]	1953–1958
	Wilton Persons[a]	1958–1961
Kennedy	None	—
Johnson	None	—
Nixon	H R. Haldeman	1969–1973
	Alexander M. Haig	1973–1974
Ford	Donald Rumsfeld	1974–1975
	Richard M. Cheney	1975–1977
Carter	Hamilton Jordan	1979–1980
	Jack Watson	1980–1981
Reagan	James A. Baker III	1981–1985
	Donald T. Regan	1985–1987
	Howard H. Baker Jr.	1987–1988
	Kenneth Duberstein	1988–1989
Bush	John H. Sununu	1989–1991
	Samuel Skinner	1991–1992
	James A. Baker III	1992–1993
Clinton	Thomas F. McLarty III	1993–1994
	Leon Panetta	1994–

Source: Michael Nelson, ed. *Congressional Quarterly's Guide to the Presidency* (Washington, D.C.: Congressional Quarterly, 1989); updated by the author.

[a] These aides carried the title of "assistant" rather than "chief of staff."

Table 6-11   Size of Executive Departments for Selected Years

Executive department	Year established	Paid civilian employees 1980	Paid civilian employees 1992
Agriculture	1889	126,139	133,049
Commerce[a]	1913	48,563	38,356
Defense[b]	1947	960,116	1,001,322
Education	1980	7,364	5,117
Energy	1977	21,557	21,351
Health and Human Services[c]	1980	155,662	134,321
Housing and Urban Development	1965	16,964	13,862
Interior	1849	77,357	84,617
Justice	1870	56,327	97,941
Labor	1913	23,400	18,111
State	1789	23,497	25,986
Transportation	1966	72,361	70,745
Treasury	1789	124,663	164,658
Veterans' Affairs[d]	1989	228,285	259,406
Total		1,942,255	2,068,842

Sources: (1980) U. S. Department of Commerce, *Statistical Abstract of the United States 1987* (Washington, D.C.: Government Printing Office, 1987); (1992) U. S. Office of Personnel Management, *Federal Civilian Work Force Statistics, 1993* (Washington, D.C.: Government Printing Office, 1993).

[a] Originally the Department of Commerce and Labor, established in 1903 and split in 1913.
[b] Originally the Department of War, established in 1789.
[c] Originally the Department of Health, Education, and Welfare, established in 1953.
[d] Originally Veterans Administration.

Table 6-12   Size of Independent Federal Agencies for Selected Years

	Paid civilian employees	
Agency	1980	1992
ACTION	1,837	421
American Battle Manuments Commission	386	401
Board of Governors, Federal Reserve System	1,498	1,594
Commission on Civil Rights	304	89
Environmental Protection Agency	14,715	18,360
Equal Employment Opportunity Commission	3,515	2,873
Export-Import Bank	385	368
Farm Credit Administration	271	486
Federal Communications Commission	2,244	1,872
Federal Deposit Insurance Corporation	3,520	22,775
Federal Emergency Management Agency	3,427	3,730
Federal Labor Relations Authority	349	252
Federal Mediation and Conciliation Service	503	322
Federal Trade Commission	1,846	993
General Services Administration	37,654	21,094
International Trade Commission	424	495
Interstate Commerce Commission	1,998	627
National Aeronautics and Space Administration	23,714	26,011
National Endowment for the Arts	362	279
National Labor Relations Board	2,936	2,199
National Science Foundation	1,394	1,352
National Transportation Safety Board	384	367
Nuclear Regulatory Commission	3,283	3,564
Office of Personnel Management	8,280	6,984
Panama Canal Commission	8,700	8,519
Railroad Retirement Board	1,795	1,812
Securities and Exchange Commission	2,056	2,610
Selective Service System	97	254
Small Business Administration	5,804	5,182
Smithsonian Institution	4,403	5,621
Tennessee Valley Authority	51,714	19,479
U.S. Postal Service	660,014	791,986
All other	20,062	24,394
Total	1,100,363	977,365

Sources: (1980) U. S. Department of Commerce, *Statistical Abstract of the United States 1987* (Washington, D.C.: Government Printing Office, 1987); (1992) U.S. Office of Personnel Management, *Federal Civilian Work Force Statistics, 1993* (Washington, D.C.: Government Printing Office, 1993).

Table 6-13   Total Executive Nominations Submitted for Senate
Confirmation, Truman to Bush

President/year	Presidential action			Senate action	
	Submitted	Rejected	Withdrawn	Unconfirmed[a]	Confirmed
Truman, I					
1945	11,056	2	11	77	10,966
1946	25,966	0	6	375	25,585
1947	40,557	0	132	570	39,855
1948	26,084	0	21	11,122	14,941
Truman, II					
1949	55,311	2	39	401	54,869
1950	25,699	4	6	99	25,590
1951	20,636	0	5	196	20,435
1952	26,284	2	40	173	26,069
Eisenhower, I					
1953	23,542	0	31	92	23,419
1954	45,916	0	12	761	45,143
1955	40,686	3	15	771	39,897
1956	43,487	0	23	667	42,797
Eisenhower, II					
1957	45,114	0	33	416	44,620
1958	59,079	0	21	367	58,691
1959	46,934	1	6	556	46,371
1960	44,542	0	22	992	43,528
Kennedy					
1961	50,770	0	1,271	538	48,961
1962	52,079	0	8	291	51,780
1963	67,456	0	21	832	66,603
Johnson[b]					
1964	54,734	0	15	1,121	53,598
1965	55,765	0	13	1,176	54,576
1966	67,254	0	160	805	66,289
1967	69,254	0	19	153	69,082
1968	50,977	0	15	1,813	49,149
Nixon					
1969	73,159	1	477	46	72,635
1970	61,305	1	10	132	61,162
1971	50,499	0	6	1,638	48,855
1972	66,554	0	5	495	66,054
1973	68,080	0	10	1,253	66,817
Nixon/Ford					
1974	66,304	0	4/46[c]	1,816	64,437
Ford					
1975	75,039	0	6/236[c]	3,521	71,276
1976	60,263	0	15	146	60,102

Table 6-13   *(Continued)*

President/year	Presidential action			Senate action	
	Submitted	Rejected	Withdrawn	Unconfirmed[a]	Confirmed
Carter					
1977	74,659	0	61	8,967	65,631
1978	62,850	0	5	3,746	59,099
1979	86,212	0	8	1,345	84,859
1980	69,929	0	10	113	69,806
Reagan, I					
1981	106,620	0	33	1,295/8[c]	105,284
1982	79,648	0	22	47/7[c]	79,562
1983	56,041	0	2	26/477[c]	55,536
1984	41,852	0	2	107	41,743
Reagan, II					
1985	59,643	0	8	3,677/34[c]	55,918
1986	39,971	0	8	70	39,893
1987	51,929	1	10	5,494/20	46,404
1988	42,758	0	13	428	41,317
Bush					
1989	48,434	1	34	2,762/52	45,585
1990	44,934	0	14	5,189	42,493
1991	45,369	0	12	167/10	45,180
1992	31,077	0	12	589	30,619

Source: Successive volumes of U.S. Congress, *Executive Proceedings of the Senate* (Washington, D.C.: Government Printing Office).

[a] Those nominations not acted upon before Senate adjournment and carried over to the next session.
[b] Includes full term from November 1963 to January 1969.
[c] Second figure indicates number of nominations that failed confirmation at adjournment under Senate rules. No final action was taken on the nominations, and they were not carried over to the next session.

Table 6-14   Presidential Appointments Confirmed by Senate, Kennedy to Clinton

President/year	Executive office	Cabinet departments	Ambassadors	Independent agencies	Total
Kennedy					
1961	6	120	12	51	249
1962	8	49	12	30	153
1963	6	31	13	45	110
Total	20	200	37	126	512
Johnson					
1964	5	28	10	24	85
1965	11	69	20	40	169
1966	10	46	22	29	167
1967	5	56	21	30	148
1968	4	37	20	46	131
Total	35	236	93	169	700
Nixon					
1969	10	160	51	48	296
1970	7	28	8	27	135
1971	7	38	4	42	154
1972	2	36	8	20	91
1973	5	109	21	39	196
1974	1	38	9	18	83
Total	32	409	101	194	955
Ford					
1974	3	16	6	20	62
1975	4	73	18	55	167
1976	4	52	9	36	132
Total	11	141	33	111	361
Carter					
1977	16	177	37	63	319
1978	4	53	16	46	158
1979	7	59	29	35	258
1980	2	48	5	23	142
Total	29	337	87	167	877
Reagan, I					
1981	13	180	28	75	337
1982	4	31	9	56	137
1983	3	51	13	39	136
1984	3	40	6	24	110
Total	23	302	56	194	720
Reagan, II					
1985	12	88	49	55	204
1986	5	74	40	42	161
1987	3	58	38	29	128
1988	3	64	39	21	127
Total	23	284	166	147	620

(Table continues)

Table 6-14   *(Continued)*

President/year	Executive office	Cabinet departments	Ambassadors	Independent agencies	Total
Bush					
1989	18	172	66	34	290
1990	5	57	40	52	154
1991	13	77	43	153	286
1992	3	38	24	45	110
Total	39	344	173	284	840
Clinton					
1993	18	209	66	28	321

Sources: (Kennedy through Reagan, I) Successive volumes of *Congressional Quarterly Almanac.* (Washington, D.C.: Congressional Quarterly); (Reagan, II, through Clinton) successive volumes of *Journal of the Executive Proceedings of the Senate.*

Table 6-15   Senate Rejections of Cabinet Nominations

Nominee	Position	President	Date	Vote
Roger B. Taney	secretary of treasury	Jackson	6/23/1834	18–28
Caleb Cushing	secretary of treasury	Tyler	3/3/1843	19–27
Caleb Cushing	secretary of treasury	Tyler	3/3/1843	10–27
Caleb Cushing	secretary of treasury	Tyler	3/3/1843	2–29
David Henshaw	secretary of navy	Tyler	1/15/1844	6–34
James M. Porter	secretary of war	Tyler	1/30/1844	3–38
James S. Green	secretary of treasury	Tyler	6/15/1844	[a]
Henry Stanbery	attorney general	A. Johnson	6/2/1868	11–29
Charles B. Warren	attorney general	Coolidge	3/10/1925	39–41
Charles B. Warren	attorney general	Coolidge	3/16/1925	39–46
Lewis L. Strauss	secretary of commerce	Eisenhower	6/19/1959	46–49
John Tower	secretary of defense	Bush	3/9/1989	47–53

Source: Congressional Quarterly's Guide to Congress, 4th ed. (Washington D.C.: Congressional Quarterly, 1991), 252.

Note: Data are current through 1994.

[a] Not recorded.

Table 6-16   Presidential Appointees from President's Party (percent)

Department	Kennedy	Johnson	Nixon	Ford	Carter[a]	Reagan[b]
Agriculture	77	80	81	100	92	94
Commerce	71	65	82	64	71	100
Defense	48	32	56	52	45	78
Education	—	—	—	—	—	82
Energy	—	—	—	—	59	94
Health, Education, Welfare/						
Health and Human Services	73	53	66	45	56	88
Housing and Urban						
Development	—	86	78	100	92	94
Interior	54	50	86	100	45	93
Justice	68	65	68	80	38	100
Labor	100	75	80	50	62	53
Post Office	100	78	56	—	—	—
State[c]	64	34	51	31	39	69
Transportation	—	27	70	70	77	96
Treasury	55	67	79	43	72	90
Executive Office of the						
President	63	43	68	82	60	87

Sources: (Kennedy through Carter) Adapted from Roger Brown, "Party and Bureaucracy: From Kennedy to Reagan," *Political Science Quarterly* 97 (Summer 1982): 279–294; (Reagan, 1981–1984) calculated by the author from *Congressional Quarterly Almanac* (Washington, D.C.: Congressional Quarterly, 1985).

Note: Major appointments as listed by *Congressional Quarterly Almanac,* including cabinet, subcabinet, and lower-level policy position.

[a] Carter figures for 1977–1978 only. Party affiliations for most of the appointees in 1979 and 1980 not available.
[b] Data available through 1984 only.
[c] Includes ambassadors.

7

Presidential Policy Making

On September 24, 1957, Dwight D. Eisenhower issued Executive Order No. 10730, directing the secretary of defense to order the Arkansas National Guard into the service of the United States. The Guard was to protect nine black teenagers who were attempting to attend Central High School in Little Rock but were being resisted by mobs of angry whites and the recalcitrant governor of the state, Orval Faubus. The Eisenhower administration acted to enforce a school desegregation order handed down by the U.S. District Court in Arkansas and, in so doing, carry out the requirements of U.S. law. Lyndon B. Johnson, under authority of the Tariff Act of 1930, enacted Executive Order No. 11377 on October 23, 1967, authorizing the U.S. Tariff Commission to monitor the annual consumption of whisk brooms in America, noting the types, numbers, and uses made of them. And under the auspices of the Agricultural Trade Development and Assistance Act (7 U.S.C. 1701), which authorizes the president "to negotiate and carry out agreements with friendly countries to provide for the sale of agricultural commodities," the Carter administration on August 28, 1979, entered into an executive agreement with Morocco. Under this agreement, the United States sold wheat and wheat flour to Morocco while the Moroccan government developed self-help measures to improve its agricultural production.

These very different uses of executive power reveal four central features of presidents' policy efforts. First, policy complexity defines the environment within which the modern presidency operates. This complexity is a reflection of the demands placed on the national government to do something about virtually everything. As a pivotal policy unit in the national government, the presidency makes a dizzying number of policies in all major issue areas and most minor ones. The presidency acts on agriculture, foreign aid, trade, health care, defense, crime, drugs, the budget, business regulations, safety, social security, welfare, nuclear power, natural resources, clean air, and civil rights. It sets policies on commemorative stamps, the length of government reports, and the shape of the national Christmas tree. The policy complexity is not only a feature of the environment but is an aspect of the presidency itself.

Second, the examples reveal independent presidential policy making. Eisenhower, Johnson, and Carter acted unilaterally, without immediate congressional approval and without any coordinate decisions by Congress. These executive orders, executive agreements, and other presidential efforts technically constitute execution of the law of the land. In these three instances, each president acted literally as chief executive. So that they may do so, Congress has granted presidents considerable discretion (and hence considerable autonomy) in the issuing of orders, agreements, and other pronouncements. Although chief executives act under authority granted them in the U.S. Constitution and federal statutes, they are not bound by any specific instructions of Congress. Thus, in many instances presidents more genuinely create law rather than simply execute it. The presidency acts as a substitute legislative policy maker—identifying a problem, establishing a procedure or program to solve it, and allocating resources and personnel to put the program into operation.

Third, individual presidents may claim a very personal role in independent policy making. Eisenhower stood firmly behind the Little Rock order. The literature on presidential policy making focuses heavily on the agendas and the successes of individual presidents; it looks upon policy making as an incumbent-specific enterprise. And, certainly, differences in presidential policy making can be significant. The differences between the economic plans of Franklin Roosevelt and Ronald Reagan are striking. Yet, these individual variations also reflect different partisan, ideological, and historical eras. These more systematic differences may be as telling as the differences among individual presidents.

Fourth, the presidency as an institution has an important, ongoing role in making presidential policy. Forced by the sheer number and varying types of decisions, spanning foreign, economic, and domestic policy spheres, presidents depend on the executive organization to get the job done. In many instances, they are only vaguely aware of the details of decisions that are made and ultimately go out under their signature. Johnson signed, but undoubtedly did not ponder, the whisk broom order. Jimmy Carter signed the executive agreement with Morocco, the language of which had been worked out by officials in the State Department. The organization of the institutional presidency routinizes the decisions and makes them less dependent on a specific individual. Thus, there is a distinction between individual presidents as policy makers and the presidency as a policy-making institution.

This chapter examines presidential policy making in four broad issue areas: diplomacy, military affairs, domestic matters, and fiscal economics. In the first three areas, the chapter concentrates on independent presidential policy decisions. In the area of fiscal economics, the chapter considers presidential efforts in relation to congressional counterefforts.

Diplomacy

Since George Washington, presidents have had relatively free rein over matters of diplomacy. In the words of then Congressman John Marshall, they are "the sole organ of the nation" in foreign affairs. Their diplomatic activity depends on two principal types of international agreements: treaties, which constitutionally require approval of the Senate by a two-thirds vote, and executive agreements, which require no congressional action. Executive agreements, which presidents simply sign into effect, are often used for relatively routine matters, for example, to enable nations to exchange postal services and to fix the tax status of foreign nationals in the United States and of American citizens abroad. However, executive agreements may significantly shape American foreign policy as well. Actions affected by executive orders have included the annexation of Texas and Hawaii, initiatives taken by the United States prior to the Japanese bombing of Pearl Harbor at the outset of World War II, the initiation and termination of U.S. involvement in the Korean War, and key escalations during the Vietnam War (Margolis, 1986). The Supreme Court has maintained that executive agreements have the same force in law as treaties (*United States v. Pink*, 315 U.S. 203, 1942). This section traces four dimensions of the presidential development of foreign policy: (1) the expansion of foreign policy activity, both by sheer numbers and by different types; (2) the relationship among different types of activities; (3) the multiplicity of policy areas within which these activities take place; and (4) the nations involved in these international negotiations.

Activity Expansion

Treaties and executive agreements have been recorded and aggregated from 1789 to the present and classified since 1949 by policy, president, party, nation, region, and regime type. Table 7-1 indicates the total number of international agreements from 1789 to 1948, while Table 7-2 records the number of international agreements since 1949.[1] As Table 7-1 shows, both treaties and executive agreements increased dramatically beginning with the McKinley administration as a result of the Spanish-American War. Theodore Roosevelt continued to expand the use of international agreements, most significantly during his second term.

A second sharp rise in the number of international agreements accompanied U.S. involvement in World War II and the postwar emergence of the United States as a superpower. The war years brought a dramatic increase in executive foreign policy activity as agreements were signed on all war fronts from Africa to the Soviet Union. This major environmental shock did more to encourage use of executive agreements than any president's isolated decisions, though the foreign policy strategies of Franklin Roosevelt and Harry S. Truman were certainly contributing factors (Schlesinger, 1973). Setting the stage for American involvement in the war, Roosevelt sold American destroyers to the British by executive agreement, without congressional approval. Foreign policy activity grew still more during Truman's second term with U.S. involvement in the Korean War and the undertaking of the Marshall Plan (see Table 7-2). The number of international agreements did not decline thereafter. Presidents since Truman have made, on average, more than nine hundred agreements over the course of their terms in office. Figure 7-1 conveniently summarizes the changes in the numbers of treaties and executive agreements negotiated since Truman's second term.

Casual observation of contemporary presidential diplomacy can be misleading. The enormous attention paid to specific actions of individual incumbents in the study of the American presidency depicts Theodore Roosevelt and Franklin Roosevelt as isolated political actors who advocated and achieved independence in presidential policy making. Systematic analysis, however, suggests that the environment was the critical "political actor." The increasing complexity of the policy environment around the turn of the century and during and after World War II placed greater demands on the presidency for the use of international agreements. For instance, William McKinley did not set about expanding the presidency; he simply confronted the exigencies of the Spanish-American War. New patterns of behavior established by one president become institutionalized, and future presidents are expected to exhibit them. The substance of these numerous proposals usually stays in place rather than being dismantled by successive White House occupants. As a result, any one president can change U.S. foreign policy only marginally.

Types of Foreign Policy Activity

Presidents and the ever-growing presidential organization generally engage in an increasing number of activities to keep up with the constant expansion of foreign policy. This suggests that increases in the use of executive agreements and treaties will occur in tandem. It has been argued that presidents use executive agreements as political devices to circumvent the Senate, especially when it is controlled by the other party (Margolis, 1986). In fact, executive agreements are convenient devices that accommodate the intricacies and details of the foreign policy environment. Tables 7-1 and 7-2 report the ratios between executive agreements and treaties. The data show no higher ratios when presidents have faced an opposition Senate than when they have enjoyed a Senate controlled by their own party. Executive agreements *and* treaties increased with Republican presidents McKinley and Theodore Roosevelt, both of whom enjoyed Republican Senate majorities. The number of executive agreements did not consistently exceed the number of treaties until the time of Calvin Coolidge, a Republican president who worked with a strongly Republican Senate. In the aftermath of World War II and at the outset of the implementation of the Marshall Plan, executive agreements increased again with President Truman, whose party generally controlled the Senate.

Table 7-3 analyzes these issues further by classifying Senate action on all international agreements submitted for ratification in the postwar period. These statistics and the list found in Table 7-4 demonstrate that since the beginning of the republic, the Senate has rejected just 22 treaties of the over 10,000 offered. In the last forty years, only four agreements have been rejected. When treaties are in danger of being rejected, presidents tend to withdraw them from consideration. The Senate may also leave an agreement pending at the end of a session. Typically ratification is thereby delayed for a session or more.

The infrequency of presidential defeat does not imply that the treaty ratification process is moribund. Although executive agreements have replaced treaties as "the official instrument of foreign policy commitment" (Johnson, 1984, 12), the number of treaties, protocols, and conventions has also increased since the administration of Franklin Roosevelt (see Table 7-2). Treaties and other agreements often involve important and controversial topics, which have included the creation of NATO, strategic arms limitations, cooperation in the Middle East, and numerous trade and tariff understandings. These tend to be negotiated, at least informally, with the Senate before final negotiations take place with the signatories. This fact may account for the very low rejection rate. Table 7-5 lists the major arms control agreements with the Soviet Union and Russia that the presidency has prepared and the Senate has reviewed since the Eisenhower administration. Both institutions appear to be responding in practical ways to an expanded policy environment: incumbent presidents have not consistently maneuvered around Congress to avoid its constitutionally prescribed check on their diplomatic powers; neither has the Senate abdicated its consent role.

In addition, the House, with no formal constitutional powers in international agreements, has recently asserted a role in diplomacy. For instance, the North American Free Trade Agreement was an executive agreement that technically did not have to receive congressional approval of any sort. Yet, the Bush administration and later the Clinton administration recognized the political costs of finalizing such an agreement without congressional approval. The executive agreement was initialed by George Bush in 1992 and then sent to the House and the Senate for enabling legislation, which passed by a close vote in each house in 1993 during the early months of the Clinton administration. Bill Clinton then signed the actual executive agreement.

In sum, the number of executive agreements seems predicated more on the exigencies of U.S. involvement in foreign affairs than on presidents' attempts to circumvent the shared powers outlined in the Constitution. Executive agreements are convenient tools that can accommodate the policy complexity created by both routine and important foreign matters, regardless of who controls the Senate or the White House.

The Multiplicity of Foreign Policies

To study the variety of international agreements in greater depth, Table 7-6 presents international agreements classified by policy area. The trade/ diplomacy category of agreements is relatively important and the number of such agreements increased beginning with the Kennedy administration. Defense agreements have been less frequent overall after reaching a peak during the first Eisenhower term (largely because of Korean War agreements). Foreign aid agreements have remained relatively small in numbers and relatively stable over time, except for an increase under John F. Kennedy that most likely reflected his commitment to Central America during the Alliance for Progress program. Together, these three "foreign policy" categories account for an average of 36 percent of the total number of international agreements made by presidents since 1949.

Most international agreements pertain to the domestic problems of the nations involved. Agreements in the area of agriculture and natural resources have increased significantly since President Truman. All presidents since Eisenhower's second term established ongoing commitments to provide U.S. support for road building, telephone lines, farm programs, commodity sales, and the construction of utility plants in the recipient country. Increases in social welfare, civil rights, and natural resources agreements took place with Gerald Ford and Carter, although social welfare agreements declined beginning with Reagan.

Individual presidents vary in policy emphases, though not dramatically. Through the Marshall Plan, the Truman administration expressed considerable interest in social welfare and civil rights agreements (accounting for 27.7 percent of the total number of agreements made during Truman's second term). In contrast, Eisenhower focused on defense during and after the Korean War (30.2 percent of his first-term total and 24.1 percent of agreements in his second term). Under the Foreign Assistance Act of 1961, the Kennedy administration signed more foreign aid agreements than were signed under any other president. Differences found here are due in part to individual interests of the presidents but also to prominent environmental factors in the international sphere. Truman and Eisenhower, especially, were responding to war and its aftermath. Some of these variations are also systematically related to the president's party (as shown at the bottom of Table 7-6). Republican presidents were more likely than Democratic presidents to sponsor military agreements: 21 percent of all Republican agreements involved defense matters, compared with only 14 percent of agreements made during Democratic administrations. Democrats concluded more agreements in the social welfare and civil rights areas. The key point here is that attention to many issue areas follows fairly stable patterns regardless of who occupies the White House and what his political party affiliation is.

Nations as Political Actors

Table 7-7 displays those regions of the globe involved in U.S. international agreements. The agreements are most likely to involve three regions: Western Europe, Asia, and Central America. The institutional preoccupation with these three regions remains even as occupants of the Oval Office change. Attention shifts among the three, but these shifts do not reflect new commitments to other regions. The contrast between agreements in these regions and the minimal commitments undertaken with Eastern Europe, the Soviet Union, and Africa highlights these patterns. Since the Cold War, the number of agreements with the Soviet Union and Eastern Europe has not substantially increased. Even after the fall of communism, agreements with Eastern Europe have remained modest. Similarly, agreements with the Soviet Union and (after 1991) the Russian Republic increased only slightly during Richard Nixon's efforts at détente but did not continue thereafter. Agreements with Africa have increased, as the relative importance of Third World nations has grown in the U.S. world outlook; however, this increase has not been steady.

For the postwar period, each international agreement has been classified by regime type characterizing the foreign partner (Table 7-8). Not unexpectedly, the results reveal that democratic regimes predominate as partners to international agreements in every presidential administration. Agreements with totalitarian regimes increased beginning with the Johnson administration but still remain a small proportion of the total number of agreements promulgated. Nonmilitary authoritarian regimes are frequent partners.

The results by party reveal little difference between the agreements sponsored by Democratic and Republican presidents. Presidents of both parties support agreements with republican and nonmilitary authoritarian regimes. This group represents a reasonable pool of known allies and dependents of the United States. Presidential diplomacy does little to build up regions that are less friendly (Eastern Europe or totalitarian regimes) or that are less well known (Africa). Furthermore, presidents do not seem to be bothered by the dictatorial, restrictive qualities of authoritarian regimes.

Presidents, as singular political figures, have only limited control of international agreements. For most of these agreements, incumbent strategies and actions appear less important than institutionalized behavior toward various regimes across specific policy areas that has been both stable and predictable over the past four decades. The independent policy making that is evident in treaties and executive agreements is run by the State Department and by the Executive Office of the President. The resulting mix of international diversity and organizational decentralization limits presidents' direct control of their own diplomatic efforts.

Military Affairs

Contemporary presidents have asserted considerable unilateral authority to engage in military actions around the globe. This, too, has taken the form of independent policy making—specifically, an independent war-making power for the presidency, which has come to supplant the dual constitutional powers of commander-in-chief for the president and the power to declare war for Congress. In many cases, presidents act without a congressional resolution sanctioning a military commitment. In other instances, presidents ask for a resolution in support of the effort while maintaining that they can act independently even if such a resolution is not in place. Table 7-9 lists instances of presidential use of military force since World War II.

The ability of any one president to march the nation off to war should not be exaggerated. Many of the actions taken by Presidents Truman through Reagan rested on an overall tenet of American foreign policy: America would use force or the threat of force to contain the spread of communism. This doctrine of global anticommunism carried different names and had different variants throughout the cold war period—containment (Truman), flexible response (Kennedy), détente (Nixon), and the evil empire (Reagan)—but its central tenets never wavered. Even after the collapse of the Soviet Union, Presidents Bush and Clinton continued to seek the protection of American interests and notions of democracy throughout the world. As a consequence, overall defense spending during the post-World War II period has been more consistent across presidents than different.

In addition to the use of military force, presidents have adopted several other techniques to enhance their role in military affairs. In the Foreign Assistance Act of 1961, Congress granted presidents independent discretion for the funding of various military operations and foreign assistance projects. The law provided that presidents may use special funding authorities without prior congressional approval when a president determines that the effort "is vital to the security of the United States" (for full details, see U.S. General Accounting Office, 1985). This is known as a presidential determination (or presidential finding). Determinations grant presidents the authority to meet emergencies or respond to situations in which formal foreign assistance agreements are not possible. The determinations are like executive agreements in that they involve independent presidential policy making. They are also like executive agreements in that the day-to-day management of a determination is coordinated between the Executive Office of the President and the State Department.

Table 7-10 documents the total number of general presidential determinations from Kennedy to Clinton. Beginning with Nixon's second term, general determinations became a relatively frequent device for both direct military support and nonmilitary support to a country. They increased somewhat during the Bush administration and the early years of Clinton's term. Much of this increase was due to determinations giving aid to countries in the Persian Gulf.

Three specific types of determinations that have been excluded from Table 7-10 are waivers, transfers, and drawdowns. The waiver is the most frequently used of these and provides for funds "without regard to any conditions as to eligibility contained in this [Foreign Assistance] Act, when the President determines that such use is important to the security of the United States" (U.S. General Accounting Office, 1985, 29). The conditions being waived are time limits, usage limits, currency requirements, and war status limitations on the funds. Waiver authority was used to undertake military operations in Laos, Vietnam, and Cambodia. These efforts would have been prohibited by the Foreign Assistance Act had waivers not been invoked. Table 7-11 reports the total number and dollar amounts of waivers, when available. More than $1.5 billion has been spent by presidents through the waiver authority.

A second form of special funding authority allows presidents, again without approval from Congress, to transfer up to 10 percent of the funds under one provision of several foreign assistance acts to another provision of any other assistance act "whenever the President determines it to be necessary" (U.S. General Accounting Office, 1985, 24). As Table 7-12 shows, these transfers have amounted to more than $450 million between various foreign assistance accounts; about half of these transfers involved U.S. efforts in Southeast Asia.

Presidents also have the "drawdown authority," which allows them to provide Department of Defense equipment to a foreign government without congressional or other budgetary authorization or appropriations. A president may draw down U.S. military stock or equipment once he has determined that the vital security of the United States is at stake. After the equipment has been sent, presidents are authorized to replace or reimburse the Defense Department for the stocks and services that have been drawn down. Subsequent foreign assistance appropriations provide for replacements and reimbursements. As Table 7-13 makes plain, much of this money was used to give material to Vietnam and Cambodia, but the drawdown procedure has also been used to fund more recent operations in El Salvador and the Persian Gulf. One of the most infamous uses of the drawdown authority, not reflected in the table, was the shipment of arms to Iran by the Reagan administration.

Domestic Matters

Presidents engage in independent policy making in domestic affairs through use of the executive order. Like executive agreements, executive orders do not require congressional approval. They are drafted in some instances in departments and agencies and in others in the Office of Management and Budget (OMB). In either case, OMB has developed a practice of "executive order clearance" in which all proposed orders are first screened by OMB to assure that they fit with the president's policy interests and existing law.

Executive orders since 1789 have been recorded and those issued since 1949 have been classified by policy area, president, and the group to which the order was addressed. The policy areas are comparable to those used for treaties, executive agreements, and congressional roll call votes (see Chapter 8). Table 7-14 shows the total number of known executive orders since Washington. Washington issued the first executive order on June 8, 1789, asking the heads of the original departments—State, War, Treasury, and the Attorney General—to make "a clear account" of affairs connected with their departments (Lord, 1979, 1). As might be expected, early executive orders were infrequent; they began to see significant use only after the Civil War. During the nineteenth century, executive orders had two primary administrative purposes. The earliest was for external administration: the disposition of public lands, especially the withdrawal of land for Indian, military, naval, and lighthouse reservations. In the 1870s executive orders were used for internal administration. Numerous orders were issued concerning Civil Service rules, including the status of government employees, their work hours, salaries, pension requirements, and federal holidays. These two administrative forms are no longer the only types of executive orders, but they remain a significant proportion of the total number.

A relatively large increase in the number of executive orders appeared in Theodore Roosevelt's first term, and an even greater increase occurred in his second term. However, these orders continued to fit the nineteenth-century administrative mode; they did not advance major policy initiatives. The increase in executive orders during Roosevelt's administration did not represent an isolated flurry of presidential activity. Presidents who succeeded Roosevelt—including those who were activists, such as Woodrow Wilson, and those who were not, such as William H. Taft, Warren G. Harding, Coolidge, and Herbert Hoover—issued executive orders at roughly the same levels as Roosevelt. The new level of executive activity begun under Roosevelt became institutionalized for subsequent chief executives and reflected an expanded federal government.

Franklin Roosevelt extended the use of executive orders beyond administrative matters to include major presidential policy initiatives. Executive orders rose sharply between 1932 and 1933 (see Table 7-14). Roosevelt closed banks during the banking emergency of 1933, wrote rules under the authority of the National Industrial Recovery Act, and established the Civilian Conservation Corps. In addition, he issued orders for defense and national security. By executive order, Roosevelt established the Office of Price Administration and the Office of Economic Stabilization and effected the internment of American citizens of Japanese ancestry living in the Pacific coastal states. The Supreme Court later declared unconstitutional the Japanese internment order, along with President Truman's order to seize the steel industry. However, the Court has usually upheld presidential executive orders, establishing them as having the same force in law as statutes.

Substantive policy making through executive orders has also focused on civil liberties. Franklin Roosevelt established the Fair Employment Practices Commission in 1943 to prevent discrimination in hiring by government agencies and military suppliers. Truman ended segregation in the armed forces. Eisenhower and Kennedy issued executive orders to enforce desegregation of schools in Arkansas, Mississippi, and Alabama. Lyndon Johnson created equal employment opportunity in federal hiring and in hiring by government contractors through a 1965 executive order. Indeed, the whole concept of affirmative action in federal employment stems from this order. The Reagan administration, which opposed affirmative action, proposed the issuance of an executive order that would have amounted to a "repeal" of Johnson's equal opportunity order though it never pursued this proposal. Clinton set off a storm of controversy when he proposed an executive order to lift the ban on gays in the military. Only after long negotiations with military commanders, Defense Department officials, and members of Congress did Clinton sign an order that was much less sweeping than the one he had originally intended.

A recent example of the use of the executive order as an independent policy device focuses on an order first signed by Reagan and then continued by Bush. This executive order prohibited family planning clinics receiving federal funds from informing their clients about abortion options. The Supreme Court upheld this so-called "gag rule" order in *Rust v. Sullivan* (1991). Congress tried several times to pass legislation to negate the order, but Bush vetoed one such attempt and threatened to veto others. Congress was unable to rally the two-thirds votes from both houses needed to override a Bush veto. Within days of taking office, however, Clinton revoked the Reagan executive order and ended the gag rule.

In sum, Franklin Roosevelt's contribution to presidential power in this area was substantial. His actions institutionalized presidents' assumptions that they could use executive orders as policy-making devices rather than merely as administrative devices. Presidents after Roosevelt followed his lead. Indeed, they had little choice.

Policy Areas and Groups

In Table 7-15 executive orders are categorized by policy type. Apart from executive orders on federal government personnel and interagency and congressional requests, presidents use these orders in five principal policy areas: defense, foreign trade, economic management, natural resources, and social welfare/civil rights. Relatively few executive orders are issued in the areas of agriculture, federalism, and foreign aid. Agricultural executive orders deal principally with farming problems, which do not provide presidents with abundant advantages for building broad constituency support. When international agreements are made, agriculture figures much more prominently because it is an easy, economical, and broad-based avenue by which to aid nations and at the same time facilitate the distribution of American farm surpluses. By comparison, numerous executive orders have covered social welfare, economic management, and natural resource issues. Table 7-15 also reveals that executive orders extend beyond domestic affairs. They cover foreign trade, defense, and, to a much lesser extent, foreign aid. Oftentimes these orders establish guidelines for carrying out earlier international agreements.

Table 7-15 analyzes the policy emphases of executive orders by individual presidents and by party. Social welfare and civil rights issues were especially prominent under Carter. Kennedy and Bush issued the most defense executive orders. Eisenhower issued the fewest executive orders on social welfare/civil rights matters. The economy received the most attention from Nixon, Truman, and Reagan. Executive orders on natural resources have declined since Truman, whereas those on foreign trade increased markedly during the Carter and Reagan administrations. Democratic presidents are generally more likely to issue executive orders in the areas of resources and social welfare/civil rights than are Republican presidents. Although variations in policy emphasis between incumbents are evident, the policy complexity within which these variations occur is even more plain. The presidency is not free to ignore any policy area and must ultimately juggle the interrelationships and inconsistencies across the several types of issues. Table 7-16 examines the diverse groups affected by executive orders. The differences here mirror differences in the policy interests of the presidents. Democratic presidents are more likely to issue executive orders affecting labor and minorities; Republican presidents target business.

Executive orders combine the interests of incumbents with programmatic priorities that attach to the institution of the presidency. The intricacies inherent in these orders are heightened by complexity across policy areas and diversity among groups. Recent presidents have faced problems of coordination and coherence. Presidents must rely on the Executive Office of the President and on departments and agencies to propose and draft executive orders. The occupant of the Oval Office is not personally issuing each executive order; instead, the institution turns this abundance of work into standard operating procedures, patterns, and expectations. The type and frequency of executive orders issued by any new president is thus predominantly a function of the institution of the presidency. Presidents do influence the direction of executive policy making, but only in incremental ways.

The Economy

Presidents since Franklin Roosevelt have portrayed themselves as budding economists who will adapt fiscal policy to promote economic prosperity. They do so by three devices: (1) adjusting taxes, typically downward; (2) adjusting spending, typically upward; and (3) attempting to balance the budget.

Taxing Politics

Presidents since Truman have offered tax cuts as the primary instrument of economic management. Presidents typically propose the cuts as swift, short-term economic solutions that give taxpayers and businesses an immediate benefit. Yet tax cuts are ultimately an uneasy blend of clear political advantages for the presidents and other politicians offering them and unclear economic effects for the consumers and corporations receiving them. Table 7-17 summarizes presidents' tax proposals and congressional enactments from Truman to Clinton. As the table shows, presidents and Congress jockey over taxes, with presidents almost never getting what they have asked for. Presidents are faced with a Congress introducing its own initiatives without a prior proposal from the White House. For instance, Truman and Eisenhower reluctantly introduced tax cuts in 1948 and 1954 to stave off larger cuts desired, and ultimately enacted, by Congress. The table also shows that every president since Truman has proposed at least one tax cut. In the span of just over two decades, tax rates for the highest income bracket dropped from 91 percent to 28 percent.

Tax cuts are the "easy" half of presidents' fiscal tax policy. How willing are presidents to adopt the "hard" part of fiscal policy—a tax increase? Table 7-17 shows that presidents have agreed to tax increases generally only in exchange for economic or other desired incentives. Johnson resisted a tax increase until 1968 when, no longer running for reelection, he acquiesced to a Vietnam tax surcharge passed by Congress. Nixon sought the continuation of the surcharge in exchange for congressionally sponsored income tax reduction and repeal of investment tax credits in 1969. Two years later Nixon changed course, asking for a large income tax reduction and the return of the investment tax credit. During the post-oil embargo recession in 1974, Ford proposed a tax increase designed to pay for anti-recessionary plans that included improved unemployment compensation and aid to the housing industry. Yet a tax cut for business also accompanied the increase. This increase was abandoned completely in 1975 in favor of a temporary tax cut to give the economy a shot in the arm. Congress and President Reagan agreed on moderate increases in excise taxes in 1982 and 1984 in response to an ever-growing budget deficit. President Bush agreed to assorted tax increases in 1990, but many of these were repealed in 1992. Clinton and Congress agreed to a tax surcharge of upper-income families in 1993, but began debate on a tax cut in 1995.

Spending Politics

Presidents also adopt programs designed to "spend" the economy back to health or to show the government's commitment to alleviating a particular problem. Table 7-18 records the differences between presidents' proposed spending totals and the amounts actually appropriated by Congress. Only Eisenhower, during his second term, met with much success in getting what he wanted. Congress has raised or lowered the requests of all other presidents since Truman. Table 7-18 reveals that presidents also advocate spending cuts. Cuts are typically offered as measures of immediate cost savings or as a matter of ideology—frugality is good. Much of the spending presidents propose and Congress approves goes to mandatory programs that have become increasingly uncontrollable aspects of the federal budget (66 percent of the total by 1995).

Presidents also use impoundment, a device by which presidents may temporarily or permanently withhold the spending of funds that Congress has appropriated. This is done to redirect or curb spending on existing programs that presidents dislike. Impoundment began in earnest with Franklin Roosevelt. Presidents from Roosevelt through Kennedy used impoundment primarily to curb military programs. Johnson and Nixon broadened the scope of this policy tool by targeting domestic appropriations. No publicly available figures exist on the total amount of funds that have been impounded.

Congress decided to place restrictions on such funding decisions in the Budget and Impoundment Control Act of 1974.[2] Presidents are now required to send special messages to Congress specifying the reasons for and the estimated effects of each proposed rescission of funds. The "rescission requests" must be approved by both houses within forty-five days (P.L. 93–844). If either house passes a resolution disapproving the rescission, the funds must be spent. Table 7-19 shows the total rescission of funds requested since 1977. Not surprisingly, the rescissions were much greater during the Reagan years than during the Carter years. The Reagan administration requested substantial cuts in already appropriated funds, particularly in education, housing and urban development, and interior. Readily available data on the number of rescissions that have been disallowed by Congress do not exist. In addition, it is not yet clear how the Supreme Court's decision in *U.S. Immigration and Naturalization Service v. Chadha*, which struck down the legislative veto, will affect the provisions of the act.

Budget Politics

Presidents' main economic policy instruments of taxing and spending ultimately depend on the budget and the budget process. The most that presidents can hope for is to modify the overall budget picture, but this is difficult to do because the budget is an amorphous document that never really exists in one place, nor is it passed at one time. The budget process is instead a confusing, fragmented, and decentralized process.

Because of the large budget deficit (Figure 7-2), budgeting increasingly goes to the core of governing. Table 7-20 indicates that the government has operated in surplus only eight times since 1947 (1947, 1948, 1949, 1951, 1956, 1957, 1960, 1969). Structural deficits—the portion of the deficit that results from a basic imbalance in spending and revenues not due to recession—are now commonplace. Deficits during the 1960s were modest, averaging $5 billion from 1961 to 1967. A $25.2 billion deficit was amassed in 1968. This was followed by the country's last surplus—$3.2 billion in 1969. A large jump in the deficit followed the first oil shock of 1974. The deficit increased tenfold from $6.1 billion in 1973 to $63.2 billion in 1975. It remained high throughout the Carter years after the oil shock of 1978. The average annual deficit from 1977 to 1980 was $58 billion. In 1981, the deficit almost doubled from the previous year to $128 billion. In 1982, it nearly doubled again to $208 billion. During the Clinton administration the deficit dropped for the first time since 1987—by $40 billion in fiscal 1993 and by over $50 billion in fiscal 1994.

The looming budget deficits point to an immense policy problem over which presidents have little control. Estimates for the deficit and plans to reduce its size are therefore matters that the institutional presidency, in the form of the Office of Management and Budget, supervises.

Conclusion

The prevailing model of presidential policy making stresses the roles of key political actors, especially presidents. As a result, less attention is paid to the institutions within which these actors behave. This chapter focuses on the institution's impact on policy making. The institutional presidency transcends individual presidents' specific actions. Although presidency watchers detail the individual idiosyncrasies of presidential officeholders, the contemporary institution is a much more complicated, though much more predictable, policy maker. It is elaborate, decentralized, and organizationally stable, with key ongoing units that have well-established practices and norms. The institution accommodates numerous policy areas that place different demands on presidents, create different incentives for them, and allow them different degrees of success. Institutional policy making occurs at the point where the predictable institution encounters the complex and unpredictable policy environment. Only within the arena defined by the institution, policy areas, and target groups are the actions of individual presidents relevant.

Notes

1. Table 7-2 and several other tables in this chapter take Truman's second term as a convenient starting point. Truman's first term was marked by activities tied to the end of World War II and is therefore somewhat anomalous.
2. Efforts by the Nixon administration to impound funds appropriated under the Federal Water Pollution Control Act Amendments of 1972 provided impetus for the act. Nixon instructed the administrator of the Environmental Protection Agency to withhold from the states $9 billion, more than one-half of the total appropriations. In *Train v. The City of New York* (1975), the Supreme Court held that the impoundment was unconstitutional.

Table 7-1   Treaties and Executive Agreements, 1789–1948

President/year	Senate majority party same as president's?	Total international agreements	Executive agreements	Treaties[a]	Ratio agreements: treaties[b]
Washington, I					
1789	Yes	0	0	0	—
1790	Yes	0	0	0	—
1791	Yes	0	0	0	—
1792	Yes	0	0	0	—
Total	—	0	0	0	—
Yearly average	—	0.00	0.00	0.00	—
Washington, II					
1793	Yes	0	0	0	—
1794	Yes	1	0	1	—
1795	Yes	2	0	2	—
1796	Yes	2	0	2	—
Total	—	5	0	5	—
Yearly average	—	1.00	0.00	1.00	—
Adams					
1797	Yes	1	0	1	—
1798	Yes	1	0	1	—
1799	Yes	1	0	1	—
1800	Yes	1	0	1	—
Total	—	4	0	4	—
Yearly average	—	1.00	0.00	1.00	—
Jefferson, I					
1801	Yes	1	0	1	—
1802	Yes	1	0	1	—
1803	Yes	3	0	3	—
1804	Yes	0	0	0	—
Total	—	5	0	5	—
Yearly average	—	1.00	0.00	1.00	—
Jefferson, II					
1805	Yes	1	0	1	—
1806	Yes	0	0	0	—
1807	Yes	0	0	0	—
1808	Yes	0	0	0	—
Total	—	1	0	1	—
Yearly average	—	0.25	0.00	0.25	—
Madison, I					
1809	Yes	0	0	0	—
1810	Yes	0	0	0	—
1811	Yes	0	0	0	—
1812	Yes	0	0	0	—
Total	—	0	0	0	—
Yearly average	—	0.00	0.00	0.00	—

Table 7-1   *(Continued)*

President/year	Senate majority party same as president's?	Total international agreements	Executive agreements	Treaties[a]	Ratio agreements: treaties[b]
Madison, II					
1813	Yes	0	0	0	—
1814	Yes	0	0	0	—
1815	Yes	1	0	1	—
1816	Yes	2	0	2	—
Total	—	3	0	3	—
Yearly average	—	0.75	0.00	0.75	—
Monroe, I					
1817	Yes	3	1	2	0.5
1818	Yes	0	0	0	—
1819	Yes	2	0	2	—
1820	Yes	0	0	0	—
Total	—	5	1	4	0.3
Yearly average	—	1.25	0.25	1.00	—
Monroe, II					
1821	Yes	0	0	0	—
1822	Yes	2	0	2	—
1823	Yes	1	0	1	—
1824	Yes	2	0	2	—
Total	—	5	0	5	—
Yearly average	—	1.00	0.00	1.00	—
J. Q. Adams					
1825	Yes	2	1	1	1.0
1826	Yes	3	1	2	0.5
1827	No	6	0	6	—
1828	No	3	0	3	—
Total	—	14	2	12	0.2
Yearly average	—	3.5	0.50	3.00	—
Jackson, I					
1829	Yes	1	0	1	—
1830	Yes	2	0	2	—
1831	Yes	2	0	2	—
1832	Yes	3	0	3	—
Total	—	8	0	8	—
Yearly average	—	2.00	0.00	2.00	—
Jackson, II					
1833	Yes	4	0	4	—
1834	Yes	0	0	0	—
1835	Yes	2	0	2	—
1836	Yes	2	0	2	—
Total	—	8	0	8	—
Yearly average	—	2.00	0.00	2.00	—

(Table continues)

Table 7-1   *(Continued)*

President/year	Senate majority party same as president's?	Total international agreements	Executive agreements	Treaties[a]	Ratio agreements: treaties[b]
Van Buren					
1837	Yes	1	0	1	—
1838	Yes	4	0	4	—
1839	Yes	3	1	2	0.5
1840	Yes	3	1	2	0.5
Total	—	11	2	9	0.2
Yearly average	—	2.75	0.50	2.25	—
W. Harrison					
1841	Yes	1	0	1	—
Tyler					
1841	Yes	0	0	0	—
1842	Yes	2	0	2	—
1843	Yes	3	1	2	0.5
1844	Yes	6	0	6	—
Total	—	11	1	10	0.1
Yearly average	—	2.75	0.25	2.50	—
Polk					
1845	Yes	4	1	3	0.3
1846	Yes	6	2	4	0.5
1847	Yes	6	1	5	0.2
1848	Yes	5	1	4	0.3
Total	—	21	5	16	0.3
Yearly average	—	5.25	1.25	4.00	—
Taylor					
1849	No	5	3	2	1.5
1850	No	2	0	2	—
Total	—	7	3	4	0.8
Yearly average	—	3.5	1.5	2.00	—
Fillmore					
1850	No	3	1	2	0.5
1851	No	2	0	2	—
1852	No	8	3	5	0.6
Total	—	13	4	9	0.4
Yearly average	—	4.33	1.33	3.33	—
Pierce					
1853	Yes	10	5	5	1.0
1854	Yes	13	4	9	0.4
1855	Yes	4	3	1	3.0
1856	Yes	5	0	5	—
Total	—	32	12	20	0.6
Yearly average	—	8.00	3.00	5.00	—

Table 7-1   *(Continued)*

President/year	Senate majority party same as president's?	Total international agreements	Executive agreements	Treaties[a]	Ratio agreements: treaties[b]
Buchanan					
1857	Yes	8	3	5	0.6
1858	Yes	10	1	9	0.1
1859	Yes	2	2	0	2.0
1860	Yes	4	2	2	1.0
Total	—	24	8	16	0.5
Yearly average	—	6.00	2.00	4.00	—
Lincoln, I					
1861	Yes	8	0	8	—
1862	Yes	7	1	6	0.2
1863	Yes	7	2	5	0.4
1864	Yes	3	0	3	—
Total	—	25	3	22	0.1
Yearly average	—	6.25	0.75	5.50	—
Lincoln, II					
1865	Yes	0	0	0	—
A. Johnson					
1865	Yes	0	0	0	—
1866	Yes	5	0	5	—
1867	Yes	7	0	7	—
1868	Yes	14	0	14	—
Total	—	26	0	26	—
Yearly average	—	6.50	0	6.50	—
Grant, I					
1869	Yes	3	1	2	0.5
1870	Yes	12	1	11	0.1
1871	Yes	5	0	5	—
1872	Yes	5	0	5	—
Total	—	25	2	23	0.1
Yearly average	—	6.25	.50	5.75	—
Grant, II					
1873	Yes	4	2	2	1.0
1874	Yes	9	5	4	1.3
1875	Yes	1	0	1	—
1876	Yes	4	2	2	1.0
Total	—	18	9	9	1.0
Yearly average	—	4.5	2.25	2.25	—
Hayes					
1877	Yes	2	1	1	1.0
1878	Yes	6	1	5	0.2

(Table continues)

Table 7-1   *(Continued)*

President/year	Senate majority party same as president's?	Total international agreements	Executive agreements	Treaties[a]	Ratio agreements: treaties[b]
Hayes (continued)					
1879	No	2	1	1	1.0
1880	No	9	2	7	0.3
Total	—	19	5	14	0.4
Yearly average	—	4.75	1.25	3.50	—
Garfield					
1881	Yes	3	1	2	0.5
Arthur					
1881	Yes	2	0	2	—
1882	Yes	14	4	10	0.4
1883	Yes	6	4	2	2.0
1884	Yes	11	3	8	0.4
Total	—	33	11	22	0.5
Yearly average	—	8.25	2.75	5.50	—
Cleveland					
1885	No	7	5	2	2.5
1886	No	8	1	7	0.1
1887	No	7	3	4	0.8
1888	No	8	2	6	0.3
Total	—	30	11	19	0.6
Yearly average	—	7.50	2.75	4.75	—
B. Harrison					
1889	Yes	3	1	2	0.5
1890	Yes	4	2	2	1.0
1891	Yes	11	6	5	1.2
1892	Yes	9	2	7	0.3
Total	—	27	11	16	0.7
Yearly average	—	6.75	2.75	4.00	—
Cleveland					
1893	Yes	2	0	2	—
1894	Yes	5	2	3	0.7
1895	No	4	2	2	1.0
1896	No	6	2	4	0.5
Total	—	17	6	11	0.5
Yearly average	—	4.25	1.50	2.75	—
McKinley, I					
1897	Yes	5	2	3	0.7
1898	Yes	11	7	4	1.8
1899	Yes	18	9	9	1.0
1900	Yes	15	7	8	0.9
Total	—	49	25	24	1.0
Yearly average	—	12.25	6.25	6.00	—

Table 7-1   *(Continued)*

President/year	Senate majority party same as president's?	Total international agreements	Executive agreements	Treaties[a]	Ratio agreements: treaties[b]
McKinley, II					
1901	Yes	4	2	2	1.0
T. Roosevelt, I					
1901	Yes	11	4	7	0.5
1902	Yes	20	9	11	0.8
1903	Yes	12	1	11	0.1
1904	Yes	20	7	13	0.5
Total	—	63	21	42	0.5
Yearly average	—	15.75	5.25	10.50	—
T. Roosevelt, II					
1905	Yes	17	10	7	1.4
1906	Yes	20	7	13	0.5
1907	Yes	25	15	10	1.5
1908	Yes	39	4	35	0.1
Total	—	101	36	65	0.6
Yearly average	—	25.25	9.00	16.25	—
Taft					
1909	Yes	11	7	4	1.8
1910	Yes	17	5	12	0.4
1911	Yes	10	2	8	0.3
1912	Yes	7	3	4	0.8
Total	—	45	17	28	0.6
Yearly average	—	11.25	4.25	7.00	—
Wilson, I					
1913	Yes	19	4	15	0.3
1914	Yes	30	7	23	0.3
1915	Yes	14	13	1	13.0
1916	Yes	9	7	2	3.5
Total	—	72	31	41	0.8
Yearly average	—	18	7.75	10.25	—
Wilson, II					
1917	Yes	5	4	1	4.0
1918	Yes	21	9	12	0.8
1919	No	18	7	11	0.6
1920	No	6	3	3	1.0
Total	—	50	23	27	0.9
Yearly average	—	12.50	5.75	6.75	—
Harding					
1921	Yes	27	14	13	1.1
1922	Yes	18	10	8	1.3
1923	Yes	14	7	7	1.0
Total	—	59	31	28	1.1
Yearly average	—	14.75	7.75	7.00	—

(Table continues)

Table 7-1   *(Continued)*

President/year	Senate majority party same as president's?	Total international agreements	Executive agreements	Treaties[a]	Ratio agreements: treaties[b]
Coolidge, I					
1923	Yes	19	6	13	0.5
1924	Yes	46	18	28	0.6
Total	—	65	24	41	0.6
Yearly average	—	32.50	12.00	20.50	—
Coolidge, II					
1925	Yes	51	38	13	2.9
1926	Yes	28	21	7	3.0
1927	Yes	24	14	10	1.4
1928	Yes	64	23	41	0.6
Total	—	167	96	71	1.4
Yearly average	—	41.75	24.00	17.75	—
Hoover					
1929	Yes	47	26	21	1.2
1930	Yes	36	19	17	1.1
1931	Yes	29	22	7	3.1
1932	Yes	46	38	8	4.8
Total	—	158	105	53	2.0
Yearly average	—	39.50	26.25	13.25	—
F. Roosevelt, I					
1933	Yes	26	19	7	2.7
1934	Yes	37	21	16	1.3
1935	Yes	32	21	11	1.9
1936	Yes	51	26	25	1.0
Total	—	146	87	59	1.5
Yearly average	—	36.50	21.75	14.75	—
F. Roosevelt, II					
1937	Yes	36	23	13	1.8
1938	Yes	47	38	9	4.2
1939	Yes	40	30	10	3.0
1940	Yes	42	29	13	2.2
Total	—	165	120	45	2.7
Yearly average	—	41.25	30.00	11.25	—
F. Roosevelt, III					
1941	Yes	60	56	4	14.0
1942	Yes	134	130	4	32.5
1943	Yes	99	98	1	98.0
1944	Yes	89	83	6	13.8
Total	—	382	367	15	24.5
Yearly average	—	95.50	91.75	3.75	—
F. Roosevelt, IV					
1945	Yes	35	35	0	35.0

Table 7-1   *(Continued)*

President/year	Senate majority party same as president's?	Total international agreements	Executive agreements	Treaties[a]	Ratio agreements: treaties[b]
Truman, I					
1945	Yes	90	85	5	17.0
1946	Yes	163	144	19	7.6
1947	No	192	174	18	9.7
1948	No	223	202	21	9.6
Total	—	668	605	63	9.6
Yearly average	—	167.00	151.25	15.75	—

Source: Adapted from Lawrence Margolis, *Executive Agreements and Presidential Power in Foreign Policy* (New York: Praeger, 1986).

[a] Treaties include protocols and conventions.
[b] The ratio is expressed as the number of executive agreements issued versus the number of treaties. In 1948, for example, 9.6 agreements were issued for every one treaty.

Table 7-2   Treaties and Executive Agreements, 1949–1993

President/year	Senate majority party same as president's?	Total international agreements	Executive agreements	Treaties[a]	Ratio agreements: treaties[b]
Truman, II					
1949	Yes	146	131	15	8.7
1950	Yes	159	144	15	9.6
1951	Yes	233	206	27	7.6
1952	Yes	310	285	25	11.4
Total	—	848	766	82	9.3
Yearly average	—	212	192	20.50	—
Eisenhower, I					
1953	Yes	178	154	24	6.4
1954	Yes	200	178	22	8.1
1955	No	343	300	43	7.0
1956	No	241	225	16	14.1
Total	—	962	857	105	8.2
Yearly average	—	240.50	214.25	26.25	—
Eisenhower, II					
1957	No	237	202	35	5.8
1958	No	207	183	24	7.6
1959	No	240	215	25	8.6
1960	No	274	248	26	9.5
Total	—	958	848	110	7.7
Yearly average	—	239.50	212.00	27.50	—
Kennedy					
1961	Yes	267	247	20	12.4
1962	Yes	320	296	24	12.3
1963	Yes	244	220	24	9.2
Total	—	831	763	68	11.2
Yearly average	—	277.00	254.33	22.67	—
Johnson[c]					
1964	Yes	226	210	16	13.1
1965	Yes	218	197	21	9.4
1966	Yes	242	216	26	8.3
1967	Yes	232	203	29	7.0
1968	Yes	194	182	12	15.2
Total	—	1112	1008	104	9.7
Yearly average	—	222.40	201.60	20.80	—
Nixon, I					
1969	No	169	151	18	8.4
1970	No	223	190	33	5.8
1971	No	235	207	28	7.4
1972	No	288	249	39	6.4
Total	—	915	797	118	6.8
Yearly average	—	228.75	199.25	29.50	—
Nixon, II					
1973	No	229	189	40	4.7
1974	No	152	130	22	5.9
Total	—	381	319	62	5.1
Yearly average	—	190.50	159.50	31.00	—

Table 7-2   *(Continued)*

President/year	Senate majority party same as president's?	Total international agreements	Executive agreements	Treaties[a]	Ratio agreements: treaties[b]
Ford					
1974	No	96	70	26	2.7
1975	No	294	255	39	6.5
1976	No	386	352	34	10.4
Total	—	776	677	99	6.8
Yearly average	—	259.67	225.67	33.00	—
Carter					
1977	Yes	370	340	30	11.3
1978	Yes	344	304	40	7.6
1979	Yes	286	238	48	5.0
1980	Yes	169	139	30	4.6
Total	—	1169	1,021	148	6.9
Yearly average	—	292.25	255.25	37.00	—
Reagan, I					
1981	Yes	249	194	55	3.5
1982	Yes	255	214	41	5.2
1983	Yes	134	113	21	5.4
1984	Yes	201	162	39	4.5
Total	—	839	683	156	
Yearly average	—	209.75	170.75	39.00	—
Reagan, II					
1985		140	d	d	—
1986		85	d	d	—
1987	No	94	d	d	—
1988	No	93	d	d	—
Total	—	412	d	d	—
Yearly average	—	103.00	d	d	—
Bush					
1989	No	95	d	d	—
1990	No	362	d	d	—
1991	No	274	d	d	—
1992	No	280	d	d	—
Total	—	1,011	d	d	—
Yearly average	—	252.75	d	d	—
Clinton					
1993	Yes	119	d	d	—

Source: (1949–1980) Calculated by the author from U.S. Department of State, *Treaties and Other International Agreements* (Washington, D.C.: Government Printing Office, 1950–1980); (1981–1993) calculated from successive volumes of *Current Treaty Index.*

[a] Refers to the total number of treaties, protocols, and conventions issued in a year.
[b] The ratio is expressed as the number of executive agreements issued versus the number of treaties. In 1983, for example, 5.4 agreements were issued for every one treaty.
[c] Includes full term from November 1963 to January 1969.
[d] Beginning in 1985 the *Current Treaty Index* no longer clearly distinguishes between treaties and executive agreements.

Figure 7-1 Number of Treaties, Executive Agreements, and International Agreements by Presidents, Truman, II, to Clinton (yearly averages)

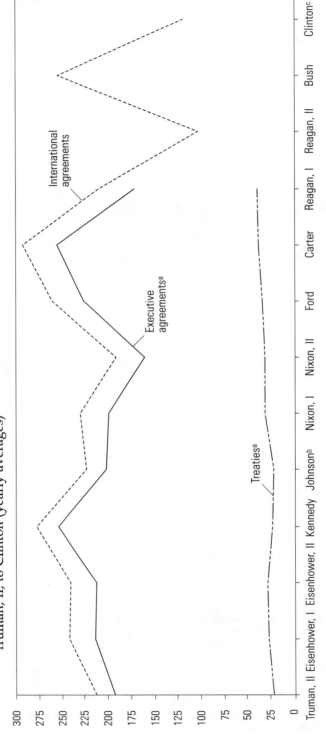

Source: Calculated by the author from (Truman through Carter) U.S. Department of State, *Treaties and Other International Agreements* (Washington, D.C.: Government Printing Office, 1950–1980); (Reagan to Clinton) *Current Treaty Index* (1981–1993).

[a] Beginning in 1985, *Current Treaty Index* no longer distinguished between treaties and executive agreements.

[b] Includes full term from November 1963 to January 1969.

[c] 1993 only.

Table 7-3   Senate Action on Treaties, Protocols, and Conventions, 1949–1993

President/year	Ratified	Pending	Withdrawn	Rejected
Truman, II				
1949	9	19	7	0
1950	14	11	0	0
1951	15	39	1	0
1952	25	7	3	0
Eisenhower, I				
1953	25	15	0	0
1954	6	24	1	0
1955	20	16	1	0
1956	12	14	0	0
Eisenhower, II				
1957	12	15	1	0
1958	3	7	7	0
1959	8	15	0	0
1960	13	13	0	1
Kennedy				
1961	9	18	0	0
1962	8	17	1	0
1963	8	27	0	0
Johnson[a]				
1964	14	14	3	0
1965	6	17	0	0
1966	9	29	0	0
1967	25	17	2	0
1968	15	14	0	0
Nixon				
1969	7	16	0	0
1970	10	18	1	0
1971	13	18	0	0
1972	18	23	0	0
1973	22	24	0	0
Nixon/Ford				
1974	9	27	0	0
Ford				
1975	15	23	0	0
1976	14	24	0	0
Carter				
1977	5	34	0	0
1978	10	31	0	0
1979	16	45	0	0
1980	19	55	0	0

(Table continues)

Table 7-3   *(Continued)*

President/year	Ratified	Pending	Withdrawn	Rejected
Reagan, I				
1981	33	37	6	0
1982	7	9	0	0
1983	14	9	0	1
1984	20	40	0	0
Reagan, II				
1985	6	45	0	0
1986	11	50	0	0
1987	3	60	0	0
1988	27	43	0	0
Bush				
1989	9	50	0	0
1990	16	49	0	0
1991	16	50	0	2
1992	31	39	0	0
Clinton[b]				
1993	20	39	0	0

Source: U.S. Congress, *Executive Proceedings of the Senate* (Washington, D.C.: Government Printing Office, 1949–1993).

[a] Includes full term from November 1963 to January 1969.

[b] 1993 only.

Table 7-4 Treaties Killed by the Senate, 1789–1994

Date of vote	President	Country	Vote Yea	Vote Nay	Subject
March 9, 1825	J. Q. Adams	Colombia	0	40	Suppression of African slave trade
June 11, 1836	Jackson	Switzerland	14	23	Personal and property rights
June 8, 1844	Polk	Texas	16	35	Annexation
June 15, 1844	Polk	German Zollverein	26	18	Reciprocity
May 31, 1860	Buchanan	Mexico	18	27	Transit and commercial rights
June 27, 1860	Buchanan	Spain	26	17	Cuban Claims Commission
April 13, 1869	Grant	Great Britain	1	54	Arbitration of claims
June 1, 1870	Grant	Hawaii	20	19	Reciprocity
June 30, 1870	Grant	Dominican Republic	28	28	Annexation
January 29, 1885	Cleveland	Nicaragua	32	23	Interoceanic canal
April 20, 1886	Cleveland	Mexico	32	26	Mining claims
August 21, 1888	Cleveland	Great Britain	27	30	Fishing rights
February 1, 1889	B. Harrison	Great Britain	15	38	Extradition
May 5, 1897	McKinley	Great Britain	43	26	Arbitration
March 19, 1920	Wilson	Multilateral	49	35	Treaty of Versailles
January 18, 1927	Coolidge	Turkey	50	34	Commercial rights
March 14, 1934	F. Roosevelt	Canada	46	42	St. Lawrence Seaway
January 29, 1935	F. Roosevelt	Multilateral	52	36	World Court
May 26, 1960	Eisenhower	Multilateral	49	30	Law of the Sea Convention
March 8, 1983	Reagan	Multilateral	50	42	Montreal Aviation Protocol
June 11, 1991	Bush	Multilateral	—	—	Annex II, international convention on load lines[a]
June 11, 1991	Bush	Multilateral	—	—	Amendments to Annex II, international convention on load lines[a]

Source: Congress A to Z (Washington, D.C.: Congressional Quarterly, 2nd ed., 1993), 395; updated by the author.

[a] Not formally rejected by a roll call vote, but instead returned to the president.

Table 7-5 Major Arms Control Agreements, Eisenhower to Clinton

President	Year signed	Agreement	Senate action	Provisions	Parties
Eisenhower	1959	Antarctic Treaty	Ratified	Prohibits all military activity, including deployment of nuclear weapons, in Antarctica	Multilateral
Kennedy	1963	Partial Nuclear Test Ban Treaty	Ratified	Prohibits nuclear tests under water, in the atmosphere, and in outer space	Multilateral
Johnson	1967	Outer Space Treaty	Ratified	Prohibits all military activity, including deployment of nuclear weapons, in outer space	Multilateral
Johnson	1968	Nuclear Nonproliferation Treaty	Ratified	Prohibits acquisition of nuclear weapons by nations not already possessing them and establishes international safeguards to prevent the spread of nuclear weapons capability	Multilateral
Nixon	1971	Sea Bed Treaty	Ratified	Prohibits deployment of nuclear weapons on the ocean floor	Multilateral
Nixon	1972	SALT I ABM Treaty	Ratified	Limits size and number (two) of antiballistic missile systems in U.S. and Soviet Union. A 1974 executive agreement reduced number of sites permitted to one.	U.S.-Soviet Union
Nixon	1972	SALT I Interim Offensive Arms Agreement	Executive agreement; no action	Established a five-year freeze on number of intercontinental ballistic missiles and submarine-launched ballistic missiles deployed by U.S. and Soviet Union	U.S.-Soviet Union
Nixon	1974	Threshold Nuclear Test Ban Treaty	Unratified	Prohibits underground nuclear test explosions greater than 150 kilotons	U.S.-Soviet Union
Ford	1976	Peaceful Nuclear Explosions Treaty	Unratified	Prohibits nuclear explosions greater than 150 kilotons for excavation and other peaceful purposes	U.S.-Soviet Union
Carter	1979	SALT II Offensive Arms Treaty	Unratified	Limits numbers and types of strategic nuclear weapons	U.S.-Soviet Union

Reagan	1987	Intermediate Nuclear Forces Treaty	Ratified	Mandates the removal and destruction of all land-based nuclear missiles with ranges between 300 and 3,400 miles	U.S.-Soviet Union
Bush	1990	Conventional Forces in Europe Treaty	Ratified	Limits conventional weapons in Europe	Multilateral
Bush	1990	Chemical weapons convention	Unratified	Bans use, development, and stockpiling of chemical weapons	Multilateral
Bush	1991	Strategic Arms Reduction Treaty (START)	Ratified	Limits numbers and types of strategic nuclear weapons	U.S.-Soviet Union
Clinton	1993	Strategic Arms Reduction Treaty, II (START, II)	Unratified	Limits numbers and types of strategic nuclear weapons	U.S.-Russia

Source: Congressional Quarterly's Guide to the Presidency (Washington, D.C.: Congressional Quarterly, 1989) 552; updated by the author.

Table 7-6 U.S. International Agreements by Policy Types, Truman, II, to Clinton

President/year	Foreign trade/ diplomacy[a]	Foreign aid	Defense[b]	Social welfare/ civil rights[c]	Government/ economic management[d]	Natural resources/ environment[e]	Agriculture[f]	Ceremonial/ cultural	Total
Truman, II									
1949	21	7	39	33	15	16	11	4	
1950	18	3	35	39	27	20	8	9	
1951	13	9	51	76	44	24	13	3	
1952	18	17	84	87	44	36	24	0	
Total	70	36	209	235	130	96	56	16	848
%	8.3	4.2	24.6	27.7	15.3	11.3	6.6	1.9	
Eisenhower, I									
1953	19	7	57	42	28	15	8	2	
1954	16	21	68	48	22	18	5	2	
1955	31	18	105	59	35	40	54	1	
1956	19	11	61	23	18	40	68	1	
Total	85	57	291	172	103	113	135	6	962
%	8.8	5.9	30.2	17.9	10.7	11.7	14.0	0.6	
Eisenhower, II									
1957	23	11	53	18	32	37	61	2	
1958	20	12	45	13	12	33	66	6	
1959	20	18	62	15	22	40	61	2	
1960	10	16	71	28	22	52	72	3	
Total	73	57	231	74	88	162	260	13	958
%	7.6	5.9	24.1	7.7	9.2	16.9	27.1	1.4	
Kennedy									
1961	21	34	40	18	18	37	95	4	
1962	54	41	36	22	17	39	107	4	

									Total
1963	36	10	28	31	28	41	68	2	
Total	111	85	104	71	63	117	270	10	831
%	13.4	10.2	12.5	8.5	7.6	14.1	32.5	1.2	
Johnson[g]									
1964	24	5	29	18	23	43	80	4	
1965	29	6	38	16	21	48	58	2	
1966	37	6	25	15	15	58	81	5	
1967	50	8	31	20	19	48	54	2	
1968	21	6	26	11	23	50	53	4	
Total	161	31	149	80	101	247	326	17	1,112
%	14.5	2.8	13.4	7.2	9.1	22.2	29.3	1.5	
Nixon, I									
1969	16	1	27	10	10	47	55	3	
1970	65	10	30	7	14	37	55	5	
1971	47	11	40	15	16	29	77	0	
1972	47	7	65	23	17	47	77	5	
Total	175	29	162	55	57	160	264	13	915
%	19.1	3.2	17.7	6.0	6.2	17.5	28.9	1.4	
Nixon, II									
1973	43	8	35	12	17	46	66	2	
1974	25	6	28	12	13	42	26	0	
Total	68	14	63	24	30	88	92	2	381
%	17.8	3.7	16.5	6.3	7.9	23.1	24.1	0.5	
Ford									
1974	14	4	18	13	7	19	20	1	
1975	38	15	36	37	34	57	73	4	
1976	39	16	34	65	36	89	105	2	
Total	91	35	88	115	77	165	198	7	776
%	11.7	4.5	11.3	14.8	9.9	21.3	25.5	0.9	

(Table continues)

Table 7-6 (Continued)

President/year	Foreign trade/diplomacy[a]	Foreign aid	Defense[b]	Social welfare/civil rights[c]	Government/economic management[d]	Natural resources/environment[e]	Agriculture[f]	Ceremonial/cultural	Total
Carter									
1977	43	12	29	53	29	111	89	4	
1978	64	8	15	62	32	88	71	4	
1979	66	7	26	42	18	79	42	6	
1980	36	1	16	25	18	34	37	2	
Total	209	28	86	182	97	312	239	16	1,169
%	17.9	2.4	7.4	15.6	8.3	26.7	20.4	1.4	
Reagan, I									
1981	29	15	40	33	22	63	42	5	
1982	35	18	38	29	22	63	47	3	
1983	16	8	19	13	10	45	23	0	
1984	16	1	42	9	41	60	28	4	
Total	96	42	139	84	95	231	140	12	839
%	11.2	5.0	16.6	10.0	11.4	27.6	16.7	1.4	
Reagan, II									
1985	11	0	53	6	8	59	3	0	
1986	5	1	33	5	17	24	0	0	
1987	12	0	29	6	21	17	9	0	
1988	13	0	9	10	35	19	6	1	
Total	41	1	124	27	81	119	18	1	412
%	10.0	0.2	30.0	6.6	19.7	28.9	4.4	0.2	
Bush									
1989	31	2	16	8	10	24	4	0	
1990	56	33	64	44	56	59	48	2	

	a	b	c	d	e	f	g	Total
1991	47	25	70	14	46	53	19	0
1992	53	23	70	20	57	50	7	0
Total	187	83	220	86	169	186	78	2	1,011
%	18.5	8.2	21.8	8.5	16.7	18.4	7.7	0.1	
Clinton[h]									
1993	15	18	83	3	24	24	2	0	119
%	12.6	15.1	27.7	2.5	20.2	20.2	1.7	0	
Democratic presidents									
Total	566	198	581	571	415	796	893	61	4,079
%	13.9	4.8	14.2	14.0	10.2	19.5	21.9	1.5	
Republican presidents									
Total	816	318	318	637	700	1,224	1,185	56	6,254
%	13.0	5.0	21.1	10.2	11.1	19.6	18.9	0.9	

Sources: (1949–1980) Coded and calculated by the author from U.S. Department of State, *Treaties and Other International Agreements* (Washington, D.C.: Government Printing Office, 1950–1980); (1981–1993) coded and calculated from *Current Treaty Index.*

Note: Includes treaties, executive agreements, protocols, and conventions.

a Includes immigration, tariffs, customs, passports, territorial waters, and navigation rights.
b Includes Strategic Arms Limitation Treaties, space or aeronautics programs designed for military purposes, and mutual defense assistance.
c Includes education, health, medical care, housing, crime, the status of prisoners, and technical cooperation among nations.
d Includes banking issues, postal services, labor issues, and business issues.
e Includes matters of energy, the environment, transportation, communications, weather and navigation stations, land transfers, and space and aeronautics programs unrelated to defense.
f Includes farming, food, and fishing issues.
g Includes full term from November 1963 to January 1969.
h 1993 only.

Table 7-7 U.S. International Agreements by Region, Truman, II, to Clinton

President/year	W. Europe/ Britain	E. Europe	Africa	Asia	Middle East	Central America	Canada	U.S.S.R.[a]	Mexico	Multilateral	Total
Truman, II											
1949	45	1	3	19	3	41	6	1	9	18	
1950	48	6	2	27	5	56	5	0	2	8	
1951	67	3	7	23	15	87	7	0	5	19	
1952	81	4	13	34	45	94	9	0	9	21	
Total	241	14	25	103	68	278	27	1	25	66	848
%	28.4	1.7	2.9	12.1	8.0	32.8	3.2	0.1	2.9	7.8	
Eisenhower, I											
1953	51	2	14	23	18	43	5	0	3	19	
1954	63	3	6	34	21	45	5	2	10	11	
1955	92	9	3	58	23	107	12	2	3	34	
1956	82	5	4	54	12	53	6	0	5	20	
Total	288	19	27	169	74	248	28	4	21	84	962
%	30.0	2.0	2.8	17.6	7.7	25.8	2.9	0.4	2.2	8.8	
Eisenhower, II											
1957	74	5	7	37	26	54	5	0	9	20	
1958	65	13	5	46	18	33	3	2	4	18	
1959	68	7	6	51	18	49	7	1	8	25	
1960	81	8	5	69	22	59	5	0	6	19	
Total	288	33	23	203	84	195	20	3	27	82	958
%	30.0	3.4	2.4	21.2	8.8	22.7	2.1	0.3	2.8	8.6	
Kennedy											
1961	70	9	23	55	26	48	9	0	8	19	
1962	72	8	35	62	29	76	7	1	6	24	

1963	48	5	20	60	27	47	7	1	6	23	
Total	190	22	78	177	82	171	23	2	20	66	831
%	23.4	2.7	9.6	21.8	10.1	21.1	2.8	0.2	2.4	8.1	
Johnson[b]											
1964	47	13	26	47	24	23	10	3	6	27	
1965	36	8	27	52	16	30	13	1	6	29	
1966	51	3	21	62	28	30	10	3	7	27	
1967	34	8	25	56	17	27	13	4	9	39	
1968	31	3	13	52	21	39	4	8	3	20	
Total	199	35	112	269	106	149	50	19	31	142	1,112
%	17.9	3.1	10.1	24.2	9.5	13.4	4.5	1.7	2.8	12.8	
Nixon, I											
1969	33	6	10	48	15	14	9	6	2	26	
1970	41	9	13	62	14	39	8	4	12	21	
1971	34	5	16	70	22	42	9	7	7	23	
1972	37	12	8	84	22	61	6	17	13	28	
Total	145	32	47	264	73	156	32	34	34	98	915
%	15.8	3.5	5.1	28.9	8.0	17.0	3.5	3.7	3.7	10.7	
Nixon, II											
1973	33	15	3	62	19	28	10	23	10	26	
1974	24	5	6	45	17	14	8	5	6	22	
Total	57	20	9	107	36	42	18	28	16	48	381
%	15.0	5.2	2.4	28.0	9.4	11.0	4.7	7.3	4.2	12.6	
Ford											
1974	15	6	1	23	10	15	2	3	8	13	
1975	45	11	14	66	43	48	11	13	12	31	
1976	49	14	28	78	65	78	16	5	19	34	
Total	109	31	43	167	118	141	29	21	39	78	776
%	14.0	4.0	5.5	21.5	15.2	18.1	3.7	2.7	5.0	10.1	

(Table continues)

Table 7-7 (Continued)

President/year	W. Europe/Britain	E. Europe	Africa	Asia	Middle East	Central America	Canada	U.S.S.R.[a]	Mexico	Multilateral	Total
Carter											
1977	42	18	37	79	80	39	17	6	19	33	
1978	47	17	41	88	58	34	10	7	24	18	
1979	40	18	14	67	43	32	15	4	25	28	
1980	22	7	23	44	21	27	3	0	11	11	
Total	151	60	115	278	202	132	45	17	79	90	1,169
%	12.8	5.1	9.8	23.6	18.1	11.2	3.8	1.4	6.8	7.6	
Reagan, I											
1981	44	13	27	42	37	35	10	2	18	21	
1982	43	8	23	61	39	42	9	3	16	11	
1983	29	8	15	28	17	18	7	2	7	3	
1984	46	15	19	22	11	44	16	3	12	13	
Total	162	44	84	153	104	139	42	10	53	48	839
%	19.3	5.2	10.0	18.2	12.4	16.6	5.0	1.2	6.3	5.7	
Reagan, II											
1985	40	3	6	27	9	25	9	2	3	7	
1986	16	3	12	10	6	22	9	2	2	3	
1987	20	4	9	18	2	19	4	4	5	9	
1988	10	5	17	10	9	8	4	5	3	22	
Total	95	15	44	65	26	74	26	13	13	41	412
%	23.0	3.6	10.7	15.8	6.3	18.0	6.3	3.2	3.2	10.0	
Bush											
1989	8	12	6	11	6	9	3	10	9	21	
1990	55	29	35	63	24	82	6	24	9	35	
1991	35	36	17	53	14	65	8	8	7	31	

											Total
1992	34	65	21	42	17	51	5	16	6	23	
Total	132	142	79	169	61	207	22	58	31	110	1,011
%	13.1	14.0	7.8	16.7	6.0	20.5	2.2	5.7	3.1	10.9	
Clinton[c]											
1993	14	28	7	22	3	26	2	6	1	10	119
%	11.8	23.5	5.9	18.5	2.5	21.8	1.7	5.0	.8	8.4	
Democratic presidents											
Total	795	159	387	849	461	756	147	45	156	374	4079
%	19.5	3.9	8.3	20.8	11.3	18.5	3.6	0.1	3.8	9.2	
Republican presidents											
Total	1276	336	356	1297	576	1202	217	171	234	589	6254
%	20.4	5.4	5.7	20.7	9.2	19.2	3.5	2.7	3.7	9.4	

Sources: (1949–1980) Coded and calculated by the author from U.S. Department of State, *Treaties and Other International Agreements* (Washington, D.C.: Government Printing Office, 1950–1980); (1981–1993) coded and calculated from *Current Treaty Index.*

Note: Includes treaties, executive agreements, protocols, and conventions.

[a] Coded as the Russian Republic after 1991.
[b] Includes full term from November 1963 to January 1969.
[c] 1993 only.

Table 7-8 U.S. International Agreements by Regime Type, Truman, II, to Clinton

President/year	Republican[a]	Totalitarian[b]	Military authoritarian[c]	Nonmilitary authoritarian[d]	Colonial[e]	Multiple regime[f]	Total
Truman, II							
1949	82	3	9	35	0	17	
1950	89	6	11	44	0	9	
1951	121	2	12	76	2	20	
1952	165	4	13	107	1	20	
Total	457	15	45	262	3	66	848
%	53.9	1.8	5.3	30.9	0.3	7.9	
Eisenhower, I							
1953	83	2	5	66	0	22	
1954	104	4	12	67	1	12	
1955	155	11	23	118	0	36	
1956	129	5	17	68	1	21	
Total	471	22	57	319	2	91	962
%	49.0	2.3	5.9	33.0	0.2	9.4	
Eisenhower, II							
1957	113	4	15	79	5	21	
1958	113	15	8	51	1	19	
1959	130	11	10	61	1	27	
1960	153	7	12	81	3	18	
Total	509	37	45	272	10	85	958
%	53.1	3.9	4.7	28.4	1.0	8.9	
Kennedy							
1961	133	9	18	83	2	22	
1962	146	14	26	103	1	30	

1963	117	8	8	85	2	24	831
Total	396	31	52	271	5	76	
%	47.7	3.7	6.3	32.6	0.6	9.1	
Johnson[g]							
1964	103	25	6	65	1	26	
1965	98	15	18	54	4	29	
1966	109	10	12	82	1	28	
1967	95	16	23	53	4	41	
1968	84	12	21	51	6	20	
Total	489	78	80	305	16	144	1,112
%	44.0	7.0	7.2	27.4	1.4	12.9	
Nixon, I							
1969	68	16	13	45	1	26	
1970	89	18	25	65	2	24	
1971	85	20	24	84	0	22	
1972	86	35	34	98	4	31	
Total	328	89	96	292	7	103	915
%	35.8	9.7	10.5	31.9	0.8	11.3	
Nixon, II							
1973	77	45	15	63	3	26	
1974	54	15	8	49	2	24	
Total	131	60	23	112	5	50	381
%	34.4	15.7	6.0	29.4	1.3	13.1	
Ford							
1974	42	9	7	24	1	13	
1975	102	27	33	97	1	34	
1976	132	22	52	142	2	36	
Total	276	58	92	263	4	83	776
%	35.6	7.5	11.9	33.9	0.5	10.7	

(Table continues)

Table 7-8 (*Continued*)

President/year	Republican[a]	Totalitarian[b]	Military authoritarian[c]	Nonmilitary authoritarian[d]	Colonial[e]	Multiple regime[f]	Total
Carter							
1977	123	29	38	139	6	35	
1978	129	27	41	126	2	19	
1979	126	31	21	76	3	29	
1980	76	14	16	50	1	12	
Total	454	101	116	391	12	95	1,169
%	38.8	8.6	9.9	33.4	0.1	8.1	
Reagan, I							
1981	109	24	25	66	3	22	
1982	116	16	32	73	2	16	
1983	65	12	19	31	3	4	
1984	100	24	21	38	5	13	
Total	390	76	97	208	13	55	839
%	46.5	9.1	11.6	24.8	1.5	6.6	
Reagan, II							
1985	90	7	12	22	2	7	
1986	49	5	8	15	5	3	
1987	51	8	10	13	3	9	
1988	31	12	9	19	0	22	
Total	221	32	39	69	10	41	412
%	53.6	7.8	9.5	16.7	2.4	10.0	
Bush							
1989	33	23	6	12	0	21	
1990	137	59	40	89	2	35	
1991	108	47	16	66	6	31	

	[a]	[b]	[c]	[d]	[e]	[f]	Total
1992	110	29	20	95	3	23	
Total	388	158	82	262	11	110	1,011
%	38.4	15.6	8.1	25.9	1.1	10.9	
Clinton[h]							
1993	48	8	9	40	4	10	119
%	40.3	6.7	7.6	33.6	3.4	8.4	
Democratic presidents							
Total	1844	233	302	1,269	40	391	4,079
%	45.2	5.7	7.4	31.1	1.0	9.6	
Republican presidents							
Total	2,714	532	531	1,797	62	618	6,254
%	43.3	8.5	8.5	28.7	1.0	9.9	

Sources: (1949–1980) Coded and calculated by the author from U.S. Department of State, *Treaties and Other International Agreements* (Washington, D.C.: Government Printing Office, 1950–1980); (1981–1993) coded and calculated from *Current Treaty Index*.

Note: International agreements include treaties, executive agreements, protocols, and conventions. Because regime types were coded at the time the executive agreement was made, changes in regime types occurring during the period covered are accommodated. For example, Poland was coded as a totalitarian regime from 1949 to 1988 and as a republican regime thereafter.

[a] Legislatures with two or more active political parties.
[b] One-party Communist or Socialist republics.
[c] Regimes led by military officers
[d] Include monarchies, dictatorships, and states controlled by other autocratic elites.
[e] Possessions of other nations.
[f] In multilateral agreements.
[g] Includes full term from November 1963 to January 1969.
[h] 1993 only.

Table 7-9 Presidential Use of Force, 1946–1994

President	Year	Action
Truman	1946	Trieste, near the Italian-Yugoslav border
Truman	1946	Bosporus Straits, Soviet threat to Turkish control
Truman	1948–1949	China, marines sent to Nanking and Shanghai during communist takeover
Truman	1950–1953	Korean War
Truman	1950–1955	Formosa (Taiwan), to prevent communist attacks from mainland
Eisenhower	1954–1955	Tachen Islands, north of Taiwan, to prevent communist bombings
Eisenhower	1956	Suez crisis, marine evacuation of Americans
Eisenhower	1957	Indonesia, marines wait to protect Americans during revolt
Eisenhower	1957	Quemoy (Taiwan), navy defends against communist shelling
Eisenhower	1958	Indonesia, marines and navy protect American citizens
Eisenhower	1958	Lebanon
Eisenhower	1959–1960	Cuba, marines protect Americans
Kennedy	1962	Cuban missile crisis, naval blockade
Kennedy	1962	Thailand, protect against communist threat
Kennedy	1963	Haiti, marines positioned off the coast
Johnson	1964	Congo, provide airlift for Congolese troops
Johnson	1964–1973	Vietnam War
Johnson	1965	Dominican Republic, troops to protect American lives
Johnson	1967	Congo, logistical support for government
Nixon	1970	Cambodia, U.S. troops invade to clear out supply depots of North Vietnam
Ford	1975	Vietnam, evacuation
Ford	1975	Cambodia, evacuation
Ford	1975	*Mayaguez,* military forces retake the ship seized by Cambodia
Ford	1976	Lebanon, evacuation
Ford	1976	Korea, forces sent after two Americans killed
Carter	1978	Zaire, logistical support
Carter	1980	Iran, unsuccessful helicopter rescue attempt of hostages
Reagan	1981	El Salvador, military advisers
Reagan	1981	Libya, U.S. planes shoot down Libyan jets
Reagan	1982	Sinai, part of multinational force
Reagan	1982	Lebanon, assist in withdrawal of Palestine Liberation force from Beirut
Reagan	1983	Chad, air force assists Chad against Libya
Reagan	1983	Grenada, marines to protect American lives
Reagan	1986	Libya, air strikes

Table 7-9   *(Continued)*

President	Year	Action
Reagan	1988	Panama, 1,000 troops to safeguard the canal zone
Bush	1989	Panama, protect American lives, bring Noriega to justice
Bush	1990–1991	Persian Gulf War
Bush	1992	Somalia, humanitarian aid effort
Clinton	1993	Bosnia, air action
Clinton	1993	Somalia, military effort to protect humanitarian relief effort
Clinton	1993	Iraq, launch missiles in retaliation for unsuccessful attempt to assassinate former President Bush
Clinton	1994	Haiti, reinstate elected government

Sources: Congressional Quarterly's Guide to the Presidency, ed. Michael Nelson (Washington, D.C.: Congressional Quarterly, 1989), 1096–1097; Ellen Collier, "Instances of Use of United States Armed Forces Abroad 1798–1993," *CRS Report to Congress*, October 7, 1993; updated by the author.

Table 7-10   Presidential Determinations (Foreign Assistance Funds),
Kennedy to Clinton

President/year	Total	Funds for military support	Funds for nonmilitary support
Kennedy			
1961	1	1	0
1962	1	0	1
1963	0	0	0
Johnson[a]			
1964	1	0	1
1965	0	0	0
1966	0	0	0
1967	3	3	0
1968	0	0	0
Nixon, I			
1969	1	1	0
1970	0	0	0
1971	0	0	0
1972	10	5	5
Nixon, II			
1973	11	10	1
1974	12	8	4
Ford			
1974	5	2	3
1975	17	10	7
1976	18	8	10
Carter			
1977	7	2	5
1978	15	7	8
1979	22	8	14
1980	21	8	13
Reagan, I			
1981	13	7	6
1982	11	5	6
1983	9	7	2
1984	10	7	3
Reagan, II			
1985	21	14	7
1986	19	7	12
1987	10	2	8
1988	26	5	21
Bush			
1989	20	10	10
1990	28	9	19
1991	30	10	20
1992	27	2	25
Clinton[b]			
1993	32	12	20

Source: From successive volumes of *Code of Federal Regulations, Title 3,* Table 3.

Note: Excludes transfers, waivers, and drawdowns.

[a] Includes full term from November 1963 to January 1969.
[b] 1993 only.

Table 7-11   Foreign Assistance Authorized by Presidential Waivers,
Kennedy to Clinton

President/fiscal year	Number of waivers	Authorization (millions)
Kennedy		
1962	10	$54.3
1963	12	85.7
Johnson[a]		
1964	12	128.2
1965	9	107.0
1966	8	114.6
1967	6	97.2
1968	4	11.7
Nixon, I		
1969	1	4.0
1970	5	62.9
1971	9	209.5
1972	8	198.6
Nixon, II		
1973	6	106.9
1974	11	194.6
Ford		
1975	2	77.6
1976	1	0.9
Carter		
1977	0	0.0
1978	0[b]	0.0
1979	2[b]	15.0
1980	2[b]	45.1
Reagan, I		
1981	5[b]	53.2
1982	2[b]	26.9
1983	1[b]	0.1
1984	2	—
Reagan, II		
1985	0	—
1986	1	—
1987	3	—
1988	2	—
Bush		
1989	1	—
1990	3	—
1991	4	—
1992	2	—
Clinton[c]		
1993	4	—

Source: (1962–1984) U.S. General Accounting Office, *Use of Presidential Authority for Foreign Assistance* (Washington, D.C.: Government Printing Office, 1985); (1985–1993) *Code of Federal Regulations, Title 3.*

Note: "—" indicates not available.

[a] Includes full term from November 1963 to January 1969.
[b] Minimum number of waivers for the year; others may not have been filed.
[c] 1993 only.

Table 7-12   Presidents' Foreign Assistance Fund Transfers,
                  Kennedy to Clinton

Date	Region/country	Use	Authorized transfer (millions)
Kennedy			
March 21, 1962	NATO	Administrative expenses	$ 2.0
March 22, 1962	Southeast Asia	Administrative expenses	3.0
June 5, 1962	Africa	Contingency funds	30.5
June 5, 1962	Africa	International organization funds	9.5
June 5, 1962	Africa	International organization funds	15.0
May 21, 1963	Central America	Alliance for Progress	10.0
Johnson			
March 21, 1964	Poland	Project Hope	1.6
May 19, 1964[a]	Not specified	Military assistance	50.0
June 26, 1964[a]	Southeast Asia/Congo/Turkey	Military assistance	25.0
June 26, 1964[a]	Southeast Asia/Congo/Turkey	Military assistance	15.0
June 29, 1964	Central America	Alliance for Progress	8.0
June 29, 1964	Central America	Alliance for Progress	6.0
June 22, 1965	Southeast Asia/Central America	Support assistance	18.0[b]
January 18, 1966[a]	Vietnam	Support assistance	28.0
January 18, 1966[a]	Vietnam	International organization funds	28.0
February 10, 1966[a]	Vietnam	Support assistance	18.0
February 10, 1966[a]	Vietnam	Support assistance	10.0
June 8, 1966	Vietnam	AID administrative expenses	1.4
November 19, 1966	Vietnam	Administrative expenses	5.0
May 16, 1968	Vietnam	Administrative expenses	7.2
Nixon, I			
May 13, 1969	Vietnam	Administrative expenses	6.4
April 14, 1970	Vietnam	Administrative expenses	5.5
June 30, 1970	Cambodia	Military assistance	1.0
July 18, 1970	Not specified	Project Hope	0.5
October 23, 1970[a]	Cambodia	Military assistance	50.0
February 11, 1971	Cambodia	Military assistance	10.0
March 23, 1971	Vietnam	Administrative expenses	3.6
March 1, 1972	Vietnam	Administrative expenses	3.6
Nixon, II			
June 13, 1973	Vietnam	Administrative expenses	2.9
April 19, 1974[a]	Egypt	Security support assistance	8.0
May 16, 1974	Egypt	Security support assistance	0.7
June 30, 1974	Egypt	Security support assistance	20.0

Table 7-12   *(Continued)*

Date	Region/country	Use	Authorized transfer (millions)
Carter			
September 13, 1979	Caribbean	Disaster relief	$ 2.2
January 24, 1980	Sinai	Air transport services	3.9
July 8, 1980	Not specified	AID expenses	7.0
Reagan, I			
September 28, 1981	Lebanon	Peace-keeping operation account	9.0
December 5, 1981	Chad	Airlift services	12.0
Bush			
June 21, 1990	Not specified	Anti-narcotics assistance	16.5
Clinton[c]			
September 28, 1993	Mexico	Economic support	0.4
September 29, 1993	Liberia	Peacekeeping	—

Sources: (1962–1983) U.S. General Accounting Office, *Use of Presidential Authority for Foreign Assistance* (Washington, D.C.: Government Printing Office, 1985), appendix I; (1984–1993) successive volumes of *Code of Federal Regulations, Title 3*, Table 3.

Note: "—" indicates not available.

[a] Transfers also demanded a waiver of the 10 percent limitation, which required that the president be allowed to move no more than 10 percent of the funds from one category to another.
[b] $13.8 million earmarked for Southeast Asia.
[c] 1993 only.

Table 7-13   Presidential Use of Drawdown Authority,
Kennedy to Clinton

Date	Country	Authorized drawdown (millions)
Kennedy		
January 3, 1963	India	$ 55.0
Johnson		
May 15, 1965	Vietnam	75.0
October 21, 1965	Vietnam	300.0
Ford		
December 24, 1973	Cambodia	200.0
May 13, 1974	Cambodia	50.0
January 10, 1975	Cambodia	75.0
Carter		
July 1, 1980	Thailand	1.1
December 9, 1980	Liberia	1.0
Reagan, I		
January 16, 1981	El Salvador	5.0
March 5, 1981	El Salvador	20.0
February 2, 1982	El Salvador	55.0
July 19, 1983	Chad	10.0
August 5, 1983	Chad	15.0
Reagan, II		
December 30, 1985	Israel (Iran arms)	15.0
Bush		
September 30, 1990	Philippines	—
January 16, 1991	Turkey	—
April 6, 1991	Persian Gulf	—
April 19, 1991	Persian Gulf	—
May 26, 1991	Bangladesh	—
February 26, 1992	Mexico	—
April 27, 1992	Israel	—
September 24, 1992	Nagorno-Karabarkh	—
September 30, 1992	Colombia	—
September 30, 1992	Pakistan	—
Clinton[a]		
March 30, 1993	Israel	—
June 24, 1993	Ecuador	—
September 30, 1993	Laos	—
December 18, 1993	Egypt	—

Sources: (1962–1983) U.S. General Accounting Office, *Use of Presidential Authority for Foreign Assistance* (Washington, D.C.: Government Printing Office, 1985), 8; (1984–1993) successive volumes of *Code of Federal Regulations, Title 3*, Table 3.

Note: "—" indicates not available.

Table 7-14   Executive Orders of Presidents, Washington to Clinton

President/year	Numbered orders[a]	Unnumbered orders[b]	Total for term	Average number per year
Washington, I				
1789	—	3		
1790	—	2		
1791	—	0		
1792	—	2	7	1.75
Washington, II				
1793	—	1		
1794	—	0		
1795	—	0		
1796	—	0	1	0.25
Adams				
1797	—	0		
1798	—	1		
1799	—	0		
1800	—	0	1	0.25
Jefferson, I				
1801	—	2		
1802	—	0		
1803	—	0		
1804	—	0	2	0.50
Jefferson, II				
1805	—	0		
1806	—	1		
1807	—	1		
1808	—	0	2	0.50
Madison, I				
1809	—	0		
1810	—	1		
1811	—	0		
1812	—	0	1	0.25
Madison, II				
1813	—	0		
1814	—	0		
1815	—	0		
1816	—	0	0	0.00
Monroe, I				
1817	—	0		
1818	—	0		
1819	—	0		
1820	—	1	1	0.25
Monroe, II				
1821	—	0		
1822	—	0		

(Table continues)

Table 7-14   *(Continued)*

President/year	Numbered orders[a]	Unnumbered orders[b]	Total for term	Average number per year
Monroe, II (continued)				
1823	—	0		
1824	—	0	0	0.00
J. Q. Adams				
1825	—	0		
1826	—	0		
1827	—	1		
1828	—	2	3	0.75
Jackson, I				
1829	—	2		
1830	—	2		
1831	—	1		
1832	—	1	6	1.50
Jackson, II				
1833	—	1		
1834	—	0		
1835	—	3		
1836	—	2	6	1.50
Van Buren				
1837	—	2		
1838	—	6		
1839	—	0		
1840	—	2	10	2.50
W. Harrison				
1841	—	0	0	0.00
Tyler				
1841	—	0		
1842	—	14		
1843	—	0		
1844	—	3	17	4.25
Polk				
1845	—	3		
1846	—	1		
1847	—	12		
1848	—	2	18	4.50
Taylor				
1849	—	4		
1850	—	1	5	3.33
Fillmore				
1850	—	1		
1851	—	4		
1852	—	7	12	5.00

Table 7-14   *(Continued)*

President/year	Numbered orders[a]	Unnumbered orders[b]	Total for term	Average number per year
Pierce				
1853	—	7		
1854	—	15		
1855	—	11		
1856	—	2	35	8.75
Buchanan				
1857	—	3		
1858	—	3		
1859	—	8		
1860	—	2	16	4.00
Lincoln, I				
1861	—	3		
1862	1	6		
1863	1	14		
1864	0	19	44	11.00
Lincoln, II				
1865	0	4	4	12.00
A. Johnson				
1865	3	17		
1866	1	14		
1867	0	23		
1868	2	19	79	19.75
Grant, I				
1869	0	29		
1870	0	27		
1871	0	18		
1872	1	15	90	22.50
Grant, II				
1873	5	31		
1874	6	27		
1875	2	36		
1876	1	19	127	31.75
Hayes				
1877	0	30		
1878	0	12		
1879	0	29		
1880	0	21	92	23.00
Garfield				
1881	0	6	6	8.00
Arthur				
1881	1	13		
1882	0	23		
1883	0	25		
1884	2	32	96	24.00

(Table continues)

Table 7-14   *(Continued)*

President/year	Numbered orders[a]	Unnumbered orders[b]	Total for term	Average number per year
Cleveland				
1885	3	35		
1886	0	25		
1887	3	15		
1888	0	32	113	28.25
B. Harrison				
1889	0	42		
1890	1	38		
1891	1	35		
1892	1	25	143	35.75
Cleveland				
1893	4	30		
1894	15	22		
1895	29	17		
1896	9	14	140	35.00
McKinley, I				
1897	10	9		
1898	10	19		
1899	12	33		
1900	16	41	150	37.50
McKinley, II				
1901	6	29	35	46.70
T. Roosevelt, I				
1901	13	13		
1902	44	39		
1903	47	25		
1904	47	23	251	77.23
T. Roosevelt, II				
1905	171	13		
1906	165	2		
1907	188	5		
1908	280	6	830	207.50
Taft				
1909	129	15		
1910	129	38		
1911	175	12		
1912	206	20	724	181.00
Wilson, I				
1913	206	20		
1914	243	6		
1915	188	12		
1916	211	10	848	212.00

Table 7-14   *(Continued)*

President/year	Numbered orders[a]	Unnumbered orders[b]	Total for term	Average number per year
Wilson, II				
1917	296	17		
1918	259	7		
1919	225	8		
1920	175	1	955	238.75
Harding				
1921	227	1		
1922	174	1		
1923	118	1	522	202.33
Coolidge, I				
1923	62	0		
1924	189	5	256	182.86
Coolidge, II				
1925	271	0		
1926	201	1		
1927	238	2		
1928	232	2	947	236.75
Hoover				
1929	239	0		
1930	268	0		
1931	247	0		
1932	214	0	968	242.00
F. Roosevelt, I				
1933	527	1		
1934	474	2		
1935	384	0		
1936	275	0	1,663	415.75
F. Roosevelt, II				
1937	257	0		
1938	249	0		
1939	287	0		
1940	258	6	1,057	264.25
F. Roosevelt, III				
1941	382	2		
1942	288	—		
1943	122	—		
1944	100	—	773	193.25
F. Roosevelt, IV				
1945	29	—	29	87.88
Truman, I				
1945	139	—		
1946	148	—		

(Table continues)

Table 7-14 *(Continued)*

President/year	Numbered orders[a]	Unnumbered orders[b]	Total for term	Average number per year
Truman, I (continued)				
1947	103	—		
1948	109	—	499	136.00
Truman, II				
1949	69	—		
1950	105	—		
1951	119	—		
1952	105	—	398	99.50
Eisenhower, I				
1953	90	—		
1954	73	—		
1955	65	—		
1956	44	—	272	68.00
Eisenhower, II				
1957	54	—		
1958	50	—		
1959	60	—		
1960	42	—	206	51.50
Kennedy				
1961	84	—		
1962	89	—		
1963	55	—	228	76.00
L. Johnson[c]				
1963	7	—		
1964	56	—		
1965	74	—		
1966	57	—		
1967	66	—		
1968	56	—	316	52.66
Nixon, I				
1969	61	—		
1970	72	—		
1971	63	—		
1972	55	—	251	62.75
Nixon, II				
1973	64	—		
1974	40	—	104	65.82
Ford				
1974	29	—		
1975	67	—		
1976	56	—	152	63.33
Carter				
1977	83	—		
1978	78	—		

Table 7-14 *(Continued)*

President/year	Numbered orders[a]	Unnumbered orders[b]	Total for term	Average number per year
Carter (continued)				
1979	77	—		
1980	73	—	311	77.75
Reagan, I				
1981	76	—		
1982	63	—		
1983	57	—		
1984	41	—	237	59.25
Reagan, II				
1985	45	—		
1986	37	—		
1987	43	—		
1988	40	—	165	41.25
Bush				
1989	36	—		
1990	43	—		
1991	46	—		
1992	40	—	165	41.25
Clinton[d]				
1993	57	—		
1994	53	—	110	55.00

Sources: (Unnumbered series, 1789–1941) Adapted from Clifford Lord, *List and Index of Presidential Executive Orders, Unnumbered Series, 1789–1941* (Wilmington, Delaware: Michael Glazier, 1979); (numbered series, 1862–1935) adapted from Lord, ed. *Presidential Executive Orders, 1862–1935,* 2 vols. (New York: Hastings House, 1944); (numbered series, 1936 to present) compiled from successive volumes of *Code of Federal Regulations.*

Note: Collation and numbering of executive orders did not begin until 1907. However, certain orders before that date were entered into the numbered series. Some unnumbered orders exist as late as 1941. In a project conducted by the Works Progress Administration in 1935 and 1936, the unnumbered orders were collected and analyzed from historical materials. This was the first and, in fact, only attempt to establish a list of unnumbered orders. Generally, such a list is difficult to compile because of a lack of agreement as to whether a document was an order, a proclamation, a land order, or some other executive communication. Those presented here are drawn from the 1935–1936 WPA project.

[a] Numbered series begins in 1862.
[b] Unnumbered series ends in 1941.
[c] Includes full term from November 1963 to January 1969.
[d] 1993–1994 only.

Table 7-15 Executive Orders by Policy Type, Truman, II, to Clinton

President/year	Foreign trade/diplomacy	Foreign aid	Defense	Social welfare/civil rights	Government/economic management	Natural resources/environment	Agriculture	Ceremonial/cultural	Federalism	Personnel, agency requests	Total
Truman, II											
1949	10	0	4	1	16	15	0	2	0	21	
1950	9	0	23	6	27	15	1	5	0	19	
1951	10	0	32	11	18	17	0	3	0	28	
1952	12	0	19	5	11	25	0	5	0	28	
Total	41	0	78	23	72	72	1	15	0	96	398
%	10.3	0.0	19.6	5.8	18.1	18.1	0.2	3.8	0.0	24.1	
Eisenhower, I											
1953	10	3	27	4	13	8	3	7	0	15	
1954	3	1	9	5	15	11	2	3	0	24	
1955	7	1	26	3	3	9	2	1	0	13	
1956	1	0	19	2	4	5	1	1	0	11	
Total	21	5	81	14	35	33	8	12	0	63	272
%	7.7	1.8	29.8	5.1	12.9	12.1	2.9	4.4	0.0	23.2	
Eisenhower, II											
1957	6	1	9	3	11	6	2	3	0	13	
1958	5	0	13	3	6	11	0	1	0	11	
1959	5	0	11	1	9	12	3	6	1	12	
1960	3	0	7	0	15	3	1	2	1	10	
Total	19	1	40	7	41	32	6	12	2	46	206
%	9.2	0.1	19.4	3.4	19.9	15.5	2.9	5.8	0.1	22.3	
Kennedy											
1961	6	2	12	5	15	19	3	5	1	16	
1962	3	2	23	9	22	12	2	5	0	11	

											Total
1963	9	0	14	12	7	2	0	5	0	13	
Total	18	4	49	26	44	33	5	15	1	40	
%	81.1	1.7	20.9	11.1	18.7	14.0	2.1	6.4	0.1	17.0	228
Johnson[a]											
1964	7	0	10	7	10	7	1	3	1	10	
1965	13	2	6	10	4	8	2	4	0	25	
1966	12	1	7	6	8	5	1	4	0	13	
1967	5	1	10	6	10	12	2	0	0	20	
1968	7	0	8	11	5	4	0	1	1	19	
Total	44	4	41	40	37	36	6	12	2	87	
%	14.2	1.3	13.3	12.9	12.0	11.7	1.9	3.9	0.1	28.2	316
Nixon, I											
1969	6	0	5	10	8	6	1	5	1	19	
1970	7	0	11	7	13	9	1	4	0	20	
1971	5	0	7	5	12	6	2	6	2	18	
1972	6	0	4	5	7	9	0	5	1	18	
Total	24	0	26	27	40	30	4	20	4	75	
%	9.6	0.0	10.4	10.8	16.0	12.0	1.6	8.0	1.6	30.0	251
Nixon, II											
1973	3	0	3	3	11	15	1	4	0	24	
1974	6	0	4	5	5	6	0	0	1	13	
Total	9	0	7	8	16	21	1	4	1	37	
%	8.7	0.0	6.7	7.8	15.4	20.2	0.1	3.8	0.1	35.6	104
Ford											
1974	7	0	2	3	4	2	0	2	0	9	
1975	8	1	11	4	7	9	0	4	0	23	
1976	11	0	3	4	3	9	0	5	0	22	
Total	26	1	16	11	14	20	0	11	0	54	
%	17.0	0.1	10.5	7.2	9.2	13.1	0.0	7.2	0.0	35.3	152

(Table continues)

345

Table 7-15 (Continued)

President/ year	Foreign trade/ diplomacy	Foreign aid	Defense	Social welfare/ civil rights	Government/ economic management	Natural resources/ environment	Agriculture	Ceremonial/ cultural	Federalism	Personnel, agency requests	Total
Carter											
1977	15	1	8	13	4	9	0	4	0	29	
1978	12	0	4	18	11	6	0	1	0	26	
1979	18	3	5	8	7	15	1	5	0	15	
1980	24	1	4	11	4	12	0	2	0	15	
Total	69	5	21	50	26	42	1	12	0	85	311
%	22.2	1.6	6.8	16.1	8.4	13.5	0.1	3.9	0.0	27.3	
Reagan, I											
1981	28	0	5	5	6	10	1	4	1	16	
1982	18	1	4	9	11	3	0	2	1	14	
1983	16	0	4	8	13	5	1	0	1	9	
1984	12	0	4	1	11	0	0	1	0	12	
Total	74	1	17	23	41	18	2	7	3	51	237
%	31.2	0.1	7.2	9.7	17.3	7.6	0.1	3.0	0.1	21.5	
Reagan, II											
1985	11	3	9	3	7	4	0	0	0	8	
1986	8	1	5	2	12	1	1	2	0	5	
1987	7	0	3	7	13	3	0	1	0	9	
1988	9	1	8	1	11	3	0	1	0	6	
Total	35	5	25	13	43	11	1	4	0	28	165
%	21.2	3.0	15.1	7.8	26.0	6.7	6.6	2.4	0.0		

Bush											
1989	3	1	5	2	6	4	0	0	0	15	
1990	10	2	8	1	1	4	2	1	0	14	
1991	10	2	8	1	1	4	2	1	0	14	
1992	8	2	5	3	2	2	0	5	1	12	
Total	31	7	26	7	10	14	4	7	1	55	162
%	19.1	4.3	16.0	4.3	6.2	8.6	2.5	4.3	0.6	34.0	
Clinton[b]											
1993	12	0	8	7	17	10	1	0	1	1	
1994	10	0	9	7	13	11	0	0	0	3	
Democratic presidents											
Total	184	13	197	146	196	193	14	54	4	309	1310
%	13.11	1.0	15.0	11.1	15.0	14.7	1.1	4.1	0.3	23.6	
Republican presidents											
Total	239	20	238	110	240	179	26	77	11	409	1549
%	15.4	1.3	15.4	7.1	15.5	11.6	1.7	5.0	0.7	26.4	

Source: Calculated by the author from successive volumes of *Code of Federal Regulations.*

Note: Policy types were coded on the basis of title descriptions and, in some cases, the text of the orders.

[a] Includes full term from November 1963 to January 1969.
[b] 1993–1994 only.

Table 7-16 Executive Orders by Affected Group, 1949–1993 (percent)

President	Nation/ consumers	Labor	Business/ industry	Minorities	Farmers	Environmentalists	States, localities	Foreign countries, citizens	Military personnel	Nonmilitary personnel	Federal agencies, Congress
Truman	9.0	14.9	2.2	1.5	0.5	1.0	16.9	10.0	15.6	17.6	10.8
Eisenhower, I	5.7	7.6	4.9	3.4	1.9	0.4	12.1	10.6	19.7	15.2	18.6
Eisenhower, II	7.8	11.5	6.4	3.7	2.8	0.5	11.0	9.6	12.8	15.1	18.8
Kennedy	6.1	19.6	1.9	9.8	2.3	0.0	8.9	11.7	7.9	7.0	24.8
Johnson	5.9	9.3	2.8	12.0	1.2	0.9	9.9	16.4	14.5	18.5	8.6
Nixon, I	13.4	5.7	2.4	7.3	0.8	4.5	8.1	8.9	10.9	23.5	14.6
Nixon, II	14.1	4.0	5.1	5.1	2.0	3.0	6.1	11.1	7.1	25.3	17.2
Ford	8.3	3.0	1.8	7.1	0.6	4.7	4.1	21.9	8.3	29.6	10.7
Carter	7.8	2.2	7.8	13.4	0.6	5.6	3.7	24.1	4.1	22.2	8.4
Reagan, I	7.1	7.1	11.1	10.9	0.0	1.9	4.7	27.0	10.9	11.4	7.1
Reagan, II	10.4	8.0	14.7	0.6	0.6	0.0	0.6	33.1	5.5	9.8	16.6
Bush	9.0	5.4	6.7	2.4	1.8	1.8	1.8	33.3	11.5	12.7	13.3
Clinton[a]	14.0	3.5	7.0	1.8	0.0	8.8	1.8	29.8	7.0	7.0	19.3
Democratic presidents[b]	7.4	11.0	3.7	8.6	1.0	2.0	10.4	15.5	11.1	17.2	12.0
Republican presidents	9.5	6.5	6.6	5.1	1.3	2.1	6.1	19.4	10.8	17.8	14.6

Source: Calculated by the author from successive volumes of *Code of Federal Regulations.*

Note: Groups classified on the basis of the title descriptions and, in some cases, the text of executive orders.

[a] 1993–1994 only.
[b] Excludes Clinton.

Table 7-17   Presidential Tax Proposals and Congressional Enactments, Truman to Clinton (in billions of 1982 dollars)

President/year	Presidential proposal		Congressional enactment		Difference	
	First year[a]	Fully effective[b]	First year[a]	Fully effective[b]	First year[a]	Fully effective[b]
Truman						
1948	−3.2	—	−4.8	—	−1.6	—
1950	5.5	—	8.8	—	3.3	—
1951	10.0	—	5.7	—	−4.3	—
Eisenhower						
1954	−1.3	—	−1.4	—	0.1	—
Johnson						
1964	−6.3	−10.3	−7.7	−11.5	−1.4	−1.2
1968	7.4	—	10.9	—	3.5	—
Nixon						
1969	c	—	−2.5	—	−2.5	—
1971	−12.9	−9.3	−11.4	−10.0	1.5	−0.7
Ford						
1975	−16.0	—	−22.8	—	−6.8	—
1976	c	—	−15.7	−6.2	−15.7	−6.2
Carter						
1977	−13.8	−15.7	−17.7	−13.8	3.9	−1.9
1978	−24.5	−34.9	−18.7	−34.1	5.8	0.8
1980	c	—	3.6	—	3.6	—
Reagan						
1981	−56.6	−129.8	−37.7	−150.0	18.9	−20.2
1982	c	—	18.0	51.8	18.0	51.8
1984	c	—	10.6	22.5	10.6	22.5
1986	11.5	−11.5	11.5	−15.1	0	−3.6
1987	6.1	—	9.4	15.8	3.3	9.7
1988	c	—	.4	—	.4	—
Bush						
1989	5.3	—	5.6	5.1	.3	−.2
1990	8.9	20.4	15.6	26.6	6.7	6.2
Clinton[d]						
1993	36.0	65.1	27.4	53.2	−8.6	−11.9

Source: Lyn Ragsdale, *Presidential Politics* (Boston: Houghton Mifflin, 1993), 326; updated by the author.

Note: In 1992, two tax cut bills passed Congress, one cutting $77.5 billion over 5 years, the other cutting $27 billion over 5 years. Both were vetoed by Bush and override attempts failed.

[a] Expected revenue change first full year after law is passed.
[b] Expected revenue change first full year after law is fully effective, if different from first column.
[c] No presidential proposal.
[d] 1993–1994 only.

Table 7-18 Differences in Appropriations Proposed by President and Passed by Congress, 1947–1994 (in billions of 1982 dollars)

President	Average annual difference[a]		
	Defense	Nondefense	Total[b]
Harry Truman (1947–1953)	17.5	–3.1	14.5
Dwight Eisenhower (1954–1957)	–4.6	–0.3	–5.3
Dwight Eisenhower (1958–1961)	–1.0	0.1	–1.0
John Kennedy/Lyndon Johnson (1962–1965)	–2.4	–7.4	–9.3
Lyndon Johnson (1966–1969)	1.0	–10.4	–10.9
Richard Nixon (1970–1973)	–16.0	2.5	–12.8
Richard Nixon/Gerald Ford (1974–1977)	–9.2	25.4	15.8
Jimmy Carter (1978–1981)	9.8	–32.3	–21.6
Ronald Reagan (1982–1984)	8.9	5.6	16.4
Ronald Reagan (1985–1988)	2.7	19.1	21.9
George Bush (1989–1992)	–2.4	4.9	2.5
Bill Clinton (1993–1994)	0	–0.9	0.9
Average			
Republican administrations	–3.2	3.1	5.8
Democratic administrations	5.2	–11.7	–5.6
All years	0.7	–0.1	1.1

Source: Lyn Ragsdale, *Presidential Politics* (Boston: Houghton Mifflin, 1993), 329; updated by the author.

[a] Positive numbers indicate Congress authorized more than the president requested, and negative numbers indicate the reverse.
[b] Includes defense, nondefense, and interest payments.

Table 7-19 Presidents' Budget Rescission Requests, Carter to Clinton (in thousands of dollars)

Item	1977	1978	1979	1980	1981	1982	1983	1984
Funds appropriated to the president								
Agriculture	−41,500	−40,200	—	—	—	−10,629	−15,133	—
Commerce	−2,025	—	—	—	−34,493	−2,000	−77,301	—
Defense-military	−878,950	—	—	—	—	−19,000	—	—
Defense-civil	−6,600	—	—	—	—	—	—	—
Education	—	—	—	—	−321,729	−1,157,205	−1,230,381	—
Energy	—	—	−50,000	—	−101,926	−20,000	−69,000	—
Health and Human services	—	—	−227,258	−104	−344,218	—	—	—
Housing	—	—	−608,167	—	−10,000	−9,421,639	—	−331,431
Interior	−47,500	00	−3,127	—	—	—	−63,500	−30,000
Justice	—	—	—	−18	—	—	—	—
Labor	—	—	—	—	−10,185	−4,095	—	−1,700
State	−12,000	−5,000	—	—	—	—	—	—
Transportation	−6,803	—	—	—	—	9,623	−28,200	—
Treasury	—	—	—	—	—	—	—	—
Independent agencies	−60,000	−10,055	−26,140	—	−433,240	−10,877	—	−25,418
Total	−1,055,378	−55,255	−914,692	−122	−1,255,791	−10,655,068	−1,483,615	−388,549

(Table continues)

Table 7-19 (*Continued*)

Item	1985	1986	1987	1988	1989	1990	1991	1992	1993	1994
Funds appropriated to the president	-105,399	-39,760	—	—	—	—	—	—	—	-144,241
Agriculture	-310,218	-1,062,681	-475,207	—	—	—	-10,000	—	—	-44,175
Commerce	-325,371	-196,632	-215,066	—	—	—	—	-21,425	—	-601,224
Defense-military	—	—	-133,750	—	—	—	-3,432,500	-7,665,195	—	—
Defense-civil	-16,200	—	—	—	—	—	—	—	—	—
Education	-173,939	-1,080,200	-2,476,422	—	—	—	—	—	—	-277,589
Energy	-21,112	—	-210,197	—	—	—	—	—	—	—
Health and Human services	-26,838	-787,417	-199,671	—	-71,651	—	—	-25,000	—	—
Housing	260,057	-4,625,677	-1,066,455	—	—	—	-780,527	-25,000	—	-225,791
Interior	72,389	-116,104	-302,737	—	-65,000	—	—	-6,198	—	—
Justice	-13,659	-122,109	-24,598	—	-5,000	—	—	—	—	—
Labor	-276,566	-416,037	-332,000	—	-1,445	—	—	—	—	—
State	-2,432	—	—	—	—	—	—	—	—	—
Transportation	-49,327	-356,051	—	—	—	—	—	-9,880	—	-290,000
Treasury	-9,530	-788,395	-62,395	—	—	—	—	—	—	-282,868
Independent agencies	-55,338	-717,995	-186,264	—	—	—	—	—	-180,000	-126,022
Total	1,718,375	-10,309,058	-5,684,762	0.0	-143,096	0.0	-4,223,027	-7,752,698	-180,000	-1,991,910

Source: Successive volumes of *Budget of the United States.*

Note: Rescissions are decisions by presidents not to spend funds already appropriated by Congress. Under the Budget and Impoundment Control Act of 1974, presidents must notify Congress by rescission requests. Congress can deny the request by a resolution passed by either house.

353

Figure 7-2 Budget Deficit, Eisenhower to Clinton (in billions)

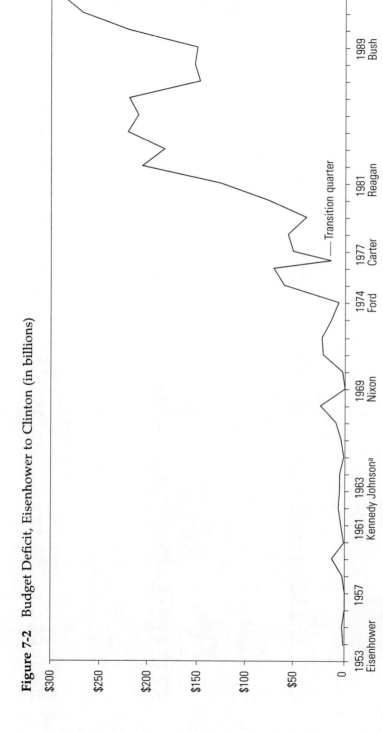

Source: (1954–1992) *Congressional Quarterly Weekly Report,* November 26, 1988, 3379; and May 9, 1992, 1235; (1993–1994) U.S. Bureau of the Census, *Statistical Abstract of the United States 1995* (Washington, D.C.: Government Printing Office, 1995).

[a] Includes full term from November 1963 to January 1969.

Table 7-20   Federal Budget Receipts and Outlays, 1924–1994
(in billions of current dollars)

Year	Receipts	Outlays	Surplus or deficit
1924	3.9	2.9	1.0
1925	3.6	2.9	0.7
1926	3.8	2.9	0.9
1927	4.0	2.8	1.2
1928	3.9	3.0	0.9
1929	3.8	2.9	0.9
1930	4.0	3.1	0.9
1931	3.2	4.1	−1.0
1932	2.0	4.8	−2.7
1933	2.1	4.7	−2.6
1934	3.1	6.5	−3.3
1935	3.8	6.3	−2.4
1936	4.2	7.6	−3.5
1937	5.6	8.4	−2.8
1938	7.0	7.2	−0.1
1939	6.6	9.4	−2.9
1940	6.9	9.6	−2.7
1941	9.2	14.0	−4.8
1942	15.1	34.5	−19.4
1943	25.1	78.9	−53.8
1944	47.8	94.0	−46.1
1945	50.2	95.2	−45.0
1946	43.5	61.7	−18.2
1947	43.5	36.9	6.6
1948	45.4	36.5	8.9
1949	41.6	40.6	1.0
1950	40.9	43.1	−2.2
1951	53.4	45.8	7.6
1952	68.0	68.0	a
1953	71.5	76.8	−5.3
1954	69.7	70.9	−1.2
1955	65.5	68.5	−3.0
1956	74.5	70.5	4.1
1957	80.0	76.7	3.2
1958	79.6	82.6	−2.9
1959	79.2	92.1	−12.9
1960	92.5	92.2	0.3
1961	94.4	97.8	−3.4
1962	99.7	106.8	−7.1
1963	106.6	111.3	−4.8
1964	112.7	118.6	−5.9
1965	116.8	118.4	−1.6
1966	130.9	134.7	−3.8
1967	149.6	158.3	−8.7
1968	153.7	178.8	−25.2
1969	187.8	184.5	3.2

Table 7-20   *(Continued)*

Year	Receipts	Outlays	Surplus or deficit
1970	193.7	196.6	−2.8
1971	187.1	210.2	−23.0
1972	207.3	230.7	−23.4
1973	230.8	245.7	−14.9
1974	263.2	269.4	−6.1
1975	279.2	332.3	−63.2
1976	298.1	371.8	−73.7
1976[b]	81.2	96.0	−14.7
1977	355.6	409.2	−53.6
1978	399.7	458.7	−59.0
1979	463.3	503.5	−40.2
1980	517.1	590.9	−78.9
1981	599.3	678.2	−127.9
1982	617.8	745.7	−207.8
1983	600.6	808.3	−185.3
1984	666.5	851.8	−222.2
1985	734.1	946.3	−212.3
1986	769.1	989.8	−220.7
1987	854.1	1,003.9	−149.8
1988	908.9	1,064.1	−155.2
1989	990.7	1,143.2	−152.5
1990	1,031.3	1,252.7	−221.4
1991	1,054.3	1,323.8	−269.5
1992	1,091.6	1,381.8	−290.1
1993	1,153.5	1,408.2	−254.7
1994	1,280.4	1,483.8	−203.4

Sources: (1929–1970) U.S. Department of Commerce, *U.S. Historical Statistics: Colonial Times to 1970*, vol. 2 (Washington, D.C.: Government Printing Office, 1971), 1105; (1971–1984) U.S. Department of Commerce, *Statistical Abstract of the United States* (Washington, D.C.: Government Printing Office, 1986), 305; (1985–1986) U.S. Executive Office of the President, *The Budget of the United States* (Washington, D.C.: Government Printing Office, 1987); (1987–1994) U.S. Department of Commerce, *Statistical Abstract* (1995, 328).

[a] Less than $50 million.
[b] Transition quarter. In 1976 the beginning of the fiscal year was changed from July 1 to October 1. A transition quarter (July 1–September 30, 1976) was used. It belonged to neither fiscal 1976 nor fiscal 1977.

8

Congressional Relations

In his eight years as president of the United States, George Washington publicly expressed an opinion on only five pieces of legislation. He recommended bills concerning the militia, the army, and a temporary commission to negotiate with the Indians, and he vetoed an apportionment bill on constitutional grounds and a bill on the military because it was poorly drafted. Washington's three recommendations were approved and his two vetoes went unchallenged. Over two hundred years later, Bill Clinton, in his first year as president, took positions on 102 pieces of legislation and signed into law 300 bills passed by Congress. The nineteenth-century norm was to minimize presidential involvement in legislative politics; the twentieth-century norm is to expect it. "The presentation of an annual program to Congress, the coordination of that program within the executive branch, the drafting of legislation, and the submission of special messages are now standard fare" (Wayne, 1982, 45).

In considering presidential involvement in legislative affairs, studies generally focus on presidents as individual policy makers rather than on the actions of the presidency as a policy-making institution. Presidents are depicted as "proximate policy makers" (Lindblom, 1968, 30n), as "policy actors," or as lone figures who try to impose a broad, national policy focus upon a parochial and wayward, if not annoying, congressional body. The image suggests that each president acts anew, asserting new legislative priorities, facing unique challenges presented by Congress, and adopting individual strategies to establish his priorities before the group.

This view belies the existence of institutional relations between the two branches of government. In fact, these institutional relations exist. They include organizational, behavioral, and structural elements of the presidency. Presidents rely on a well-developed organization in the Executive Office of the President to execute many of their legislative decisions. The Office of Management and Budget (OMB) monitors incoming requests for legislation, outgoing legislative proposals, and final bills from Congress. The Office of Legislative Affairs (formerly the Office of Congressional Relations) develops strategies to pass bills that the president promotes. While much of this appears to be undertaken by presidents single-handedly (indeed, the White House itself may wish to give this impression), these activities are ultimately carried out by dozens of people in the presidential organization.

The policy programs presidents initiate and the positions they take on legislation reflect institutional behavior. Presidents annually present policy proposals to Congress in their State of the Union messages. Each year, too, presidents submit the federal budget, as required by the Budget and Accounting Act of 1921. Although these actions are undertaken by individual executives, the expectations upon which they are based rest on institutional behavior. One of these expectations is that presidents handle the policy complexity of the political environment by proposing, or at least supporting, legislation to solve national problems in an array of issue areas. Harry Truman began a practice of using the State of the Union message to submit an annual legislative program to Congress. Although Dwight Eisenhower had no desire to follow Truman's lead, congressional Republicans criticized him for failing to submit a set of priorities, and Eisenhower relented. Truman's precedent became institutional behavior for future presidents.

Three structural features of the presidency influence its relations with Congress. These features are time, the political party system, and the U.S. Constitution. An institutional time line guides presidents' policy programs in Congress. The presidential cliché about "hitting the ground running" is not trite, merely good advice. Time, calibrated by the next election, establishes a cycle of influence whereby the ability of presidents to succeed with Congress declines the longer they are in office.

The political party system is one of the primary institutional connections between Congress and the presidency. Table 8-1 documents the party composition of Congress since Washington. Party provides a basis of communication between the two institutions and helps to reconcile some of their differences, especially when the president's party holds a majority in one or both houses. But even during the years that the president's party did not have a majority in at least one house, party still served to narrow the debate. Independent partisanship, the modern configuration of party first introduced in Chapter 2, plays a distinct role in the operation of the two institutions and their interrelationships. The concept pertains to politicians who seek election and reelection by devising independent campaign organizations, bases of support, and media strategies, but still associate with a party label. This means that much of the support presidents get (or do not get) in Congress flows through the political parties, but the parties are made up of members who do not feel beholden to the president. This independent partisanship affects contemporary presidents' relations with Congress no matter who the president is, no matter what the issue is, and no matter what the president's policy position is.

The Constitution also establishes institutional relations between presidents and Congress. One of the president's most powerful mechanisms in his dealings with Congress is the veto—its use or the threat of its use. The efficacy of this mechanism is not accidental, but stems from the constitutional requirement that two-thirds of both houses vote to override a veto. The veto offers a structural advantage for the presidency since getting two-thirds of all members of Congress to agree on a controversial action is a herculean task, again no matter who the president, what the issue, or what the president's position. Thus, although presidents individually engage in certain activities, their efforts are neither new nor unique. Knowing who the president is may be less important than the ability to identify the organizational, behavioral, and structural types of institutional patterns that now exist.

Organizational Relations with Congress

Organizational units within the White House undertake two key congressional activities: legislative liaison efforts that sell presidential proposals to Congress and legislative management that supervises the flow of legislation, legislative requests, and budget proposals to and from the White House. As staff and resources have increased, the formal congressional liaison staff has expanded. Since the days of Washington personnel in the executive branch have sporadically helped presidents communicate with Congress. Herbert Hoover tentatively formalized such assistance by relying on one staff member to supervise congressional liaison. Truman, who wanted help in pursuing annual legislative programs, introduced a staff with official legislative liaison responsibilities. Yet the two junior presidential assistants assigned the task were primarily messengers who did not speak for the president (Holtzman, 1970, 231–234). Not until Eisenhower was the Office of Congressional Relations established. It was renamed the Office of Legislative Affairs in 1981. Its size is depicted in Table 8-2. The office has become a well-developed unit in the White House, with separate offices that handle the House and Senate. These units did not change, for instance, when Democratic president Clinton took over from Republican George Bush.

The task of legislative management involves two processes that are handled within the OMB: legislative clearance and the handling of enrolled bills. The former was initiated in 1924, with the first Budget of the United States; the latter in 1938. Figures 8-1 and 8-2 depict these two processes, respectively. A classic instance of the legislative clearance process at work, and its detachment from presidents' own involvement, took place on August 9, 1974, when Richard Nixon announced his resignation. A congressional staff member called a high-ranking White House official during the day to inquire as to whether a minor piece of legislation was "in accordance with the president's program" (reported by Heclo, 1981, 3). Neither a president nor a presidential program existed in those hours, but the institution of the presidency continued to operate. Likewise, the handling of enrolled bills (bills passed by the House and Senate that are awaiting a presidential signature) is very much an institutional process. Except in the case of particularly visible legislation or items the White House initiates, presidents are unlikely to keep tabs on legislation passed on Capitol Hill. The OMB steps in to determine whether the president should sign or veto a bill, presenting its own recommendations, which presidents typically adopt (Wayne, Cole, and Hyde, 1979).

The tasks of legislative liaison and management have become sufficiently elaborate that presidents exert less than full control over their processes or content. The use of proposals made by the executive bureaucracy that are channeled by the OMB, itself a large bureaucratic unit, and advocated by a good-sized liaison staff largely determines the extent of a president's involvement in the legislative process.

Institutional Behavior: Presidential Priorities and Congressional Concurrence

Contemporary presidents have fashioned two distinct types of institutional behavior by which to identify policy priorities. They both submit legislation unrelated to their programs, and they engage in a type of institutional behavior involving presidential-congressional relations that establishes the level of concurrence between the positions held by members and the positions held by presidents on the same legislation.

Presidential Programs

Since Truman presidents have used State of the Union messages to capture congressional and national attention for their legislative programs. The size and scope of these legislative programs are depicted in Table 8-3. The analysis indicates that presidents typically have made most of their policy requests in their first year in office. In later years, new requests generally decline and repeat requests increase. Ronald Reagan proved an exception: he made far fewer requests than did the other presidents and also had a fairly uniform number of requests each year during his two terms. As Table 8-4 indicates, the majority of policy requests during the first year of a president's tenure occur in the first six months. Indeed, except in Nixon's first term, the first-year requests occur most frequently between January and March.[1]

These tables provide evidence that timing is a critical structural element of the presidency. Presidents face, in Paul Light's words, "a cycle of decreasing influence" (1991, 36). This cycle affects all presidents. They enter office with a complement of political capital: their popularity is at its highest point for the term, they can claim a mandate for policy initiatives based on their election victory, and their party often picks up seats in Congress during the presidential election. Yet, the political honeymoon soon ends: popularity declines, people forget about the election and turn their attention to governance, and the president's party loses congressional seats in the midterm elections. The gloomy circumstances of this cycle of decreasing influence mean that presidents must act early in their terms to secure major legislative victories in Congress.

Presidential Positions

Another way of evaluating presidential priorities is to observe the preferences that presidents reveal in the positions they take on congressional legislation. Position taking not only encompasses presidents' own initiatives and desires but also measures responses to congressional legislation in which presidents are not fully involved. Table 8-5 reports the total number of House roll call votes and the number of votes on which presidents have taken public positions from 1957 to 1994.

The most dramatic trend revealed in Table 8-5 is the sharp drop in position taking after Lyndon Johnson's tenure as president. Presidents since Johnson have taken positions on roughly one-quarter of the total roll call legislation voted on by the House. An initial drop is not surprising; we would expect Johnson to feel more comfortable taking a position on legislation produced by the large Democratic congressional majority than would the Republican president Nixon while he was in the White House. However, the drop persisted. Democrats Jimmy Carter and Clinton did not approach the pre-Nixon percentage of position taking. Whereas Presidents Eisenhower, John F. Kennedy, and Johnson took positions on an average of 52 percent of congressional roll call votes, presidents since Johnson took positions on an average of only 21 percent of roll call votes. The change may be partly explained by the dramatic increase in roll call votes, which nearly doubled in the early 1970s. But this shift cannot provide a full answer, since the number of roll call votes declined again beginning in 1981.

Another part of the explanation may be that presidents, wary of an increasingly independent-minded congressional membership, have come to actively support legislation only when it is of particular importance to them, in an attempt to minimize defeat. Presidents must build new legislative coalitions among independent partisans in Congress for each bill on which they take a position, bill after bill. Thus, limited position taking may be a form of institutional behavior that presidents of both parties have adopted to establish legislative priorities and ensure success.

Policy Complexity in the Political Environment

The political environment constrains the institutional behavior presidents undertake. One key aspect of this environment is policy complexity. Because of the scope of modern government, presidents take positions and Congress pursues legislation on a vast array of policy issues. This occurs regardless of whether the president and Congress are Democrat or Republican, liberal or conservative. Table 8-6 reports the number of bills on which presidents since Eisenhower have taken positions in seven policy categories—foreign trade, foreign aid, defense, social welfare, economic management, resources, and agriculture. Not surprisingly, presidents have taken greatest interest in policy areas that strongly define the core of government activity—social welfare and economic management. Since Eisenhower, all presidents have taken numerous positions in these two policy areas. This suggests the extent to which the political environment shapes presidents' legislative decisions and minimizes differences among them on policy issues.

Table 8-6 shows another equally clear pattern: all presidents since Eisenhower have taken fewer positions on agriculture than on any other policy area. Incentives to take stands on agriculture, especially for recent presidents who find the proportion of the population working on farms declining, are low. Instead, this type of policy better fits institutional behavior patterns found in Congress. The specialization and reciprocity that characterize Congress suggest that the positions taken by legislators representing agricultural regions will have greater importance than those taken by presidents.

Beyond these two strong general patterns, individual differences exist. Presidents Gerald Ford and Carter gave sustained emphasis to energy policy, while President Reagan took more positions on defense than any other president under study. Overall, however, the similarities outweigh the differences. Considerable consistency exists in the presidential attention given these policy types—indeed, the consistency is such that it seems appropriate to refer to "presidential attention" generically rather than discuss the attention given by any individual president.

Congressional Concurrence with Presidents

Writers often comment on presidential success, or support, in Congress. Yet, this is not only a problematic concept to measure, but the notion of success itself is misleading. One might think of presidential success as how well the president does on legislative measures that actually originate in the White House. Many pieces of legislation on which the White House puts its stamp, however, have been developed for years in Congress, making it difficult to determine what in fact originates from the presidency. Too, presidents may be actively involved with bills that did not originate at the White House, and such a measure of success would not capture those efforts. Another way of thinking about presidential success is to examine how well presidents do on major legislation dealt with by a given Congress. While this may adequately deal with the prominent issues that connect presidents and Congress, it does not encompass the smaller issues that also define presidential-congressional relations.

Thus, in considering presidents' relations with Congress, it is important to consider the range of issues on which the president takes a position. This includes the major pieces of legislation originating from the White House, those which come from Capitol Hill, and many less crucial bills that nonetheless constitute the work of Congress in any given term. This concept is most aptly termed congressional (or presidential) concurrence. It is measured here in two ways: vote concurrence and member concurrence. Vote concurrence is measured by the number of times a majority of members of Congress vote with the president's position on roll call votes. Member concurrence is the percentage of members who agree with the president's position on a roll call vote. Unlike the usual scholarly focus on success or support, the concurrence measures acknowledge that it is impossible to judge who influenced whom. Information is simply inadequate to ascertain the direction of influence. Members of both parties overwhelmingly support many roll call votes regardless of whether the president has a position.

Vote Concurrence.   Figure 8-3 charts the vote concurrence rates for Congress since Eisenhower. Generally, presidents did best in the first year of their first elected term, regardless of their party or the majority parties of the two houses of Congress. This reflects the benefit of presidents hitting the ground running. President Johnson garnered the highest levels of vote concurrence: in 1965, a majority of the Congress concurred with Johnson's position 93 percent of the time. President Reagan's seemingly magical legislative success during the 1981 Congress was not exceptional in comparison with the records of other presidents. Eisenhower, Kennedy, Johnson, and Clinton all exceeded Reagan's record. Kennedy, Nixon, and Carter did slightly better in their second years, but differences between the first and second years were not substantial. Nor did divided government necessarily inhibit high degrees of vote concurrence. Eisenhower (1953) and Reagan (1981) faced divided government but had high concurrence rates.

Table 8-7 permits a more careful examination of the total vote concurrence rates for both houses. The data make clear that congressional vote concurrence has stayed fairly modest over the terms of the last nine presidents. These rates rarely dipped below the 50 percent mark (except for Reagan in 1987 and 1988 and Bush in 1990 and 1992) and only infrequently exceeded 80 percent.

Table 8-7 also permits a separate analysis of House and Senate vote concurrence. It reveals that the House and Senate concurred with presidents since Eisenhower at fairly similar levels, with the exceptions of Reagan and Bush. During the twelve years covered by their terms, only six of which saw Republican control of the Senate, the Senate was much more likely to concur with Reagan's or Bush's position than was the House. As an example, the Senate concurred with Bush nearly 66 percent of the time, while the House only agreed with the president on 40 percent of his legislative positions. One explanation for these exceptions may be that during the Reagan and Bush years conservative coalition victories were higher in the Senate than in the House, meaning that Republicans and Southern Democrats voted together more often in the Senate, presumably in ways that these two administrations supported (Ornstein et al., 1994, 203).

Tables 8-7 and 8-8 suggest several generalizations about party as a structural link between the presidency and Congress. First, as one would expect, Democratic presidents were more successful in the Democratic House and Senate than Republican presidents (Table 8-7). The results, however, were not completely uniform. Although congressional vote concurrence with Carter was generally higher than for the Republican presidents, it was consistently lower than for Presidents Kennedy, Johnson, and Clinton. Table 8-8 reveals what presidents and members of Congress have long known—Southern Democrats are more likely to concur with Republican presidents than with the chief executives of their own party. While their support of Republican positions was not as high as Republicans' own support, it was nonetheless substantial enough to give Republican presidents room to maneuver and Democratic presidents reason to complain.

Member Concurrence.   Table 8-9 provides initial evidence about member concurrence. While vote concurrence determines whether a majority of congressional members supported the president's position on a roll call vote, member concurrence involves the actual percentage of members who concurred with the president's position on the roll call. This provides a more precise measure of agreement between individual members and the president. The high first-year pattern noted for vote concurrence is less clear for member concurrence. Especially for members of the out party, concurrence was typically not at its highest during the president's first year in office. Out-party members may have wished to assert their autonomy from the new president. For members of the in party, concurrence was fairly consistent across the president's term. Among the presidents studied, Ford obtained the highest level of member concurrence in 1974, largely due to very high out-party support in the aftermath of Watergate. Indeed, in that year concurrence from congressional Democrats exceeded that from congressional Republicans. In general, member concurrence rates, like vote concurrence rates, stayed within a relatively narrow range—from 50 to 70 percent concurrence among all members. Reagan, in the latter part of his first term and throughout his second term, proved an exception, falling below the 50 percent mark.

The implication of this narrow range observed for both measures is that the institutions of the presidency and Congress shape individual presidents' success in Congress. Congressional decentralization, committee strength, and constituent policy interests place a ceiling on presidential support, whereas party loyalty, regularized liaison efforts, and strategic veto threats prevent this support from dropping too low. The congressional and executive institutions place constraints on and provide resources for actors within them, thereby narrowing the degree of difference and the variation in feasible behavior.

Tables 8-10 through 8-12 examine member concurrence by issue areas. The results indicate key policy similarities across presidents. Presidents consistently did well in matters of foreign trade and defense. From 1957 to 1993, the member concurrence rate was 62.4 percent on trade and 60.9 percent on defense. In addition, for 23 of the 38 years presented in Table 8-10, member concurrence with the president was highest in one of the three foreign policy areas (although the second highest category was one of the domestic policy areas roughly 40 percent of the time). This is most notable among members of the out party whose concurrence with the president was highest in one of the three foreign policy areas in 25 of the 38 years under study (Table 8-12). The nine presidents studied also obtained reasonably strong concurrence among all members on economic management issues (55.6 percent). Member concurrence in the other areas was more varied.

These results point to a mixing of issue content with institutional advantages and limitations. Presidents are constitutionally mandated to act in areas of diplomacy and defense. Statutes such as the Budget and Accounting Act of 1921 and the Full Employment Act of 1946 also give them an active role in economic policy. With these constitutional and statutory bases for action, presidents may commit greater resources to legislative efforts in these areas, and congressional members may be more willing to support presidential positions. In contrast, the remaining areas are characterized more by changing political stakes than by stable institutional attributes.

Structural Politics: Vetoes and Congressional Overrides

In his classic book, *Congressional Government,* Woodrow Wilson wrote that a president's "power of veto . . . is, of course, beyond all comparison, his most formidable prerogative" (1973, 53). It is "the president's ultimate legislative weapon in that it gives him the weight of two-thirds of the members of each house of Congress" (Watson and Thomas, 1983, 257). It is also a "weapon" that is understood in notably structural terms within the institution. It is exercised infrequently and, by constitutional design, it is overridden rarely. Indeed, overuse of the veto power is sometimes identified as a sign of presidential weakness. Table 8-13 summarizes veto data since Washington. Presidents Ulysses Grant, Grover Cleveland, Theodore Roosevelt, Franklin Roosevelt, Truman, and Ford used the veto most often; Presidents Franklin Pierce, Andrew Johnson, Truman, and Ford saw their vetoes overridden most frequently. Table 8-13 also reveals that presidential expansion of legislative activity in the twentieth century has produced a concomitant increase in vetoes. Even when Cleveland is included, nineteenth-century presidents averaged some 32 vetoes during their terms (only 14 vetoes per term if Cleveland is excluded); twentieth-century presidents, beginning with Theodore Roosevelt, averaged 72 vetoes per term.

Table 8-14 examines vetoes by issue area. It shows a dramatic decline in the number of private bills vetoed after Eisenhower. Apparently presidents no longer saw such minor matters as worthy of presidential attention. Policy complexity can be observed in the other categories. The largest number of vetoes appears in the social welfare, economic management, and resources categories, the areas in which presidents take their greatest numbers of positions (see Table 8-6). Among the other areas, from 1946 to 1994 there was only one presidential veto of foreign aid legislation and only scattered vetoes in foreign trade. Defense policy vetoes occurred less frequently than vetoes in some of the domestic policy areas. Very few vetoes on agricultural matters are evident.

Congressional attempts at overriding presidential vetoes, along with the total number of vetoes, appear in Table 8-15. Congress has overridden presidents' regular vetoes just over one hundred times in over two hundred years—a mere seven-tenths of 1 percent. Despite the strong unilateral power the veto gives presidents, it is largely a negative institutional power. Presidents stop what they do not want, but do not necessarily get what they want.

Presidents and Group Interests

Table 8-16 presents a look at how interest groups view presidents' legislative activities. The relationship between interest groups and presidents, while becoming much more developed than it once was, does not yet appear to be a structural feature of the institution in the way that party is. Observers seldom consider how interest groups view presidents' legislative activities. Scholars write detailed accounts of "iron triangles" to account for the communication and influence patterns manifested by a specific interest group, a congressional committee, and an executive department or agency. So much time is spent drawing the triangles that presidents are usually treated as irrelevant to interest groups within the halls of Congress. These groups are presumed to enjoy the access and support they need as clients of committees and executive departments, neither of which presidents can easily control.

Nevertheless, presidents do pay attention to interest groups, and interest groups do pay attention to presidents. Of greatest importance in understanding the attention given by interest groups to presidents is the concept of intergroup variation. Just as congressional members differ by party and region in their support of presidential positions on legislation, so, too, do interest groups. However, their differences are the product of varying ideological stances not necessarily related to party or region.

The data in Table 8-16 offer an opportunity to explore group ratings of presidents' positions on roll call votes. The reconstructed group ratings included are from the Americans for Democratic Action (ADA), considered a barometer of liberal thinking; the Committee on Political Education (COPE), a group associated with the AFL-CIO that monitors the positions members of Congress take on labor legislation; the Americans for Constitutional Action (ACA) and the American Conservative Union (ACU), the ADA's conservative counterparts; and the Chamber of Commerce of the United States (CCUS), a pro-business interest group. These organizations do not assign interest group scores to presidents when they announce the ideological scores given members of Congress. But such scores can be reconstructed for presidents from the positions presidents have taken on the same legislation used by these interest groups to compile their congressional rankings.

Table 8-16 presents the calculations of presidential interest group ratings for roll call votes from 1960 to 1991. The table displays a liberal-conservative continuum for the presidents studied. It ranges from Lyndon Johnson, who received the highest ADA scores (liberal), to Reagan and Bush, who received the lowest ADA scores and very high ACA, ACU, and CCUS (conservative) scores. Although Bush attempted to offer a "kinder, gentler" presidency to distinguish his tenure from the Reagan legacy, his positions were no less consistently conservative. Nixon, Ford, and Carter were more nearly moderates with scores that varied over their terms. As more data become available about presidents' ideologies, it may be possible to ascertain the role of ideology not only in presidential appeals to interest groups, but also in their appeals to members of Congress and the public as a whole. Ideology may well be another structural component of the institution that, like party, guides presidential behavior and the reactions of other political actors to it.

Conclusion

The data in this chapter suggest three points about presidential relations with Congress. First, the presidency, not the officeholder, is the "policy actor" to watch. Many of the president's efforts are handled by a well-developed organization within the White House. Presidents must grapple with the presidential institution as it coordinates legislative proposals, legislative liaison work, and strategies to achieve legislative success. Presidents must engage in institutional behavior by advancing a presidential program even if they would prefer to minimize their role in the policy-making process. Structural constraints within the presidency, such as the cycle of declining influence and independent partisanship, influence the initiatives presidents propose, when they are proposed, and what degree of success they ultimately achieve.

Second, the impact of the institution is similar for presidents across various policy areas. The complexity of the policy environment affects different presidents in very similar ways. This institutional policy making can be placed in clearer perspective by considering together the several types of policy behavior in which presidents engage. Figures 8-4 through 8-7 show presidents' legislative positions, vetoes, and, from data in Chapter 7, executive orders across all policy areas, and then separately for foreign, defense, and domestic policy since 1957. (A similar display for international agreements appears in Figure 7-1.) These figures provide a startling view of the many policy demands placed on the presidency and the many policy techniques available to presidents through both executive and legislative avenues. The complexity of policy types, the conflicts among techniques, and the diversity among targeted groups promote a reliance on institutional rather than personal decision making.

Finally, institutional relations between the presidency and Congress define the success of a president's performance on any single occasion. The organizational, behavioral, and structural elements of Congress establish these interinstitutional connections as much as do the same elements of the presidency. The organization of Congress is larger and more decentralized than the presidency, which itself is large and decentralized. The congressional organization places pressure on the presidency to be everywhere at once, creating greater distance between the presidential organization and the president (see Chapter 6). The slow pace of congressional activity means that presidents must be masters of timing in spotlighting their programs. Party and the Constitution structure both Congress and the presidency, and the two elements tie the two institutions together while at the same time pulling them apart. After all the political speeches are made and the congressional votes are done, presidents are apparently *not* "chief legislators" who "guide Congress in much of its lawmaking activity" (Rossiter, 1960, 26), though the presidency is surely one of the two chief legislative institutions.

Note

1. A distinction should be noted here between the number of proposals submitted to Congress by the White House and the importance attached to any one proposal. The frequency with which proposals are submitted within a policy area provides one indication of the breadth of attention given the issue category by a president, but a single proposal may be viewed as a major priority by the chief executive. For example, although Lyndon Johnson did not submit numerous proposals on civil rights, a few central measures did show concerted attention to this policy area.

Table 8-1 Political Parties of Presidents and Congress, 1789–1995

Year	President	President's party	Congress	House Majority (N)	House Majority Party	House Opposition (N)	House Opposition Party	House Other	Senate Majority (N)	Senate Majority Party	Senate Opposition (N)	Senate Opposition Party	Senate Other	Unified/divided government
1789–1791	Washington	F	1st	38	F	26	OP	—	17	F	9	OP	—	UG
1791–1793		F	2d	37	F	33	DR	—	16	F	13	DR	—	UG
1793–1795		F	3d	57	DR	48	F	—	17	F	13	DR	—	DG-H
1795–1797		F	4th	54	F	52	DR	—	19	F	13	DR	—	UG
1797–1799	J. Adams	F	5th	58	F	48	DR	—	20	F	12	DR	—	UG
1799–1801		F	6th	64	F	42	DR	—	19	F	13	DR	—	UG
1801–1803	Jefferson	DR	7th	69	DR	36	F	—	18	DR	13	F	—	UG
1803–1805		DR	8th	102	DR	39	F	—	25	DR	9	F	—	UG
1805–1807		DR	9th	116	DR	25	F	—	27	DR	7	F	—	UG
1807–1809		DR	10th	118	DR	24	F	—	28	DR	6	F	—	UG
1809–1811	Madison	DR	11th	94	DR	48	F	—	28	DR	6	F	—	UG
1811–1813		DR	12th	108	DR	36	F	—	30	DR	6	F	—	UG
1813–1815		DR	13th	112	DR	68	F	—	27	DR	9	F	—	UG
1815–1817		DR	14th	117	DR	65	F	—	25	DR	11	F	—	UG
1817–1819	Monroe	DR	15th	141	DR	42	F	—	34	DR	10	F	—	UG
1819–1821		DR	16th	156	DR	27	F	—	35	DR	7	F	—	UG
1821–1823		DR	17th	158	DR	25	F	—	44	DR	4	F	—	UG
1823–1825		DR	18th	187	DR	26	F	—	44	DR	4	F	—	UG
1825–1827	J.Q. Adams	I	19th	105	IDR	97	JDR	—	26	IDR	20	JDR	—	DG
1827–1829		I	20th	119	JDR	94	IDR	—	28	JDR	20	IDR	—	DG
1829–1831	Jackson	D	21st	139	D	74	NR	—	26	D	22	NR	—	UG
1831–1833		D	22d	141	D	58	NR	14	25	D	21	NR	2	UG
1833–1835		D	23d	147	D	53	NR	60	20a	D	20a	NR	8	UG
1835–1837		D	24th	145	D	98	W	—	27	D	25	W	—	UG
1837–1839	Van Buren	D	25th	108	D	107	W	24	30	D	18	W	—	UG
1839–1841		D	26th	124	D	118	W	—	28	D	22	W	—	UG

(Table continues)

Table 8-1 (Continued)

				House					Senate					
				Majority		Opposition			Majority		Opposition			Unified/divided
Year	President	President's party	Congress	(N)	Party	(N)	Party	Other	(N)	Party	(N)	Party	Other	government
1841–1845	W. Harrison/Tyler	W	27th	133	W	102	D	6	28	W	22	D	2	UG
1843–1845	Tyler	W	28th	142	D	79	W	1	28	W	25	D	1	DG-H
1845–1847	Polk	D	29th	143	D	77	W	6	31	D	25	W	—	UG
1847–1849		D	30th	115	W	108	D	4	36	D	21	W	1	DG-H
1849–1851	Taylor/Fillmore	W	31st	112	D	109	W	9	35	D	25	W	2	DG
1851–1853	Fillmore	W	32d	140	D	88	W	5	35	D	24	W	3	DG
1853–1855	Pierce	D	33d	159	D	71	W	4	38	D	22	W	2	UG
1855–1857		D	34th	108	R	83	D	43	40	D	15	R	5	DG-H
1857–1859	Buchanan	D	35th	118	D	92	R	26	36	D	20	R	8	UG
1859–1861		D	36th	114	R	92	D	31	36	D	26	R	4	DG-H
1861–1863	Lincoln	R	37th	105	R	43	D	30	31	R	10	D	8	UG
1863–1865		R	38th	102	R	75	D	9	36	R	9	D	5	UG
1865–1867	A. Johnson	R	39th	149	R	42	D	—	42	R	10	D	—	UG
1867–1869		R	40th	143	R	49	D	—	42	R	11	D	—	UG
1869–1871	Grant	R	41st	149	R	63	D	—	56	R	11	D	—	UG
1871–1873		R	42d	134	R	104	D	5	52	R	17	D	5	UG
1873–1875		R	43d	194	R	92	D	14	49	R	19	D	—	UG
1875–1877		R	44th	169	D	109	R	14	45	R	29	D	2	DG-H
1877–1879	Hayes	R	45th	153	D	140	R	—	39	R	36	D	1	DG-H
1879–1881		R	46th	149	D	130	R	14	42	D	33	R	1	DG
1881–1883	Garfield/Arthur	R	47th	147	R	135	D	11	39	R	37	D	1	UG
1883–1885	Arthur	R	48th	197	D	118	R	10	38	R	36	D	2	DG-H
1885–1887	Cleveland	D	49th	183	D	140	R	2	43	R	34	D	—	DG-S
1887–1889		D	50th	169	D	152	R	4	39	R	37	D	—	DG-S
1889–1891	B. Harrison	R	51st	166	R	159	D	—	39	R	37	D	—	UG
1891–1893		R	52d	235	D	88	R	11	47	R	39	D	2	DG-H
1893–1895	Cleveland	D	53d	218	D	127	R	7	44	D	38	R	3	UG

Years	President	Party	Congress	House Maj. party	House Maj. seats	House Min. party	House Min. seats	House Other	Senate Maj. party	Senate Maj. seats	Senate Min. party	Senate Min. seats	Senate Other	Government
1895–1897		D	54th	R	244	D	105	40	R	43	D	39	6	DG
1897–1899	McKinley	R	55th	R	204	D	113	9	R	47	D	34	7	UG
1899–1901		R	56th	R	185	D	163	9	R	53	D	26	8	UG
1901–1903	McKinley/T. Roosevelt	R	57th	R	197	D	151	—	R	55	D	31	4	UG
1903–1905		R	58th	R	208	D	178	—	R	57	D	33	—	UG
1905–1907	T. Roosevelt	R	59th	R	250	D	136	—	R	57	D	33	—	UG
1907–1909		R	60th	R	222	D	164	—	R	61	D	31	—	UG
1909–1911	Taft	R	61st	R	219	D	172	—	R	61	D	32	—	UG
1911–1913		R	62d	D	228	R	161	1	R	51	D	41	1	DG-H
1913–1915	Wilson	D	63d	D	291	R	127	17	D	51	R	44	—	UG
1915–1917		D	64th	D	230	R	196	9	D	56	R	40	—	UG
1917–1919		D	65th	D	216	R	210	6	D	53	R	42	—	UG
1919–1921		D	66th	R	240	D	190	3	R	49	D	47	2	DG
1921–1923	Harding	R	67th	R	301	D	131	1	R	59	D	37	1	UG
1923–1925	Coolidge	R	68th	R	225	D	205	5	R	51	D	43	1	UG
1925–1927		R	69th	R	247	D	183	4	R	56	D	39	1	UG
1927–1929		R	70th	R	237	D	195	3	R	49	D	46	1	UG
1929–1931	Hoover	R	71st	R	267	D	167	1	R	56	D	39	1	UG
1931–1933		R	72d	D	220	R	214	1	R	48	D	47	1	DG-H
1933–1935	F. Roosevelt	D	73d	D	310	R	117	5	D	60	R	35	1	UG
1935–1937		D	74th	D	319	R	103	10	D	69	R	25	2	UG
1937–1939		D	75th	D	331	R	89	13	D	76	R	16	4	UG
1939–1941		D	76th	D	261	R	164	4	D	69	R	23	4	UG
1941–1943		D	77th	D	268	R	162	5	D	66	R	28	2	UG
1943–1945		D	78th	D	218	R	208	4	D	58	R	37	1	UG
1945–1947	Truman	D	79th	D	242	R	190	2	D	56	R	38	1	UG
1947–1949		D	80th	R	245	D	188	1	R	51	D	45	—	DG
1949–1951		D	81st	D	263	R	171	1	D	54	R	42	—	UG
1951–1953		D	82d	D	234	R	199	1	D	49	R	47	—	UG
1953–1955	Eisenhower	R	83d	R	221	D	211	1	R	48	D	47	1	UG
1955–1957		R	84th	D	232	R	203	—	D	48	R	47	1	DG
1957–1959		R	85th	D	233	R	200	—	D	49	R	47	—	DG
1959–1961		R	86th	D	283	R	153	—	D	64	R	34	—	DG
1961–1963	Kennedy	D	87th	D	263	R	174	—	D	65	R	35	—	UG
1963–1965	Kennedy/L. Johnson	D	88th	D	258	R	177	—	D	67	R	33	—	UG

(Table continues)

Table 8-1 (*Continued*)

Year	President	President's party	Congress	House Majority (N)	Party	House Opposition (N)	Party	Other	Senate Majority (N)	Party	Senate Opposition (N)	Party	Other	Unified/divided government
1965–1967	L. Johnson	D	89th	295	D	140	R	—	68	D	32	R	—	UG
1967–1969		D	90th	246	D	187	R	—	64	D	36	R	—	UG
1969–1971	Nixon	R	91st	245	D	189	R	—	57	D	43	R	—	DG
1971–1973		R	92d	254	D	180	R	—	54	D	44	R	2	DG
1973–1975	Nixon/Ford	R	93d	239	D	192	R	1	56	D	42	R	2	DG
1975–1977		R	94th	291	D	144	R	—	60	D	37	R	2	DG
1977–1979	Carter	D	95th	292	D	143	R	—	61	D	38	R	1	UG
1979–1981		D	96th	276	D	157	R	—	58	D	41	R	1	UG
1981–1983	Reagan	R	97th	243	D	192	R	—	53	R	46	D	1	DG-H
1983–1985		R	98th	269	D	165	R	—	54	R	46	D	—	DG-H
1985–1987		R	99th	252	D	182	R	—	53	R	47	D	—	DG-H
1987–1989		R	100th	259	D	176	R	—	55	D	45	R	—	DG
1989–1991	Bush	R	101st	260	D	175	R	—	55	D	45	R	—	DG
1991–1993		R	102d	267	D	167	R	1	56	D	44	R	—	DG
1993–1995	Clinton	D	103d	261	D	173	R	—	58	D	42	R	—	UG

Sources: (1789–1970) Adapted from U.S. Department of Commerce, *U.S. Historical Statistics: Colonial Times to 1970* (Washington, D.C.: Government Printing Office, 1971), 204–210; (1971–1995) U.S. Department of Commerce, *Statistical Abstract of the United States* (Washington, D.C.: Government Printing Office, various years).

Note: D—Democrats, DG—Divided Government, DG-H—Divided Government (House only), DG-S—Divided Government (Senate only), DR—Democratic-Republicans, IDR—Independent Democratic-Republicans, JDR—Jacksonian Democratic-Republicans, NR—National Republicans, OP—Opposition, R—Republicans, U—Unified Government, W—Whig.

[a] Eight members not affiliated with either main party gave their support, and thus a majority, to the Democrats.

Table 8-2   Size of the Office of Legislative Affairs, Reagan to Clinton

President/year	Size of staff	President/year	Size of staff
Reagan, I		Bush	
1981	39	1989	12
1982	39	1990	13
1983	34	1991	14
1984	28	1992	14
Reagan, II		Clinton[a]	
1985	24	1993	21
1986	25	1994	18
1987	22		
1988	27		

Source: Successive volumes of *Federal Staff Directory* (Mt. Vernon, Va.: Staff Directories, Ltd.).

Note: Annual data not available prior to Reagan.

[a] 1993–1994 only.

Figure 8-1   The Legislative Clearance Process

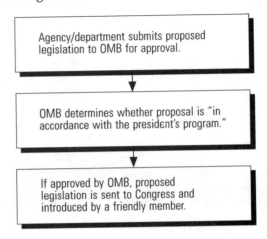

Agency/department submits proposed legislation to OMB for approval.

OMB determines whether proposal is "in accordance with the president's program."

If approved by OMB, proposed legislation is sent to Congress and introduced by a friendly member.

Figure 8-2   The Enrolled Bill Process

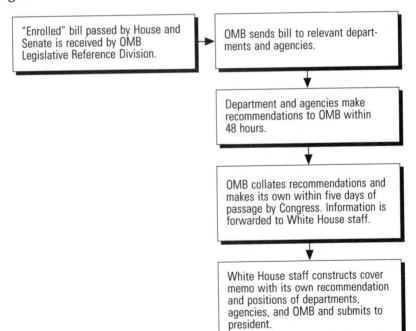

"Enrolled" bill passed by House and Senate is received by OMB Legislative Reference Division.

OMB sends bill to relevant departments and agencies.

Department and agencies make recommendations to OMB within 48 hours.

OMB collates recommendations and makes its own within five days of passage by Congress. Information is forwarded to White House staff.

White House staff constructs cover memo with its own recommendation and positions of departments, agencies, and OMB and submits to president.

Table 8-3   Number of Presidential Requests of Congress in State of the Union Messages, Truman to Clinton

President/year	Total requests[a]		First-time requests		Repeat requests	
Truman, I						
1945	—		—		—	
1946	41	(36)	16	(12)	25	(24)
1947	23	(20)	21	(18)	2	(2)
1948	15	(11)	6	(5)	9	(6)
Truman, II						
1949	28	(26)	17	(15)	11	(11)
1950	20	(19)	9	(9)	11	(10)
1951	11	(9)	5	(5)	6	(5)
1952	19	(18)	7	(6)	12	(12)
Eisenhower, I						
1953	14	(13)	14	(13)	0	
1954	39	(30)	35	(26)	4	(4)
1955	32	(25)	19	(11)	14	(14)
1956						
Eisenhower, II						
1957	14	(10)	6	(3)	8	(7)
1958						
1959	16	(14)	14	(12)	2	(2)
1960	6	(5)	1	(1)	5	(4)
Kennedy						
1961	25		25	0		
1962	24		16	8		
1963	18		6	12		
Johnson[b]						
1964	17		6	11		
1965	38		34	4		
1966	31		24	7		
1967	27		19	8		
1968	26		14	12		
Nixon, I						
1969	17		17	0		
1970	21		12	9		
1971	20		8	12		
1972	17		3	14		
Nixon, II	23		20	3		
1973	23		20	3		
1974	16		5	11		
Ford						
1975	13		10	3		
1976	13		6	7		

(Table continues)

Table 8-3   *(Continued)*

President/year	Total requests[a]		First-time requests		Repeat requests	
Carter						
1977	21		21	0		
1978	11		8	3		
1979	13		8	5		
1980	11		4	7		
Reagan, I						
1981	8		8	0		
1982	8		7	1		
1983	14		11	3		
1984	9		4	5		
Reagan, II						
1985	7		0	7		
1986	5		0	5		
1987	5		0	5		
1988	4		0	4		
Bush						
1989	24	(23)	24	(23)	0	(0)
1990	18	(18)	15	(15)	3	(3)
1991	20	(17)	12	(9)	8	(8)
1992	24	(22)	13	(13)	11	(9)
Clinton[c]						
1993	30	(29)	30	(29)	0	(0)
1994	22	(22)	15	(15)	7	(7)

Sources: (Kennedy through Reagan, II) Paul Light, *The Presidential Agenda,* rev. ed. (Baltimore: Johns Hopkins University Press, 1991), 42, 241, reprinted by permission of the Johns Hopkins University Press, updated by the author.

Note: The tallies for Truman, Eisenhower, Bush, and Clinton were taken from State of the Union messages. Those for Kennedy through Reagan are from the legislative clearance records of the OMB and from State of the Union messages. The counts involve items that had cleared in accordance with the president's program and had been mentioned in at least one State of the Union message.

[a] Numbers in parentheses refer to domestic legislative proposals submitted to Congress. The difference between the first entry in a column and the entry in parentheses is the number of foreign policy legislative proposals submitted to Congress. For example, Truman submitted five foreign policy proposals in 1946. Light does not distinguish between foreign and domestic policy proposals in his data for Kennedy through Reagan.
[b] Includes full term from November 1963 to January 1969.
[c] 1993–1994 only.

Table 8-4   First-Year Requests for Legislation, Truman, II, to Clinton

President/year	January–March	April–June	July–September	October–December	Total number of requests
Truman, II					
1949	68%	0%	32%	0%	41
Eisenhower, I					
1953	52	41	7	0	27
Eisenhower, II					
1957	51	46	0	3	39
Kennedy					
1961	76	24	0	0	25
Johnson					
1965	94	6	0	0	34
Nixon, I					
1969	12	41	41	6	17
Nixon, II					
1973	40	30	15	15	20
Ford					
1974	—	—	28	72	18
Carter					
1977	33	57	10	0	21
Reagan, I					
1981	63	18	19	0	8
Reagan, II					
1985	31	61	0	0	7
Bush					
1989	79	0	21	0	24
Clinton					
1993	52	0	48	0	30

Sources: (Truman, Eisenhower, Ford, Reagan, Bush, Clinton) Calculated by the author from all major addresses to the nation delivered during prime time, carried by the major networks, and preempting regular programming; (Kennedy through Carter) OMB Legislative Reference Division clearance records in Paul Light, *The Presidential Agenda,* rev. ed. (Baltimore: Johns Hopkins University Press, 1991), 45, reprinted by permission of the Johns Hopkins University Press.

Table 8-5 Presidential Position Taking on House Roll Calls, Eisenhower, II, to Clinton

President/year	Total roll calls	Positions[a]	Positions as percentage of roll calls[b]
Eisenhower, II			
1957	100	54	54.0
1958	93	48	51.6
1959	87	53	60.9
1960	91	41	45.1
Kennedy			
1961	113	65	57.5
1962	124	60	48.4
1963	119	71	59.7
Johnson[c]			
1964	113	52	46.0
1965	201	112	55.7
1966	193	102	52.8
1967	245	126	51.4
1968	233	101	43.3
Nixon, I			
1969	177	47	26.6
1970	266	64	24.1
1971	320	61	19.1
1972	329	37	11.2
Nixon, II			
1973	541	125	23.1
1974	476	107	22.5
Ford			
1974	61	0	0.0
1975	612	89	14.5
1976	661	49	7.4
Carter			
1977	706	75	10.6
1978	834	115	13.8
1979	672	143	21.3
1980	604	114	18.9
Reagan, I			
1981	353	75	25.8
1982	459	75	20.5
1983	498	80	20.7
1984	408	111	31.1
Reagan, II			
1985	439	80	18.2
1986	451	90	20.0

Table 8-5   (*Continued*)

President/year	Total roll calls	Positions[a]	Positions as percentage of roll calls[b]
Reagan, II (continued)			
1987	488	99	20.3
1988	451	104	23.1
Bush			
1989	379[d]	86	22.7
1990	536[d]	108	20.1
1991	444[d]	111	25.0
1992	488[d]	105	21.5
Clinton[e]			
1993	597	102	17.1
1994	464	78	16.8

Source: Coded by the author from annual volumes of *Congressional Quarterly Almanac* (Washington, D.C.: Congressional Quarterly).

[a] Number of House roll calls on which president took a clear position.
[b] Total number of positions presidents have taken as a percentage of the total number of House roll calls.
[c] Includes full term from November 1963 to January 1969.
[d] Includes quorum calls.
[e] 1993–1994 only.

Table 8-6 Presidential Position Taking in the House by Issue Area, Eisenhower, II, to Clinton

President/year	Foreign trade	Foreign aid	Defense	Social welfare	Economic management	Resources	Agriculture
Eisenhower, II							
1957	2	6	4	18	9	10	5
1958	5	4	9	13	7	8	2
1959	1	7	3	9	11	15	7
1960	3	7	1	15	6	5	4
Kennedy							
1961	5	10	5	12	18	9	6
1962	3	10	6	10	19	8	4
1963	3	9	8	14	23	9	5
Johnson[a]							
1964	4	9	5	14	9	10	1
1965	5	10	10	36	30	16	5
1966	7	13	4	24	36	18	0
1967	5	12	9	42	43	11	4
1968	5	10	7	29	26	18	4
Nixon, I							
1969	1	4	2	18	18	2	2
1970	1	5	2	21	20	13	2
1971	9	2	9	25	9	7	0
1972	3	3	7	8	11	5	0
Nixon, II							
1973	10	3	15	20	36	26	15
1974	2	11	15	23	35	21	0
Ford							
1974	0	0	0	0	0	0	0
1975	7	4	10	14	22	27	5
1976	3	1	5	11	10	19	0

Carter							
1977	4	9	11	10	15	25	1
1978	13	19	20	11	31	20	1
1979	32	21	14	31	17	28	0
1980	10	19	11	14	31	22	7
Reagan, I							
1981	4	1	15	4	21	15	15
1982	3	4	22	6	15	20	5
1983	5	6	27	20	8	9	5
1984	19	1	20	26	19	22	4
Reagan, II							
1985	6	13	19	4	14	12	12
1986	15	4	25	20	13	9	4
1987	12	4	27	13	18	25	0
1988	9	7	29	31	14	13	1
Bush							
1989	4	13	12	16	24	17	0
1990	13	6	12	32	24	16	5
1991	7	14	21	29	27	12	1
1992	13	3	13	27	29	20	0
Clinton[b]							
1993	3	7	17	22	41	10	2
1994	7	0	15	19	26	11	0

Source: Coded by the author from annual volumes of *Congressional Quarterly Almanac* (Washington, D.C.: Congressional Quarterly).

Note: Figures are the number of roll calls in which the president took a position in each issue area. Foreign trade—foreign trade, diplomacy, or immigration; foreign aid—various forms of assistance to other countries; defense—military, defense, veterans issues; social welfare—social welfare, civil rights, Indian affairs, and education; economic management—government and economic management, income tax issues; resources—energy, natural resources, environment, and transportation; agriculture—agriculture and farm policy.

[a] Includes full term from November 1963 to January 1969.
[b] 1993–1994 only.

Figure 8-3 Congressional Concurrence with Presidents, Eisenhower to Clinton

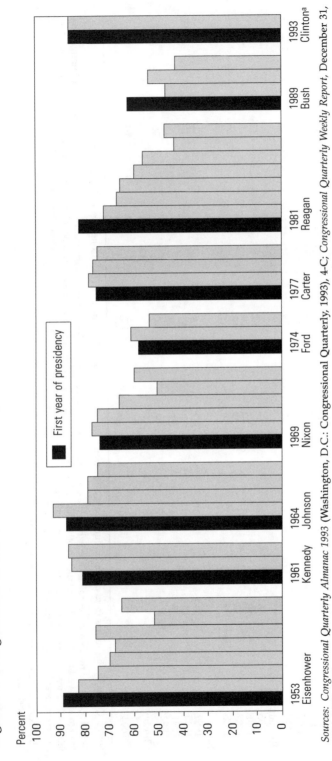

Sources: Congressional Quarterly Almanac 1993 (Washington, D.C.: Congressional Quarterly, 1993), 4-C; *Congressional Quarterly Weekly Report,* December 31, 1994, 3652–3653.

Note: Concurrence is defined by the number of times a majority in Congress supported the president's position on legislation. Congressional Quarterly has tracked presidential positions since 1953. However, the decision rules and methods of recording positions were altered in 1957. Therefore, data from 1953 to 1956 may not be comparable with data after 1957.

[a] 1993–1994 only.

Table 8-7   House and Senate Concurrence with Presidents,
Eisenhower to Clinton

President (political party)/year	Total House and Senate concurrence	House		Senate	
		Concurrence rate	Number of votes	Concurrence rate	Number of votes
Eisenhower (R)					
1953	89.2%	91.2%	34	87.8%	49
1954	82.8	78.9	38	77.9	77
1955	75.3	63.4	41	84.6	52
1956	69.2	73.5	34	67.7	65
1957	68.4	58.3	60	78.9	57
1958	75.7	74.0	50	76.5	98
1959	52.9	55.6	54	50.4	121
1960	65.1	65.1	43	65.1	86
Average	69.9	68.4		70.7	
Total			354		605
Kennedy (D)					
1961	81.5	83.1	65	80.6	124
1962	85.4	85.0	60	85.6	125
1963	87.1	83.1	71	89.6	115
Average	84.6	83.7		85.2	
Total			196		364
Johnson (D)[a]					
1964	87.9	88.5	52	87.6	97
1965	93.1	93.8	112	92.6	162
1966	78.9	91.3	103	68.8	125
1967	78.8	75.6	127	81.2	165
1968	74.5	83.5	103	68.9	164
Average	82.2	85.9		79.7	
Total			497		713
Nixon (R)					
1969	74.8	72.3	47	76.4	72
1970	76.9	84.6	65	71.4	91
1971	74.8	82.5	57	69.5	82
1972	66.3	81.1	37	54.3	46
1973	50.6	48.0	125	52.4	185
1974	59.6	67.9	53	54.2	83
Average	64.3	68.2		61.5	
Total			384		559
Ford (R)					
1974	58.2	59.3	54	57.4	68
1975	61.0	50.6	89	71.0	93
1976	53.8	43.1	51	64.2	53
Average	58.3	51.0		65.0	
Total			194		214

(Table continues)

Table 8-7 *(Continued)*

President (political party)/year	Total House and Senate concurrence	House		Senate	
		Concurrence rate	Number of votes	Concurrence rate	Number of votes
Carter (D)					
1977	75.4	74.7	79	76.1	88
1978	78.3	69.6	112	84.8	151
1979	76.8	71.7	145	81.4	161
1980	75.1	76.9	117	73.3	116
Average	76.6	73.1		79.7	
Total			453		516
Reagan (R)					
1981	82.4	72.4	76	88.3	128
1982	72.4	55.8	77	83.2	119
1983	67.1	47.6	82	85.9	85
1984	65.8	52.2	113	85.7	77
1985	59.9	45.0	80	71.6	102
1986	56.5	33.3	90	80.7	83
1987	43.5	33.3	99	56.4	78
1988	47.4	32.7	104	64.8	88
Average	62.2	45.6		77.9	
Total			721		760
Bush (R)					
1989	62.6	50.0	86	73.3	101
1990	46.8	32.4	108	63.4	93
1991	54.2	43.2	111	67.5	83
1992	43.0	37.1	105	53.3	60
Average	51.8	40.2		65.6	
Total			410		337
Clinton (D)[b]					
1993	86.4	87.3	102	85.4	89
1994	86.3	87.2	78	85.5	62

Source: Harold Stanley and Richard Niemi, *Vital Statistics on American Politics,* 4th ed. (Washington, D.C.: CQ Press, 1993), 274–275.

Note: R—Republican; D—Democrat. Percentages based on the number of congressional votes supporting the president divided by the total number of votes on which the president had taken a position.

[a] Includes full-term from November 1963 to January 1969.
[b] 1993–1994 only.

Table 8-8   House and Senate Concurrence with Presidents by Party,
Eisenhower to Clinton (percent)

	House			Senate		
President/year	All Demo-crats	Southern Demo-crats	Repub-licans	All Demo-crats	Southern Demo-crats	Repub-licans
Eisenhower, I						
1953	55	N/A	80	55	N/A	78
1954	54	N/A	80	45	N/A	82
1955	58	N/A	67	65	N/A	85
1956	58	N/A	79	44	N/A	80
Eisenhower, II						
1957	54	N/A	60	60	N/A	80
1958	63	N/A	65	51	N/A	77
1959	44	N/A	76	44	N/A	80
1960	49	N/A	63	52	N/A	76
Kennedy						
1961	81	N/A	41	73	N/A	42
1962	83	71	47	76	63	48
1963	84	71	36	77	65	52
Johnson[a]						
1964	84	70	42	73	63	52
1965	83	65	46	75	60	55
1966	81	64	45	71	59	53
1967	80	65	51	73	69	63
1968	77	63	59	64	50	57
Nixon, I						
1969	56	55	65	55	56	74
1970	64	64	79	56	62	74
1971	53	69	79	48	59	76
1972	56	59	74	52	71	77
Nixon, II						
1973	39	49	67	42	55	70
1974	52	64	71	44	60	65
Ford						
1974	48	52	59	45	55	67
1975	40	48	67	53	67	76
1976	36	52	70	47	61	73
Carter						
1977	69	58	46	77	71	58
1978	67	54	40	74	61	47
1979	70	58	37	75	66	51
1980	71	63	44	71	69	50

(Table continues)

Table 8-8   (*Continued*)

President/year	House			Senate		
	All Demo-crats	Southern Demo-crats	Repub-licans	All Demo-crats	Southern Demo-crats	Repub-licans
Reagan, I						
1981	46	60	72	52	63	84
1982	43	55	70	46	57	77
1983	30	45	74	45	46	77
1984	37	47	64	45	58	81
Reagan, II						
1985	31	43	69	36	46	80
1986	26	37	69	39	56	90
1987	26	37	65	38	43	67
1988	28	34	61	51	58	73
Bush						
1989	38	49	72	56	66	84
1990	26	35	65	39	49	72
1991	35	43	74	42	53	84
1992	27	38	75	33	40	75
Clinton[b]						
1993	77	78	39	87	82	29
1994	75	75	47	86	84	42

Source: Harold Stanley and Richard Niemi, *Vital Statistics on American Politics,* 4th ed. (Washington, D.C.: CQ Press, 1994), 276–277; updated by the author.

Note: N/A—not available. Percentages indicate number of congressional votes supporting the president divided by the total number of votes on which the president took a position. The percentages are calculated to eliminate the effects of absences as follows: support = (support)/(support + opposition).

[a] Includes full term from November 1963 to January 1969.
[b] 1993–1994 only.

Table 8-9 Average Annual Roll Call Support for the President by Members of the House, Eisenhower, II, to Clinton

President/year	All members		Out party		In party	
	Number voting	Percent with president	Number voting	Percent with president	Number voting	Percent with president
Eisenhower, II						
1957	386	56.0	208	53.7	178	59.3
1958	375	64.4	199	63.1	175	65.6
1959	395	57.3	258	46.7	138	77.1
1960	392	53.3	251	47.5	141	63.6
Kennedy						
1961	391	65.2	157	40.8	235	81.4
1962	382	68.5	155	47.7	227	82.6
1963	379	65.2	157	36.5	220	85.4
Johnson[a]						
1964	383	67.4	161	43.2	222	84.8
1965	384	71.3	124	46.4	260	83.1
1966	343	69.8	114	46.3	228	81.6
1967	380	67.6	167	51.8	213	79.8
1968	363	69.9	161	60.0	202	77.9
Nixon, I						
1969	376	59.8	210	56.1	166	64.4
1970	359	71.4	201	66.1	158	78.3
1971	386	64.2	224	53.1	162	79.5
1972	366	64.0	215	56.4	153	74.5
Nixon, II						
1973	395	51.6	219	39.1	176	67.3
1974	381	55.8	214	48.8	166	64.8

(Table continues)

Table 8-9 (Continued)

President/year	All members		Out party		In party	
	Number voting	Percent with president	Number voting	Percent with president	Number voting	Percent with president
Ford						
1974	369	72.4	207	76.4	162	67.4
1975	406	50.2	270	40.8	136	69.0
1976	389	48.1	259	37.3	131	69.5
Carter						
1977	394	60.7	132	43.6	261	69.4
1978	384	58.9	130	39.7	254	68.7
1979	399	58.6	146	36.7	253	71.3
1980	387	60.5	143	44.4	244	70.1
Reagan, I						
1981	404	57.0	224	45.3	180	71.4
1982	393	55.4	218	43.8	175	69.9
1983	410	46.6	251	29.9	159	72.9
1984	402	47.7	246	37.2	156	64.3
Reagan, II						
1985	421	48.9	245	33.8	179	73.5
1986	397	42.5	211	29.7	169	68.7
1987	411	41.2	239	26.0	168	64.0
1988	400	42.0	233	27.0	165	62.0
Bush						
1989	413	52.0	244	42.1	169	70.9
1990	416	42.0	247	26.2	170	65.1

1991	395	50.6	241	37.3	152	71.5
1992	411	50.6	247	27.3	159	74.5
Clinton[b]						
1993	423	63.5	171	40.2	236	84.2
1994	426	61.2	153	48.3	252	64.3

Source: Each roll call individually coded by the author from annual volumes of *Congressional Quarterly Almanac* (Washington, D.C.: Congressional Quarterly).

[a] Includes full term from November 1963 to January 1969.

[b] 1993–1994 only.

Table 8-10 Percentage of Support for the President on House Roll Calls by Issue Area, Eisenhower, II, to Clinton

President/year	Foreign trade	Foreign aid	Defense	Social welfare	Economic management	Resources	Agriculture
Eisenhower, II							
1957	70.1	54.4	50.6	56.9	56.3	55.4	54.1
1958	70.1	60.0	80.6	63.2	62.8	51.4	50.3
1959	99.5	70.3	49.4	55.6	69.0	46.0	50.3
1960	56.1	58.3	46.3	55.6	34.8	55.2	72.5
Kennedy							
1961	84.2	71.6	85.1	70.1	55.6	51.9	60.1
1962	71.7	61.7	83.1	78.8	70.0	58.3	49.2
1963	69.6	54.5	71.3	74.9	62.7	65.6	55.0
Johnson[a]							
1964	74.3	64.5	49.4	65.3	63.0	84.6	51.0
1965	81.5	68.9	68.7	72.7	66.6	81.7	56.0
1966	75.5	69.9	53.1	69.4	67.1	77.1	—
1967	59.7	58.7	79.5	69.9	68.0	62.7	62.8
1968	68.6	70.0	77.2	72.5	61.7	75.4	72.5
Nixon, I							
1969	85.9	56.2	86.1	59.3	59.9	45.6	44.6
1970	76.3	64.8	68.2	58.1	82.8	80.5	56.0
1971	66.1	51.2	65.6	61.7	73.5	60.7	—
1972	80.1	65.2	68.0	55.9	61.7	66.2	—
Nixon, II							
1973	51.3	72.5	44.2	47.6	57.5	50.5	48.2
1974	55.3	49.4	48.6	54.9	57.7	67.0	—
Ford							
1975	69.9	61.8	52.7	30.5	49.0	52.5	57.2
1976	52.5	60.3	56.5	45.2	43.1	48.9	—

Carter							
1977	67.7	49.2	73.6	61.5	56.0	60.5	75.7
1978	55.0	52.8	58.5	54.9	64.3	62.8	64.1
1979	60.7	53.9	59.9	64.8	58.0	55.4	—
1980	72.8	50.8	66.2	55.4	59.9	59.3	72.7
Reagan, I							
1981	54.7	31.7	52.3	55.6	59.1	73.0	42.9
1982	67.7	61.6	47.6	65.8	41.1	56.1	46.6
1983	43.3	57.5	38.8	57.8	39.8	30.7	47.0
1984	56.5	50.6	38.7	55.5	47.4	41.2	62.5
Reagan, II							
1985	51.7	53.6	28.9	50.2	48.5	42.6	52.5
1986	37.4	40.3	40.9	49.5	47.3	41.8	—
1987	39.5	43.5	39.3	53.4	28.3	34.8	—
1988	39.4	68.0	32.4	53.3	27.3	31.2	95.5
Bush							
1989	58.4	55.2	48.9	51.5	58.5	39.6	—
1990	34.0	47.6	42.5	57.1	43.0	33.3	36.6
1991	52.1	43.2	48.5	58.6	48.5	43.3	93.6
1992	32.5	—	46.0	50.1	45.4	48.6	—
Clinton[b]							
1993	68.6	62.2	73.0	55.3	62.5	56.5	—
1994	66.2	—	52.7	56.4	50.7	98.8	—

Source: Coded by the author from annual volumes of *Congressional Quarterly Almanac* (Washington, D.C.: Congressional Quarterly).

Note: Foreign trade—foreign trade, diplomacy, or immigration; foreign aid—various forms of assistance to other countries; defense—military, defense, veterans issues; social welfare—social welfare, civil rights, Indian affairs, and education; economic management—government and economic management, income tax issues; resources—energy, natural resources, environment, and transportation; agriculture—agriculture and farm policy. "—" indicates that no votes were taken in that area.

[a] Includes full term from November 1963 to January 1969.

[b] 1993–1994 only.

Table 8-11 Percentage of In-Party Support for the President on House Roll Calls by Issue Area, Eisenhower, II, to Clinton

President/year	Foreign trade	Foreign aid	Defense	Social welfare	Economic management	Resources	Agriculture
Eisenhower, II							
1957	70.3	55.9	56.1	47.7	67.5	70.0	66.8
1958	59.1	59.2	93.1	58.1	62.9	52.4	82.4
1959	100.0	65.1	81.6	70.1	83.8	74.7	87.0
1960	63.0	63.2	63.0	60.3	50.8	79.2	92.4
Kennedy							
1961	93.5	81.2	87.1	86.9	78.8	71.9	77.7
1962	96.1	76.9	92.0	82.7	85.1	76.1	74.0
1963	88.9	80.7	85.9	84.3	87.0	86.2	85.6
Johnson[a]							
1964	89.4	82.8	66.2	85.1	84.3	94.3	84.8
1965	85.4	83.5	80.0	85.9	77.9	89.6	76.6
1966	84.0	80.8	66.2	81.2	81.7	84.9	—
1967	65.8	76.6	76.4	81.0	83.8	76.0	70.9
1968	80.0	78.1	93.2	78.2	68.4	85.2	79.4
Nixon, I							
1969	99.4	40.1	92.9	63.3	69.9	51.1	40.5
1970	71.0	63.4	92.8	73.1	88.4	79.8	50.8
1971	85.3	59.0	80.6	82.9	82.1	61.2	—
1972	77.2	58.8	91.4	68.9	76.4	63.6	—
Nixon, II							
1973	56.3	75.9	65.3	56.7	81.4	63.1	62.4
1974	78.3	52.1	60.1	59.4	68.1	74.6	—
Ford							
1975	59.9	73.1	67.3	50.6	73.3	76.1	76.1
1976	67.4	86.7	81.2	65.1	59.9	73.5	—

Carter							
1977	67.1	58.5	71.7	85.5	59.9	71.1	92.4
1978	63.7	58.1	65.3	68.2	77.4	72.3	70.7
1979	78.4	68.6	69.0	73.0	68.7	65.9	—
1980	81.2	65.0	53.5	75.6	74.2	66.2	77.7
Reagan, I							
1981	66.4	21.9	68.7	76.7	92.0	76.2	43.8
1982	94.1	72.8	80.5	63.0	57.1	68.4	59.2
1983	71.3	51.3	87.7	69.3	64.1	65.8	62.5
1984	69.9	71.6	84.9	56.7	54.7	52.8	92.6
Reagan, II							
1985	70.8	85.5	75.5	27.3	62.8	54.7	70.0
1986	62.2	79.0	49.5	40.9	47.3	41.8	53.2
1987	48.8	79.9	80.9	78.3	48.3	45.8	—
1988	72.8	87.2	53.3	49.5	44.7	40.9	93.1
Bush							
1989	65.0	71.0	73.5	48.9	58.5	39.6	—
1990	45.3	90.0	85.8	68.0	69.9	50.7	41.1
1991	53.4	47.8	78.3	82.6	85.7	70.4	93.9
1992	59.9	54.6	84.0	71.2	85.3	73.2	—
Clinton[b]							
1993	73.5	72.1	57.4	93.4	89.3	58.6	—
1994	65.2	—	71.8	75.9	66.2	98.4	—

Source: Coded by the author from annual volumes of *Congressional Quarterly Almanac* (Washington, D.C.: Congressional Quarterly).

Note: Foreign trade—foreign trade, diplomacy, or immigration; foreign aid—various forms of assistance to other countries; defense—military, defense, veterans issues; social welfare—social welfare, civil rights, Indian affairs, and education; economic management—government and economic management, income tax issues; resources—energy, natural resources, environment, and transportation; agriculture—agriculture and farm policy. "—" indicates that no votes were taken in that area.

[a] Includes full term from November 1963 to January 1969.
[b] 1993–1994 only.

Table 8-12 Percentage of Out-Party Support for the President on House Roll Calls by Issue Area, Eisenhower, II, to Clinton

President/year	Foreign trade	Foreign aid	Defense	Social welfare	Economic management	Resources	Agriculture
Eisenhower, II							
1957	70.2	53.3	46.3	65.2	46.7	44.4	43.1
1958	79.6	60.7	69.8	67.6	62.7	50.2	20.7
1959	99.2	73.2	31.8	47.6	61.1	30.5	29.9
1960	52.2	55.5	40.9	52.9	25.9	41.2	61.4
Kennedy							
1961	71.0	56.0	81.3	45.2	21.4	22.4	34.1
1962	37.2	39.4	69.6	73.1	47.5	31.9	12.4
1963	42.8	17.0	50.3	61.6	28.0	37.6	12.3
Johnson[a]							
1964	54.1	39.4	26.9	37.8	32.7	71.1	5.7
1965	73.6	38.1	45.1	44.4	43.3	64.6	11.8
1966	58.0	48.0	28.6	45.4	38.0	62.1	—
1967	52.4	35.2	83.3	55.5	47.6	46.1	52.2
1968	54.3	59.7	58.3	65.2	53.4	63.3	64.0
Nixon, I							
1969	75.0	69.1	80.5	56.0	52.2	41.2	47.9
1970	80.8	65.7	47.9	46.5	78.4	81.5	60.1
1971	52.2	45.6	54.4	46.5	67.2	60.5	—
1972	82.2	69.8	51.2	45.9	51.4	68.1	—
Nixon, II							
1973	47.6	69.9	27.2	40.1	38.5	40.4	36.8
1974	37.5	47.4	40.0	51.3	49.6	60.9	—
Ford							
1975	74.9	56.3	45.3	20.4	36.6	40.6	47.7
1976	44.7	46.8	43.9	35.3	34.4	36.6	—

Carter							
1977	69.6	31.2	41.4	50.4	48.6	39.2	43.4
1978	38.0	42.8	33.9	39.6	39.3	44.0	51.7
1979	30.4	28.4	57.6	37.2	39.2	37.4	—
1980	58.7	26.8	58.6	50.2	35.9	47.8	64.1
Reagan, I							
1981	45.4	39.6	45.2	32.6	32.7	70.3	42.0
1982	47.1	52.6	54.1	35.5	28.2	46.3	36.2
1983	25.3	61.5	38.8	19.3	24.7	8.82	36.9
1984	48.2	37.3	36.8	27.3	42.4	33.9	44.1
Reagan, II							
1985	37.9	28.0	31.6	30.1	37.4	33.7	39.6
1986	20.0	10.7	29.8	21.4	29.2	34.0	39.3
1987	33.0	18.0	34.0	12.2	18.3	27.0	—
1988	16.5	54.4	34.6	17.7	15.3	28.2	97.1
Bush							
1989	53.7	44.2	36.4	23.4	48.9	25.6	—
1990	26.2	18.6	36.8	25.0	25.6	21.3	33.4
1991	51.3	40.3	46.2	28.3	24.6	26.5	93.3
1992	13.1	67.6	28.7	30.2	21.3	33.1	—
Clinton[b]							
1993	61.6	47.9	52.5	43.3	22.9	53.4	—
1994	68.3	—	39.8	23.3	27.8	99.4	—

Source: Each roll call individually coded by the author from annual volumes of *Congressional Quarterly Almanac* (Washington, D.C.: Congressional Quarterly).

Note: Foreign trade—foreign trade, diplomacy, or immigration; foreign aid—various forms of assistance to other countries; defense—military, defense, veterans issues; social welfare—social welfare, civil rights, Indian affairs, and education; economic management—government and economic management, income tax issues; resources—energy, natural resources, environment, and transportation; agriculture—agriculture and farm policy. " — " indicates that no votes were taken in that area.

[a] Includes full term from November 1963 to January 1969.
[b] 1993–1994 only.

Table 8-13 Presidential Vetoes, Washington to Clinton

Years	President	Total vetoes	Regular vetoes	Pocket vetoes	Vetoes overridden	Veto success rate
1789–1797	George Washington	2	2	0	0	100.0%
1797–1801	John Adams	0	0	0	0	—
1801–1809	Thomas Jefferson	0	0	0	0	—
1809–1817	James Madison	7	5	2	0	100.0
1817–1825	James Monroe	1	1	0	0	100.0
1825–1829	John Quincy Adams	0	0	0	0	—
1829–1837	Andrew Jackson	12	5	7	0	100.0
1837–1841	Martin Van Buren	1	0	1	0	—
1841–1841	William H. Harrison	0	0	0	0	—
1841–1845	John Tyler	10	6	4	1	83.3
1845–1849	James K. Polk	3	2	1	0	100.0
1849–1850	Zachary Taylor	0	0	0	0	—
1850–1853	Millard Fillmore	0	0	0	0	—
1853–1857	Franklin Pierce	9	9	0	5	44.4
1857–1861	James Buchanan	7	4	3	0	100.0
1861–1865	Abraham Lincoln	7	2	5	0	100.0
1865–1869	Andrew Johnson	29	21	8	15	28.6
1869–1877	Ulysses S. Grant	93	45	48	4	91.1
1877–1881	Rutherford B. Hayes	13	12	1	1	91.7
1881–1881	James A. Garfield	0	0	0	0	—
1881–1885	Chester A. Arthur	12	4	8	1	75.0
1885–1889	Grover Cleveland	414	304	110	2	99.3
1889–1893	Benjamin Harrison	44	19	25	1	94.7
1893–1897	Grover Cleveland	170	42	128	5	88.1
1897–1901	William McKinley	42	6	36	0	100.0
1901–1909	Theodore Roosevelt	82	42	40	1	97.6
1909–1913	William H. Taft	39	30	9	1	96.7
1913–1921	Woodrow Wilson	44	33	11	6	81.8
1921–1923	Warren G. Harding	6	5	1	0	100.0
1923–1929	Calvin Coolidge	50	20	30	4	80.0
1929–1933	Herbert Hoover	37	21	16	3	85.7
1933–1945	Franklin D. Roosevelt	635	372	263	9	97.6
1945–1953	Harry S Truman	250	180	70	12	93.3
1953–1961	Dwight D. Eisenhower	181	73	108	2	97.3
1961–1963	John F. Kennedy	21	12	9	0	100.0
1963–1969	Lyndon B. Johnson	30	16	14	0	100.0
1969–1974	Richard M. Nixon	43	26	17	7	73.1
1974–1977	Gerald R. Ford	66	48	18	12	75.0
1977–1981	Jimmy Carter	31	13	18	2	84.6
1981–1989	Ronald Reagan	78	39	39	4	77.8
1989–1993	George Bush	46	27	19[a]	1	96.3
1993–1994	Bill Clinton	0	0	0	0	—

Sources: Calculated by the author from *Presidential Vetoes, 1789–1976* (Washington, D.C.: Government Printing Office, 1978) and *Presidential Vetoes, 1977–1984* (Washington, D.C.: Government Printing Office, 1985); updated from successive volumes of *Congressional Quarterly Almanac* (Washington, D.C.: Congressional Quarterly).

[a] Two pocket vetoes were not recognized by Congress, which passed subsequent legislation that did not encounter vetoes.

Table 8-14 Annual Number of Presidential Vetoes by Issue Area, Truman to Clinton

President/year	Private	Foreign trade	Foreign aid	Defense	Social welfare	Economic management	Resources	Agriculture
Truman, I								
1946	36	0	0	3	2	4	4	0
1947	16	0	0	2	2	8	3	1
1948	29	0	0	1	3	5	5	0
Truman, II								
1949	22	0	0	2	1	2	5	0
1950	34	1	0	4	1	3	2	1
1951	10	0	0	4	0	1	0	0
1952	1	2	0	1	0	2	2	0
Eisenhower, I								
1953	8	0	0	0	0	1	1	0
1954	25	2	0	2	2	8	3	0
1955	4	0	0	1	0	4	2	0
1956	9	0	0	1	1	3	8	1
Eisenhower, II								
1957	8	0	0	1	0	2	1	0
1958	27	0	0	3	1	5	2	1
1959	9	0	0	0	3	2	4	2
1960	11	1	0	0	2	8	2	0
Kennedy								
1961	3	0	0	0	1	3	1	0
1962	8	1	0	0	0	2	1	0
1963	2	1	0	0	0	0	0	0
Johnson[a]								
1964	6	0	0	0	0	0	1	0
1965	4	0	0	1	1	0	1	0
1966	2	0	0	0	1	2	2	0

(Table continues)

Table 8-14 (*Continued*)

President/year	Private	Foreign trade	Foreign aid	Defense	Social welfare	Economic management	Resources	Agriculture
Johnson (continued)								
1967	1	1	0	0	1	0	0	0
1968	2	1	0	0	0	0	1	1
Nixon, I								
1969	0	0	0	0	0	0	0	0
1970	2	0	0	0	2	5	0	0
1971	0	0	0	0	2	2	1	0
1972	1	0	0	2	7	2	5	0
Nixon, II								
1973	0	0	0	2	2	4	2	0
1974	3	1	0	0	2	7	4	2
Ford								
1974	0	1	0	0	1	3	3	2
1975	0	2	0	1	3	4	4	2
1976	2	2	0	2	4	7	4	2
Carter								
1977	0	0	0	0	0	0	1	1
1978	1	2	0	3	0	7	4	0
1979	0	0	0	0	0	0	0	0
1980	2	0	0	1	1	4	4	0
Reagan, I								
1981	0	0	0	0	0	2	0	0
1982	1	0	0	0	0	7	3	0
1983	0	1	0	0	2	2	2	2
1984	4	0	0	0	2	6	5	0

Reagan, II								
1985	0	1	0	0	2	1	1	1
1986	2	1	0	1	2	2	6	0
1987	0	0	0	0	0	1	2	0
1988	0	2	0	1	7	3	3	0
Bush								
1989	0	2	1	1	1	4	1	0
1990	1	2	0	1	4	2	1	0
1991	0	0	0	0	2	1	1	0
1992	0	2	0	0	6	7	5	1
Clinton[b]								
1993	0	0	0	0	0	0	0	0
1994	0	0	0	0	0	0	0	0

Source: Calculated by the author from *Presidential Vetoes, 1789–1976* (Washington, D.C.: Government Printing Office, 1978) and *Presidential Vetoes, 1977–1984* (Washington, D.C.: Government Printing Office, 1985); updated from successive volumes of *Congressional Quarterly Almanac* (Washington, D.C.: Congressional Quarterly).

Note: Private—bills specifically providing relief for a named individual or individuals (all other categories include only public bills); foreign trade—foreign trade, diplomacy, or immigration; foreign aid—various forms of assistance to other countries; defense—military, defense, veterans issues; social welfare—social welfare, civil rights, Indian affairs, and education; economic management—government and economic management, income tax issues; resources—energy, natural resources, environment, and transportation; agriculture—agriculture and farm policy.

[a] Includes full term from November 1963 to January 1969.
[b] 1993–1994 only.

Table 8-15 Congressional Challenges to Presidential Vetoes, Truman to Clinton

President/year	Vetoes			Veto challenges		Percentage to override[d]	
	Total[a]	Pocket[b]	No challenge[c]	Sustained	Successful	House	Senate
Truman, I							
1946	49	16	30	3	0	60.38	—
1947	32	19	10	2	1	73.25	67.20
1948	43	14	23	1	5	78.64	80.04
Truman, II							
1949	32	2	29	0	1	86.65	88.24
1950	46	6	35	3	2	88.53	70.44
1951	15	5	7	1	2	83.71	86.71
1952	8	4	3	0	1	71.28	68.67
Eisenhower, I							
1953	10	6	4	0	0	—	—
1954	42	25	17	0	0	—	—
1955	11	8	2	1	0	—	58.06
1956	23	14	8	1	0	48.91	—
Eisenhower, II							
1957	12	9	3	0	0	—	—
1958	39	24	14	1	0	52.88	77.53
1959	20	10	5	4	1	67.31	66.05
1960	24	12	9	2	1	72.44	65.38
Kennedy							
1961	8	2	6	0	0	—	—
1962	12	7	5	0	0	—	—
1963	3	2	1	0	0	—	—

Johnson[e]							
1964	6	2	4	0	0	—	—
1965	7	0	7	0	0	—	—
1966	7	4	3	0	0	—	—
1967	3	1	2	0	0	—	—
1968	5	5	0	0	0	—	—
Nixon, I							
1969	0	0	0	0	0	—	—
1970	9	3	0	4	2	62.51	71.35
1971	5	2	1	2	0	—	60.00
1972	17	13	1	1	2	78.27	88.28
Nixon, II							
1973	10	1	0	8	1	60.70	69.48
1974	19	2	8	5	4	80.19	84.27
Ford							
1974	10	9	1	0	0	—	—
1975	16	0	5	7	4	73.72	68.53
1976	23	7	6	6	4	73.42	65.57
Carter							
1977	2	0	2	0	0	—	—
1978	17	13	2	2	0	51.11	—
1979	0	0	0	0	0	—	—
1980	12	5	5	0	2	94.97	93.87
Reagan, I							
1981	2	1	1	0	0	—	—
1982	11	3	3	3	2	68.92	72.92
1983	9	3	5	0	1	70.38	100.00
1984	17	14	2	0	1	79.23	87.76

(Table continues)

Table 8-15 (*Continued*)

President/year	Vetoes			Veto challenges		Percentage to override[d]	
	Total[a]	Pocket[b]	No challenge[c]	Sustained	Successful	House	Senate
Reagan, II							
1985	6	0	5	0	1	92.22	92.71
1986	14	7	5	1	1	79.04	72.36
1987	3	0	1	0	2	88.35	76.50
1988	16	11	2	2	1	66.43	70.16
Bush							
1989	10	2	4	5	0	67.08	64.32
1990	11	5	0	6	0	66.44	65.00
1991	4	2	0	2	0	63.89	65.00
1992	21	10	2	8	1	68.32	65.37
Clinton[f]							
1993	0	0	0	0	0	0	0
1994	0	0	0	0	0	0	0

Sources: Calculated by the author from *Presidential Vetoes, 1789–1976* (Washington, D.C.: Government Printing Office, 1978) and *Presidential Vetoes, 1977–1984* (Washington, D.C.: Government Printing Office, 1985); updated from successive volumes of *Congressional Quarterly Almanac* (Washington, D.C.: Congressional Quarterly).

[a] Total number of vetoes of all types: public, private, pocket, and regular.

[b] There is no possibility of a congressional challenge for pocket vetoes in the legislative process, although there have been several unsuccessful court challenges.

[c] Number of bills not challenged among those that might have been challenged.

[d] Average percentage of the members of the House and Senate who vote to override on veto challenge motions; dashes indicate no challenges.

[e] Includes full term from November 1963 to January 1969.

[f] 1993–1994 only.

Table 8-16 Reconstructed Interest Group Ratings of the President, Eisenhower to Bush

President/year	Percentage of agreement				Number of roll calls				Percentage of positions			
	ADA	COPE	ACA/ACU	CCUS	ADA	COPE	ACA/ACU	CCUS	ADA	COPE	ACA/ACU	CCUS
Eisenhower												
1960	42.86	—	—	—	9	—	—	—	77.78	—	—	—
Kennedy												
1961	88.89	—	—	—	10	—	—	—	90.00	—	—	—
1963	100.00	—	—	—	12	—	—	—	83.33	—	—	—
Johnson[a]												
1964	100.00	—	—	—	13	—	—	—	84.62	—	—	—
1965	100.00	—	—	—	19	—	—	—	52.63	—	—	—
1966	90.00	—	—	—	17	—	—	—	58.82	—	—	—
1967	90.00	—	—	—	15	—	—	—	66.67	—	—	—
1968	100.00	—	—	—	12	—	—	—	66.67	—	—	—
Nixon, I												
1969	20.00	—	—	—	15	—	—	—	33.33	—	—	—
1970	50.00	—	—	—	14	—	—	—	28.57	—	—	—
1971	8.33	—	—	—	37	—	—	—	32.43	—	—	—
1972	33.33	—	—	—	16	—	—	—	37.50	—	—	—
Nixon, II												
1973	11.11	0.00	81.82	—	25	11	27	—	36.00	63.64	40.74	—
1974	12.50	0.00	60.00	—	23	11	15	—	34.78	9.09	33.33	—
Ford												
1975	28.57	11.11	75.00	90.91	18	23	28	17	38.89	39.13	42.86	64.71
1976	0.00	12.50	100.00	100.00	20	23	28	16	25.00	34.78	35.71	37.50
Carter												
1977	66.67	85.71	25.00	28.57	21	23	26	17	42.86	30.43	65.38	41.18
1978	77.78	100.00	18.18	16.67	20	20	27	18	45.00	25.00	40.74	33.33

(Table continues)

Table 8-16 (Continued)

President/year	Percentage of agreement				Number of roll calls				Percentage of positions			
	ADA	COPE	ACA/ACU	CCUS	ADA	COPE	ACA/ACU	CCUS	ADA	COPE	ACA/ACU	CCUS
Carter (continued)												
1979	72.73	57.14	11.11	33.33	20	20	26	17	55.00	35.00	34.62	52.94
1980	72.73	83.33	11.76	58.82	17	11	21	34	64.71	54.55	66.67	50.00
Reagan, I												
1981	0.00	22.22	80.00	93.75	20	15	24	19	60.00	60.00	62.50	84.21
1982	11.11	22.22	100.00	88.89	20	20	23	22	45.00	45.00	47.83	40.91
1983	7.69	0.00	89.47	88.89	20	17	28	20	65.00	29.41	67.86	45.00
1984	0.00	0.00	83.33	85.71	20	13	21	16	45.00	23.08	57.14	43.75
Reagan, II												
1985	0.00	8.33	100.00	84.00	21	12	22	25	52.50	31.58	55.00	49.02
1986	5.00	8.33	100.00	85.71	20	12	16	7	50.00	41.38	40.00	18.92
1987	0.00	8.33	96.00	100.00	28	12	25	12	70.00	46.75	59.52	36.36
1988	0.00	0.00	100.00	100.00	22	14	11	27	55.00	50.00	39.29	61.56
Bush[b]												
1989	0.00	0.00	76.19	100.00	26	12	21	8	65.00	54.55	42.86	44.44
1990	0.00	7.69	92.59	88.89	23	13	27	18	63.89	61.90	62.79	69.23
1991	0.00	18.18	94.44	92.31	28	11	18	13	70.00	45.83	47.37	65.00

Source: Calculated by the author from successive volumes of *Congressional Quarterly Almanac* (Washington, D.C.: Congressional Quarterly).

Note: ADA—Americans for Democratic Action, COPE—Committee on Political Education (AFL-CIO), ACA—Americans for Constitutional Action, ACU—American Conservative Union, CCUS—Chamber of Commerce of the United States. In 1985 Congressional Quarterly replaced ACA ratings with ACU ratings. Presidential ratings are calculated based on the votes used by interest groups to construct their own ratings. Presidents' positions for and against the interest group's position are calculated from presidents' positions, as recorded by Congressional Quarterly.

[a] Includes full term from November 1963 to January 1969.
[b] Data available through 1991 only.

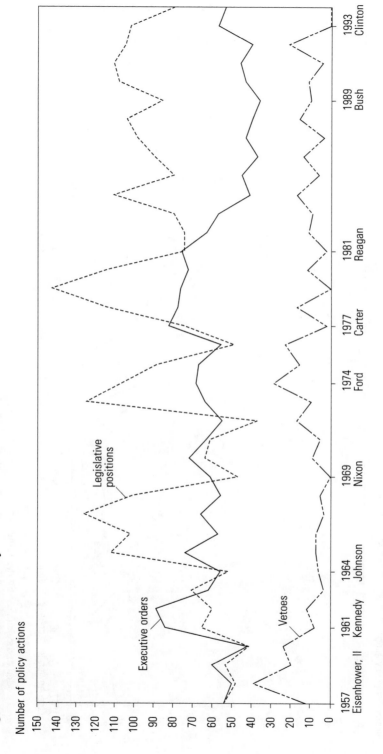

Figure 8-4 Presidential Policy Behavior, Eisenhower, II, to Clinton

Number of policy actions

Legislative positions

Executive orders

Vetoes

1957	1961	1964	1969	1974	1977	1981	1989	1993
Eisenhower, II	Kennedy	Johnson	Nixon	Ford	Carter	Reagan	Bush	Clinton

Source: Coded and calculated by the author.

Figure 8-5 Presidential Behavior on Foreign Policy, Eisenhower, II, to Clinton

Number of policy actions

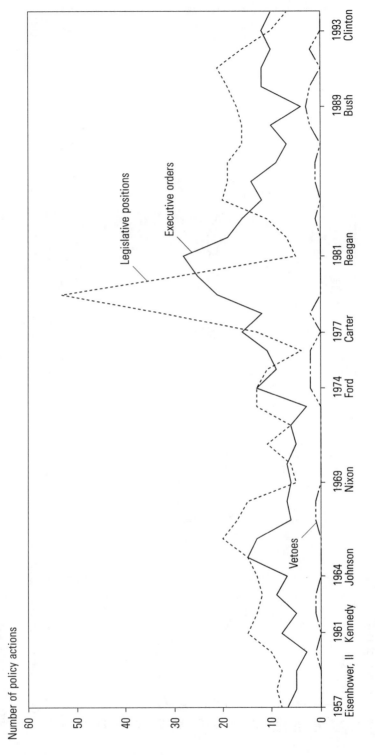

Source: Coded and calculated by the author.

Figure 8-6 Presidential Behavior on Defense Policy, Eisenhower, II, to Clinton

Number of policy actions

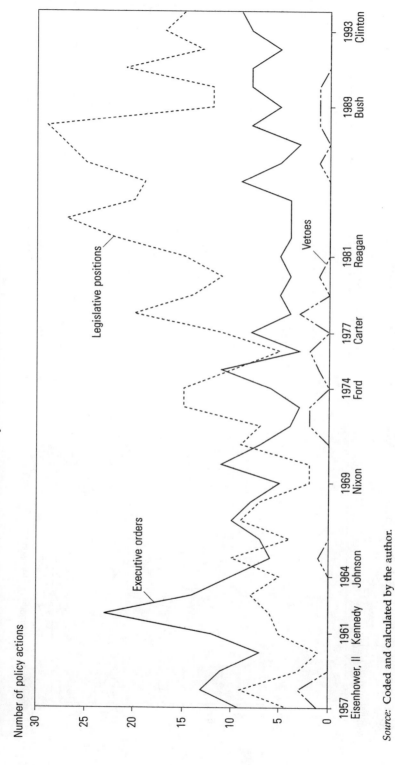

Source: Coded and calculated by the author.

Figure 8-7 Presidential Behavior on Domestic Policy, Eisenhower, II, to Clinton

Number of policy actions

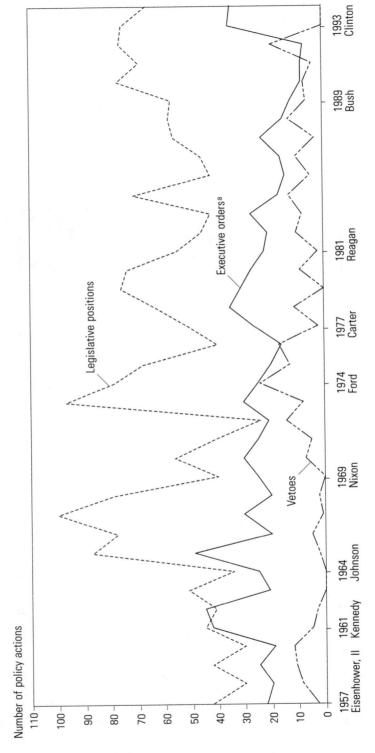

Source: Coded and calculated by the author.

[a] Excludes ceremonial, personnel, and federalism orders.

9

The Presidency and the Judiciary

Although presidential relations with the judiciary are more sporadic and less visible than those with Congress, they nonetheless rest on structural, organizational, and behavioral elements of the institutional presidency. The U.S. Constitution provides one key structural element of the presidential-judicial relationship: it specifies that presidents nominate and, with the advice and consent of the Senate, appoint judges to the federal courts, including the U.S. Supreme Court. The White House organization is heavily involved in screening potential nominees and running the confirmation process in the Senate. Senatorial courtesy—the practice of allowing senators to have control over lower court appointments—is a form of institutional behavior that links the presidency, the Senate, and the courts.

Data on presidential-judicial relations are more scarce than data documenting the connections between the presidency and Congress. This absence of data limits understanding of the presidential-judicial relationship. This chapter surveys four aspects of this relationship: Supreme Court nominations, lower court nominations, the degree of governmental success before the Supreme Court, and the Court's decisions as they relate to the presidency.

Supreme Court Nominations

High political drama typically accompanies a president's nominations to the Supreme Court. These decisions are commonly viewed as very personal. The chief executive is depicted as heavily involved—culling a list of potential nominees, scrutinizing the credentials of the finalists, personally interviewing them, and announcing the selection with some fanfare. There is some truth to this portrayal. Presidents are often personally associated with their Court nominees. Franklin Roosevelt, Harry

Truman, John F. Kennedy, and Lyndon Johnson had a personal relationship with nearly every Court nominee they submitted to the Senate. Richard Nixon, Ronald Reagan, George Bush, and Bill Clinton, all of whom were more concerned with the ideological credentials of their candidates, were less likely to know their nominees personally. Yet, presidents' nominations to the Court are more rooted in the presidential organization than this personal depiction suggests. Candidates face lengthy background checks, interviews, and analyses of their writings, carried out by the Justice Department, the Office of the White House Counsel, the White House personnel office, and the Office of the White House Chief of Staff. In addition, many of the nominations reflect internal conflict. Opposing camps within the presidential organization will champion one contender over another. For instance, after the defeat of Robert Bork's nomination to the Supreme Court, two camps in the Reagan administration battled over whether a moderate choice (Douglas Ginsburg) or a conservative one (Anthony Kennedy) should be next. Reagan ultimately decided to go with Ginsburg, whom he met for the first time only thirty minutes before announcing the nomination. Nine days later Ginsburg withdrew his nomination upon admitting that he had once smoked marijuana; Kennedy's nomination was then sent to the Senate and confirmed. There was also considerable jockeying between those officials in the Clinton administration who wanted Judge Stephen Breyer (the eventual nominee) to replace Associate Justice Harry Blackmun and those who supported Secretary of the Interior Bruce Babbitt. A similar contest between the Breyer and Babbitt camps had also preceded the appointment of Clinton's first nominee to the Court, Ruth Bader Ginsburg.

The clearest structural pattern discernible in Court nominations is that presidents overwhelmingly choose members of their own party as nominees to the Court. This is true regardless of the president, his party, the Court vacancy, or any other qualifications a prospective nominee may have. Although people often like to say that the Supreme Court is "above politics," it is in fact strongly tied to politics at least through the party affiliations of presidents and justices. Evidence of this pattern is made clear in Table 9-1, which examines the number of appointments presidents since George Washington have made to the high court. Presidents have nominated someone of the other party to the Supreme Court only 12 times in 112 appointments.

Beyond party, presidents also consider other representational qualifications in making their Court nominations. This involves the extent to which a nominee can be identified with a significant portion of the American public. Region, religion, race, and gender have all been relevant attributes. Presidents, particularly in the nineteenth century, sought regional balance on the Court. Washington commented on his appointment of

North Carolinian James Iredell to the Court in 1790 that no one from North Carolina had yet received a judicial appointment. Abraham Lincoln expressed dismay at having to fill two "southern seats," created at the start of the Civil War, with northerners. Franklin Roosevelt told Wiley Rutledge of Iowa upon his nomination to the court that "we had a number of candidates for the Court who were highly qualified, but they didn't have geography—you have that" (Scigliano, 1971, 111).

A rise in religious, racial, and gender qualifications has accompanied the decline in regionalism. Observers refer to a "Catholic seat," a "Jewish seat," "a black seat," and, most recently, a "woman's seat." Since William McKinley's appointment of Joseph McKenna in 1898, there has been a Roman Catholic sitting on the bench almost continuously. Woodrow Wilson appointed the first Jew to the Court—Louis Brandeis. Brandeis' appointment in 1916 was followed by Benjamin Cardozo in 1932 (Hoover), Felix Frankfurter in 1938 (Roosevelt), Arthur Goldberg in 1963 (Kennedy), Abe Fortas in 1965 (Johnson), Ruth Bader Ginsburg in 1993, and Stephen Breyer in 1994 (both Clinton). Bush continued to reserve a seat for an African-American jurist when he nominated conservative Clarence Thomas to replace liberal civil rights advocate Justice Thurgood Marshall, who in 1967 became the first African-American appointed to the Court. Reagan nominated the first woman, Sandra Day O'Connor, in 1981; Clinton appointed the second woman, Ginsburg, in 1993.

Table 9-1 also reveals that there is little way of telling how many appointments a president will make. Only four presidents—William Henry Harrison, Zachary Taylor, Andrew Johnson, and Jimmy Carter—did not make any Supreme Court appointments. Among those, Carter was the only full-term president in history to be denied this opportunity. By contrast, William Howard Taft, also a one-term president, appointed six justices. Presidents average one appointment every twenty-two months.

Table 9-2 shows Senate rejections of presidential nominations to the Court. Twenty-nine nominees were rejected for 19 seats on the Court; this amounts to roughly 17 percent of the total appointments made. (Four of those rejected were later confirmed.) Are there any patterns to these rejections? First, 22 of the 29 problems occurred in the nineteenth century, when the Senate had a history of asserting strong power over presidential appointments. It is also clear that when a president runs into a problem with one nominee, he may also encounter trouble with subsequent nominees for the same seat. For instance, John Tyler, who had great difficulty with Congress after he became president upon the death of William Henry Harrison, nominated five people to a vacancy on the Court, each of whom encountered problems. Tyler did not succeed until his sixth try. Nixon also failed in two successive nominations—Clement Haynsworth and G. Harrold Carswell—before succeeding in his appointment of Harry

Blackmun. One strategy that presidents adopt when their nominations run into trouble is to withdraw them from the Senate calendar. This has occurred 9 of the 29 times a nomination has run into trouble.

Lower Court Nominations

Presidents have far less control over selecting lower court judges than they do in choosing nominees to the Supreme Court. In the 95 federal district courts, there are 525 judges. The 13 courts of appeals, or circuit courts, have a corps of 159 full-time judges. Table 9-3 records the number of lower court positions presidents since Kennedy have filled. With 50 or more judicial vacancies to fill in a year, presidents turn to the White House organization and the Justice Department to evaluate the candidates, make recommendations, and see that the eventual nominees are confirmed by the Senate. Of equal importance is the tradition of "senatorial courtesy," which influences the appointment of district court judges in particular. Based on an informal reciprocal arrangement among senators, this institutional behavior allows senators of the president's party from the state where the district court vacancy occurs to sponsor candidates they like and veto candidates they do not like. Other senators go along, knowing that they, too, will have an opportunity to recommend nominations at some point. Senatorial courtesy thus limits presidents' control over their own appointments to the federal district bench.

Consistent with the party pattern observed for the Supreme Court, Table 9-4 reveals the partisanship on the federal district courts, while Table 9-5 presents evidence of partisanship on the federal circuit courts. The percentage of district court nominees of the president's party exceeded 90 percent for all presidents from Grover Cleveland to Bush, with the exceptions of Taft, Gerald Ford, and Bush. Party was slightly less important in appointments to the circuit courts.

Tables 9-6 and 9-7 examine some of the other characteristics of presidents' appointees to federal district courts and federal circuit courts, respectively. The backgrounds of the district court judges and appeals court judges have been very similar under the six presidents from Lyndon Johnson to Bush. Nominees to the courts are mostly white male lawyers. No president has been especially noteworthy in his efforts to appoint African Americans, other ethnic minorities, or women to the federal bench. President Carter's record exceeds those of the others in appointing blacks and hispanics, but even he appointed just 21 percent minorities to federal district courts and 21 percent minorities to federal circuit courts. As shown in Table 9-8, from Lyndon Johnson to Bush, over 90 percent of the judicial appointees were men. Carter and Bush did best in appointing women; 16

percent of Carter's appointments were women, while 20 percent of Bush's appointments to the federal bench were women.[1] In other respects, the Carter and Bush nominees looked much like each other and much like those of the other presidents.

Figure 9-1 shows how the judicial appointments of presidents since Franklin Roosevelt shaped the federal bench. Franklin Roosevelt, Dwight Eisenhower, and Reagan made more nominations relative to the total number of judgeships than did the other presidents studied.

The Government and the Supreme Court

The presidency has some ability to influence what cases the Supreme Court hears and how it decides those cases through the Office of the Solicitor General in the Justice Department. The solicitor general is a presidential appointee who supervises the litigation of the executive branch. Put simply, the solicitor general is the lawyer for the executive branch. The Office of the Solicitor General can influence the Court's decisions in two ways. First, when the government is a party to a lawsuit, the solicitor general's office decides which of the cases lost by the government will be appealed to the Court and thus receive the considerable resources of the federal government. Although the Court controls its docket, it is much more likely to accept cases filed by the solicitor general than from others. In recent years, the federal government has been a party to about half of the cases heard before the Court. As shown in Table 9-9, its success rate in these cases averaged 63 percent for the period 1953 to 1991.

Second, the solicitor general's office participates in cases to which it is not directly a party. It files amicus curiae (friend of the court) briefs supporting or opposing the positions of other parties before the Court. As seen in Table 9-10, the solicitor general's office is very successful in advancing the position the Court ultimately upholds. Although the success rate has declined from highs during the Eisenhower, Kennedy, and Johnson years, it still remains quite strong.

In these two ways, the solicitor general's office has developed a fairly close working relationship with the Court. It clearly has more expertise and greater resources in dealing with the Court and its members than do other litigants. Although the solicitor general's office is independent of the presidency, presidents and presidential staff members nonetheless keep in close contact with it. On occasion, the White House has lobbied the solicitor general to take a particular case before the Court or handle a brief in a specific way. Thus, through the solicitor general's office, the presidency has an organizational avenue of influence to the Supreme Court.

The Supreme Court's Impact on the Presidency

While the presidency shapes the judiciary primarily through the appointments process, the courts also have the ability to shape the presidency. In particular, the Supreme Court throughout its history has handed down various decisions that have done far more to expand presidential power than to restrict it. The Court has interpreted presidential power broadly in the areas of diplomacy, war, and domestic unrest. When the Court has stopped or chastised presidential action, it has often done so after an incident is over or a crisis has passed.

Table 9-11 examines the impact of the Court on the presidency. Although the Court generally upholds presidential actions, the table lists the number of times the Court has ruled against presidents from Washington to Clinton. It shows that in only seventy-three instances have presidents been rebuffed by the Court.

Conclusion

Although data on relations between the presidency and judiciary are sparse, those that are available reveal three patterns, two that arise from institutional elements of the presidency and a third that emerges from the political environment. First, just as party connects the presidency and Congress, so, too, does it connect the presidency and the judiciary. Party is a structural component of the presidency that provides an indicator of how closely a nominee's views will match those of a president. Although the stamp placed on the courts may look like that of an individual president, it is in fact the product of this much larger institutional partisanship. The data reveal no evidence of independent partisanship in presidents' judicial appointments. If this were so, an increase in the number of appointments of judges from the opposition party might be evident. Instead, the partisanship looks decidedly old-fashioned and one-sided. Since judges serve for good behavior, the presidents' appointments draw party lines in the federal judiciary that are longstanding.

Second, the recruitment environment within which the presidency operates strongly affects the types of nominations presidents make. Presidents rely on a readily available pool of candidates from the upper echelons of the law profession and law schools, and from lower courts to fill open slots. Their appointments mirror the make-up of the legal profession in general and judgeships more specifically. Presidents do very little to rock the legal boat in their appointments, so the white-men-only profile still holds.

Finally, in its decisions the Supreme Court respects the presidency as a co-equal branch. This is a structural aspect of the presidency's relations with the judiciary implied in the Constitution. While presidents make individual appointments to the federal bench and the Court makes significant decisions for and against the actions of individual presidents, institutional dynamics nonetheless guide these incumbent-specific dealings.

Note

1. Note that Table 9-8 refers to nominations for Bush's entire term, while Tables 9-6 and 9-7 list the nominations for 1989–1990 only, hence the different percentages for women, blacks, and hispanics for these tables.

Table 9-1 Presidents and Supreme Court Justices, Washington to Clinton

President/seat number and justice	Total appointees	Party	Home state	Years on Court	Age at nomination	Years of previous judicial experience
Washington	10					
1 John Jay		Federalist	New York	1789–1795	44	2
2 John Rutledge		Federalist	South Carolina	1789–1791	50	6
3 William Cushing		Federalist	Massachusetts	1789–1810[a]	57	29
4 James Wilson		Federalist	Pennsylvania	1789–1798[a]	47	0
5 John Blair, Jr.		Federalist	Virginia	1789–1796	57	11
6 James Iredell		Federalist	North Carolina	1790–1799[a]	38	0.5
2 Thomas Johnson		Federalist	Maryland	1791–1793	59	1.5
2 William Paterson		Federalist	New Jersey	1793–1806[a]	47	0
1 John Rutledge		Federalist	South Carolina	1795	55	6[b]
5 Samuel Chase		Federalist	Maryland	1796–1811[a]	55	8
1 Oliver Ellsworth		Federalist	Connecticut	1796–1800	51	5
J. Adams	3					
4 Bushrod Washington		Federalist	Virginia	1798–1829[a]	36	0
6 Alfred Moore		Federalist	North Carolina	1799–1804	44	1
1 John Marshall		Federalist	Virginia	1801–1835[a]	45	3
Jefferson	3					
6 William Johnson		Jeffersonian[c]	South Carolina	1804–1834[a]	32	6
2 H. Brockholst Livingston		Jeffersonian	New York	1806–1823[a]	49	0
7 Thomas Todd		Jeffersonian	Kentucky	1807–1826[a]	42	6
Madison	2					
5 Gabriel Duvall		Jeffersonian	Maryland	1811–1835	58	6
3 Joseph Story		Jeffersonian	Massachusetts	1811–1845[a]	32	0
Monroe	1					
2 Smith Thompson		Jeffersonian	New York	1823–1843[a]	55	16
J. Q. Adams	1					
7 Robert Trimble		Jeffersonian	Kentucky	1826–1828[a]	49	11

President / Justice	Appts.	Party	State	Term		
Jackson	5					
7 John McLean		Democrat	Ohio	1829–1861[a]	44	6
4 Henry Baldwin		Democrat	Pennsylvania	1830–1844[a]	50	0
6 James Wayne		Democrat	Georgia	1835–1867[a]	45	5
1 Roger B. Taney		Democrat	Maryland	1836–1864[a]	59	0
5 Philip P. Barbour		Democrat	Virginia	1836–1841[a]	52	8
Van Buren	3					
8 John Catron		Democrat	Tennessee	1837–1865[a]	51	10
9 John McKinley		Democrat	Alabama	1837–1852[a]	57	0
5 Peter V. Daniel		Democrat	Virginia	1841–1860[a]	57	0
W. Harrison	0					
Tyler	1	Whig				
2 Samuel Nelson		Democrat	New York	1845–1872	52	22
Polk	2					
3 Levi Woodbury		Democrat	New Hampshire	1845–1851[a]	55	6
4 Robert C. Grier		Democrat	Pennsylvania	1846–1870	52	13
Taylor	0	Whig				
Fillmore	1	Whig				
3 Benjamin R. Curtis		Whig	Massachusetts	1851–1857	41	0
Pierce	1	Democrat				
9 John A. Campbell		Democrat	Alabama	1853–1861	41	0
Buchanan	1	Democrat				
3 Nathan Clifford		Democrat	Maine	1858–1881[a]	54	0
Lincoln	5					
7 Noah H. Swayne		Republican	Ohio	1862–1881	57	0
5 Samuel F. Miller		Republican	Iowa	1862–1890[a]	46	0
9 David Davis		Republican	Illinois	1863–1877	47	14
10 Stephen J. Field		Democrat	California	1863–1897	46	6
1 Salmon P. Chase		Republican	Ohio	1864–1873	56	0

(Table continues)

417

Table 9-1 (*Continued*)

President/seat number and justice	Total appointees	Party	Home state	Years on Court	Age at nomination	Years of previous judicial experience
A. Johnson	0	Republican				
Grant	4					
4 William Strong		Republican	Pennsylvania	1870–1880	61	11
6 Joseph P. Bradley		Republican	New Jersey	1870–1892[a]	56	0
2 Ward Hunt		Republican	New York	1873–1882	62	8
1 Morrison R. Waite		Republican	Ohio	1874–1888[a]	57	0
Hayes	2					
9 John M. Harlan		Republican	Kentucky	1877–1911[a]	44	1
4 William B. Woods		Republican	Georgia	1880–1887[a]	56	12
Garfield	1	Republican				
7 Stanley Matthews		Republican	Ohio	1881–1889[a]	56	4
Arthur	2					
3 Horace Gray		Republican	Massachusetts	1881–1902	53	18
2 Samuel Blatchford		Republican	New York	1882–1893[a]	62	15
Cleveland (first term)	2	Democrat				
4 Lucius Q. C. Lamar		Democrat	Mississippi	1883–1893[a]	62	0
1 Melville W. Fuller		Democrat	Illinois	1888–1910[a]	55	0
B. Harrison	4					
7 David J. Brewer		Republican	Kansas	1889–1910[a]	52	19
5 Henry B. Brown		Republican	Michigan	1891–1906	54	16
6 George Shiras, Jr.		Republican	Pennsylvania	1892–1903	60	0
4 Howell E. Jackson		Democrat	Tennessee	1893–1895[a]	60	7
Cleveland (second term)	2	Democrat				
2 Edward D. White		Democrat	Louisiana	1894–1910[a]	48	1.5
4 Rufus W. Peckham		Democrat	New York	1895–1909[a]	57	9

		Party	State	Years	Age	
	McKinley					
1	8 Joseph McKenna	Republican	California	1898–1925	54	5
	T. Roosevelt					
3	3 Oliver W. Holmes	Republican	Massachusetts	1902–1932	61	20
	6 William R. Day	Republican	Ohio	1903–1922	53	7
	5 William H. Moody	Republican	Massachusetts	1906–1910	52	0
	Taft					
6	4 Horace H. Lurton	Democrat	Tennessee	1909–1914[a]	65	26
	7 Charles E. Hughes	Republican	New York	1910–1916	48	0
	1 Edward D. White	Democrat	Louisiana	1910–1921[a]	65	1.5[b]
	2 Willis Van Devanter	Republican	Wyoming	1910–1937	51	8
	5 Joseph R. Lamar	Democrat	Georgia	1910–1916[a]	53	2
	9 Mahlon Pitney	Republican	New Jersey	1912–1922	54	11
	Wilson					
3	4 James C. McReynolds	Democrat	Tennessee	1914–1941	52	0
	5 Louis D. Brandeis	Democrat	Massachusetts	1916–1939	59	0
	3 John H. Clarke	Democrat	Ohio	1916–1922	59	2
	Harding					
4	1 William H. Taft	Republican	Ohio	1921–1930	63	13
	7 George Sutherland	Republican	Utah	1922–1938	60	0
	6 Pierce Butler	Democrat	Minnesota	1923–1939[a]	56	0
	9 Edward T. Sanford	Republican	Tennessee	1923–1930[a]	57	14
	Coolidge					
1	8 Harlan Fiske Stone	Republican	New York	1925–1941	52	0
	Hoover					
3	1 Charles E. Hughes	Republican	New York	1930–1941	67	0
	9 Owens J. Roberts	Republican	Pennsylvania	1930–1945	55	0
	3 Benjamin N. Cardozo	Democrat	New York	1932–1938[a]	61	18
	F. Roosevelt					
9	2 Hugo L. Black	Democrat	Alabama	1937–1971[a]	51	1.5
	7 Stanley F. Reed	Democrat	Kentucky	1938–1957	53	0

(Table continues)

Table 9-1 (*Continued*)

President/seat number and justice	Total appointees	Party	Home state	Years on Court	Age at nomination	Years of previous judicial experience
F. Roosevelt (continued)						
3 Felix Frankfurter		Independent	Massachusetts	1939–1962	56	0
5 William O. Douglas		Democrat	Connecticut	1939–1975	40	0
6 Frank Murphy		Democrat	Michigan	1940–1949[a]	49	7
4 James F. Byrnes		Democrat	South Carolina	1941–1942	62	0[b]
1 Harlan Fiske Stone		Republican	New York	1941–1946[a]	68	0
9 Robert H. Jackson		Democrat	New York	1941–1954[a]	49	0
4 Wiley B. Rutledge		Democrat	Iowa	1943–1949[a]	48	4
Truman	4					
9 Harold H. Burton		Republican	Ohio	1945–1958	57	0
1 Fred M. Vinson		Democrat	Kentucky	1946–1953[a]	56	5
6 Tom C. Clark		Democrat	Texas	1949–1967	49	0
4 Sherman Minton		Democrat	Indiana	1949–1956	58	8
Eisenhower	5					
1 Earl Warren		Republican	California	1953–1969	62	0
8 John M. Harlan		Republican	New York	1955–1971	55	1
4 William J. Brennan		Republican	New Jersey	1956–1990	50	7
7 Charles E. Whittaker		Democrat	Missouri	1957–1962	56	3
9 Potter Stewart		Republican	Ohio	1958–1981	43	4
Kennedy	2					
7 Byron R. White		Democrat	Colorado	1962–1993	44	0
3 Arthur J. Goldberg		Democrat	Illinois	1962–1965	54	0
L. Johnson	2					
3 Abe Fortas		Democrat	Tennessee	1965–1969	55	0
6 Thurgood Marshall		Democrat	New York	1967–1991	59	4
Nixon	4					
1 Warren E. Burger		Republican	Minnesota	1969–1986	61	13
3 Harry A. Blackmun		Republican	Minnesota	1970–1994	61	11

		Party	State	Years		
2 Lewis F. Powell, Jr.		Democrat	Virginia	1971–1987	64	0
8 William H. Rehnquist		Republican	Arizona	1971–1986	47	0
Ford	1					
5 John Paul Stevens		Republican	Illinois	1976–	55	5
Carter	0					
Reagan	4					
9 Sandra Day O'Connor		Republican	Arizona	1981–	51	6.5
1 William H. Rehnquist		Republican	Arizona	1986–	61	0[b]
8 Antonin Scalia		Republican	Illinois	1986–	50	4
2 Anthony Kennedy		Republican	California	1988–	51	12
Bush	2					
4 David H. Souter		Republican	New Hampshire	1990–	50	13
6 Clarence Thomas		Republican	Georgia	1991–	43	1
Clinton[d]	2					
2 Ruth Bader Ginsburg		Democrat	New York	1993–	60	13
3 Stephen G. Breyer		Democrat	Massachusetts	1994–	55	14

Source: Adapted from Harold Stanley and Richard Niemi, *Vital Statistics on American Politics*, 4th ed. (Washington, D.C.: CQ Press, 1994); updated by the author.

Note: Seat number 1 is always held by the chief justice of the United States.

[a] Died in office.
[b] Prior to appointment to associate justice.
[c] Jeffersonian Party also known as Democratic-Republican Party.
[d] 1993–1994 only.

Table 9-2 Supreme Court Nominees with Senate Problems, Washington to Clinton

President/year	Nominee	Action
Washington		
1793	William Paterson	Withdrawn[a]
1795	John Rutledge	Rejected[a]
Madison		
1811	Alexander Wolcott	Rejected
John Adams		
1828	John J. Critinden	Postponed
Jackson		
1835	Roger B. Taney	Postponed[a]
Tyler		
1844	John G. Spencer	Rejected
1844	R. H. Walworth	Withdrawn
1844	Edward B. King	Withdrawn
1844	R. H. Walworth	Withdrawn
1845	John M. Read	Postponed
Polk		
1846	G. W. Woodward	Rejected
Fillmore		
1852	Edward A. Bradford	Postponed
1853	George E. Badger	Postponed
1853	William C. Micou	Postponed
Buchanan		
1861	Jeremiah S. Black	Rejected
A. Johnson		
1866	Henry Stanbery	Postponed
Grant		
1870	Ebenezer R. Hoar	Rejected
1874	George H. Williams	Withdrawn
1874	Caleb Cushing	Withdrawn
Hayes		
1881	Stanley Mattheys	Postponed
Cleveland		
1894	W. B. Hornblower	Rejected
1894	W. H. Peckham	Rejected[a]
Hoover		
1930	John J. Parker	Rejected
L. Johnson		
1968	Abe Fortas[b]	Withdrawn
1968	Homer Thornberry	Withdrawn
Nixon		
1969	Clement F. Haynsworth	Rejected
1970	G. Harrold Carswell	Rejected

Table 9-2   *(Continued)*

President/year	Nominee	Action
Reagan		
1987	Robert H. Bork	Rejected
1987	Douglas H. Ginsburg	Withdrawn

Source: Adapted from *Congressional Quarterly's Guide to the U.S. Supreme Court* (Washington, D.C.: Congressional Quarterly, 1979), 946–948; updated by the author. Data current as of 1995.

[a] Later confirmed.
[b] Associate justice nominated for chief justice.

Table 9-3   Presidential Nominations to the Lower Courts,
Kennedy to Clinton

President/year	Number of nominations	President/year	Number of nominations
Kennedy		Carter	
1961	60	1977	26
1962	52	1978	39
1963	15	1979	128
Total	127	1980	64
		Total	257
Johnson[a]			
1964	18	Reagan, I	
1965	28	1981	40
1966	60	1982	37
1967	35	1983	30
1968	24	1984	37
Total	165	Total	144
		Reagan, II	
Nixon, I		1985	95
1969	26	1986	54
1970	64	1987	52
1971	61	1988	46
1972	25	Total	247
Total	176		
		Bush	
Nixon, II		1989	17
1973	22	1990	61
1974	17	1991	63
Total	39	1992	67
		Total	208
Ford			
1974	17	Clinton[b]	
1975	17	1993	42
1976	30	1994	95
Total	64	Total	137

Note: Includes only district and circuit court appointments.

Source: Successive volumes of *Congressional Quarterly Almanac* (Washington, D.C.: Congressional Quarterly).

[a] Includes full term from November 1963 to January 1969.
[b] 1993–1994 only.

Table 9-4 Presidential Appointments to the U.S. District Courts by Political Party, Cleveland to Bush

President	Party affiliation	Appointees				Total
		Member of same party	Member of other party or independent	Unknown party affiliation	Percentage from president's party	
Cleveland	Democrat	30	0	0	100.0	30
B. Harrison	Republican	18	1	0	94.7	19
McKinley	Republican	19	0	0	100.0	19
T. Roosevelt	Republican	55	0	0	100.0	55
Taft	Republican	26	6	0	81.2	32
Wilson	Democrat	54	1	0	98.2	55
Harding	Republican	37	1	0	97.4	38
Coolidge	Republican	49	2	0	96.1	51
Hoover	Republican	30	3	0	90.9	33
F. Roosevelt	Democrat	151	10	0	93.8	161
Truman	Democrat	105	10	0	91.3	115
Eisenhower	Republican	116	9	0	92.8	125
Kennedy	Democrat	93	10	0	90.3	103
L. Johnson	Democrat	115	7	0	94.3	122
Nixon	Republican	166	13	0	92.7	179
Ford	Republican	41	11	0	78.8	52
Carter	Democrat	187	15	0	92.6	202
Reagan	Republican	270	20	0	93.1	290
Bush	Republican	131	17	0	88.5	148

Note: Data for Clinton not yet available.

Source: Adapted from Lee Epstein, Jeffrey A. Segal, Harold J. Spaeth, and Thomas G. Walker, *The Supreme Court Compendium* (Washington, D.C.: Congressional Quarterly, 1994), 657.

Table 9-5 Presidential Appointments to the Circuit Courts and Courts of Appeal by Political Party, Cleveland to Bush

President	Party affiliation	Appointees			Percentage from president's party	Total
		Member of same party	Member of other party or independent	Unknown party affiliation		
Cleveland	Democrat	6	1	5	50.0	12
B. Harrison	Republican	8	2	2	66.7	12
McKinley	Republican	3	2	0	60.0	5
T. Roosevelt	Republican	14	3	3	70.0	20
Taft	Republican	11	2	0	84.6	13
Wilson	Democrat	19	1	0	95.0	20
Harding	Republican	6	0	0	100.0	6
Coolidge	Republican	15	2	0	88.2	17
Hoover	Republican	12	4	0	75.0	16
F. Roosevelt	Democrat	45	3	0	93.8	48
Truman	Democrat	23	3	0	88.5	26
Eisenhower	Republican	42	3	0	93.3	45
Kennedy	Democrat	20	1	0	95.2	21
L. Johnson	Democrat	38	2	0	95.0	40
Nixon	Republican	42	3	0	93.3	45
Ford	Republican	11	1	0	91.7	12
Carter	Democrat	46	10	0	82.1	56
Reagan	Republican	76	2	0	97.4	78
Bush	Republican	33	4	0	89.2	37

Note: Data for Clinton not yet available.

Source: Adapted from Lee Epstein, Jeffrey A. Segal, Harold J. Spaeth, and Thomas G. Walker, *The Supreme Court Compendium* (Washington, D.C.: Congressional Quarterly, 1994), 646.

Table 9-6 Characteristics of District Court Appointees, Johnson to Bush (percent)

Characteristics	Johnson	Nixon	Ford	Carter	Reagan, I	Reagan, II	Bush[a]
Race							
White	93.4	95.5	88.5	78.7	93.0	91.9	95.8
Black	4.1	3.4	5.8	13.9	0.8	3.1	2.1
Hispanic	2.5	1.1	1.9	6.9	5.4	4.3	2.1
Asian	0.0	0.0	3.9	0.5	0.8	0.6	0.0
Sex							
Male	98.4	99.4	98.1	85.6	90.7	92.5	89.6
Female	1.6	0.6	1.9	14.4	9.3	7.4	10.4
Religious background							
Protestant	58.2	73.2	73.1	60.4	61.2	60.9	64.9
Catholic	31.1	18.4	17.3	27.2	31.8	27.3	22.9
Jewish	10.7	8.4	9.6	12.4	6.9	11.2	12.5
Party							
Democratic	94.3	7.2	21.2	94.1	3.3	6.2	4.2
Republican	5.7	92.8	78.8	4.5	96.9	90.7	93.8
Independent	0.0	0.0	0.0	1.5	0.0	3.1	2.1
Law school education							
Public institution	40.2	41.9	44.2	50.5	34.1	36.6	41.7
Private (non-Ivy)	36.9	36.9	38.5	32.2	49.6	50.9	50.0
Ivy League	21.3	21.2	17.3	17.3	16.3	12.4	8.3
Experience							
Judicial	34.3	35.1	42.3	54.5	50.4	43.5	50.0
Prosecutorial	45.8	41.9	50.0	38.6	43.4	44.7	37.5
Neither	33.6	36.3	30.8	28.2	28.7	27.9	27.1

(Table continues)

Table 9-6 (*Continued*)

Characteristics	Johnson	Nixon	Ford	Carter	Reagan, I	Reagan, II	Bush[a]
Occupation							
Politics/government	21.3	10.6	21.2	4.4	7.8	16.8	10.4
Judiciary	31.1	28.5	34.6	44.6	40.3	34.8	47.9
Law firm	44.3	58.2	44.3	47.7	52.0	46.6	39.5
Professor of law	3.3	2.8	0.0	3.0	2.3	1.9	2.1
Other	0.0	0.0	0.0	0.5	1.6	0.0	0.0
Total appointees	N=122	N=179	N=52	N=202	N=129	N=161	N=48

Source: Adapted from Sheldon Goldman, "The Bush Imprint on the Judiciary," *Judicature* 74 (April–May 1991): 298.

[a] 1989–1990 only. Data for the remainder of Bush's term and for Clinton not yet available.

Table 9-7 Characteristics of Circuit Court Appointees, Johnson to Bush (percent)

Characteristics	Johnson	Nixon	Ford	Carter	Reagan, I	Reagan, II	Bush[a]
Race							
White	95.0	97.8	100.0	78.6	93.5	100.0	88.9
Black	5.0	0.0	0.0	16.1	3.2	0.0	5.6
Hispanic	0.0	0.0	0.0	3.6	3.2	0.0	5.6
Asian	0.0	2.2	0.0	1.8	0.0	0.0	0.0
Sex							
Male	97.5	100.0	100.0	80.4	96.8	93.6	88.9
Female	2.5	0.0	0.0	19.6	3.2	6.4	11.1
Religious background							
Protestant	60.0	75.6	58.3	60.7	67.7	46.8	55.6
Catholic	25.0	15.6	33.3	23.7	22.6	36.2	33.3
Jewish	15.7	8.9	8.3	16.1	9.7	17.0	38.9
Party							
Democratic	95.0	6.7	8.3	89.3	0.0	0.0	0.0
Republican	5.0	93.3	91.7	5.4	100.0	95.7	94.4
Independent	0.0	0.0	0.0	5.4	0.0	4.2	5.6
Law school education							
Public institution	40.0	37.8	50.0	39.3	29.0	42.6	22.2
Private (non-Ivy)	32.5	26.7	25.0	19.6	45.2	29.8	44.4
Ivy League	27.5	35.6	25.0	41.1	25.8	27.7	33.3
Experience							
Judicial	65.0	57.8	75.0	53.6	70.9	53.2	55.6
Prosecutorial	47.5	46.7	25.0	32.1	19.3	34.0	33.3
Neither	20.0	17.8	25.0	37.5	25.8	40.4	38.9

(*Table continues*)

Table 9-7 (Continued)

Characteristics	Johnson	Nixon	Ford	Carter	Reagan, I	Reagan, II	Bush[a]
Occupation							
Politics/government	10.0	4.4	8.3	5.4	3.2	8.5	11.1
Judiciary	57.5	53.3	75.0	46.4	61.3	51.1	55.6
Law firm	30.0	35.5	16.6	32.3	19.4	37.6	33.4
Professor of law	0.0	6.7	0.0	14.3	16.1	10.6	0.0
Other	0.0	0.0	0.0	1.8	0.0	2.1	0.0
Total appointees	N=40	N=45	N=12	N=56	N=31	N=47	N=18

Source: Adapted from Sheldon Goldman, "The Bush Imprint on the Judiciary," *Judicature* 74 (April–May 1991): 299.

[a] 1989–1990 only. Data for the remainder of Bush's term and for Clinton not yet available.

Table 9-8   Women and Minorities Appointed to Judgeships,
Johnson to Bush

	Women		Black		Hispanic	
President	Number	Percentage of total	Number	Percentage of total	Number	Percentage of total
Johnson	3	1.9	7	4.3	3	1.9
Nixon	1	0.4	6	2.7	2	0.9
Ford	1	1.6	3	4.7	1	1.6
Carter	40	15.5	37	14.3	16	6.2
Reagan	28	7.6	7	1.9	15	4.1
Bush	36	19.4	12	6.5	8	4.3

Note: Total reflects only appointments to U.S. District Court and U.S. Courts of Appeal. Data for Clinton not yet available.

Source: Congressional Quarterly Almanac (Washington, D.C.: Congressional Quarterly, 1992), 324.

Figure 9-1 Total Number of Judicial Appointments, F. Roosevelt to Bush

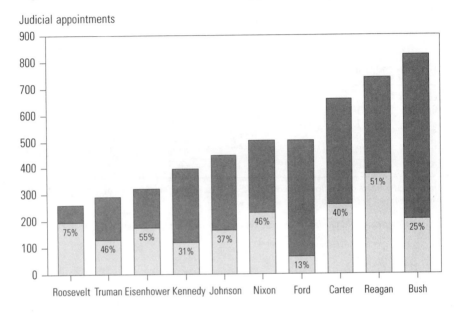

Judicial appointments

President	Supreme Court	Court of Appeals[a]	District Courts[b]	Total	Total Judgeships
F. Roosevelt (1933–1945)	9	52	136	197	262
Truman (1945–1953)	4	27	102	133	292
Eisenhower (1953–1961)	5	45	127	177	322
Kennedy (1961–1963)	2	20	102	124	395
L. Johnson (1963–1969)	2	41	125	168	449
Nixon (1969–1974)	4	45	182	231	504
Ford (1974–1977)	1	12	52	65	504
Carter (1977–1981)	0	56	206	262	657
Reagan (1981–1989)	3	83	292	378	740
Bush (1989–1993)	2	60	148	210	825

Source: Congressional Quarterly Almanac (Washington, D.C.: Congressional Quarterly, 1990), 517. Updated by the author.

Note: Light portion of the bar indicates percentage of judgeships appointed by a president; remainder of bar denotes judgeships appointed by previous presidents.

a Does not include the appeals court for the Federal Circuit.
b Includes district courts in the territories.

Table 9-9   Success Rate of the United States as a Party to a Case Before the Supreme Court, Eisenhower to Bush

President/year	Total number of cases[a]	Percentage of cases won
Eisenhower, I		
1953	26	61.5
1954	34	61.8
1955	41	46.3
1956	59	44.1
Eisenhower, II		
1957	48	58.3
1958	35	62.9
1959	56	62.5
1960	51	68.6
Kennedy		
1961	36	44.4
1962	36	61.1
1963	37	56.8
Johnson[b]		
1964	24	79.2
1965	39	56.4
1966	30	60.0
1967	40	65.0
1968	31	61.3
Nixon, I		
1969	26	65.4
1970	40	70.0
1971	23	43.5
1972	40	72.5
Nixon, II		
1973	31	71.0
Ford		
1974	38	68.4
1975	33	84.8
1976	30	50.0
Carter		
1977	33	57.6
1978	20	65.0
1979	38	65.8
1980	16	66.8
Reagan, I		
1981	18	72.2
1982	25	52.0
1983	30	83.3
1984	25	76.0

(Table continues)

Table 9-9   (*Continued*)

President/year	Total number of cases[a]	Percentage of cases won
Reagan, II		
1985	25	88.0
1986	26	61.5
1987	24	66.7
1988	15	80.0
Bush[c]		
1989	23	56.5
1990	14	64.3
1991	21	57.1
Total	1,237	63.0

Source: Lee Epstein, Jeffrey A. Segal, Harold J. Spaeth, and Thomas G. Walker, *The Supreme Court Compendium* (Washington, D.C.: Congressional Quarterly, 1994), 569.

[a] Includes those cases where the *U.S. Reports* names the United States a party to the case, and criminal and habeas corpus cases where the *U.S. Reports* lists as the party the name of the official or office of the person who prosecutes or has custody of the accused or convicted person. If the United States is not the first named party in multiple party litigation, the case is not included.
[b] Includes full term from November 1963 to January 1969.
[c] 1992 data not available. Clinton not yet available.

Table 9-10   Success Rate of the Solicitor General as an Amicus Curiae in Cases Before the Supreme Court, Eisenhower to Bush

President	Total number of cases[a]	Percentage of cases won
Eisenhower	42	83.3
Kennedy	48	87.5
Johnson	41	82.9
Nixon	79	70.9
Ford	38	71.1
Carter	86	65.1
Reagan[b]	123	67.5
Bush[c]	99	75.8

Source: Lee Epstein, Jeffrey A. Segal, Harold J. Spaeth, and Thomas G. Walker, *The Supreme Court Compendium* (Washington, D.C.: Congressional Quarterly, 1994), 571.

[a] Includes all cases where solicitor general filed an amicus curiae brief and the Court decided the case with an opinion on the merits.
[b] Includes 1980–1982 and 1986–1987 terms.
[c] Includes 1988–1990 terms only. Remaining years for Bush and Clinton years not available.

Table 9-11   Supreme Court Rulings Against Presidents,
Washington to Clinton

President	Number of decisions
Washington	0
Adams	0
Jefferson	2
Madison	3
Monroe	1
J. Q. Adams	0
Jackson	0
Van Buren	0
Harrison	0
Tyler	1
Polk	0
Taylor	0
Fillmore	1
Pierce	0
Buchanan	0
Lincoln	5
A. Johnson	2
Grant	0
Hayes	1
Garfield	0
Arthur	2
Cleveland	1
Harrison	0
McKinley	0
T. Roosevelt	0
Taft	0
Wilson	2
Harding	2
Coolidge	3
Hoover	1
F. Roosevelt	8
Truman	3
Eisenhower	3
L. Johnson	2
Nixon	25
Ford	3
Carter	2
Reagan	0
Bush	0
Clinton[a]	0
Total	73

Source: Michael A. Genovese, *The Supreme Court, the Constitution and Presidential Power* (Lanham, Md.: University Press of America, 1980), 264. Used by permission. Updated by the author.

[a] 1993–1994 only.

References

Aldrich, John. 1980. *Before the Convention.* Chicago: University of Chicago Press.

Alford, John, and David Brady. 1993. "Personal and Partisan Advantages in Congressional Elections." In *Congress Reconsidered,* 5th ed., ed. Lawrence Dodd and Bruce Oppenheimer. Washington, D.C.: CQ Press.

Aristotle. 1943. *Politics.* New York: Modern Library.

Berman, Larry. 1979. *The Office of Management and Budget and the Presidency.* Princeton: Princeton University Press.

Brace, Paul, and Barbara Hinckley. 1992. *Follow the Leader.* New York: Free Press.

Brown, Roger. 1982. "Party and Bureaucracy: From Kennedy to Reagan." *Political Science Quarterly* 97 (Summer): 279–294.

Burke, John. 1992. *The Institutional Presidency.* Baltimore: Johns Hopkins University Press.

Chambers, William. 1963. *Political Parties in a New Nation: The American Experience, 1776–1809.* New York: Oxford University Press.

Cornwell, Elmer. 1965. *Presidential Leadership of Public Opinion.* Bloomington: Indiana University Press.

Corwin, Edward. 1957. *The President: Office and Powers.* New York: New York University Press.

Cronin, Thomas. 1987. "The Swelling of the Presidency." In *American Government: Reading and Cases,* 9th ed., ed. P. Woll. Boston: Little, Brown.

DeGrazia, Alfred. 1965. *Republic in Crisis: Congress Against the Executive Force.* New York: Federal Legal Publications.

Dennis, Jack. 1988. "Political Independence in America, Part I: On Being an Independent Partisan Supporter." *British Journal of Political Science* 18 (Winter): 77–109.

DiClerico, Robert. 1985. *The American President,* 2d ed. Englewood Cliffs, N.J.: Prentice-Hall.

DiMaggio, Paul. 1991. "Constructing an Organizational Field as a Professional Project: U.S. Art Museums, 1920–1940." In *The New Institutionalism in Organizational Analysis,* ed. W. Powell and P. DiMaggio. Chicago: University of Chicago Press.

Edwards, George, III. 1989. *At the Margins: Presidential Leadership of Congress.* New Haven: Yale University Press.

Edwards, George, III, John Kessel, and Bert Rockman, eds. 1993. *Researching the Presidency.* Pittsburgh: University of Pittsburgh Press.

Eisenstadt, S. N. 1964. "Institutionalization and Change." *American Sociological Review* 29 (April): 235–247.

Epstein, Leon. 1986. *Political Parties in the American Mold.* Madison: University of Wisconsin Press.

Fenno, Richard. 1959. *The President's Cabinet.* New York: Vintage.

Ford, Paul. 1892-1899. *The Writings of Thomas Jefferson.* 8 vols. New York: Putnam.

Garand, James, and Donald Gross. 1984. "Changes in the Vote Margins for Congressional Candidates: A Specification of Historical Trends." *American Political Science Review* 78 (March): 17–30.

Grossman, Michael, and Martha Kumar. 1981. *Portraying the President.* Baltimore: Johns Hopkins University Press.

Hart, John. 1987. *The Presidential Branch.* New York: Pergamon.

Heclo, Hugh. 1981. "Introduction: The Presidential Illusion." In *The Illusion of Presidential Government,* ed. H. Heclo and L. Salamon. Boulder, Colo.: Westview Press.

Helmer, John. 1981. "The Presidential Office: Velvet Fist in an Iron Glove." In *The Illusion of Presidential Government,* ed. H. Heclo and L. Salamon. Boulder, Colo.: Westview Press.

Herring, Pendleton. 1940. *Presidential Leadership.* New York: Harcourt Brace.

Hershey, Marjorie. 1989. "The Campaign and the Media." In *The Election of 1988,* ed. G. Pomper. Chatham, N.J.: Chatham House.

Hess, Stephen. 1976. *Organizing the Presidency.* Washington, D.C.: Brookings Institution.

Holtzman, Abraham. 1970. *Legislative Liaison: Executive Leadership in Congress.* New York: Crowell and Readers Digest Press.

Huntington, Samuel. 1965. "Political Development and Political Decay." *World Politics* 17 (April): 235–247.

Johnson, Lock. 1984. *The Making of International Agreements: Congress Confronts the Executive.* New York: New York University Press.

Kernell, Samuel. 1978. "Explaining Presidential Popularity." *American Political Science Review* 72 (June): 506–522.

Kernell, Samuel. 1984. "The Presidency and the People: The Modern Paradox." In *The Presidency and the Political System,* ed. M. Nelson. Washington, D.C.: CQ Press.

Ketcham, Ralph. 1984. *Presidents above Party: The First American Presidency, 1789-1829*. Chapel Hill: University of North Carolina Press.

King, Gary. 1993. "The Methodology of Presidential Research." In *Researching the Presidency*, ed. G. Edwards, J. Kessel, and B. Rockman. Pittsburgh: University of Pittsburgh Press.

King, Gary, Robert Keohane, and Sidney Verba. 1994. *Scientific Inference in Qualitative Research*. Princeton: Princeton University Press.

Kissinger, Henry. 1979. *The White House Years*. Boston: Little, Brown.

Koenig, Louis. 1964. *The Chief Executive*. New York: Harcourt, Brace, and World.

Krehbiel, Keith. 1987. "Why are Congressional Committees Powerful?" *American Political Science Review* 81 (September): 929–935.

Ladd, Everett C. 1981. "The Proper Role of Parties in Presidential Nominee Selection." *Commonsense* 4: 33–39.

La Follette, Robert. 1913. *La Follette's Autobiography*. Madison, Wis.: R. La Follette.

Light, Paul. 1991. *The President's Agenda: Domestic Policy Choice from Kennedy to Reagan*, rev. ed. Baltimore: Johns Hopkins University Press.

Lindbolm, Charles. 1968. *The Policy-Making Process*. Englewood Cliffs, N.J.: Prentice-Hall.

Lorant, Stefan. 1951. *The Presidency: A Pictorial History of Presidential Elections from Washington to Truman*. New York: Macmillan.

Lord, Clifford, ed. 1979. *List and Index of Presidential Executive Orders, Unnumbered Series, 1789–1941*. Wilmington, Del.: Michael Glazier.

MacKenzie, G. Calvin. 1981. *The Politics of Presidential Appointments*. New York: Free Press.

Malek, Fred. 1978. *Washington's Hidden Tragedy*. New York: Free Press.

March, James, and Johan Olsen. 1984. "The New Institutionalism: Organizational Factors in Political Life." *American Political Science Review* 78 (September): 734–749.

Margolis, Lawrence. 1986. *Executive Agreements and Presidential Power in Foreign Policy*. New York: Praeger.

Meyer, John, and Brian Rowan. 1991. "Institutionalized Organizations: Formal Structure as Myth and Ceremony." In *The New Institutionalism in Organizational Analysis*, ed. W. Powell and P. DiMaggio. Chicago: University of Chicago Press.

Moe, Terry. 1985. "The Politicized Presidency." In *The New Direction in American Politics*, ed. J. Chubb and P. Peterson. Washington, D.C.: Brookings Institution.

Moe, Terry. 1993. "Presidents, Institutions, and Theory." In *Researching the Presidency*, ed. G. Edwards, J. Kessel, and B. Rockman. Pittsburgh: University of Pittsburgh Press.

Mueller, John. 1970. "Presidential Popularity from Truman to Johnson." *American Political Science Review* 64 (March): 18–34.

Nathan, Richard. 1983. *The Administrative Presidency.* New York: Wiley.

Neustadt, Richard. 1960. *Presidential Power.* New York: Wiley.

Neustadt, Richard. 1975. "The Constraining of the President." In *Perspectives on the Presidency,* ed. A. Wildavsky. Boston: Little, Brown.

North, Douglass. 1990. *Institutions, Institutional Choice, and Economic Performance.* Cambridge: Cambridge University Press.

Norrander, Barbara. 1992. *Super Tuesday.* Lexington: University Press of Kentucky.

Ornstein, Norman, Thomas Mann, and Michael Malbin. 1994. *Vital Statistics on Congress 1993–1994.* Washington, D.C.: CQ Press.

Ostrom, Charles, and Brian Job. 1986. "The President's Use of Force." *American Political Science Review* 80 (June): 541–566.

Ostrom, Charles, and Dennis Simon. 1985. "Promise and Performance: A Dynamic Model of Presidential Popularity." *American Political Science Review* 79 (June): 334–358.

Pika, Joseph. 1988. "Management Style and The Organizational Matrix." *Administration and Society* 20 (May): 3–29.

Polsby, Nelson. 1968. "The Institutionalization of the U.S. House of Representatives." *American Political Science Review* 62 (March): 144–168.

Powell, Woodward, and Paul DiMaggio, eds. 1991. *The New Institutionalism in Organizational Analysis.* Chicago: University of Chicago Press.

Ragsdale, Lyn. 1984. "The Politics of Presidential Speechmaking." *American Political Science Review* 78 (December): 971–984.

Ragsdale, Lyn. 1993. *Presidential Politics.* Boston: Houghton Mifflin.

Ragsdale, Lyn. 1994. "Studying the Presidency: Why Presidents Need Political Scientists." In *The Presidency and the Political System,* 4th ed., ed. Michael Nelson. Washington, D.C.: CQ Press.

Roosevelt, Theodore. 1913. *Theodore Roosevelt: An Autobiography.* New York: Macmillan.

Rossiter, Clinton. 1960. *The American Presidency.* New York: Mentor Books.

Rubin, Richard. 1981. *Press, Party, and Presidency.* New York: Norton.

Schlesinger, Arthur, Jr., ed. 1973a. *The History of U.S. Political Parties.* 3 vols. New York: Chelsea House.

Schlesinger, Arthur, Jr. 1973b. *The Imperial Presidency.* Boston: Houghton Mifflin.

Schlozman, Kay, and John Tierney. 1986. *Organized Interests and American Democracy.* New York: HarperCollins.

Scigliano, Robert. 1971. *The Supreme Court and the Presidency.* New York: Free Press.

Selznick, Philip. 1957. *Leadership in Administration.* Evanston, Ill.: Row, Peterson.

Shepsle, Kenneth, and Barry Weingast. 1987. "The Institutional Foundations of Committee Power." *American Political Science Review* 81 (March): 85–104.

Sigelman, Lee, and Kathleen Knight. 1983. "Why Does Presidential Popularity Decline? A Test of the Expectation/Disillusion Theory." *Public Opinion Quarterly* 47 (Fall): 310–324.

Sorauf, Frank, and Paul Beck. 1992. *Party Politics in America.* New York: HarperCollins.

Stanley, David, Dean Mann, and Jameson Diog. 1967. *Men Who Govern.* Washington, D.C.: Brookings Institution.

Stimson, James. 1976. "Public Support for American Presidents: A Cyclical Model." *Public Opinion Quarterly* 40 (Spring): 1–21.

Taft, William Howard. 1916. *The Presidency.* New York: Charles Scribner.

Theis, John J. 1994. *Split-Ticket Voting and the Origins of Divided Government.* Ph.D. dissertation. University of Arizona.

U.S. General Accounting Office. 1985. *Use of Special Presidential Authority for Foreign Assistance.* Washington, D.C.: Government Printing Office.

Watson, Richard, and Norman Thomas. 1983. *The Politics of the Presidency.* New York: Wiley.

Wayne, Stephen. 1978. *The Legislative Presidency.* New York: Harper and Row.

Wayne, Stephen. 1982. "Congressional Liaison in the Reagan White House: A Preliminary Assessment of the First Year." In *President and Congress,* ed. N. Ornstein. Washington, D.C.: American Enterprise Institute.

Wayne, Stephen, Richard Cole, and James Hyde. 1979. "Advising the President on Enrolled Legislation: Patterns of Executive Influence." *Political Science Quarterly* 94 (Summer): 303–317.

Weber, Max. 1947. *The Theory of Social and Economic Organization.* Glencoe, Ill.: Free Press.

West, William, and Joseph Cooper. 1985. "The Rise of Administrative Clearance." In *The Presidency and Public Policy Making,* ed. G. Edwards, S. Shull, and N. Thomas. Pittsburgh: University of Pittsburgh Press.

Wilson, Woodrow. 1973. *Congressional Government.* Cleveland: World Publishing.

Index